Preface

SCOPE OF THE BOOK

Better Software Practice for Business Benefit: Principles and Experience was written by 30 authors from 11 different European Union (EU) countries with contributions from leading European companies. This book combines theory with industrial experience and provides a comprehensive overview of different improvement methodologies. The experience part of the book was written by authors from both large and small companies.

The reader must understand that there is no silver bullet. The same process improvement experiment in different organisational environments might lead to different results. What, in general, is the same is the evolution of companies along the capability level scale, but the medicine used in each company might differ. This is the reason why you will find a large set of different improvement methodologies and not only one presented in this book.

For instance, Chapters 9 and 10 compared to Chapter 12 show such an example. Italtel and Alcatel contributed experience reports from the same application domain (digital switching systems) and both organisations used different approaches to achieve significant results concerning quality and productivity. What both companies had in common was the use of the Capability Maturity Model (CMM) as a general model for the evolution of organisations from a chaotic process to a well-defined, predictable, and optimising process.

TARGET AUDIENCE

Process groups and quality engineers are a prime audience for this book. Consultants are a relevant group with vital interest in basic information about structured evaluation and improvement. Software professionals are another group which we would like to address, yet this group cannot be precisely defined.

Managers on various levels within all organisations dealing with software should be a further main audience. Especially, the role of middle management and project leaders is crucial because these people are the ones who decide which methods are to be implemented.

THE BOOK'S ARCHITECTURE

The figure on the following page illustrates the general architecture of the book. *Roadmap* describes Chapter 1, which provides a road map for readers, summarises the experiences presented, and gives recommendations. *Principles* describes a set of business strategies and improvement methodologies. *Experience* includes industrial case studies from different companies to illustrate how these methodologies were implemented and used.

Note: The Capability Maturity Model (CMM) is a service mark and a registered trademark (U.S. Patent and Trademark Office) of Carnegie Mellon University.

Road Map

Selecting Proper Routes by
Reader's Background
Improvement Approach
Industry Size

Principles

Business Principles
Organisational Systems
Improvement Catalogue

Experience

Improvement Programmes
Actual Improvement Stories
Leading Companies

Principles

Chapter 2 discusses process improvement from the business manager's viewpoint, speaking about return on investment (ROI), fixed cost, variable cost, break-even point, market share, and leveraging. The process improvement movement originally was a very technical one dealing with process architectures and software development. However, if top management does not provide commitment and resources any technical initiative will fail. Therefore it is necessary to start from business goals, plan the improvement aiming at return on investment, and to measure the success.

Chapter 3 is about process models, process evolution, and process analysis paradigms and defines the basic technical terms used when starting a process improvement initiative.

Chapter 4 outlines the currently available methodologies for process analysis and assessment. Due to the fact that all industrial case studies in this book started with process analysis this chapter is relevant for all experience chapters.

Chapter 5 deals with improvement strategies for action planning, illustrated by the ami approach as a framework for goal-based improvement planning and measurement.

Chapter 6 focuses on a basic set of process and product metrics which are used in measuring productivity, size and complexity, and quality. It specifically discusses how to establish measurement programmes in a company to achieve a quantitative view of the processes.

Chapter 7 illustrates the measured ROI from a set of case studies and internationally published data.

Experience

Chapter 8 presents Siemens's assessment and improvement programme, and Chapters 9 and 10 illustrate the experience with improvement projects starting with the Siemens and the BOOTSTRAP assessment approach. Chapter 12 discusses Alcatel's experience in the same application domain as presented in Chapters 9 and 10 by Italtel.

Chapter 13 deals with experience with the ISO 12207 process modelling standard for which a well-defined reference to the architecture of the Software Process Improvement and

Better Software Practice for Business Benefit

Principles and Experience

Richard Messnarz
Editor

Colin Tully
Co-editor

Original contributions by

G. Bazzana	R. Delmiglio	P. Kuvaja	G. Rumi
M. Biro	S. DiMuro	H.B. Lambert	G. Rutschek
L. Briand	K. El Emam	S. Lanzerstorfer	H. Scherzer
G. Caielli	E. Fagnoni	A. Lora	D. Scrignaro
D. Courtel	N. Fuchs	E. McGuinness	J.M. Simon
G. Damele	P. Fusaro	T. Mehner	B. Smith
C. Debou	M. Haux	R. Messnarz	C. Tully
	S. Humml	M. Piotti	

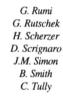

IEEE

COMPUTER
SOCIETY

Los Alamitos, California

Washington • Brussels • Tokyo

Library of Congress Cataloging-in-Publication Data

Better software practice for business benefit : principles and
  experience / [edited by] Richard Messnarz, Colin Tully.
       p.   cm.
  Based on the results of three international conferences organised by
the International Software Collaborative Network since 1994.
  Includes bibliographical references.
  ISBN 0-7695-0049-8.
  1. Industrial management – Data processing.   2. Computer
software – Development.   3. Computer software – Quality control.
I. Messnarz, Richard.   II. Tully, C. J. (Colin J.).   III. International
Software Collaborative Network.
  H030.2.B47 1999
  658' .0553 — dc21

                                                        99-31768
                                                        CIP

IEEE Computer Society Press Order Number BP00049
Library of Congress Number 99-31768
ISBN 0-7695-0049-8

Additional copies may be ordered from:

IEEE Computer Society Press	IEEE Service Center	IEEE Computer Society
Customer Service Center	445 Hoes Lane	Watanabe Building
10662 Los Vaqueros Circle	P.O. Box 1331	1-4-2 Minami-Aoyama
P.O. Box 3014	Piscataway, NJ 08855-1331	Minato-ku, Tokyo 107-0062
Los Alamitos, CA 90720-1314	Tel: +1-732-981-0060	JAPAN
Tel: +1-714-821-8380	Fax: +1-732-981-9667	Tel: +81-3-3408-3118
Fax: +1-714-821-4641	mis.custserv@computer.org	Fax: +81-3-3408-3553
cs.books@computer.org		tokyo.ofc@computer.org

Publisher: Matt Loeb
Manager of Production, CS Press: Deborah Plummer
Advertising/Promotions: Tom Fink
Production Editor: Denise Hurst
Printed in the United States of America

Capability dEtermination (SPICE) methodology is available, and Chapter 16 presents practical experience with the SPICE trials.

Chapters 11, 14, 15, and 17 represent industrial case studies from Small and Middle-sized Enterprises (SMEs) and Very Small Enterprises (VSMEs) covering process analysis, improvement planning, measurement, and benefit analysis.

Summary and Outlook

Chapter 18 concludes that most process improvement initiatives are based on new technical approaches and still lack business orientation. To bridge the gap, the technical movement must be changed into a business movement so that top executives start to invest in process and product quality aiming at Return on Investment.

BACKGROUND AND HISTORY

The book is based on the results of three international conferences organised by the International Software Collaborative Network (ISCN) since 1994. Conferences on "Practical Improvement of Software Processes and Products," which were held in 1994 (ISCN'94, Dublin), 1995 (ESI and ISCN'95, Vienna), and 1996 (ISCN'96/SP'96, Brighton/London), brought together three types of players: large users (companies with major software process improvement programmes), methods providers (small companies offering specific methods and techniques in process/product analysis, measurement, and improvement), and individual experts (independent consultants, experts from companies acting on behalf of their companies in ISCN projects, or academic researchers).

The ISCN conference series focuses on "Practical Improvement of Software Processes and Products" and each conference has a structure including four major components: Strategies and Cooperation, Methodologies, Industrial Experience, and a Workshop about "How will this work for me?" A requirement for acceptance of contributions is that, for each presented methodology, there must be an industrial case study presenting the experience with the use of that methodology. This way the methodology portion is interfaced with the experience portion of the conference. The book project reused the same integrated architecture as the ISCN conference series.

The book was partly supported by the European Union under the Process Improvement Combined apprOach (PICO) project. It provides a handbook for process engineers and quality and project managers, and basic reference material for PICO training courses.

PICO's mission is to develop a comprehensive set of configurable training courses packaged with a book as a basic information pool and with a tool for supporting automated generation of analysis data covering "Process Improvement from Analysis to Success."

PICO is based on the "learning by doing" training principle and on the paradigm of a learning organisation. Only those systems that are able to continuously adapt themselves to new situations and environments have a chance to survive. Learning and dealing with these new situations is a key success factor. A life form that stops learning stops living.

Since 1998 the ISCN conference series has continued under the European Software Process Improvement Initiative (EuroSPI) with EuroSPI'98 in Sweden, and further conferences in the Scandinavian area in the years until 2002.

The PICO project is carried out with the financial support of the Commission of European Communities (CEC) under the Leonardo da Vinci Programme.

Contents

Chapter 3   Software Process Analysis and Improvement: Concepts and Definitions

Chapter 4   Software Process Analysis and Improvement: A Catalogue and Comparison of Models

PART II—EXPERIENCE

Chapter 1

Road Map for Readers and How to Use the Book

Dr. Richard Messnarz
International Software Consulting Network (ISCN), Ireland

INTRODUCTION

This chapter classifies the experience presented in this book and provides a road map to guide the reader to extract the experience which is most applicable and beneficial. It starts with a structural analysis illustrating dependencies, links, and relevance for certain phases of the improvement cycle, and finally offers decision support for identifying which parts of the book are usable in the context of the reader's organisation.

While Chapters 2 to 17 present principles and experience, Chapter 1 will make it easy for different target groups in an organisation to select reusable experience and to draw from a large set of data from European process improvement initiatives and projects.

MOTIVATION UNDERLYING THE BOOK

Combined Use of Methodologies

Many process improvement experts are too convinced from only one (their own) approach, leading to statements such as: Only Capability Maturity Model (CMM) will work; or, Only BOOTSTRAP will work; or, Just skip all assessment methods and use goal-based metrics, and so forth. This book is a collection of different experiences with different projects and proposes a combined use of methodologies. This combination of business aspects with pragmatic improvement approaches is essential in order to make the right improvement decisions. It is senseless to make process improvement with just a pragmatic goal to formalize. Return on investment (ROI) and the support of the organization's business success must be the real drivers of any process improvement action.

A big electronics company in Europe, for instance, made an assessment resulting in maturity levels for different areas of the organization and the identification of weaknesses such as unrealistic planning, no process for design reviews, and weak configuration management. The organization was already International Organization for Standardization (ISO) 9001 certified but only 30 percent actually accepted the guidelines due to missing practicability (formally well documented but not realistic for projects in the field [7]). A formal pragmatic assessment and improvement approach would then, for example, decide about introduction of configuration management and so forth, but does this really now meet the organization's business goals? Without any additional data than the normal assessment methodologies (CMM, BOOT-STRAP, etc.) this unfortunately cannot be answered.

So this electronics company decided to run a goal analysis based on the Goal Question Metrics Methodology (GQM) approach, in parallel interviewing business managers, department heads, Information Technology (IT) managers, and project managers to design a consistent goal tree from top to bottom. See Figure 1.1.

One of the specific business policies was to create a financial framework for the next years which allows the funding of a reserve budget to be used to introduce new products to the market. To establish this marketing budget, the business managers decided to stabilize the development effort from divisions at x percent so that, with all other overheads and cost, a certain percentage is saved every year. This enables the marketing budget to be available at the time the product is announced. At this moment, the divisions were certainly higher than x percent and the improvement actions (based on the previously identified weaknesses from the assessment) had three years to demonstrate the success of achieving this business goal.

The technical staff were frightened and thought that people would be dismissed but the truth was that a proper interpretation of the business goals led to a completely different view. The business managers expected that process improvement provides a better work process and environment so that with the same staff more projects and tasks can be done and over

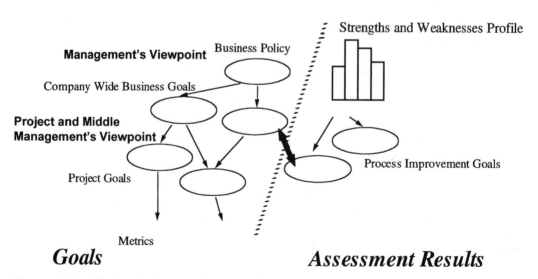

Figure 1.1 Aligning business goals [10] with improvement of weaknesses found in assessments [6].

time the development effort is stabilized at x percent. Under this perspective the three process weaknesses were again analyzed and further interviews showed a potential of reuse because in all systems in the sector nearly 80 percent of the functionality was always the same. So the improvement plan focused on an integration of design, and on configuration management and review of a reuse pool of these 80 percent functions; and reduction of the development for each project to the only 20 percent additions—thus enhancing productivity and achieving the effort stabilization.

Now, let us assume that only a pragmatic assessment would have been performed. Three weaknesses would have been identified and without reuse orientation would have led to a pragmatic proposal to first run a pilot project to identify a configuration management system and field test it, to disseminate it to other projects, and to help make it a divisionwide standard. Sounds simple, but unfortunately the business context is lost. What then happens is that management sees additional effort, the development effort further increases and, with no vision of decrease of the development effort, the business manager after one year (before benefits can be made visible) would really decide about things like dismissals.

A More People-Oriented Process View

The book, of course, in general follows the principle that an improved process will lead to higher product quality. However, the book also adds to the statement "A fool with a tool is still a fool (so a tool is less important than having a process)" and a further one, "A fool with a process is still a fool." And it is not so much the maturity of each single person itself, it is the teamwork capability that is decisive.

Therefore, in Chapter 3 the book makes a teamwork scenario based definition of management processes in which people identify themselves with roles, people in these roles communicate, and people work together in a team. The workflow (process steps) is then just a waste product of the information flows in the team work (Chapters 3 and 14).

An Inclusion of the Business Context in General

Sometimes people are told that process improvement is a simple step by step pragmatic approach and can be described with technical checklists and levels of maturity. However, as business is dynamic also the requirements for improvement are continuously changing so that the improvement paths themselves underly a continuous adaptation.

Well, in this respect the book demonstrates a number of different viewpoints which might easily be misinterpreted as contradictions. Practice shows that the same strengths and weaknesses profile (as an output from assessments) at different organisations (depending on the business goals, the current infrastructure, the available resources, the cultural approach to change—very different in Japan and Germany compared to the United States) leads to different action plans and results.

So my answer to the above opinion is: I sometimes see persons that accelerate to full speed with confidence although they are directed toward a heavy wall. These are different roads to follow, even with the same starting situation, in different organisations depending on a number of factors, and the most important one is the business context.

Different Process Improvement Languages and Target Groups

Business managers, project managers, and practitioners speak different languages and might have different viewpoints on the same situation [9]. Business managers speak about fixed cost, variable cost, return on investment, leveraging, market trends, product sales, and customer satisfaction.

Middle and project managers speak about budget, work plans, quality plans, configuration management, requirements analysis and structured analysis, and always fear to be delayed or to overrun the budget provided by the business managers. Practitioners deal with modules, design them, implement, and test them, and deliver them so that they can be integrated into the system architecture planned by the project manager.

It is the nature of process improvement methodologies that measurement and control functions are installed which again will be seen differently by the different target groups. Business managers—not understanding that software process improvement (SPI) needs investment with a return on investment (ROI) in about 3 years—sometimes demand that process improvement is performed without any assignment of budget to it: let's do quality but it should not cost any dollars. This certainly leads to a disaster and top management commitment is the number one success criteria for starting an improvement program. Middle managers will like the process improvement most because it provides them with methodologies and facilities to better define the processes, to better visualize the productivity and quality, and to improve the predictability which leads to the fact that schedules and budget (which are set by the business managers) are better kept. At the beginning, the practitioners usually see the implementation of a process improvement program as a dirty trick of middle and project management to better control their performance. However, after some time they start to realize that more reliable plans give them enough time for design, and that better design reduces the rework and maintenance stress. Formalized reports help them to identify the root cause of problems and to track the correction, and they can learn and improve themselves based on measures [5].

It is a key to success to have all groups behind the initiative and to act as a translator of the different viewpoints [2].

STRUCTURAL ANALYSIS OF THE BOOK

Basically there are three types of relationships in this book outlined in Table 1.1.

Table 1.1.   Types of Relationships in the Book

Type of Link	Explanation
Principles ⇔ Experience	Linking principles with experience to provide illustrations
Principles ⇔ Principles	Establishing a framework into which the methodologies fit, avoiding redundancies and contradictions
Experience ⇔ Experience	Any variety is allowed; with the same starting situation, sets of different improvement methodologies were used in the industrial cases

Structure of Part I—Principles

Part I—Principles (see Figure 1.2) provides two basic clusters of chapters. A "process" cluster makes a role and teamwork-based software process definition (Chapter 3), introduces goal and process analysis, and provides an overview of currently existing models and methods for software process analysis and improvement (Chapter 4).

A "business" cluster describes the business managers views and return on investment principles (Chapter 2), approaches for goal analysis starting from business goals and breaking down

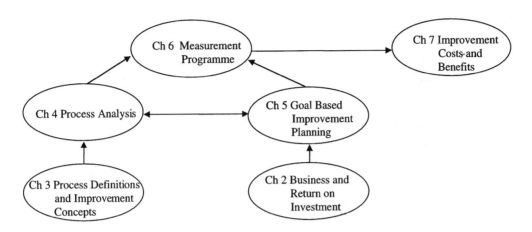

Process   + Business + Results

Figure 1.2. *Principles ⇔ Principles* relationships in Part I.

into improvement goals (Chapter 5), and a set of metrics to quantitatively measure if the goals are achieved (Chapter 6). It also provides an overview of cost and benefits in software process improvement (Chapter 7).

It is important to note (Figure 1.2) that the process analysis results and proposed improvement actions must be aligned with the business goals (thus there is a double arrow between Chapter 4 and Chapter 5) resulting in ROI.

Structure of Part II—Experience

Part II—Experience contains three basic clusters of chapters (see Figure 1.3). Chapter 8 discusses Siemens's assessment and improvement programme, and Chapters 9 and 10 illustrate the experience with improvement projects at Italtel, one starting with the Siemens assessment approach and one starting with the BOOTSTRAP assessment approach. Chapter 12 discusses Alcatel's experience in the same application domain as presented in Chapters 9 and 10 by Italtel.

Chapter 13 discusses experience with the ISO 12207 process modeling standard which formed the basis for the Software Process Improvement and Capability Determination (SPICE) methodology, and Chapter 16 presents the experience with the SPICE trials.

Chapters 11, 14, 15, and 17 represent industrial case studies from small- and medium-sized enterprises (SMEs) and very small enterprises covering process analysis, improvement planning, measurement, and benefit analysis.

Principles and Experience—Links between Chapters of Parts I and II

Table 1.2 illustrates which company contributed experience with which approach. Plan Do Check Act Cycle (PDCA), Goal Question Metrics Methodology (GQM), and Application of Metrics in Industry (ami) are in one category. This is because practice showed that ami is a framework to do GQM and that goal-oriented methodologies usually refer to a general improvement framework like PDCA. This is the curious reason why these three categories are combined into one in this book.

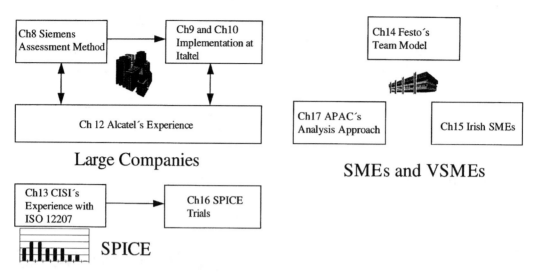

Figure 1.3. *Experience ⇔ Experience* relationships in Part II.

Table 1.2. *Principles ⇔ Experience* Relationships

	Chapter 8 Siemens	Chapter 9 and 10 Italtel	Chapter 11 Onion	Chapter 12 Alcatel	Chapter 13 AQT, CISI	Chapter 14 FESTO	Chapter 15 AIMware	Chapter 16 Fraunhofer	Chapter 17 APAC
Chapter 1 Business and ROI	✓			✓					
Chapter 2 Process models	✓			✓	✓	✓	✓	✓	✓
Chapter 3 Process analysis	✓	✓	✓	✓	✓	✓	✓	✓	✓
Chapter 4 GQM-Driven improvement		✓	✓	✓					
Chapter 5 Measurement programme		✓	✓				✓		
Chapter 6 Improvement cost/benefit	✓	✓		✓		✓	✓		✓

Note: Siemens, Italtel, Onion, AQT, CISI, AIMware, Alcatel, Fraunhofer, and APAC are company names.

Table 1.3. Process Analysis Approaches

	Chapter 8 Siemens	Chapter 9 Italtel	10 Italtel	Chapter 11 Onion	Chapter 12 Alcatel	Chapter 13 AQT, CISI	Chapter 14 FESTO	Chapter 15 AIMware	Chapter 16 Fraunhofer	Chapter 17 APAC
ami, PDCA, GQM			✓	✓	✓	✓				
BICO										✓
BOOTSTRAP		✓						✓		
CMM				✓	✓			✓		
EQA					✓					
ISO					✓			✓		✓
SPICE						✓			✓	
Siemens method	✓		✓							
TickIT					✓				✓	

Abbreviations: Benchmark and ISO combined (BICO), European Quality Award (EQA)

TYPES OF IMPROVEMENT PROJECTS

There are different types of improvement projects such as

- technology transfer based process improvement
- process modeling based process improvement
- training based process improvement

A process improvement project usually consists of a group of miniprojects combining the three types mentioned above. This could, for instance, be (1) to analyse and model a work scenario for configuration management, (2) to select and introduce a proper technology for supporting the work, and (3) to train the people to effectively follow the guidelines and use the infrastructure. However, in some cases you only need a better process model, or there might be a process already in place but the technology is missing, or there might be a proper technology in place but due to cultural issues the acceptance was missing. Thus, a process improvement project does not always cover all three components.

Technology Transfer Based Improvement

The selection and introduction of new technologies and platforms is a complex process and the required effort is often underestimated [2]. All recent improvement models emphasise that organisational aspects are most important, and that methodology is more important than technology. This means that before selecting any technology the work scenario must be designed and discussed with the engineers and, based on a defined organisational process, technology requirements are established to support certain process steps—and only then a technology is selected which satisfies the defined requirements. In BOOTSTRAP profiles, for instance, this becomes visible when the technology satisfaction is high, whereas the methodology level is low. Usually engineers also do not accept a new technology if it is not an integrated part of their work environment.

Therefore a technology transfer based improvement project is like a professional development project, with phases like:

- Analyse and design the work scenario (process modeling based process improvement)
- Identify the process steps which should be supported by technology
- Identify quantitative goals (expected benefits) in terms of quality and productivity
- Establish a list of requirements for the technology
- Evaluate the technology available on the market against the established requirements
- Select one (or more) candidates and implement them in pilot projects
- Measure the impact of the new technology on quality and productivity
- Extract best practices from the pilot projects
- Prepare the best practice for internal dissemination and training
- Train and transfer best practices to all other projects in the organisation

Process Modeling Based Improvement

Problems resulting from the increasing complexity of software systems were budget and schedule overruns, and reliability and quality problems leading to extremely high maintenance costs. In the early eighties Boehm [3] discussed the so-called "S-curve," which shows that software is becoming increasingly expensive, whereas hardware is getting cheaper. The "S-curve" was investigated in the United Kingdom (U.K.) [4] and it was found that in 1985 the distribution of the percent of total cost was as follows: 10 percent hardware, 90 percent software, with about 60 percent of the software activities being maintenance related.

All approaches to process improvement at the beginning of the eighties to cope with the software crisis were of a technocratic type, and the promises of the CASE manufacturers (including analysis and design components as well as code generators and 4GL facilities) have not been fulfilled. The above-mentioned study [4] continued the analysis of the "S-curve" until 1991, and it was shown that the high maintenance costs of 1985 could not be reduced. Moreover, a Canadian study [1] pointed out that in 1989, due to the international software crisis, the distribution of the percent of total effort was: 55 percent maintenance, 35 percent enhancements, and only 10 percent for new applications.

Because of the failure of the technology-driven approaches the interest in process-driven approaches started to increase in the mid-eighties. This led to the SEI technical report from Humphrey at 1987, the ISO 9001 standards, the IEEE software engineering standards, the ESA PSS05 software engineering standards, the different CMMs, and methodologies such as ami, BOOTSTRAP, etc. which were then developed between 1987 and 1993. And with SPICE this initiative is continuing.

These 10 years of experience with organisational analysis clearly highlighted that the root causes of technical problems usually are organisational problems such as

- Unrealistic planning
- Unclear responsibilities and roles

- Inefficient work processes
- Missing motivation and cultural problems
- Missing quality commitment

Therefore all current improvement initiatives first start with an organisational analysis, identify weaknesses, define work scenarios (with roles, responsibilities, process steps, workflows, results, etc.) for missing processes, and only then introduce supporting technology.

Training Based Improvement

From the technician's point of view the improvement is done when finishing the improvement experiment and by presenting the quality and productivity indicators. This, however, is not true for the business managers who have a much broader view of the improvement process. They provide resources to increase fixed cost in order to reduce, in the long term, variable cost caused by poor quality.

The business manager sees the experiment as a multiplication factor for his organisation. If by using a new process x in the domain y a productivity increase of z percent was shown in the experiment then the next step will be to use this approach in all projects in the domain to multiply the z percent productivity increase. This finally helps to achieve a productivity increase of z percent for the entire domain y of the company and not only for one experiment. And this transfer process from the experiment to different sites and projects in the organisation is also a very complex process.

Important factors here are:

- To create awareness before confronting the people with new processes and technologies
- To have quantitative and objective indicators to convince the managers
- To have process descriptions which are easy to understand
- Workshops—to let the experiment team present the project to other sites and projects and to discuss "But how will this work for me?"
- To provide training from practitioners for practitioners
- To found a kind of user club in the organisation that continuously refines the process
- To establish a close cooperation between the user club and the Software Engineering Process Group (SEPG)
- And so forth

THE ESSI PROCESS IMPROVEMENT MODEL

It is important to mention this model because it provided funds to many hundreds of process improvement experiments across Europe up to now, and will still be used for further years in the fifth framework program of the European Union. Process Improvement Experiments (PIEs) (see Figure 1.4) are forming the bulk of the Software Best Practice actions of ESSI European Systems and Software Initiative (ESSI)[8]. Their aim is to demonstrate the benefits of software process improvement through user experimentation. The results will be disseminated both internally within the user organizations to improve software production and externally to the wider community to stimulate adoption of process improvement at a European level.

The emphasis is on continuous improvement through small, stepped actions. During a PIE, a user organisation undertakes a controlled, limited experiment in process improvement,

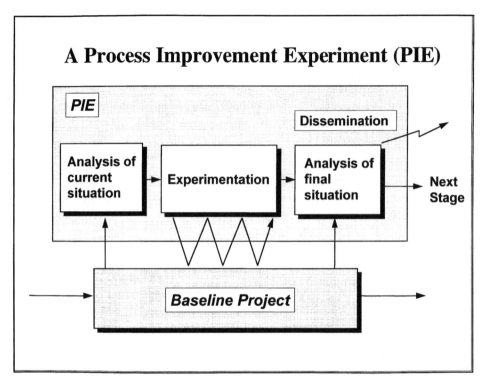

Figure 1.4.   The basic architecture of a PIE.

based on an underlying baseline project. The *baseline project* is a typical software project undertaken by the user organisation as part of its normal business and the results of the experiment should therefore be replicable.

For a PIE to be performed, it is required that the current status of software engineering be known (organisational process analysis) along with the organisational profile that one plans to achieve. The company's strengths and weaknesses profile is translated into a number of process improvement actions which are process modeling, technology transfer, or training based. The experiment (use of new work scenarios, technologies, know-how) is employed in a baseline project of the organisation (a small and not too critical software development project) and the impact on people, process, products is measured. The analysis of the final situation (good and bad experience) is then disseminated internally as well as in working groups externally.

Chapters 11, 14, and 15 document the experience with ESSI PIEs. In Chapter 15 the PIEs were running as TRI-SPIN projects which were a special Irish way of starting and performing mini-PIEs in Ireland.

ASSIGNMENT OF CHAPTERS TO PHASES OF THE IMPROVEMENT PROCESS

A major goal of the book was not to concentrate on one approach or on one aspect of process improvement but to discuss the process improvement issues from business to success. Therefore at least one chapter can be assigned to each of the phases of the improvement process (Figure 1.5), and Chapters 8–17 form a resource pool of experiments and reusable practice.

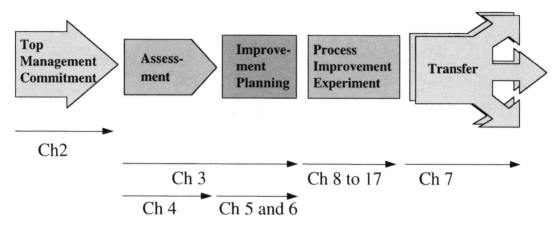

Figure 1.5.   Phases of the improvement process.

DECISION SUPPORT

First, it is recommended that you read the book from the beginning to the end. However, a feature of the modern world is that time gets shorter and shorter and becomes more precious every second. Business processes are becoming faster and business managers no longer read entire books but select the ten most significant pages, and if these pages do not seem to be interesting they skip the book. This is the reason why in this section a road map is established for different target groups for selecting the most interesting parts.

Target Groups

Table 1.4.   Different Target Groups

Question	Characteristics
Are you a business manager?	Your day-to-day language contains words like: revenue, profit, fixed cost, variable cost, total cost, leveraging, break-even, customer satisfaction, return on investment
Are you a project manager?	Your day-to-day language contains words like: requirements, work plan, quality plan, schedule, milestones, system architecture, etc.
Are you a practitioner?	Your day-to-day language contains words like: module, design, unit test, problem report, correction report, version, test protocol, etc.

Road Map for Business Managers

Start with the business cluster to read about business and SPI, business goal driven improvement planning, improvement cost, and how to measure success (Chapter 2 $\Rightarrow$ Chapter 5 $\Rightarrow$ Chapter 6 $\Rightarrow$ Chapter 7).

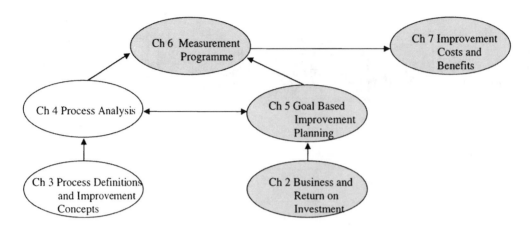

Figure 1.6.   Principles path for the business manager.

In Part II, Experience (Chapters 8 to 17) read:
   Are you a business manager from a large company?
    Read Chapters 8 and 12.
   Are you a business manager from a small company?
    Read Chapters 14, 15, and 17.

Road Map for Middle, Project, or Quality Managers

Start with the process cluster outlined in Figure 1.7 to read about process models, process analysis methodologies, benchmarking approaches, and how to use the analysis results for goal-based improvement planning. Be aware that Chapter 5 forms the interface to your business manager and thus is the most important aspect when you plan to align your goals with that of the business manager (Chapter 3 $\Rightarrow$ Chapter 4 $\Rightarrow$ Chapter 5 $\Rightarrow$ Chapter 6).

In Part II, Experience, read:
   Are you a project or middle manager from a large company?
    Read Chapters 8 to 10, and 12.
   Are you a project manager from a small company?
    Read Chapters 11, 13, 15, and 17.

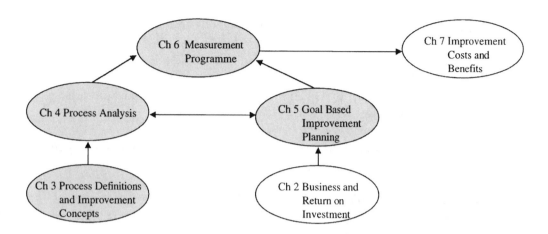

Process   + Business + Results

Figure 1.7.   Principles path for the project, middle, and quality manager.

REFERENCES

Chapter 1 is an overview of all the other chapters in this book, therefore it would be redundant to repeat here the references supplied in Chapters 2 to 17. Each of the chapters has its own reference list. Therefore only a few additional references are listed here, and the references that deal with the different methodologies are omitted. These works are discussed and documented in detail in Chapters 2 to 17.

1. A. Abran and H. Nguyenkim, "Analysis of Maintenance Work Categories Through Measurement," *Proceedings of the Conference on Software Maintenance 1991*, J. C. Munson et al., eds. IEEE Computer Soc., Sorrento, Italy, Oct. 1991, pp. 98–103.

2. W.L. Andersen, "Technology Transfer is a Social Phenomenon," *Transferring Software Engineering Tool Technology*, S. Przybylinsky and P. J. Fowler, eds., IEEE Computer Soc. Press, 1987, pp. 56–57.

3. B.W. Boehm, *Software Engineering Economics*, Prentice Hall, Englewood Cliffs, N.J., 1981.

4. J. Foster, "Program Lifetime: A Vital Statistic for Maintenance," *Proceedings of the Conference on Software Maintenance 1991*, J. C. Munson et al., eds., IEEE Computer Soc., Sorrento, Italy, Oct. 1991, pp. 98–103.

5. W.S. Humphrey, "The Personal Software Process in Software Engineering," *Proceedings of the Third International Conference on the Software Process*, Oct. 1994, pp. 69–77.

6. R. Messnarz et. al., BOOTSTRAP: Fine Tuning Process Assessment, *IEEE Software*, July 1994, pp. 25–35.

7. R. Messnarz and H.J. Kugler, "BOOTSTRAP and ISO 9000: From the Software Process to Software Quality," *Proceedings of the APSEC'94 Conference*, Computer Soc. Press of the IEEE, Tokyo, Japan, 1994.

8. M. Rohen, ESSI—"The European Systems and Software Initiative," *Proceedings of the ESI-ISCN'95 Conference on Practical Improvement of Software Processes and Products in September 1995 in Vienna*, ISCN, Ltd., Dublin, Ireland, 1995.

9. H.J. Thamhain and D.L. Wilemon, "Criteria for Controlling Projects According to Plan," *Software Engineering Project Management*, E. Nahouraii et al. eds., IEEE Computer Soc. Press, 1990, pp. 15–54.

10. R. Messnarz and P. Kuvaja, "Practical Experience with the Establishment of Improvement Plans," *Proceedings of the ISCN'96/SP'96 Congress on December 1996 in Brighton*, ISCN Ltd., Dublin, Ireland, pp. 155–169.

Chapter 2

The Software Process in the Context of Business Goals and Performance

Miklós Biró
SZTAKI, HU

Colin Tully
CTA, U.K.

INTRODUCTION

This chapter attempts to achieve a double goal. On the one hand, it synthesizes for the engineer the motivations of business managers when considering process improvement measures. On the other hand, it presents the benefits or drawbacks of process improvement for the business manager in a business strategy oriented integrated framework. The focus of this section, as is that of the book itself, is software development, nevertheless, many ideas presented here have a much broader scope.

The fact that engineers and business managers have different motivations is well known. For example, quality, one of the major themes of this book, is not a direct business goal. It is perceived quality which is a fundamental means of achieving customer satisfaction resulting in marketing leverage, an ultimate business goal to be explained below. Everybody knows examples from the software industry where there is a gap between real quality and perceived quality and where marketing leverage is determined by the latter.

It is of strategic importance to explain the differences in motivations to both sides, since engineers cannot directly contribute to the business objectives, just as business managers are unlikely to be able to contribute to engineering solutions. If this situation is properly recognized, however, the possible conflicts can be turned into synergy.

After the discussion of the business motivations for process improvement, a new business decision oriented viewpoint is presented to justify the existence of the basic notions of process assessment and improvement as compared to product quality in the case of software. We will make use of the terminology of Multiple-Criteria Decision Making (MCDM) which is self-explanatory in itself but is briefly presented anyway for the sake of completeness.

In this chapter, all ideas will be introduced at a conceptual level, thus avoiding analytical definitions and technical details which could be discouraging as well as practically unnecessary at this point for either engineers or business managers.

WINDS OF CHANGE

Software: Critical Success Factor and Crisis

The volume of work which we delegate to software is rising inexorably. There is no foreseeable fall in the rate at which our dependency on software is growing.

Software is implanted in more and more products, in a greater and greater part of the service infrastructure of the modern world, and in more and more business processes. In addition, there is a rapidly growing market for commodity software—software as a product in its own right. Software thus directly represents, and indirectly underpins, an increasing proportion of organisations' activity, output, turnover, profit, and real worth.

If they are to be successful in bringing products to market, in winning contracts and in running their internal operations, and if they are to be adaptive and to survive in complex and rapidly changing markets, organisations must be sure of having the right software. Software, that is, which does the right job for its users, costs the right amount, and is ready at the right time.

Getting the right software requires an enterprise to mobilise effectively a wide range of build and buy activities and internal and external resources. Except in the case of specialist software houses, those activities and resources are alien to what the enterprise considers its mainstream business. It is estimated that, in Europe, 70 percent of software development is carried out by organisations whose core activity is not software.

Here in a nutshell lies a fundamental explanation of the "software crisis" which has occupied our attention, but has defied attempted solutions, for nearly three decades.

- On the one hand, software is a critical success factor, with enterprises demanding an insatiably escalating volume of software functionality for their products and processes.
- On the other hand, to develop software of the size and complexity which will meet those demands is a task of great technical and management difficulty, requiring strengths which lie outside the culture and resource of most enterprises.

In the large number of organisations for which that is true, senior executives (whose training and experience has rarely been acquired in information technology [IT]) have, in general, been unable to understand the nature or the seriousness of the software problem, or to evaluate proposed solutions to it. Action has been left by default to software practitioners, who have generally perceived the problem as one of technology, and have tried to solve it with technology. Since technology is usually the least significant of the ingredients in the total problem brew, and since technological solutions often make things worse rather than better (at least in the short term), such attempts have rarely led to success.

Between the two groups, corporate management and software practitioners, there has existed a communication gap, a chasm of mutual incomprehension, which was recognised even before the software crisis which it feeds. The two groups have different languages, perceptions, objectives, loyalties, problems, and values. Their mutual incomprehension has fatally distorted most attempts to formulate problems and solutions.

There is now, however, substantial evidence that winds of change are blowing. They affect both the practitioner side and the management side of the divide, and will lead to both a better understanding of the business needs by the technical managers, and a better understanding of process improvement needs by business managers.

BUSINESS MOTIVATIONS

Experiences describing engineering and business benefits of software process improvement were hard to find during the early days of software maturity models. The reason is clear. It is far from being in the interest of a low-maturity-level commercial company to make this fact public. The situation changes as soon as there is notable improvement in the maturity level. Indeed, publication of an enhanced level of maturity may have a significant effect on the marketing leverage of the firm. It is not surprising, consequently, that the final outcome of software process improvement (SPI) experiments, mostly published by U.S. firms up to now, is positive. The reported problems and pitfalls represent, however, invaluable experiences. The second part of this book is unique in that it contains a large amount of experiences and that they are, in addition, primarily from Europe.

One of the most pertinent questions a business manager can ask is the following: "How can I make my firm succeed where another has failed?" Managers with financial, operating, production, marketing, human behavioural, or other orientations will give a variety of answers to this question and will arduously argue for their valuable ideas. Here, we will outline a framework integrating and structuring several orientations.

The key concept of the approach is the notion of the lever. *Levers* are means used by a firm to increase its resource generating ability, just as a mechanical lever is used for increasing the force applied to an object. The analogy goes even further. Just as a force can be applied in many different ways to the object resulting in a similar displacement, the use of the different levers can increase the resource generating ability of the firm resulting in similar business benefits. Finally, the resources are used to increase the assets of the firm and to reward employees and stockholders.

Let us analyse the ways SPI can provide leverage to a firm from the financial, operating, production, marketing, and human behavioural perspectives.

Financial Leverage

Financial leverage means borrowing funds and investing them with a return higher than the cost of the debt. If a company is able to exploit financial leverage, it can make money on funds it does not own. Can SPI provide financial leverage to a firm? The answer is clearly yes if the return is high enough to make it worth borrowing money for achieving it. In other words, is the return on investment (ROI) for SPI high enough?

This issue is discussed in more detail in Chapter 7. Here, we only mention a few determining numbers which allow the reader to form an idea about the magnitude of the leverage that can be achieved. ROI is considered as "the bottom-line figure of most interest to many practitioners and managers" in a pioneering report [1] of the Software Engineering Institute (SEI) of Carnegie Mellon University. [20] The value of this report lies in the fact that it contributes to the satisfaction of the major need of companies for quantitative information regarding the benefits of SPI before committing resources and investing into it. There were 13 organisations, where CMM-based SPI occurred prior to 1990, which agreed to provide their highly sensitive and confidential data to the SEI for anonymous or identified reporting according to their own decision. The companies were the following:

- Bull HN
- GTE Government Systems

- Hewlett Packard
- Hughes Aircraft Co.
- Loral Federal Systems (formerly IBM Federal Systems Company)
- Lockheed Sanders
- Motorola
- Northrop
- Schlumberger
- Siemens Stromberg-Carlson
- Texas Instruments
- United States Air Force Oklahoma City Air Logistics Centre
- United States Navy Fleet Combat Direction Systems Support Activity

The report does not claim that its results are typical. It only shows the potential benefits of SPI in a favourable environment. And these benefits in terms of ROI are more than impressive. The range of the ratio of measured benefits to measured costs is between $4x$ and $8.8x$ over periods of software process improvement ranging from 3.5 to 6 years. Benefits include savings from productivity gains and fewer defects, but do not include the value of enhanced competitive position which will be examined below under the title marketing leverage. Costs include the cost of a Software Engineering Process Group (SEPG), assessments, and training, but do not include indirect costs such as incidental staff time to put new procedures into place.

In [2], Capers Jones reports a return on investment (ROI) of $3x$ to $30x$ with the returns measured over a 48-month period using the Software Productivity Research (SPR) assessment method and baseline studies. Exceptionally in the literature, Capers Jones also reports a negative and alarming record: "Several companies and government agencies have managed to spend in excess of $10,000 per capita with no tangible benefits accruing."

The conclusion of this section is that yes, SPI can provide significant financial leverage to the firm, making it worth borrowing money for investing into it. Nevertheless, the effect can be adverse if the company does not pay appropriate attention to accrued costs and to immediate exploitation.

Operating Leverage

The profitability of a firm highly depends on its cost structure, that is, the distribution between its fixed costs and variable costs. *Operating leverage* (Figures 2.1 and 2.2) means the relative change in profit induced by a relative change in volume, which is clearly higher for a firm with lower variable costs. Nevertheless, the achievement of a low variable cost production usually presumes high fixed costs, that is, a capital-intensive process.

Software process improvement clearly means an increase in fixed costs, which include training, consulting fees, equipment, software licenses, and improvements in office conditions. However, the question is whether the company is really able to use it for decreasing its variable costs. Measuring the variable costs of software production is not a straightforward issue. The notion of function point had to be invented to resolve this problem among others. Function point analysis is discussed in more detail in Chapter 6 of the book.

Function points are results of well-defined calculations based on different characteristics of a software product that are of interest to users: inputs, outputs, data groups, inquiries, interfaces. The cost of the average number of person-months necessary for delivering a fixed quantity of function points is an appropriate measurement for the variable costs of software production (person-months/function point). However, the measurement mostly used in reports on software process improvement is development productivity (function points per person-

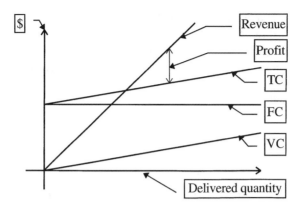

Figure 2.1.   Firm with high fixed costs (FC) and low variable costs (VC). The total cost is TC = FC + VC.

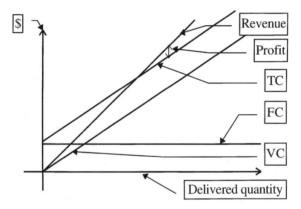

Figure 2.2.   Firm with low fixed costs (FC) and high variable costs (VC). The total cost is TC = FC + VC.

month) which is in fact the reciprocal of the above number. In the following, reported results are presented in terms of development productivity whose increase is, consequently, equivalent to the decrease of the variable cost of software production.

If, due to software process improvement, a software firm is able to deliver the same quantity of function points using less person-months than its competitors, then it will have the potential to take advantage of operating leverage. Nevertheless, real profit will only be generated if the revenue resulting from actually delivered function points exceeds the total of the cost (TC) of software process improvement (FC) and the cost of person-months used for generating them (VC). This means that bigger firms with a larger number of delivered function points will have a better chance to enjoy the operating leverage resulting from software process improvement.

Productivity gains per year measured in lines of code (LOC) per unit of time are reported in [1] to be between 9 percent and 67 percent at the examined organisations. Another form of productivity gain particularly relevant to software is due to the earlier detection of defects also presented in [17]. The figures show a 6 to 25 percent increase in the number of early detected defects. This represents enormous savings if we consider that "the cost of fixing a defect pre-release is approximately $50 per line of code, while the cost of fixing a defect discovered post-release is about $4000 per line of code."

It is important to highlight at this point that the major European company Siemens is a worldwide pioneer in measuring and publishing information related to productivity gains resulting from software process improvement. They report the following experimental reductions in error costs based on maturity levels [3]:

- 17 percent from Level 1 to Level 2,
- 22 percent from Level 2 to Level 3,
- 19 percent from Level 3 to Level 4, and
- 44 percent from Level 4 to Level 5.

Siemens also reports productivity increases in terms of lines of code, but at this point it is more appropriate to refer to Chapter 8 of this book which gives a direct account of Siemens experiences.

Another report accounting for productivity gains due to process improvement in European software development organisations originates from the results of a questionnaire developed by IBM Europe [4]. This report compares, among others, the performance of leaders to that of laggards from among 360 responding organisations from 15 countries. As summarized in Table 2.1, leaders "achieve a development productivity of 25 function points per person-month; remove over 95% of defects before delivery; estimate consistently to within 10% of the actual cost and duration of a project; and spend less than 1% of the development effort on defect correction in the first 12 months after delivery." Laggards "have a development productivity below 5 function points per person months; remove less than 50% of defects before delivery; have projects which often exceed estimates by more than 40%; and spend more than 10% of the development effort on defect correction in the first 12 months after delivery."

Production Leverage

Production leverage is the rate of growth of profits resulting from cost declines due to the accumulation of production. It is an empirical fact that unit production costs decline exponentially when experiences are accumulated and the steady reuse of these experiences is well managed by the firm.

The graph of the unit costs in function of the cumulative quantity produced is known as the experience curve which is usually represented as a straight line in a logarithmic scaled system of coordinates. The existence of the experience curve is essentially due to economies of scale, learning, improvements, and reuse [5].

The accumulation of experiences and the management of their steady reuse is clearly one of the primary objectives of software process improvement. Interestingly, this aspect of soft-

Table 2.1. Data from Leaders and Laggards

	Leaders	Laggards
Development productivity (function points per person-month)	25	<5
Defects removed before delivery	95%	<50%
Inaccuracy of cost and duration estimates	10%	>40%
Percentage of development effort spent on defect correction in the first 12 months after delivery	<1%	>10%

ware process improvement has not been analysed directly. Nevertheless, [1] acknowledges that the techniques useful for tracking the cost changes over time do not specify what is causing the changes. The cause may be the process improvement, but it may also be increased experience, new analysis and design methods, new tools, and so on.

Marketing Leverage

Marketing leverage means the effect of higher prices and innovative distribution on profits. Software process improvement, maturity achievement, ISO 9000, or TickIT certification have an important impact on the perceived capability of the company and on the perceived value of its products, which contributes to improved customer satisfaction and makes it possible to achieve higher prices. Quality and process improvement are part of a differentiation strategy in which the business delivers and is perceived to deliver a product or service superior to that of competitors. In a study of 248 distinct businesses in the service and high-technology industries referred to in [5], "a reputation for quality was the most frequently mentioned sustaining competitive advantage."

In line with the above U.S. study, a major European company, Lloyds Bank Plc. lists the demonstration of competitiveness through the CMM/SPICE/TickIT schemes as one of the key drivers for software process improvement [6].

The experiences of Siemens, another major European company, were already mentioned and are described in more detail in Chapter 8 of this book. The "promotion of the external visibility of Siemens' software competence" is listed as an important area to focus on [3]. They also report that "highly-predictable quality regarding system releases and costs led to greater market acceptance."

Herbsleb et al. [1] acknowledge the importance of "improved reputation, good will, and brand name recognition" as intangible benefits of process improvement arising from the "impact of SPI on customers," but they present no actual results relating to these findings.

A survey reported in [7] provides the feedback of more than 50 companies on the benefits gained from the TickIT certification scheme. One of the major benefits is formulated in the following way: "Customers have increased confidence in the quality of our products. With the advent of TickIT the U.K. Ministry of Defence (and many other influential purchasers) have ceased their second party assessment activity, while many other large organisations now insist that their suppliers and product resale partners achieve ISO 9001 certification by a TickIT accredited certification body."

One of the rare reports which provide a measurement of the direct effect of SPI on the marketing leverage of a company was presented in [8]. The report is based on 560 SEI software process assessments through December 1995 whose results were provided to the SEI by March 1996. The statistics give the percent of respondents reporting "excellent" or "good" customer satisfaction when improving software processes from the initial level (around 80 percent) through the repeatable level (a surprising decrease to 70 percent) up to the defined level (around 100 percent).

Human Leverage

Human leverage means the effect of employee motivation on profits. It is widely known that employee motivation can be significantly influenced by immaterial means like management styles and organisational structures. Huge individual energies can be released, for example, in an appropriate teamwork environment where team members are simply given the responsibility to do their jobs as well as they can, instead of enduring close surveillance. Nevertheless, attention must be paid to the differences in the collective mental programming of people in different national cultures [9].

The exploitation of human leverage is particularly important in SPI since software development is a fundamentally human mental process. Herbsleb et al. [1] classify the "impact of the SPI effort on the organisation's employees," including "better morale, improved understanding of the corporate mission and vision, fewer crises, less stress, less turnover, and better communication within the organisation," among the intangible benefits of SPI. Actually, no measurements are presented relating to these benefits in this report.

The above-mentioned report presented in [8] also shows statistics giving the percent of respondents reporting "excellent" or "good" staff morale when improving software processes from the initial level (around 20 percent) through the repeatable level (around 50 percent) up to the defined level (around 60 percent).

We have already mentioned above an important study [4], initiated by IBM Europe, which gives a measurement of the impact of employee morale on the level of performance of a company. The statistics, based on 360 responding organisations from 15 European countries, show that employee morale correlates strongly with both delivery performance and quality performance levels.

An ultimate recognition of the importance of human leverage is the development of models directly addressing this issue: the People Capability Maturity Model (P-CMM) [10], and the Personal Software Process (PSP).

FROM PRODUCT QUALITY TO PROCESS IMPROVEMENT— A BUSINESS DECISION ORIENTED APPROACH

The objective of this section is to justify, from a business decision point of view, the existence of the basic notions of process assessment and improvement as compared to product quality in the case of software, and to show how Software Product Evaluation and Software Process Assessment and Improvement methods can benefit from the systematic application of MCDM theory and techniques.

MCDM is a classical applied research field whose objective is the improvement of decision-maker performance when there are several alternatives and a variety of criteria for evaluating and comparing them. The fundamental notions of the MCDM field are introduced in the following section with a focus on software quality. The questions analysed afterward are the following:

- What kinds of decisions are supported by software product quality evaluations based on more or less defined systems of decision criteria?
- Are there critical decisions which are not supported by software product quality evaluations?

Multiple-Criteria Decision Making (MCDM)

MCDM research starts back in the eighteenth century with Daniel Bernoulli [11]. He argued that a person's utility of wealth is not a linear function of the money measure of his wealth. In our century, it was first von Neumann and Morgenstern [12] who gave a scientific articulation to MCDM. They referred to "several conflicting maximum problems." Since then, due in part to the general successes of the operations research/management science field, the literature of MCDM has exhibited a huge growth.

With a mind trained in the traps of the software development process, we can discover, however, that many approaches are strongly biased by the solution methods they offer themselves. An analogous problem is encountered within the software life cycle, when user requirements specification is not expressly separated from software requirements specification.

There are of course approaches which discipline themselves to focus first on the analysis of the real nature of decision problems. These include [13] and [14]. In this paper, we introduce the MCDM approach following [14], but focus on the concepts relevant to Software Product and Process Assessments.

Multiple-criteria decisions involve alternatives which are usually evaluated on the basis of a hierarchical system of criteria. There is a large variety of evaluation process types. The alternatives for example are most of the time to be ranked, but there are cases where only a single alternative has to be accepted.

The starting point of the introduction to MCDM must be the clarification of the fundamental concepts which are *attributes*, *objectives*, *goals*, *criteria*, *strategies*, and *alternatives*. The subject of the following sections is essentially the discussion of the high relevance of these notions to software quality and process assessment. These terms are typically used but not defined in the otherwise meticulous standards.

Attributes are the descriptors of reality. They can be identified and measured essentially independently from the decision maker's or user's requirements. *Objectives* consist of individual attributes or sets of attributes together with their directions of preference. They are clearly identifiable with the decision maker's or user's requirements. Two or more objectives can form higher-level objectives resulting in a hierarchy which helps overcoming the cognitive psychological barriers in case of more than 7 ± 2 simultaneous objectives [15]. *Goals* mean target levels of achievement defined in terms of either attributes or objectives. They are determined by the decision maker's or user's requirements. *Criteria* is a general term for the attributes, objectives, or goals which are judged relevant in a given decision situation by an individual or a group. A quality standard can be considered as the result of a group consensus on a system of relevant quality criteria.

Strategies are the means of changing the current situation. *Alternatives* are strategies which are candidates to be employed for changing the current situation according to a current system of criteria. Alternatives are usually expected to be mutually exclusive. Nevertheless, if the decision situation allows for the simultaneous selection of several alternatives, then it is enough to state that there is at least one pair of alternatives which are mutually exclusive, otherwise there is no real decision to be made.

Product Quality Evaluation

The evaluation of the quality of a software product is one of the basic issues in information technology. Many books [16–18] and papers deal with this subject, never explicitly but practically suggesting MCDM approaches. A system of decision criteria is summarised in the ISO/IEC 9126 standard further analysed in Chapter 6. The first level of the criterion hierarchy contains the following elements: functionality, reliability, usability, maintainability, portability, and efficiency. This standard should be considered as the result of a group consensus on a system of relevant criteria. Nevertheless, there was no consensus about subcharacteristics for example, which are only provided as an illustrative annex to the current standard, but will be fully integrated in its forthcoming revision after the consensus is reached. In MCDM terms, the current standard defines high level objectives only without specifying the corresponding lower-level measurable attributes themselves. In this way, it fails to satisfy its fundamental purpose of assisting consistent

Table 2.2. Characterisation by Weighting and Scaling ISO 9126 Quality Attributes

Alternatives	
Product 1 Product 2 Product n	Result: Status Related to the ISO/IEC 9126 Standard
Criteria	
Functionality Reliability Usability Maintainability Portability Efficiency	Evaluation: scaling, weights

software product quality evaluation. Approaches to filling this gap are provided by the forthcoming revision of ISO/IEC 9126 and by the SCOPE guide for software product quality evaluation [19], which is one of the sources of the draft international standard ISO/IEC DIS 14598.

The decisions that ISO/IEC 9126 intends to support are the following:

- Does the software requirements specification adequately reflect the user requirements?
- Does the developed software satisfy the user requirements?

From the MCDM point of view, the alternatives are software products which can be evaluated and ranked by calculating the weighted average of their scores with respect to the different criteria (see Table 2.2). The weighted average is also called *status* of the alternative. The weights and value scales should be carefully determined so that the status represents a true characterisation of the alternatives on the basis of the hierarchical system of criteria.

There are fundamental business decisions which are not supported by ISO/IEC 9126 or other systems of product quality criteria, and which are in the focus of the following sections.

Decisions Depending on Sustainable Reliability

The fact that a company was able to eliminate defects from some of its products does not mean that those same defects will not reoccur in future software products. A fundamental business issue is, consequently, the customer's decision problem:

- Is the supplier able to sustain the reliability of its production?

ISO-9000 certification is intended to support the above decision by focusing on the process rather than on the product. The standard generally applied to the software development process is ISO 9001 which is complemented by the ISO 9000-3 notes for guidance on the application of ISO 9001 to software development (see Table 2.3). ISO 9001 lists 20 quality system requirements which can be considered as a set of high-level criteria for the above decision problem.

These criteria have more or less detailed subcriteria spelled out in the standard's subparagraphs on multiple levels. Thus, we are again faced with a hierarchical system of criteria.

Table 2.3.   ISO 9001 and ISO 9000-3 as a Guidance for ISO 9001 Certification

	ISO 9001	**ISO 9000-3**
Alternatives	Certification (Yes or No)	Certification to ISO 9001 (Yes or No)
Criteria	• Tree structure • 20 elements (high-level criteria) • Multiple subparagraphs (lower-level criteria)	Same as ISO 9001 in a different structure.
Result	Certificate	Certificate

Here the lowest-level attributes are mostly measurable in binary terms, that is, only the existence of required policies and practices has to be checked. ISO 9000-3, formulated in the form of guidelines for the application of ISO 9001 to the development, supply and maintenance of software, is essentially a restructuring and reformulating of the system of criteria from top to bottom but finally covering all of the ISO 9001 requirements.

DECISIONS RELATED TO SOFTWARE PROCESS ASSESSMENT AND IMPROVEMENT

Certification provides little support for improvement. The system of requirements is rather large and their simultaneous satisfaction may mean an inhibitory burden to the company. In addition, conformance must be maintained after registration as well, which can be best achieved by implementing continuous improvement. Consequently, the natural question before or after certification is how a company can improve its capability for reliably producing high quality products. This is the supplier's decision problem:

- How can we improve the reliability of the production?

While the customer's decision problem discussed in the preceding section involved only two alternatives (yes or no), this decision problem admits a large number of alternative courses of action the choice among which is supported by the action plan resulting from software process assessment.

Contrary to the yes/no conclusions of ISO 9000, software process assessment and capability evaluation methods provide an ordinal scale for measuring process maturity, which makes it possible to set priorities for improvement efforts.

In the well-known capability maturity model, the maturity levels are decomposed into key process areas which are targeted by specific yes/no questions during assessment. From the decision-making perspective, the key process areas are high-level criteria which lead to the decision to be made about the maturity level of the evaluated software producing unit as a whole. The decision alternatives in this case are the maturity levels themselves as outlined in Table 2.4.

It must be mentioned that there are also methodologies which provide a refined maturity level status for detailed process-quality attributes. When, instead of evaluation, the decision problem is improvement related, a strategy must be worked out. The key process areas or

Table 2.4.   Maturity Levels as Results of Software
Capability Evaluations

	Capability Evaluation
Alternatives	Five maturity levels
Criteria	Key process areas
Result	Maturity level status (integer)

Table 2.5.   Characteristic Profiles as Results
of Maturity Level Ratings for Individual
Key Process Areas

	Improvement Action Plan
Alternatives	Key process areas or process-quality attributes to include into the action plan
Criteria	Maturity level or maturity level status for detailed process-quality attributes
Result	Action plan

detailed process-quality attributes become decision alternatives as the potential components of the improvement action plan. The decision problem is the following:

- Which key process areas or which attribute(s) should be improved in order to achieve a higher maturity level?

In this case, the number of alternatives is considerable and leads to a refinement of Table 2.4 to the structure shown in Table 2.5. In mathematical terms, the number of alternatives is the number of subsets of the set of key process areas.

CONCLUSION

Winds of change are blowing in the software development arena. This chapter was a gust of wind unveiling the motivations of business managers to software engineers in the form of financial, operating, production, marketing, and human leverages as well as showing to business managers the potential of software process improvement to increase these leverages.

When the motivation is there, goals have to be identified and decisions have to be taken. The second part of the chapter gave a structured viewpoint of the fundamental business decisions addressed by the book.

REFERENCES

1. J. Herbsleb et al., "Benefits of CMM-Based Software Process Improvement: Initial Results," Software Engineering Institute, Carnegie Mellon University, Technical Report CMU/SEI-94-TR-13.

2. "The Pragmatics of Software Process Improvement," *Software Process Newsletter*, No. 5, Winter 1996, pp. 1–4.

3. A. Völker and M. Gonauser, "Why Maturity Matters," *European Software Engineering Process Group Conference* (C305), 1996.

4. P. Goodhew, "Achieving Real Improvements in Performance from Software Process Improvement Initiatives. European Software Engineering Process Group Conference (C306), 1996.

5. D. A. Aaker, *Strategic Market Management*, John Wiley & Sons, 1995.

6. C. Larner, "More Practical Experiences and Lessons Gained by the Software Engineering Process Group of a Major European Bank: A Question of Ownership," *European Software Engineering Process Group Conference* (C304), 1996.

7. "TickIT Provides Proven Quality Benefits to Both Customers and Suppliers of Software Systems," Computer Services Association (CSA) Position Paper, Pub. No. 32, 1994.

8. B. Peterson, "Software Process Improvement Trends," *European Software Engineering Process Group Conference* (C306), 1996.

9. Geert Hofstede, "Motivation, Leadership, and Organisation: Do American Theories Apply Abroad?" *Organisational Dynamics*, Summer 1980, pp. 42–63.

10. B. Curtis, W. E. Hefley, and S. Miller, *Overview of the People Capability Maturity Model*. Software Engineering Institute, Carnegie Mellon University, Maturity Model CMU/SEI-95-MM-01.

11. D. Bernoulli, "Specimen Theoriae Novae de Mensura Sortis." *Comment. Acad. Sci. Imper. Petropolitanae*, Vol. 5, 1738, pp. 175–192. English translation by L. Sommer, "Exposition of a New Theory on the Measurement of Risk," *Econometrica*, Vol. 22, 1954, pp. 23–36.

12. J. von Neumann and O. Morgenstern, *Theory of Games and Economic Behaviour*, Princeton University Press, Princeton, N.J., 1944.

13. A. Tversky, "Intransitivity of Preferences," *Psychological Review*, Vol. 76, 1969, pp. 31–48.

14. M. Zeleny, *Multiple Criteria Decision Making*, McGraw-Hill, 1982.

15. M. Biró and I. Maros, "The Use of Deep Knowledge from the Perspectives of Co-operative Problem Solving, Systems Modeling, and Cognitive Psychology," *Shifting Paradigms in Software Engineering* (R. Mittermeir ed.,) Springer-Verlag, Vienna, New York, 1992, pp. 56–67.

16. T. Gilb, *Principles of Software Engineering Management*, Addison-Wesley, 1988.

17. A.C. Gillies, *Software Quality Theory and Management*, Chapman & Hall, 1992.

18. *Software Engineering Economics*, Prentice Hall, Englewood Cliffs, N.J., 1981.

19. J. Boegh, "SCOPE: A Guide for Software Product Quality Evaluation," *Proceedings of the ISCN '94 Conference on Practical Improvement of Software Processes and Products*, Dublin, Ireland, 1994.

20. J. Herbsleb and W. Hayes, "Performance Profile: Measuring the Business Value of Software Process and Technology Improvements," European Software Engineering Process Group Conference (C317), 1996.

Chapter 3

Software Process Analysis and Improvement:

Concepts and Definitions

Dr. Richard Messnarz
ISCN, Ireland

INTRODUCTION

Nowadays process analysis has become a widespread practice and many engineers speak about it without understanding the basic principles of what terms like *process, system,* and *analysis* really mean. Even if methodologies such as CMM, BOOTSTRAP, SPICE, TickIT, Goal-Question-Metric (GQM), etc. are used, it is helpful to understand the basic paradigms underlying all the different methodologies, and to know about the differences between the various paradigms and methodologies to be able to select the appropriate methodology for a specific organisational environment.

In this introductory chapter the relevance of different philosophical paradigms for software engineering and process analysis approaches will be outlined and discussed. This discussion will be based on the evolutionary stages of the software industry over the last 30 years, thus making the evolution of the concept of *process* understandable. This shall help to understand the basic principles underlying the methodologies and it results in a definition of the terms *software system, process model, software process, organisational system, analysis, software system analysis,* and *software process analysis.*

SOFTWARE ENGINEERING PHILOSOPHY

Plato (428–347 B.C.) believed in an eternal and immutable reality and that humans perceive reflections of this reality (the myth of the cave). Plato's pupil Aristotle (384–322 B.C.) divided the world into categories and identified a logic system to describe the world, and as a consequence the world then could be expressed mathematically. He concentrated on understanding the real world instead of believing in an ideal one as Plato did [30].

This above view was dominant in the software industry in the sixties and the beginning of the seventies. Different programming languages were developed and people believed in the fact that every problem can be described mathematically and automated by computer programmes. However, this view of reality fails to take into account a number of important facts and difficulties:

- The complexity of software systems [1, 16, 29, 79–81]
- The fact that all the world is not immutable but is rapidly changing and thus the maintenance problem was severely underestimated [1]
- The fact that the level of abstraction using only a programming language as means of description is not sufficient for designing and understanding systems [15, 49, 56]
- The fact that systems are developed by humans who are error prone [40, 70]

The Complexity of Problems

Even if there was an immutable world or a mathematically describable world it would be preposterous to believe that humans can completely understand it. In fact the problem starts with the requirements analysis and the architectural design. If a requirement is defined incorrectly and then implemented the mathematical implementation of the requirement might be correct but the model of the underlying reality will be wrong. Even today there are research groups who believe that with programming languages you can solve any problem but they fail to realise that problems might arise much earlier in the organisation, the management, the requirements definition or the architectural design before a single line of code is written [14].

In the late seventies U.S. companies in the aerospace and defence sector became aware of this problem and started to measure software development, estimating the complexity of programs, comparing effort with the complexity, collecting first test and defect data. Between 1974 and 1981 a number of well-known articles were published illustrating that with the growing complexity of a software system the effort was increasing exponentially [33]. And with the increasing complexity the maintenance effort dramatically increased [1].

A Rapidly Changing World

The innovation cycle in industry is becoming shorter and shorter [40]. After delivering a product version to a customer the following things might change:

- The customer requirements (additional functions needed, change in organisational environment)
- The market demand
- The underlying technology platform
- The system and operational environment
- Product changes due to problems
- The underlying software environment (new versions from Microsoft appear every 6 months)
- The management requirements (ISO 9001, subcontractor capabilities)
- The development team changes
- Business factors (a developing company stops further development because revenue can rather be made by other services and products)
- The politics (e.g., in the defence sector the budget is reduced by half)
- etc.

In fact, as Heraklith (540–475 B.C.) said, "all things flow"; the world is rapidly changing, adapting, and underlies a continuous evolution [30]. So instead of believing that software products describe fixed and immutable realities it seems more adequate to perceive reality as something that can change rapidly and that one must be prepared for continuous change management [8, 25, 54, 60, 73].

A Higher Level of Abstraction

Aristotle even proposed a higher level of abstraction for modeling realities than the use of programming languages. To this end Aristotle defined terms like *form* and *logic*.

First, Aristotle classified things in different groups—"I see a horse, then I see another horse, and another. The horses are not exactly alike, but they have something in common, and this common something is the horse's *form*" [30]. This is comparable to the object-oriented paradigm which holds that the world consists of object classes comprising objects with common features [15]. In order to describe the relationship between objects Aristotle defined object hierarchies, the *forms* dog and horse, for example, are both living things.

Second, the *logic* describes the relationship between the different forms. An example of logical rules used by Aristotle is: "All living things are mortal." "Aristotle's dog Hermes is a living thing." "Hermes is mortal." This logic leads to a conceptual view of the world which consists of a number of object classes and relationships. This approach is similar to the object-oriented paradigm in software engineering, in which also additional types of relationships have been identified (see section below, "Dynamic Process Architectures").

Humans Are Error Prone

As has been mentioned above, technology, organisational environment, etc. are rapidly changing. However, many people have a natural aversion to change that manifests itself as excuses like: "We don't have time to learn all this new stuff"; "It looks too complicated"; "We heard that this would not work for us because . . ." [2].

People are generally reluctant to give up their investment in the current solution, especially if it is an ingenious use of existing resources which they discovered for themselves after much effort and for which they have been given recognition. This is known as the not-invented-here syndrome.

Sometimes the new technology is a closed system—a black box—that the users do not fully understand, either because they have not had the opportunity or because it is beyond their technical ability. Given a choice between using this technology or something that may not work as well but which they understand, they will almost always choose the latter. This is the so called black-box-syndrome.

Therefore to continuously adapt organisational systems and software processes to up-to-date requirements the human factor is most important. And it is a key success factor

- To provide effective training
- To motivate people for using new approaches, methodologies, and technologies
- To identify clear roles and responsibilities and to enable all people to enhance and adapt their skills continuously

Researchers have found a wide range in programmer performance [70], from a low of 5:1 to a high of 100:1. This means that programmers at the same level, with similar backgrounds and comparable salaries might take from 1 to 5 days to complete the same tasks. In studies conducted by Bill Curtis, the ratio of programmer performance was 22:1 [22]. This was both for source lines of code produced and for debugging times, which include both defect detection rate and defect removal efficiency. This means that negative programmers with every change (or correction of a previous fault) insert new faults into the system, which then exponentially multiplies the effect of negative programmers.

However, the above programmer performance data stem from old studies (not based on the modern 4GL and code-generating environments), and focus only on the programmer's role and its influence on productivity and the defect rate. But what about the humans' responsibility for project planning, capacity planning, requirements definition, etc.? A study, for instance, which represents a survey of 72 projects has shown that more than 40 percent of problems are caused by error-prone project and capacity planning [31].

This proves that problems may be dealt with at the wrong phase, or problems might be phrased as solutions. It is therefore very important that organisational systems, responsibilities, procedures, and methodologies are defined and checked across the entire work and that tailorable models such as CMM, BOOTSTRAP, ISO 9001, etc. are used as a framework [19, 38, 57, 61, 62, 64].

Aristotle differentiated between two main categories, living and nonliving things. However, he did not see such a dynamic interaction of living and nonliving things as there turns out to be nowadays between nature, organisational systems, software processes, and human beings.

DYNAMIC PROCESS ARCHITECTURES

At the beginning of the eighties, people still believed that all problems could be solved technically. Software development was seen as a technical process and not as an organisational human management process.

This led to the establishment and use of structured design methodologies and the development of software engineering tools (CASE tools) to solve the software complexity problem, to make software more understandable, and to provide engineers with a higher level of abstraction for describing software before starting the implementation.

The CASE approach [49, 56] describes software systems as networks of data processes with data- and control-flows, databases, and interfaces. Figure 3.1 shows a sample collection of elements used to describe software systems with Structured Analysis (SA) based on the Yourdon/De Marco notation guidelines. The system in Figure 3.1 reads machine variables online from a machine interface, stores data records in a database from which the records are analysed online. User 1 switches the software system on/off and the status of the system, for example, active/nonactive/waiting is displayed. If the system is activated the data records are analysed and the machine behaviour is calculated and displayed to user 2. User 2 uses the displayed data to control the machine from which the data are retrieved online. Please note the regulative cycle between the user 2, the machine, and the software system.

This example illustrates that by using SA techniques the system architecture is made more visible and humans mainly are seen as user interfaces to a technical process. Another interesting paradigm behind SA is the "levelling" principle, each process itself might consist of a cluster of further processes (Figure 3.2).

The SA-based software engineering approach still failed to take into account the following aspects:

- Many organisations bought a CASE tool not taking into account the organisational requirements. People must be convinced to describe systems with extensive graphical and formal design methods before any development of code, people must be trained, and the organisational and teamwork procedures must integrate the new methodology efficiently.

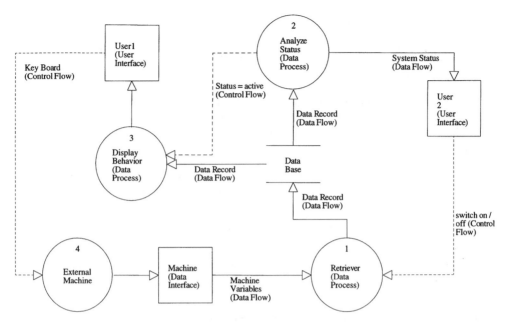

Figure 3.1.   A part of a sample software system description using SA.

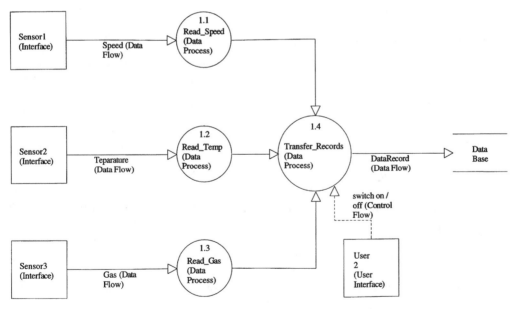

Figure 3.2.   An example for "levelling" the data process "retriever" in Figure 3.1.

- If the requirements management fails the design will also fail.
- The design is only as good as the person's capability who transforms the customer requirements into a software system architecture: "A fool with a tool is still a fool".
- If the project and resource planning fails the design will either not be performed or will be done under time pressure leading to many problems in later phases.
- If there are no design reviews (also involving a technically competent person from the customer) errors will be found in testing or maintenance which could be found earlier.
- If the CASE approach is not integrated into an overall development process which is part of a company culture it will not be used.

So it became necessary to create a "systems thinking" approach which takes all organisational and management aspects into account in addition to software systems.

SYSTEMS THINKING

The radical constructivism defines the world as a dynamic network of processes which highly interact with each other. Humans are seen as part of this network, the human brain itself acting as a process. And like human beings every process in the world underlies a continuous evolution.

This means that change is a natural requirement of a never-stopping evolution of the world. And any evolution of a process leads to an adaptation of its interfaces to all other processes.

So it is completely wrong to believe that a stable and never-changing software system can be achieved. The development and management of software systems must rather concentrate on the adaptability of software systems and change management as a key organisational process.

Process Models and Views

At the end of the eighties people started to develop management guidelines and standards such as SEI/CMM, ISO 9001, Trillium, ESA PSS 05 Software Engineering Standards, BOOT-STRAP, etc. [28, 42, 45, 46–48, 55, 58, 61, 62, 64, 75, 76] which deal with the architecture of a comprehensive organisational and management system which is able to guarantee the development of reliable software systems meeting customer satisfaction and expectation. The paradigm followed was: "The quality of a software system is governed by the quality of the process used to plan, manage, develop, and evolve it."

Most of these models comprised practices, workflows, document flows, templates, and procedures but many of them did not cover all possible process views for description. Therefore at the beginning of the nineties process modeling guidelines were published such as the ESA Process Modeling Standard, or the German V-model [32] which is part of the EURO-METHOD approach, etc. clearly outlining all different submodels, viewpoints, and aspects that can be taken into account to establish defined organisational systems and (software) management processes for software development firms.

A process model might cover one, many, or all of the following aspects

- The activities and process steps
- The workflow (network of activities)
- The results
- The overall data architecture (relations between the results)
- The roles and responsibilities
- The resources (and different types of resources)

of an organisational and management process [32, 43, 51, 52]. People are assigned to roles, roles are assigned to activities, activities produce results, and activities are part of a workflow architecture. Results are part of an overall data architecture. Resources are assigned to activities and roles, and resources are used by the people playing a certain role. Software systems as described in the previous chapter are either regarded as resources (in the case that tools are applied for development) or as the result of software development related workflows.

The Fine-Graining of Process Models

This is one of the major problems in process modeling. Metamodels describe major process steps but do not describe activities, roles, and resources in detail. The Waterfall Model, for instance, is such a metamodel. Different companies might use the same metamodel but would implement the major process steps by other sets of activities, roles, and resources. Framework models describe detailed activities and expected results but leave open to define roles, responsibilities and resources to employ the required activities for achieving the results. The CMM, for instance, is such a framework model. And very detailed models use all aspects for describing a process including detailed activities, expected results, roles, responsibilities, and resources. Such detailed models are usually applied in safety-critical applications to ensure a complete software engineering process.

The German V-model (Figure. 3.3), for instance, is such a detailed model which describes four main process models: quality system, software engineering, project management, and

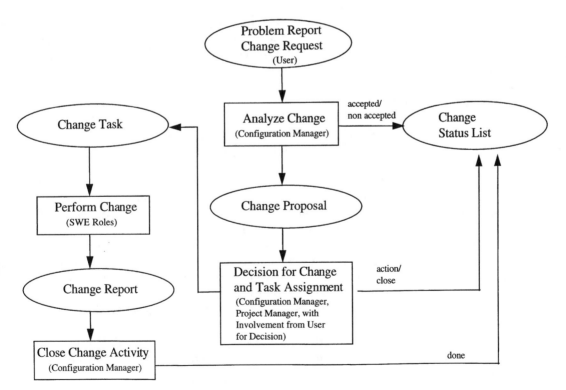

Figure 3.3. V-model—part of the submodel for configuration management.

configuration management. For these four submodels all activities, workflows, results, and roles are described. The V-model includes a tailoring guideline about how to adapt the models for your own organisation.

The squares in Figure 3.3 represent activities, the ellipses represent results, roles are described within brackets, and by using arrows a workflow is constructed.

A user identifies and documents problems and, with the support of a technician, produces a change request. The configuration manager analyses the change request then creates an entry in the change status list to indicate whether the change request was "accepted" or "not accepted." If "accepted" was chosen, the configuration manager produces a change proposal. The change proposal is discussed with the responsible project manager and, if needed, the customer is involved; then, the configuration manager makes a decision. If "action" is decided a "perform change" process is created and submitted to Software Engineering (SWE) and a change report is produced. When the change has been performed, documented, and reported the new version is released and archived and a "done" is inserted into the change status list. Figure 3.3 illustrates only parts of the V-model's change management process; the complete V-model also contains the configuration management plan and further protocols [32].

Roles and Ownership

At the end of the eighties people sometimes interpreted standards and guidelines such as CMM, ISO 9001, etc. using wrong statements like: "You need a standardised process to document the work done, and knowledge of, an employee so that dependence on the specific individual is minimized and the focus is more on the process." As you see in Figure 3.3, roles are an element of process models, and process models are used to describe effective practices of an organisation to make them understandable across different divisions and projects, therefore becoming a standard. If you do not assign roles to activities there will be no actors employing the activity. In fact roles are like organisational variables which can be filled with people [65].

In this way, a management and organisational process becomes like a theatre in which people are playing different roles. Employee morale and skills are an important factor for the success of an organisation [72, 78].

This is the reason why roles usually are defined by responsibilities and skill requirements. If a role R is assigned to an Activity A which uses a computer programme P as a resource then role A must be capable of efficiently using the methodology and technology underlying the programme P.

Thus the people factor became more and more important and the SEI started to think about a people CMM clearly outlining people skills for different evolutionary levels of an organisation. Detailed models like the V-model or the one presented in Chapter 14 describe role names and requirements within certain work scenarios.

This way an organisation becomes a collection of different use cases and work scenarios [15] each of which can be described by process models. If people then get involved in one of those work scenarios they select one or many roles and start to own these roles with all related responsibilities (and skill requirements). And this ownership feeling leads to the psychological effect that people find themselves as responsible and active parts of a process which leads to higher motivation.

Another major advantage is the fact that role models allow multifunctional team structures which is very much necessary if development is done by distributed small teams and not by one large monolithic team.

Resources

Resources are assigned to activities, and resources can be:

- People who are assigned to roles
- Effort of people acting as roles
- Software systems and tools that are used by a role within an activity
- Access rights related to roles (e.g., time constraints)
- Fixed and variable cost related with the implementation of the process
- etc.

Process Evolution

Process models are used to describe work scenarios of an organisational system and form the basis for defining software development and management processes. Such processes run through different evolutionary stages when starting a continuous improvement programme. These evolutionary stages have first been defined decades ago by Crosby [20] with the maturity grid. Later the SEI refined it to a maturity level model [39, 66] with five evolutionary stages, and recently SPICE refined this model to six evolutionary levels [26, 63].

When you first start to think about modeling your best practices and standardising them across projects and divisions there is usually a lack of practices. After introducing lacking practices the practices can be integrated into work scenarios which are established with process models, thus reaching a defined level in which the roles, responsibilities, activities, results, and dependencies are understandable and visible. However, the next question then is: "Is the process which I established really the most effective one?" To find this out you need quantitative data, thus metrics definition [25, 39, 50, 67, 68, 69, 71, 74], data collection, and benefit analysis must become part of the process. And in the final evolutionary stage all quantitative data are used to make objective decisions about changing the processes and procedures established.

All Things Flow—Change as a Natural Requirement

It is very important to have a positive view on change. Systems in general consist of many complex elements, links, and interfaces and each element itself is underlying a continuous evolution which is a natural principle (see previous sections).

DEFINITION OF SOFTWARE PROCESS

Based on the evolution of the notion process over the last 30 years the term *software process* can be defined on four different levels:

- On a technical system level
- On a development level
- On a management
- And on an organisational system level

A *software process on the technical system level* (according to SA) [56] is a data process with defined input and output criteria, and function that reads from interfaces/other processes/databases and provides results to interfaces/other processes/databases (Figure 3.1). Each process can again consist of a network of processes (Figure 3.2).

A *software development process* [42, 45] describes a set of phase-specific activities (phases according to, e.g., the waterfall model, spiral model, evolutionary development model, etc. [11–13]), methods and practices used by people for developing and maintaining a software system, guidelines for documenting throughout the life cycle (planning, product related, quality related, maintenance related, etc.) [46], verifiable milestones and checkpoints and measurable quality goals [3, 34–37, 53].

A *software system* consists of a cluster of software processes on the technical system level, represents the outcome of a software development process, provides features defined by requirements management, fulfils or fails the quality attributes defined in ISO 9126 [7, 10, 48] concerning the established requirements, and is part of an operational environment interacting with users and interfaces that are integrated into an *organisational system.*

An *organisational system* [18] consists of clusters of different work scenarios which can be described with process models comprising activities, workflows, results, roles, and resources. People are assigned to roles, roles are assigned to activities, activities are part of a workflow, activities produce results, and roles use resources to perform the activities. Resources can also be software systems used by a role to produce the required result. This way software systems are integrated into organisational systems, the users of a software system represent roles in the organisational system.

In ISO 9000-3 three clusters are differentiated: quality system, supporting activities, and life cycle. The life cycle activities are the software development process. The quality system describes the organisational system and how the processes and standards are developed and maintained. And the support function defines all management activities around the life cycle activities employing the standards and processes defined in the quality system. This viewpoint is similar to the previous definition of a software development process, an organisational system, and the following definition:

> A *(software) management process* is an instance of a collection of work scenarios of the organisational system related with the management and support of (software) development. Applicable work scenarios are selected, and real effort and people are assigned to practically carry out the work according to the process models defined in the organisational system.

Note: An organisational system usually comprises a number of work scenarios which are not directly related with software development.

These definitions can also be applied for SPICE [26, 63], with the SPICE process categories representing organisational systems, the SPICE processes representing the work scenarios (e.g., how to plan a project), and the base practices defining the activities that must be performed within a work scenario.

PROCESS ANALYSIS PARADIGMS

Definition of Software Process Analysis

The term "process analysis" can be described

- on a software system level, or
- on an organisational system level.

In addition for each of the two levels different methodologies can be applied to perform the analysis. Most parts of the book deal with the analysis of organisational systems and how to improve them.

Software System Analysis [45] is the process of studying a software system by partitioning it into parts (functions or objects) and determining how the parts relate to each other to understand the whole. For this approach Structured Analysis (SA) or Object-Oriented Analysis (OOA) methodologies can be applied.

(Software) Process Analysis is the process of studying the different work scenarios of an organisational system, to identify activities, workflows, roles, resources, results, and relationships between all components and to establish models, quantitative data, or any illustrative results that make the current status of the organisational system visible and point out areas for change and improvement.

Concerning software process analysis three main streams stemming from philosophy are currently applied in industry.

Empirical Approaches

The empirical approach was a very important step to claim the power of experimental science. Instead of creating ideal theoretical models, a new theorem is first tried out in the small, proved in experiments, and theoretically described after the proof. So the world is not understood as a whole but by experiments pieces are understood and integrated into a whole.

This philosophy formed the basis for the experimental software engineering approach aiming at an experience factory (Figure 3.4).

To set up an experiment the Goal-Question-Metric (GQM see Chapters 5 and 6 [3, 4–6]) approach usually is applied to identify business goals, derive from that organisational system goals, derive from that project and software system goals. A metric is assigned to each goal which helps to quantitatively verify if the defined goals have been achieved. The next step is to define a number of experiments which change/adapt/improve parts of the organisational

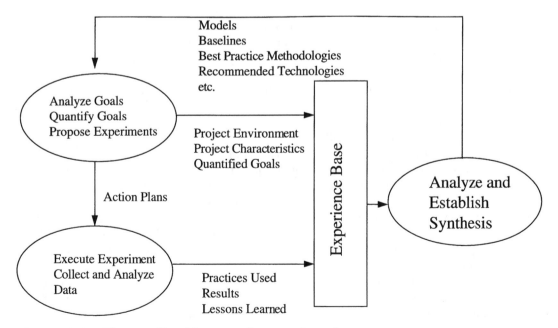

Figure 3.4. The overall architecture of an experience factory.

system and to use the defined metrics to measure the impact of change on the organisational system. All experiments and measured results are kept in an "experience database" and successful experience is applied for all further projects.

Chapters 5 and 12 deal with this approach and illustrate by practical case studies how to efficiently employ it.

Assessment and Benchmarking Approaches

Assessment models [44, 57, 77] represent an interesting combination of Plato's world taking into account the evolution of this ideal world over time.

Each software process assessment and improvement model (see Chapter 4) has three dimensions: functionality, capability, and improvement. The functionality dimension contains the processes to be evaluated, the *capability* dimension comprises the capability levels against which the processes will be evaluated. The *improvement* dimension makes use of the assessment results (capability values for features of the functionality dimension), takes into account business goals and priorities, and establishes a number of improvement projects (experiments) resulting in an improvement strategy.

The functionality dimension is like Plato's world and describes the architecture of an ideal organisational system against which all companies shall be evaluated. The capability dimension describes evolutionary levels along which the processes of the functionality dimension undergo an evolution. And the improvement dimension describes procedures which enable the organisation to continuously adapt itself to up-to-date requirements and situations.

In contrast to the experimental software engineering approach it is assumed that the functionality dimension already describes the whole world and that organisations are analysed to identify how many practices are missing to also establish a complete organisational system.

The main disadvantage of this approach is that it is a wrong assumption to believe that all organisations can be compared with the same model.

On the other hand this approach allows organisations to get tips about missing practices, to achieve a fast overview about the current status in comparison with international practices, and to compare its profile with that of other organisations in the same market segment. This benchmarking idea is a key motivating factor for organisations to perform an assessment.

Different assessment models are described in more detail in Chapter 4 and many of the practical experiences deal with how assessment results were used to plan, start, and measure improvement actions.

Figure 3.5 shows a typical example from a BOOTSTRAP assessment. In the functionality dimension of BOOTSTRAP the process clusters represent organisational systems, process attributes correspond to work scenarios (e.g., project management), and the questions relate to activities in the work scenario (see above definition of an organisational system). Each process attribute is measured on a maturity level scale from one to five. 1 means that practices are missing, 2 means that practices are in place and efficiently employed, 3 means that an effective process model and work scenario has been established, 4 means that the productivity and quality are measured, and 5 means that that the quantitative data are used to continuously improve the process.

An assessment results in a profile illustrated in Figure 3.5 and is used as a first overview about strengths and weaknesses in comparison with the ideal architecture of an organisational system.

Practical experience with the use of such profiles to establish action plans is described in Part II of this book.

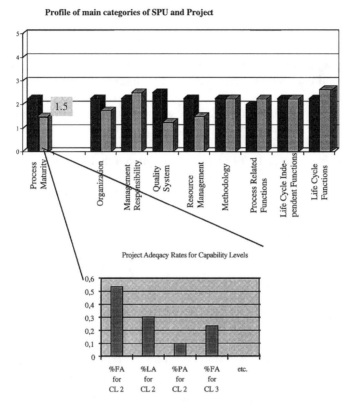

Figure 3.5. Typical assessment results.

Tailoring and Reengineering

There are three ways for tailoring, two moderate ones and one radical:

- To select a standard (e.g., the German V-model) and to adapt practices that are applicable
- To select different approaches and to combine them to a new model
- Complete reengineering

The moderate tailoring philosophy bases on the idea that every organisational system has its own key competencies. The process analysis then focuses on identifying the key practices and enhancing the software engineering capabilities in those areas which further strengthen the key competencies.

The radical tailoring philosophy says that an improvement project shall throw away all old practices and directly start with more efficient processes. However, mostly this approach fails either because you loose your previous key competencies (they are substituted by a new model with another focus) or because a model introduced from outside tries to radically change the work culture of the people.

So it is a key success factor to take into account practices that are already in place, to consider the business objectives of the organisation, and only then use the assessment results to establish an action plan for the organisation based on quantified goals.

The following case study describes a process modeling project which was performed for a middle-sized Austrian company (see Chapter 14). It aimed at the development of an effective team and process model for small software engineering teams tailoring the ESA software engineering standards [28] to their needs. In this company most development is performed by small and competent teams with multi-functional roles. People must be able to play different roles in one team—designer and developer, sales representative and requirements engineer, project leader and developer of most critical modules, etc.—following the demands of small and multi-functional teams. This is in contrast to the old paradigm of "management by function" in which one person is assigned to one job and does not play any other role. This can only be done in very large companies and even there such a system lacks flexibility. Therefore the paradigm of "management by processes," in which one person can play many roles which are clearly defined within work scenarios, was employed in this project [32].

During the modeling project

- Nine different work scenarios from project acquisition and requirements engineering to maintenance
- 11 roles
- 25 result types
- 40 activities (process steps)

were identified.

The modeling project had a duration of 7 months (Feb. 1995 through Aug. 1995) and comprised

- One consulting team (one expert plus two junior consultants)
- One field test team (five people working in a multifunctional environment)

who held

- Five workshops following the rules detailed below:
- Each workshop had to have an agenda (a minimum set of questions to be discussed)
- Each workshop aimed to include all the personnel involved
- Each workshop resulted in graphical models
- Each workshop resulted in minutes
- Each workshop had a duration of 2 days
- Each workshop resulted in homework to be done by the consultants and to be reviewed by the field test team.

One of the most critical success factors was motivating the engineers to cooperate with the external consulting team and to use the new guidelines and models. This was due to the fact that managers and software engineers had different viewpoints. The goal of the managers in this project was to gain better insight into the work done by the teams. The goal of the engineers was to improve their workplace and to facilitate their work, but they also saw the visibility of the work processes as a means of control that could be used against them by management. Therefore it seems to be of critical importance that modeling is not done with the managers alone. Consultants should include all software engineers and managers in solution-oriented discussions identifying roles, responsibilities, work scenarios, and data objects.

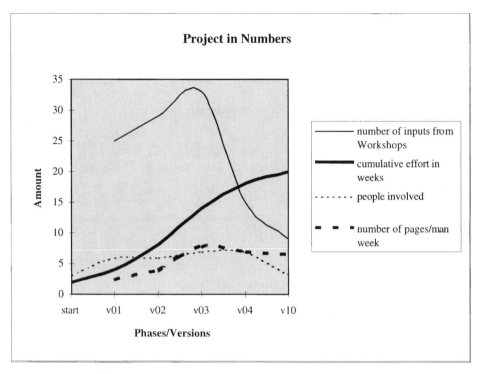

Figure 3.6.   Quantitative data of the above modeling project.

The quantitative project data can show whether the modeling project proceeded properly:

- *Number of inputs from the workshop.* If key people are left out from the workshop discussions, problems will be detected very late, usually when the engineers complain that they cannot work with the model. Therefore it is a good sign if the input-curve increases in the first phases of the project and decreases towards the end of the project. The sooner you realise the requirements and problems the sooner you will get on the right track.

- *Cumulative effort in weeks and number of pages per person-week.* Let us look at Figure 3.6. In the beginning the consulting and the field test team had a lot of discussions and interviews because it really took time to understand the existing procedures and to deal with people's wishes and suggestions. So the modeling in the first 2 months was very slow. Once the goals, procedures, and missing practices were well understood and a team spirit was established, the modeling speed doubled (compare versions v02 and v03 in Figure 3.6). If you are on the right track, there must be a jump in your effort and productivity curve, otherwise you have not reached the "point of no return" when suddenly all engineers and the modeling team start to work toward a shared vision.

Table 3.1 illustrates the steps performed, the main questions that were discussed, and the results achieved. Figure 3.6 summarises some quantitative project data.

Table 3.1. General Project Schedule

Step	Activity	Product
Planning (Jan.–Feb. 1995)	Planning project and allocating resources	Purpose, scope
Workshop 1 (Apr. 1995)	Identification of different scenarios/use cases scenarios	
Modelling 1	Identification of roles involved Documenting the use cases/scenarios Documenting the roles and their interaction	*Version 0.1:* Describing roles and interface objects and how they inter- act
Workshop 2 (Apr. 1995) Modeling 2	Identification of data objects Scenario diagrams Drawing scenario diagrams	
Workshop 3 (May 1995) Modeling 3	Refining roles Refining scenario diagrams Refining the role descriptions, the data object descriptions, and the scenario diagrams	*Version 0.2:* Version 0.1 plus graphical representation of scenarios *Version 0.3:* Clear and agreed • Roles and responsibilities • Data objects • Work scenarios
Workshop 4 (May 1995) Modeling 4	Definition of standard planning templates based on the scenario diagrams Establishment of a data collection and analysis plan for process and product measurement Discussion of reuse concepts Drawing the MS Project templates Documenting the standard data collection plan Refining the scenario diagrams to include data collection, analysis Including the aspect of reuse in the scenario diagrams	*Version 0.4:* Standard planning templates Data collection and analysis plan
Workshop 5 (July 1995) Modeling 5 Acceptance (Aug. 1995)	Review of the overall model Acceptance test protocol Final refinements Final Acceptance	*Version 1.0* *Version 1.0* released

CREATING A FRAME OF MIND

The goal of this chapter was to create a frame of mind: a good improvement manager and assessor understands that

- Every process model has its limitations
- There are complex relations between systems, humans, and organisations

- Improvement mostly directly relates to the reengineering of work scenarios of organisational systems to do the same work in less time, with less cost, producing higher quality.

Also this chapter points out that all the world, all humans, and all systems underlie a continuous evolution and it is a natural process that everything changes all the time. So it is much more important to address the design of systems which are adaptable, tailorable, and configurable than to believe that a stable never-changing system can be achieved.

REFERENCES

1. A. Abran and H. Nguyenkim, "Analysis of Maintenance Work Categories Through Measurement," *Proceedings of the Conference on Software Maintenance 1991*, J. C. Munson et al., eds., IEEE Computer Soc., Sorrento, Italy, Oct. 1991, pp. 98–103.

2. W.L. Anderson, "Technology Transfer is a Social Phenomenon," *Transferring Software Engineering Tool Technology*, S. Przyblinski and P. J. Fowler, eds. IEEE Computer Soc. Press, 1987, pp. 56–57.

3. AMI Consortium, ESPRIT Project 5494, *Application of Metrics in Industry: A Quantitative Approach to Software Management*, June 1992.

4. V.R. Basili, "Recent Advances in Software Measurement," *12th International Conference on Software Engineering*, IEEE Computer Soc. Press, Los Alamitos, Calif., 1990, pp. 44–51.

5. V. Basili, "An Experience Factory," *Proceedings of the International Conference on Lean Software Development*, Stuttgart, Germany, Oct. 1992.

6. V. Basili, "Software Process Evolution at the SEL," *IEEE Software*, July 1994, pp. 58–66.

7. G. Bazzana, O. Andersen, and T. Jokela, "ISO 9126 and ISO 9000—Friends or Foes?" *Proceedings of the Software Engineering Standards Symposium 1993*, IEEE Computer Soc. Press, Los Alamitos, CA, pp. 79–88.

8. E.H. Bersoff, "Elements of Software Configuration Management," *Software Engineering Project Management*, E. Nahouraii et al., eds., Computer Soc. Press of the IEEE, Washington, D.C., 1988, pp. 430–438.

9. M. Biro, H.J. Kugler, and R. Messnarz et al., "BOOTSTRAP and ISCN—A Current Look at a European Software Quality Network," *The Challenge of Networking, Proceedings of the CON'93 Conference*, Oldenbourg, Vienna, 1993.

10. J. Boegh, "SCOPE—A Guide for Software Product Quality Evaluation," *Proceedings of the ISCN'94 Conference on Practical Improvement of Software Processes and Products*, ISCN Ltd., Dublin, Ireland, 1994.

11. B.W. Boehm, "Improving Software Productivity," eds. *Software Engineering Project Management*, E. Nahouraii et al., eds. Computer Soc. Press of the IEEE, Washington, D.C., 1988, pp. 93–107.

12. B.W. Boehm, "A Spiral Model of Software Development and Enhancement," *Software Engineering Project Management*, E. Nahouraii et al., eds. Computer Soc. Press of the IEEE, Washington, D.C., 1988, pp. 128–142.

13. B.W. Boehm, *Software Engineering Economics*, Prentice Hall, Englewood Cliffs, N.J., 1981.

14. B.W. Boehm, "Risk Management Practices—The Six Basic Steps," *Software Risk Management*, IEEE Computer Soc. Press, Los Alamitos, Calif., 1989, pp. 115–150.

15. G. Booch, *Object Oriented Design*, 2d ed., Benjamin Cummings, 1994.

16. F.P. Brooks, "The Mythical Man-Month," *Datamation*, Addison-Wesley, 1973.

17. D.N. Card and R.L. Glass, *Measuring Software Design Quality*, Prentice Hall, Englewood Cliffs, London, Sydney, Tokyo, 1990.

18. G. Chroust, "Computer Integrated Work Management," *Shifting Paradigms in Software Engineering*, R. Mittermeir, ed., Springer Verlag, Vienna, New York, 1992, pp. 4–13.

19. F. Coallier and B. Canada, "How ISO 9001 Fits Into the Software World," *IEEE Software*, Jan. 1994, pp. 98–100.

20. P. B. Crosby, *Quality is Free—The Art of Making Quality Certain*, McGraw-Hill, New York, 1979.

21. B. Curtis, Maintaining the Software Process, *Proceedings of the Conference on Software Maintenance 1992*, IEEE Computer Soc. Press, Orlando, Fla., 1992, pp. 2–8.

22. B. Curtis, "Substantiating Programmer Variability," *Human Factors in Software Development*, IEEE Computer Soc. Press, 1981, pp. 533–534.

23. C. Debou, "ami—A New Paradigm for Software Process Improvement," *Proceedings of the ISCN'94 Conference on Practical Improvement of Software Processes and Products*, ISCN Ltd., Dublin, Ireland, 1994.

24. C. Debou, N. Fuchs, and M. Haux, "ami—A Tailor-able Framework for Software Process Improvement," *Proceedings of the ESI-ISCN'95 Conference on Practical Improvement of Software Processes and Products in September 1995 in Vienna*, ISCN Ltd., Dublin, Ireland, 1995.

25. T. DeMarco, *Controlling Software Projects*, Yourdon Press Computing Series, Prentice Hall, Englewood Cliffs, London, Sydney, Tokyo, 1982.

26. A. Dorling, "SPICE—Software Process Improvement and Capability Determination," *Software Quality Journal*, Vol. 2, 1993, pp. 209–224.

27. W.K. Ehrlich, J.P. Stampfel, and J.R. Wu, "Application of Software Reliability Modeling to Product Quality and Test Process," *12th International Conference on Software Engineering*, IEEE Comput. Soc. Press, Los Alamitos, Calif., 1990, pp. 108–117.

28. ESA Board for Standardisation and Control, *ESA PSS 05 Software Engineering Standards*, European Space Agency, Paris, 1991.

29. J. Foster, "Program Lifetime: A Vital Statistic for Maintenance," *Proceedings of the Conference on Software Maintenance 1991*, J. C. Munson, et al., eds., IEEE Computer Soc., Sorrento, Italy, Oct. 1991, pp. 98–103.

30. J. Gaarder, *Sophie's World—An Adventure in Philosophy*, Phoenix House, London, 1995.

31. M. Genuchten, "Why is Software Late ?—An Empirical Study for Delay in Software Development," *IEEE Trans. Software Engineering*, June 1991, pp. 582–590.

32. German Interior Ministry, *German V-Model*, Bonn, Aug. 1992.

33. R.L. Glass, "The Software Crisis—Is it a Matter of Guts-Management," *Software Management*, 4th ed., D. J. Reifer, ed., IEEE Computer Soc. Press, Los Alamitos, Calif., 1993.

34. P. Goodman, *Practical Implementation of Software Metrics*, McGraw-Hill Book Company, London, New York, Sydney, 1992.

35. R.B. Grady, *Practical Software Metrics for Project Management and Process Improvement*, Prentice Hall, Englewood Cliffs, London, Sydney, Tokyo, 1992.

36. R.B. Grady, "Work Product Analysis: The Philosopher's Stone of Software," *IEEE Software*, March 1990, pp. 26–34.

37. R.B. Grady, Caswell D. C., *Software Metrics: Establishing a Company-Wide Program*, Prentice Hall, Englewood Cliffs, N.J., 1986.

38. V. Haase, et al., "BOOTSTRAP: Fine Tuning Process Assessment," *IEEE Software*, July 1994, pp. 25–35.

39. V. Haase et al., "Software Process Improvement by Measurement," *Shifting Paradigms in Software Engineering*, R. Mittermeir, ed., Springer Verlag, Vienna, New York, Sept. 1992, pp. 32–41.

40. V. Haase and R. Messnarz, *A Survey Study on Approaches in Technology Transfer, Software Management and Organisation*, Report 305, Institutes for Information Processing, Graz, June 1991.

41. W.S. Humphrey and W.L. Sweet, *A Method for Assessing the Software Engineering Capability of Contractors*, Software Engineering Institute, CMU, Technical Report CMU/SEI-87-TR-23, 1987.

42. W.S. Humphrey, *Managing the Software Process*, Software Engineering Institute (U.S.A.), Addison-Wesley Publishing Company, New York, Wokingham, Amsterdam, Bonn, Madrid, Tokyo, 1989.

43. W.S. Humphrey, "The Personal Software Process in Software Engineering," *Proceedings of the Third International Conference on the Software Process*, October 1994, pp. 69–77.

44. W.S Humphrey, T.R. Snyder, and R.R. Willis, "Software Process Improvement at Hughes Aircraft," *IEEE Software*, July 1991, pp. 11–23.

45. IEEE *Software Engineering Standards Collection*, IEEE Standards for Software Quality Assurance Plans (IEEE 730-1989), Quality Assurance Planning (IEEE 983-1986), Project Management Plans (IEEE 1058.1-1987), Configuration Management Plans (IEEE 828-1990), Software Verification and Validation Plans (IEEE 1012-1986), IEEE Computer Soc. Press, 1991.

46. ISO 9001, *Model for Quality Assurance in Design, Development, Production, Installation and Servicing*, 1987.

47. ISO 9000-3, *Quality Management and Quality Assurance Standards*, Part 3: Guidelines for the Application of ISO 9001 to the Development, Supply, and Maintenance of Software, 1991.

48. ISO 9126, *Information Technology—Software Product Evaluation—Quality Characteristics and Guidelines for Their Use*, 1990.

49. I. Jacobson, *Object Oriented Software Engineering: A Use Case Driven Approach*, Addison-Wesley, 1992.

50. J.M. Juran, *Juran's Quality Control Handbook*, 4th ed., McGraw-Hill, New York, 1988.

51. K. Inoue et al., "Modeling Method for Management Process and Its Application to CMM and ISO 9000-3," *Proceedings of the Third International Conference on the Software Process*, Oct. 1994, pp. 85–98.

52. M.I. Kellner, "A Method for Designing, Defining, and Evolving Software Processes," *Proceedings of the European Software Engineering Process Group Conference 1996*, Software Engineering Institute, Carnegie Mellon University, May 1996.

53. M. Kelly, "METKIT—Approaches, Experiences and Results," *Proceedings of the ISCN'94 Conference on Practical Improvement of Software Processes and Products*, ISCN Ltd., Dublin, Ireland, 1994.

54. M. Kelly, *Configuration Management—The Changing Image: The Changing Image*, McGraw-Hill, 1996.

55. P. Kuvaja et al., *The BOOTSTRAP Approach—Software Process Assessment & Improvement*, Blackwell Business, Oxford, UK, 1994.

56. S. McMenamin and J.F. Palmer, *Essential Systems Analysis*, Yourdon, New York, 1984.

57. R. Messnarz and H.J. Kugler, "BOOTSTRAP and ISO 9000: From the Software Process to Software Quality," *Proceedings of the APSEC'94 Conference*, Computer Soc. Press of the IEEE, Tokyo, Japan 1994.

58. R. Messnarz and H.J. Kugler, "Bootstrap and ISO 9000—A Quantitative Approach to Objective Quality Management, in: *Proceedings of the ISCN'94 Conference on Practical Improvement of Software Processes and Products*, K&M Technologies, Dublin, Ireland, 1994.

59. R. Messnarz and H. Scherzer, "The Evolution of a Quantitative Process Analysis—the BOOTSTRAP–Approach," *Interdisciplinary Informational Management Talks*, G. Chroust and P. Doucek, eds., Oldenbourg, Vienna, Munich, 1995.

60. W.B. Miller, "Fundamentals of Project Management," *Software Engineering Project Management*, E. Nahouraii et al., eds., Computer Soc. Press of the IEEE, Washington, D.C., 1988, pp. 178–185.

61. M.C. Paulk, B. Curtis, and M.B. Chrissis, eds., *Capability Maturity Model for Software*, Software Engineering Institute (U.S.A.), Technical Report CMU/SEI-91-TR-24, Carnegie Mellon University, Pittsburgh, Pa., 1991.

62. M.C. Paulk et al., *Key Practices of the Capability Maturity Model*, Version 1.1, Technical Report CMU/SEI-93-TR-25, Software Engineering Institute, Pittsburgh, Pa., 1993.

63. M.C. Paulk and M.D. Konrad, "An Overview of ISO's SPICE project." *American Programmer*, February 1994.

64. M. Paulk et al., Capability Maturity Model for Software, Version 1.1, CMU/SEI-93-TR-24, Feb. 1993.

65. D.E. Perry et al., "People, Organisations, and Process Improvement," *IEEE Software*, July 1994, pp. 36–45.

66. S. Pfleeger and C. McGowan, "Software Metrics in the Process Maturity Framework," *Journal Systems and Software*, Volume 12, 1990, pp. 255–261.

67 PYRAMID Consortium, ESPRIT Project 5425, *Quantitative Management: Get a Grip on Software!*, Dec. 1991.

68. N.F. Schneidewind, "Setting Maintenance Quality Objectives and Prioritising Maintenance Work by Using Quality Metrics," *Proceedings of the Conference on Software Maintenance 1991*, J. C. Munson, ed., IEEE Computer Soc., Sorrento, Italy, Oct. 1991, pp. 240–249.

69. N.F. Schneidewind, *Standard for a Software Quality Metrics Methodology*, IEEE Computer Soc., 1993.

70. G.G. Schulmeyer, "The Net Negative Producing Programmer," *Software Management*, 4th ed., IEEE Computer Soc. Press, 1993, pp. 307–313.

71. S.A. Sherer, "Cost Benefit Analysis and the Art of Software Maintenance," *Proceedings of the Conference on Software Maintenance 1992*, IEEE Computer Soc. Press, Orlando, Fla., 1992, pp. 70–77.

72. B. Shneiderman, *Software Psychology: Human Factors in Computer and Information Systems*, Winthrop Publishers, Cambridge, Mass., 1980.

73. R.H. Thayer, "Software Engineering Project Management: A Top-Down View," *Software Engineering Project Management*, E. Nahouraii et al., eds., Computer Soc. Press of the IEEE, Washington, D.C., 1988, pp. 15–54.

74. S. Treble and N. Douglas, *Sizing and Estimating Software in Practice, Series in Software Engineeing*, McGraw-Hill, 1995.

75. J. Vincent, A. Waters, and J. Sinclair, *Software Quality Assurance—Practice and Implementation*, Vol. I, Prentice Hall, Englewood Cliffs, London, 1988.

76. J. Vincent, A. Waters, and J. Sinclair, *Software Quality Assurance—Practice and Implementation*, Vol. II, Prentice Hall, Englewood Cliffs, London, 1988.

77. A. Völker, "Software Process Assessments at Siemens as a Basis for Process Improvement in Industry," *Proceedings of the ISCN'94 Conference on Practical Improvement of Software Processes and Products*, ISCN Ltd., Dublin, Ireland, 1994.

78. R. Witty, "Executive Fast Track, Business Manager Tutorial," *Proceedings of the European Software Engineering Process Group Conference 1996*, Software Engineering Institute, Carnegie Mellon University, May 1996.

79. H.K. Zuse, *Software Complexity: Measures and Methods*, Walter de Gruyter, Berlin, New York, 1991.

80. H.K. Zuse, *Software Metrics, Conference on Software Maintenance 91*, Tutorial 4, IEEE Computer Soc., Sorrento, Italy, Oct. 1991.

81. H.K. Zuse, "How to Cope with Software Complexity," *Proceedings of the ISCN'94 Conference on Practical Improvement of Software Processes and Products*, ISCN Ltd., Dublin, Ireland, 1994.

RECOMMENDED READING

The Proceedings of the Third International Conference of the Software Process 1994, IEEE Computer Society Press contain a set of articles from leading experts about strategies, notations, and methodologies for process modeling. It can be used as a reference guide for engineers who plan to employ process modeling in their own organisation.

The *ESA PSS-05 Software Engineering Standards, European Space Agency, France 1992* represent a tailored version of all IEEE software engineering standards including a life cycle model with document flows, templates, and describing both, development and management procedures.

The *German V-Model, German Interior Ministry, 1992* [32] is a very detailed process model including four different submodels with roles, activities, workflows, and results which is used for development in the German defence sector. It is a very good example for a process model which covers many of the aspects previously discussed in this chapter.

The *Proceedings of the European SEPG 1996 Conference* contain up-to-date contributions about software processes [52] and business and people factors in software management [78].

The books from Booch [15] and Jacobson [49] and McMenamin [56] contain a huge number of additional relationships and element types applied for describing software systems which could also be used for designing and describing work scenarios.

Humphrey's new book [43] *The Personal Software Process in Software Engineering* describes a role-based process model emphasising the role of a module developer within the software development process who learns to measure his own performance, to estimate effort, and to draw conclusions for improving his own work.

The ISCN Proceedings, *ISCN'94—Practical Improvement of Software Processes and Products*, *ISCN'95—Practical Improvement of Software Processes and Products: Measurement and Training Based Process Improvement, ISCN Ltd. Dublin, Ireland*, contain a selection of contributions dealing with approaches, methodologies, and technologies practically tried out, field tested, and measured in industry.

CHAPTER 4

Software Process Analysis and Improvement:

A Catalogue and Comparison of Models

Colin Tully
CTA, UK

Pasi Kuvaja
University of OULU, Finland

Richard Messnarz
ISCN, Ireland

INTRODUCTION

This book can be thought of as a collection of travellers' tales, told by some of the bold early explorers in the newfound land of software process. In that overall context, the purpose of this chapter is to provide some maps of that territory, which may help the reader understand those stories of exploration and discovery.

While Chapter 3 spoke about basic principles underlying the concept and definition of *software system, process model, software process, organisational system, analysis, software system analysis, software process analysis,* Chapter 4 is *a catalogue of most currently existing models and approaches.* In little more than 10 years, the software process movement has generated a rich variety of models and methods for the purposes of analysis and improvement. If those models are thought of as plant species, then the present chapter is like the work of the early botanical taxonomists, starting with Linnaeus in the eighteenth century, who moved through the plant kingdom describing and classifying what they found.

The three main sections of the chapter represent three different scales, or levels of detail, in examining software process models and methods.

- The section entitled *Catalogue of Models and Methods* provides a depiction at the smallest scale (widest scope, least detail). It identifies a rather large sample from the whole range, with brief informal descriptions of some of the defining characteristics of each.

- *Classification of Measurement Models* presents an intermediate-level view (reduced scope, more detail). The scope in this section is a sample from just one group out of the whole range of models and methods. This group comprises models which offer the ability to make simple *measurements* of the software process (sometimes in conjunction with other factors influencing the quality of the delivered software product). The models which make up the sample in this section are classified and described in terms of a set of more formal characteristics for such models (which, following the botanical analogy, constitutes a simple taxonomy).
- *Detailed Comparison of BOOTSTRAP, CMM, and SPICE*, does exactly what it says. Here the scope is narrowest and the detail greatest. From the measurement models classified in the preceding section, the three leading examples are examined closely.

Before embarking on those three substantial sections, however, a hors d'oeuvre is offered, telling the story of the SEI Capability Maturity Model for Software. Why? The reason is that the "Software CMM" (as it will be called for short) had an ancestral position for many of the models and methods with which we are concerned in this and subsequent chapters.

THE SOFTWARE CAPABILITY MATURITY MODEL

The Software CMM [30, 33, 35, 36] emerged from work done primarily by Watts Humphrey [12], and it is impossible to exaggerate the influence of that one man and his model on the field of software process analysis and improvement.

Humphrey grounded his ideas [13] firmly in the tradition of Total Quality Management (TQM), starting with Shewhart's work on statistical process control at Bell Labs between the wars, and carried on by the postwar prophets of the industrial quality movement: Crosby [4], Deming [5] and Juran [21]. According to a detailed account of the evolution of the Software CMM [36], Humphrey found his initial inspiration in the Quality Management Maturity Grid of Philip Crosby.

Anyone looking at Crosby's Maturity Grid, and comparing it with the Software CMM, will find little similarity between the two. It is interesting to outline the process by which one became metamorphosed into the other.

The Crosby Grid is a very simple (and correspondingly powerful) device for managers to evaluate rapidly the quality status of their organisations. It proposes six measurement categories, in each of which an organisation may progress through five maturity stages: "uncertainty," "awakening," "enlightenment," "wisdom," and "certainty." The Grid then defines, in brief narrative form, the meaning of each maturity stage for each of the measurement categories.

Figure 4.1 is an illustrative extract from the complete Grid. It shows all six measurement categories, but only shows the first and last maturity stages ("uncertainty" and "certainty").

How then did Humphrey adapt the Crosby Grid? The adaptation seems to have been in two main stages [36]. (It should be emphasised that what follows is a personal interpretation of the observed results of Humphrey's innovations: it is in no way an attempt to explain his actual processes of thought at the time.)

The first stage of the adaptation was carried out under Humphrey's leadership in 1985, while he was still at IBM. This in effect created a Crosby-like grid for each of 12 life-cycle phases (requirements, product level design, component level design, module level design, code, unit test, functional verification test, product verification test, system verification test, package and release, early support programme, and general availability). The grid, as applied to each of the 12 phases, comprised 11 attributes and a five-point scale; see Figure 4.2.

Measurement Categories	Maturity Stages		
	Stage 1: Uncertainty	Stages 2,3,4	Stage 5: Certainty
Management understanding and attitude	No comprehension of quality as a management tool. Tend to blame quality department for "quality problems."		Consider quality management an essential part of company system.
Quality organisational status	Quality is hidden in manufacturing or engineering departments. Inspection probably not part of organisation. Emphasis on appraisal and sorting.		Quality manager on board of directors. Prevention is main concern. Quality is a thought leader.
Problem handling	Problems are fought as they occur; no resolution; inadequate definition; lots of yelling and accusations.		Except in the most unusual cases, problems are prevented.
Cost of quality as % of sales	Reported: unknown. Actual: 20%		Reported: 2.5%. Actual: 2.5%
Quality improvement actions	No organised activities. No understanding of such activities.		Quality improvement is a normal and continued activity.
Summation of company quality posture	"We don't know why we have problems with quality."		"We know why we don't have problems with quality."

Figure 4.1.   Illustrative extract of Crosby's Quality Maturity grid.

11 Attributes	5–Point Scale				
	1	2	3	4	5
	Traditional	Awareness	Knowledge	Skill and wisdom	Integrated management system
Process					
Methods					
Adherence to practices					
Tools					
Change control					
Data gathering					
Data communication and use					
Goal setting					
Quality focus					
Customer focus					
Technical awareness					

Figure 4.2.   First stage of the adaptation from Crosby grid to CMM.

The two five-point scales are very similar. Crosby's six measurement categories and Humphrey's 11 attributes (applied in common to each of the 12 life cycle phases) are also similar, being fairly broad properties capable of mainly subjective assessment. The main difference is that Crosby's categories are general to the whole organisation, while Humphrey's attributes were software–specific.

Overall, Humphrey replaced Crosby's–dimensional grid (6×5) with a much bigger three–dimensional one $(12 \times 11 \times 5)$. In addition to adding a dimension, the size was increased by a factor of 22.

This increase in size was justified because a far finer–grained picture could be obtained of the organisation's software maturity. But there was a corresponding disadvantage: in the face of 132 "measurements," determining an improvement path presented a major decision–making problem.

It was the perceived importance of providing a standard improvement path that drove the second, and far more radical, stage of the adaptation away from Crosby. This second stage started in 1986 when Humphrey moved from IBM to the Software Engineering Institute (SEI), at Carnegie Mellon University, Pittsburgh Pa. It carried on for several years, through several subsidiary transformations [36], until the present Software CMM structure stabilised with Version 1.1 in 1993. It is only to this current version that reference will now be made.

The end result of the series of transformations is that the twelve lifecycle phases with their set of eleven common attributes have been repackaged into a set of eighteen "key process areas" (KPAs). The KPAs are hypothesised to be a first–level breakdown of the software process. Each KPA is further decomposed into a set of "key practices" (316 in all, across all the KPAs). The KPAs and their key practices constitute a comprehensive conjecture of the activities which make up the total software process.

The five-point scale is preserved in the form of five levels. Their names are changed, but they remain similar to their forerunners. They are "initial," "repeatable," "defined," "managed," and "optimising."

The really radical change lies in the way in which the five levels are used. They are not used like the earlier five–point scale, to measure the maturity of the KPAs. That is now measured simply by whether a sufficient number of the key practices defined for each KPA are being performed. In other words, KPA maturity is an amalgamation of a number of simple binary "present/absent" tests.

In that case, where have the five levels gone? Instead of measuring the maturity of KPAs, they now measure the overall software maturity of the organisation. That change is achieved by partitioning the set of eighteen KPAs between the five levels. The result is that the path to maturity becomes a well defined one of ensuring that the KPAs are satisfactorily in place for each of the levels in turn. This can be seen in Figure 4.3.

Figure 4.3 also shows that the model has become one–dimensional. The single dimension is the path defined by the partially ordered set of KPAs, starting at level 1 (chaotic) and ending at level 5 (continuously improving, fully instrumented, controlled, fit for purpose).

While the dimensionality has shrunk from three to one, the "size" in terms of number of evaluation objects has further increased. The 132 attributes have been replaced by 316 key practices. Finally, the measurement granularity has been reduced, from five points for the old attributes to two points for the new key practices.

So much for the pedigree of the Software CMM. It remains to say something about its impact and authority.

During the development period, a number of pilot appraisals based on an intermediate version of the model were conducted on leading Department of Defence software contractors.

18 KPAs Organised in 5 Levels

Level 1 Initial (no KPAs)	
Level 2 Repeatable (6 KPAs)	Requirements management Software project planning Software project tracking and oversight Software subcontract management Software quality assurance Software configuration management
Level 3 Defined (7KPAs)	Organisation process focus Organisation process definition Training programme Integrated software management Software product engineering Intergroup coordination Peer reviews
Level 4 Managed (2KPAs)	Quantitave process management Software quality management
Level 5 Optimising (3KPAs)	Defect prevention Technology change management Process change management

Improvement in Maturity

Figure 4.3.   Second stage of the adaptation from Crosby Grid to CMM.

These results were published, and had a shock effect on the U.S. software industry. DoD contractors might naturally be assumed to be among the best software producers. On the contrary, the results were devastatingly bad, with over 80 percent being assessed at level 1 (chaotic).

At that time, the SEI still had a predominantly defence and academic image, based on its being funded by DoD and hosted by Carnegie Mellon University. Since then, SEI has been able to exploit the shock effect of the early process assessments, to the point where software process improvement, based on CMM–style assessments, is pervasive throughout the U.S. software industry. The CMM levels have become part of management and practitioner language, and are the basis of managers' new faith that software need not remain in crisis.

The SEI's role with respect to the CMM is

- to be the development authority,
- to promote, and to exercise quality control over, its application,
- to maintain a data repository of results,
- to publish and disseminate information, and
- to provide and license training.

The development authority role is exercised through collaborative mechanisms such as working groups, reviewer groups and correspondence groups. Quality control extends to such things as the licensing of training courses and the registration of lead assessors. This role has not yet been developed so as to function effectively outside the United States.

The CMM version 2.0 effort started on July 1, 1995. On that date the commenting period on version 1.1 ended. It was planned that the revision process would last about 18 months, but the release of version 2.0 has been delayed. A core team of four people is leading the revision effort.

In the United States there is a flourishing marketplace for CMM–based services, in which around a dozen specialist vendors offer assessment, training, and consultancy to many hundreds of clients. The corresponding European market is tiny by comparison. The SEI effectively regulates the marketplace. Any appraisal may only be termed an SEI appraisal if it is led by an SEI–authorised lead assessor. The requirements for becoming a lead assessor are the completion of a lead assessor course and approved assessment experience. Lead assessor courses are run only by the SEI, and approved assessment experience can be gained only under the leadership of a lead assessor. The SEI itself has a special and dominant position in the marketplace, offering a wide range of courses, events, and publications.

On the basis of the widespread take-up of the Software CMM, a family of related models has sprung into being. Some of them include the term CMM in their names, others do not. Some are in the field of software, others are not. Many of them, but by no means all, are included in the catalogue in the next section. Much experience in using the CMM is reported in subsequent chapters of this book.

Before concluding this section, some readers may be interested in the earlier history of staged maturity models. Crosby and Humphrey are only recent perpetuators of a long tradition.

In a seminal book in 1960, the distinguished economist Walt Whitman Rostow, later to become special assistant to the U.S. president, proposed a theory of economic growth in five stages: the traditional society, the preconditions for take–off, the take–off, the drive to maturity, and the age of high mass consumption (equated with maturity). As with Crosby and Humphrey, the purpose of the theory or model was to aid improvement by having a better understanding of the path to maturity.

Rostow contrasted his stage model with an earlier, and even more influential one, that of Karl Marx, to which it was intended as an antidote. In Marxist theory, societies develop through four stages, from feudalism, through bourgeois capitalism and socialism, to communism.

The origin of all stage models could perhaps be said to lie in Plato. His related metaphors of the Line and the Cave are subject to endless detailed interpretations; but roughly they describe a four–staged ascent of the mind from illusion, through belief and mathematical/scientific reasoning, to the ultimate insight into first principles and the "Idea of the Good."

In those images, and in many other places in his writings, Plato was the original utopian. He gave rise to a vast corpus of utopian thought and writing, describing how humankind can climb to some perfect state. The stage models, whether of philosophers, economists, quality gurus, or software engineers, can be seen as occupying a respectable place in that utopian tradition.

But do not forget the dangers and the limitations of idealism, the pitfalls that lie along the road to perfection, and the number of utopias that are closer to nightmares!

CATALOGUE OF MODELS AND METHODS

The purpose of the following catalogue is no more than to illustrate the range of models and methods currently available. It does not pretend to be complete, but rather offers a representative selection. It comprises 34 entries, each of which is described as briefly as is consistent with giving an adequate overall impression of what it is and what it does. Some are covered in more detail elsewhere in this book, and in those cases the reader should treat what follows as just a "taster."

The models and methods are grouped according to their origins, as follows:

- Software Engineering Institute (SEI)
- Software Engineering Laboratory (SEL)
- U.S. Department of Defence (DoD)
- International Council on Systems Engineering (INCOSE)
- International Organisation for Standardisation (ISO)
- International Standards Group for Software Engineering (ISO/IEC JTC1/SC7)
- Commission of the European Communities (CEC)
- European Space Agency (ESA)
- UK Government Department of Trade and Industry (DTI)
- quality awards
- commercial proprietary
- corporate in–house

Software Engineering Institute (SEI), Carnegie Mellon University, Pittsburgh, PA

CMM–Based Appraisal for Internal Process Improvement (CBA IPI)

A CBA IPI is a method for self–assessment (first–party appraisal), for the purpose of subsequent improvement. Its scope may be the whole process or selected parts of the process.

CMM–Based Appraisal for Software Capability Evaluation (CBA SCE)

A CBA SCE is primarily a method for procurement organisations to evaluate contractors (second–party appraisal), for the purposes of source selection or contract monitoring for a specific project. Its main user in this mode is DoD. Its secondary use is for self-assessment, again in the context of a specific project. Its scope is limited to selected parts of the process relevant to the project.

Note: the term "evaluation" often has the specific connotation of second–party appraisal.

Interim profiles

An interim profile is a CMM–compatible method for monitoring the progress and success of improvement programmes, typically in the intervals between more formal CBA IPI/SCE appraisals.

Software Process Assessments (SPAs)

An SPA is a self-assessment which is based not on Version 1.1 but on an earlier version of the CMM. SPAs are still performed under license from SEI, but are being phased out.

Software Acquisition Maturity Model (SAMM)

The SAMM is a CMM–compatible model focusing on the processes performed by software acquisition organisations. It is being developed by a multiorganisation collaborative team, facilitated by SEI. Work started in 1994.

Trusted CMM

The Trusted CMM is an extension of CMM Version 1.1, with increased specificity in the domain of trusted software. Trusted software handles sensitive or classified information; it must be developed according to a defined security policy and adopting appropriate integrity measures. Work started in 1994, and pilot appraisals have been carried out in the intelligence community.

Personal Software Process (PSP)

The PSP is Watts Humphrey's latest initiative [15], which he is working on with SEI collaboration. In contrast to the Software CMM's focus on organisational maturity, the PSP focuses on the individual skill of the software engineer in design, coding, and testing. It represents a new process–oriented and quality–oriented approach to professional development. It has been piloted with students, and is now being used in both industrial and university courses.

Systems Engineering Capability Maturity Model (SE–CMM)

The SE–CMM is an adaptation of the Software CMM to the related process of systems engineering. Systems engineering is defined (adopting the definition in U.S. Army Field Manual 770–78) as follows.

Systems engineering is the selective application of scientific and engineering efforts to

- transform an operational need into a description of the system configuration which best satisfies the operational need according to the measures of effectiveness;
- integrate related technical parameters and ensure compatibility of all physical, functional and technical interfaces in a manner which optimises the total system definition and design;
- integrate the efforts of all engineering disciplines and specialities into the total engineering effort.

The SE–CMM is being developed by a multiorganisation collaborative team called Enterprise Process Improvement Collaboration (EPIC), facilitated by SEI. Work started in 1993. A first version of the model was published in late 1994, and a number of pilot appraisals have been carried out. A final release is currently delayed within the Capability Maturity Model Integration (CMMI) project.

In architectural terms, the SE–CMM adopted the SPICE model of base and generic practices (described later in this chapter) unchanged.

There is substantial demand for the SE–CMM from leading organisations, in government and industry, who have experience of the Software CMM. Among the main reasons are

- that a great deal of software engineering takes place within a systems engineering setting (whether or not the term systems engineering is actually used), and a mature software process can often be subverted by an immature systems process;
- that one of the primary justifications for the CMM approach is that process complexity and novelty cause difficulties in process management—and the systems process is at least as complex and novel as the software process;
- that there is a substantial area of intersection between the two processes, and therefore there is an economy in their linked development and application.

More detail on the SE–CMM is given in the next section.

Integrated Product Development Capability Maturity Model (IPD–CMM)

The IPD–CMM is an adaptation of the Software CMM to the related process of IPD. IPD is defined as follows.

IPD is a systematic approach to product development that achieves a timely collaboration of necessary disciplines throughout the product life cycle to better satisfy customer needs. IPD thus involves two things:

- setting up and managing multidisciplinary work units (e.g., teams) charged with developing a product, and
- integrating the disciplines needed to conduct the technical work.

IPD clearly has a lot in common with systems engineering, and the IPD–CMM is being developed by the same multiorganisation collaborative team, EPIC, facilitated by SEI, that is working on the SE–CMM. Work started in 1995.

People Capability Maturity Model (P–CMM)

The P–CMM is an adaptation of the Software CMM to the related process of the professional development of software practitioners. It is expected to be equally applicable to systems engineers. It addresses the tasks of attracting, growing, motivating, deploying, and retaining the specialist talent necessary to enact the software (or systems) process. This is an in–house SEI initiative. A final release is currently delayed within the Capability Maturity Model Integration (CMMI) project.

Software Engineering Laboratory (SEL), University of Maryland

Experience Factory

The SEL, under the leadership of Victor Basili, has worked in close collaboration with Natonal Aeronatics and Space Administration (NASA) Goddard Space Flight Centre for many years to evolve a software development environment which integrates models and metrics (of products, processes and resources), permits maximum reuse (of products, processes and knowledge), and stimulates feedback (for control and for learning). Two methods are particularly associated with this work: the Quality Improvement Paradigm (QIP), and the Goal/Question/Metric (GQM) Paradigm; but these are subsidiary to the central concept of the Experience Factory.

To quote Basili [2]:

The Experience Factory is a logical and/or physical organisation that supports project developments by analysing and synthesising all kinds of experience, acting as a repository for such experience, and supplying that experience to various projects on demand. It packages experience by building, informal, formal, or schematised, and product based models and measures of various software processes, products, and other forms of knowledge via people, documents and automated support.

It is a very wide–ranging and well–founded approach. While the QIP and GQM methods are reasonably well known and accepted, the central Experience Factory model deserves to be more widely adopted.

See also the CEC ami project in Chapter 5.

U.S. Department of Defence (DoD)

Software Development Capability Evaluation (SDCE)

SDCE is used by DoD for evaluating software contractors against specific capability require-ments. It is applicable to large mission–critical projects in the defence sector. DoD based it on early versions of the Software CMM and on DoD standards [DoD88] and it is a precursor to SEI's CBA SCE.

International Council on Systems Engineering (INCOSE)

INCOSE/CAWG Interim Model for Capability Assessment of Systems Engineering

The Capability Assessment Working Group (CAWG) is a working group of INCOSE. It pub-lished an Interim Model for Systems Engineering Capability Assessment (often referred to as SECAM) in 1995.

There was some overlap, both in time and personnel, between the development of SECAM and of the EPIC SE–CMM (see earlier entry in this catalogue). The SECAM is an excellent model, but it has not yet received as much field piloting as the SE–CMM. There is also some possibility, at the time of writing, that the two models may be combined and sub-mitted for standardisation.

More detail on SECAM is given in the next section.

International Organisation for Standardisation (ISO)

International Standard ISO 9001 Quality Systems

ISO Standard 9001: 1987 [17] defines a generic standard for quality management systems (QMS). The standard relates to the activities of design/development, production, installation, and servicing for any product. It can be applied relatively straightforwardly to normal indus-trial products.

The characteristics of software, however, are sufficiently different that guidance is neces-sary in the application of the standard to software development, supply, and maintenance. Such guidance is provided in ISO 9000 Part 3 (9000–3) [16]. ISO 9000–3 is not itself a standard, but a set of guidelines for the application of the 9001 standard.

An organisation may use ISO 9001 as the basis for first–party appraisal (self-assessment) of its QMS. If software activities come within the scope of that QMS, then the 9000–3 guidelines apply.

More importantly, however, an organisation may submit its QMS for third–party appraisal (independent audit) under 9001. A successful audit, undertaken by accredited auditors, leads to the QMS being eligible for ISO 9001 certification. Such independent and objective certifi-cation can then be relied upon by all an organisation's clients, and avoids the need for a num-ber of separate second–party appraisals. The use of 9000–3 to facilitate the certification of soft-ware QMS has been an important advance since the start of the 1990s.

It should be clearly appreciated that ISO 9001 directly addresses only the QMS compo-nent of the total process. The purpose of any QMS, of course, is to ensure that processes are in place which will produce quality products, and that those processes are consistently followed and continuously improved. A 9001 auditor, therefore, should be concerned with the fitness of the total process and with observable product quality; and any inadequacies in those should ring alarm bells. The audit does not directly address the total process or the product, however, and noncompliances can only be raised against the QMS requirements set out in the standard, not against process or product inadequacies *per se*.

The predominant drive for ISO 9001 certification (both generally and for software) has been in Europe. (The standard was originally developed in the UK as a British Standard, BS 5750.) US and other non–European software developers are increasingly realising, nevertheless, that certification can be a significant aid to doing business, especially in European markets.

ISO 9001 was revised in 1994, and ISO 9000-3 was revised in 1997.

More detail on ISO 9000–3 is given in the next section. See also the entry for TickIT later in the section.

International Standards Group for Software Engineering (ISO/IEC JTC1/SC7)

ISO and the International Electrotechnical Commission (IEC) collaborate through their Joint Technical Committee 1 Subcommittee 7 (JTC1/SC7) on the development of software engineering standards.

International Standard ISO/IEC 9126 Software Product Evaluation

ISO Standard 9126: 1991 [3] defines a model of software product quality in terms of 6 main characteristics and 21 subcharacteristics, together with an outline method for software product quality evaluation.

The six characteristics in the quality model are

- functionality,
- reliability,
- usability,
- efficiency,
- maintainability, and
- portability.

The three steps in the method are

- quality requirement definition,
- evaluation preparation (quality metrics selection, rating level definition, assessment criteria definition), and
- evaluation procedure (measurement, rating, assessment).

See also the CEC SCOPE project in Chapter 6.

International Standard ISO/IEC 12207 Software Life Cycle Processes

ISO 12207 [19] provides a definition of the software process, to serve as a framework for the management and engineering of software. It is a voluntary standard, which may be used internally within an organisation or as the basis of contractual agreements between organisations. Nothing is said about certification.

The software process as a whole is defined as a set of processes (equivalent to process areas in many other models); each process is further subdivided into activities, and each activity into tasks.

The processes are grouped into three classes:

- Primary processes
  - Acquisition,
  - Supply,
  - Development,
  - Operation, and
  - Maintenance;
- Supporting processes
  - Documentation,
  - Configuration management,
  - Quality assurance,
  - Joint review,
  - Audit,
  - Verification,
  - Validation, and
  - Problem resolution;
- Organisational processes
  - Management,
  - Infrastructure,
  - Improvement, and
  - Training.

The standard has a strong TQM orientation and commitment. In addition to the specific quality–directed processes (quality assurance, joint review, audit, verification, validation, and improvement), each process has a built–in plan–do–check–act (PDCA) quality cycle.

More information on ISO 12207 is given in Chapter 13.

Proposed International Standard ISO/IEC 15288 System Life Cycle Processes

ISO 15288 is intended as a companion in the systems engineering domain to ISO 12207 in the software engineering domain. Work on the standard, at the time of writing, is at an early stage.

As in 12207, processes are divided into activities and further into tasks. The proposed processes, grouped into four classes, are as follows.

- Technical processes
  - Development,
  - Production,
  - Operations, and
  - Support;
- Management processes
  - Planning,
  - Assessment, and
  - Control;
- Enterprise processes
  - Project investment,
  - Process management,
  - Enabling infrastructure, and
  - Human resource;

- Agreement processes
  - Acquisition, and
  - Supply.

Software Process Improvement and Capability Determination (SPICE)

SPICE [7], [31], [34] is an international project, approved by ISO/IEC JTC1/SC7/WG10, to develop such a standard to the point where it can be submitted for adoption. Work started in 1993. International pilot trials started in 1995. It is hoped that adoption by ISO will take place within the next couple of years.

Work on the project is managed through the following four regional Technical Centres:

- Software Engineering Institute, Pittsburgh Pa. (United States)
- Bell Canada, Montreal, Quebec (Canada)
- Defence Research Agency, Malvern, UK (Europe)
- Software Quality Institute, Griffith University, Queensland, Australia (Pacific Rim)

The standard aims to take account of the features of, and experience with, existing first–generation methods for appraisal and improvement, such as SEI's Software CMM, BOOTSTRAP (Europe), STD (UK), and Bell Canada's Trillium, all of which are referenced in this catalogue It is not intended to be a replacement for those methods, however, but rather a standard against which such methods, or their successors or future competitors, can be measured for compliance. It can therefore be expected that the main players in this field will have SPICE–compliant products and services ready for launch if and when the standard is adopted.

The distinctive characteristic of the SPICE architecture is the distinction between *base practices* and *generic practices,* and the hypothesis that the improvement of process areas (each of which comprises a set of base practices) can be measured by the extent to which they effectively employ generic practices. This architecture was adopted unchanged by SE–CMM.

More detail on SPICE is given in the next two sections, and in a subsequent chapter.

Commission of the European Communities (CEC)

With one exception, all the following approaches were initially developed by projects of the European Commission's European Strategic Programme for Research in Information Technology (ESPRIT). The exception is Euromethod, which was developed with support from a different CEC initiative.

SCOPE (ESPRIT Project 2151, 1989–1993)

SCOPE developed a metrics–based model and method for the evaluation, certification, and improvement of software product quality, based on the ISO 9126 standard (see Chapter 6). The project involved 16 partners from eight countries. An important innovation in SCOPE is the concept of modular evaluation, carried out by the use of so–called "bricks" (evaluation modules) which can be accumulated into libraries.

A substantial amount of piloting of SCOPE results has been carried out through industrial case studies [1]. Some results (e.g., the Evaluator's Guide and the Documentation Guide for Evaluation Modules) are being submitted for ISO adoption in support of the 9126 standard. Commercial product quality evaluation services are available, with initial emphasis on evaluation of Commercial Off-The Shelf Software **COTS** packages and object-oriented (OO) code.

More information on SCOPE is given in Chapter 6.

Metrics Educational Toolkit (METKIT) (ESPRIT Project 2384, 1989–1992)

METKIT involved eight partners from four countries. The project developed modular instruction packages on software quality and productivity metrics. An industrial package (17 modules) for practitioners and managers was complemented by an academic package (eight modules) for students; some of the modules are available in multiple European languages. A supporting textbook [9] was produced, together with Computer Assisted Instructions **CAI** and video material and training versions of metrics tools.

The project developed original material on the planning and implementation of measurement and improvement programmes, which has been further developed since the end of the project.

BOOTSTRAP (ESPRIT Project 5441, 1990–1994)

The project involved seven partners from five countries. It developed the BOOTSTRAP software development process assessment and improvement method [10], [23], [24], [28], [29]. At the end of the project the partners set up the BOOTSTRAP Institute, a nonprofit organisation with the legal form of a European Economic Interest Group (EEIG). Its role with respect to BOOT-STRAP is the same as the SEI's role with respect to the CMM: to be the development authority; to promote, and to exercise quality control over, its application; to maintain a data repository of results; to publish and disseminate information; and to provide and license training.

BOOTSTRAP combines the following approaches: the Software CMM; ISO 9001/9000–3; European Space Agency Software Engineering Standard PSS–05–0; and DoD–STD–2167A software process standard. It claims to be equally applicable and cost–effective for software organisations of any size and in any application domain. That is in contrast to the CMM, which has a natural or perceived bias (due to its origins) toward large organisations and toward defence and other real–time applications.

BOOTSTRAP assessments are mostly first–party, normally with third–party assistance (assisted self–assessments). BOOTSTRAP is usable, however, for second–party (client–contractor) assessments.

An essential part of the BOOTSTRAP approach is that assessments lead to improvement action plans. A means of developing action plans is an integral part of the method. A strong feature is the provision of full tool support, not only for carrying out the assessment itself and for processing and presenting the results, but also for tasks such as questionnaire and license maintenance.

The primary output of a BOOTSTRAP assessment is a maturity profile, which shows the maturity of each of the component parts of the total process. It is, however, possible to convert the maturity profile to the CMM single–figure maturity level.

Following is some data indicating the current status of BOOTSTRAP.

- Membership of the BOOTSTRAP Institute: 14 full members (voting rights, full benefits, license to practice); 3 corporate members (no commercial interest); 4 licensees (license to practice only)
- Number of organisations currently performing assessments under license: 15 in 10 countries
- Individual assessors: about 70 trained, about 30 certified and operating commercially
- Organisations assessed: about 100, with probably an average of around two assessments per organisation (taking account of reassessments and multiple sites)
- National distribution: most assessments in Germany and Italy, with smaller numbers in UK, Spain, France, Scandinavia, and Austria; a few in the United States and South America; interest from India

More detail on BOOTSTRAP is given in the next two sections, and in subsequent chapters.

ami (ESPRIT Project 5494, 1990–1993)

ami (Application of Metrics in Industry) is a method for selecting, applying, and acting on software metrics, so as to achieve efficiency and effectiveness in the software development process. The ami project brought together nine partners from six countries. It produced the ami Handbook, which has achieved wide distribution internationally, and a new edition of which has been published by Addison–Wesley [37]. It also produced an ami tool to support use of the method.

Since the end of the project, the ami User Group has functioned as a means of information exchange between users of the method. Among other things it publishes a quarterly newsletter and World Wide Web (WWW) pages, and runs an electronic discussion group (over 500 members) and an annual meeting.

The method is based on the GQM Paradigm (see Chapter 5). Metrics are thus coupled to business goals. The method comprises four main activities (assess, analyse, metricate, improve), subdivided into 12 steps.

Euromethod

The Euromethod project is run by the Eurogroup consortium, comprising ten main partners from eight countries, together with five associated partners. The project has been running, in a series of discontinuous phases, since 1989. It is funded by the European Commission on behalf of the Public Procurement Group, a pan–European grouping of public procurement bodies.

Euromethod applies to the domain of information systems development, and is relevant where there is a contractual relationship between a customer and supplier (both of which may be within the same organisation). It is intended to contribute to a more effective open market in the procurement and supply of information systems in Europe, taking into account the differences of practice that exist across national boundaries in terms of culture, process, methods and training: people, in other words, speak different technical languages as well as different natural languages, and that can present an additional layer of difficulty in already–difficult contractual relationships. Euromethod may also, of course, help to improve the competitive position of European information systems contractors in the world market.

The goal of the project is well expressed as the creation of a virtuous circle "in which better requirements elicitation, better communications, better decision making, and better matching of customers with suppliers, result in the provision of more appropriate information systems to the customer." There is a strong emphasis on customer–supplier partnership.

The following are some important features of Euromethod.

- It breaks down the procurement process as a whole into three main subprocesses: tendering, production, and completion. These are further subdivided into nine sub-subprocesses. The process is described from the two different viewpoints of customer and supplier in the Customer Guide and the Supplier Guide.
- The emphasis in describing processes is on transactions, decisions, and deliverables. Models for each of these are developed in three concepts manuals, entitled Transaction Model, Strategy Model, and Deliverable Model. The concept of a delivery plan underpins the whole process, and is described in the Delivery Planning Guide.
- It distinguishes between the contract level and the project level in the customer–supplier relationship. That distinction gives rise to four role classes within which role assignment is to be carried out: customer contract roles, supplier contract roles, customer project roles, and supplier project roles.

- It offers a means of "method bridging" between its own concepts and the concepts of the various different methods that may be mandated by customers and used by suppliers. This is described in the Method Bridging Guide.
- The above guides and concepts manuals are supported by a case study and a dictionary of terms.

European Space Agency (ESA)

ESA Software Engineering Standards (PSS–05–0)

These standards [8] are developed from two linked models, one for the software life cycle (the basis for a set of product standards) and one for management of the software life cycle (the basis for a set of procedure standards).

The software life cycle comprises six phases:

- User requirements definition
- Software requirements definition
- Architectural design
- Detailed design and production
- Transfer
- Operations and maintenance.

Each phase has a defined set of activities, deliverables, and reviews, and terminates in a major milestone.

Management of the software life cycle comprises four processes:

- software project management,
- software configuration management,
- software verification and validation, and
- software quality assurance.

Each process has a defined set of activities, and generates a management plan which evolves through the first four phases of the life cycle.

Throughout the definitions of the phases and processes, a set of around 200 mandatory practices are laid down.

The complete model defines just under 50 activities, intermediate in level between the process areas and practices of CMM–style models. The 200 or so mandatory practices are not dissimilar to CMM–style practices.

Document structures are given for each of the major product documents and management plans.

UK Government, Department of Trade and Industry (DTI)

TickIT

The TickIT Initiative ran, with DTI sponsorship, from about 1988 to about 1993. It developed and promoted the TickIT Scheme [39], TickIT Guide, Guide to SW Quality Management System Construction and Certification Using 1509001, DISC TickIT Office, 1992, the purpose of which is to regulate third–party certification of software quality management systems under ISO 9001/9000–3, so as to improve professional practice and market confidence in software QMS audit. It cannot be too strongly emphasised that TickIT in no way alters the ISO standard; it only provides a means for regulating the certification process.

The TickIT uniform accreditation arrangements provide for the following.

- Accreditation of certification bodies (i.e., companies which offer QMS audits) against defined standards of competence and practice for undertaking ISO 9001 audits of software QMS. Accreditation is controlled by the National Accreditation Council for Certification Bodies.
- Registration of individual auditors against defined standards of competence and practice for undertaking ISO 9001 audits of software QMS. Registration is controlled by the Institute of Quality Assurance and the British Computer Society.
- Award of a certificate carrying the TickIT mark, and entry in the DTI Register of Assessed Companies, for companies which have passed audit by an accredited certification body using registered auditors. An audit is always carried out against a defined scope of business activity, and this scope is stated on the certificate and in the Register entry.

The TickIT Scheme applies to the UK. It is, however, available for adoption in other countries, and Sweden, for instance, has now implemented a full-fledged TickIT system.

Determining an Evaluation Methodology for Software Methods and Tools (DESMET)

DESMET (1990–1994) [22] was a collaborative project, partially funded by the DTI and the UK Science and Engineering Research Council under the Information Engineering Advanced Technology Programme. It involved four partners, with the National Computing Centre (NCC) as lead partner.

DESMET's goal was to provide a methodology (set of methods) by which software practitioners could evaluate the effects and effectiveness of software development methods and tools, and to conduct trials to validate the methodology. It identifies various types of evaluation methods, and describes some of them:

- quantitative methods (objective evaluations aimed at establishing measurable effects of using methods or tools), comprising formal experiment, case study, survey, and cost modelling;
- qualitative methods (subjective evaluations aimed at establishing the appropriateness of using methods or tools), comprising feature analysis, qualitative effects analysis, and benchmarking.

It offers guidance on important process issues relating to method and tool evaluation:

- issues in selecting an evaluation method from the above set;
- maturity assessment issues, relating to an organisation's capability to undertake evaluations; and
- managerial and sociological issues.

Finally, it describes key aspects of a measurement system:

- measurement goals;
- data collection and storage;
- data analysis.

The DESMET material was developed in a series of draft manuals. The exact status of these manuals since the end of the project is not clear; it is hoped, however, that they will be published.

Quality Awards

Malcolm Baldrige National Quality Award (MBNQA)

The MBNQA [38] was established in 1987 by U.S. public law (Malcolm Baldrige National Quality Improvement Act), and the first awards were made in 1988. One award may be made annually in each of three categories (manufacturing, service, and small business). Principal support comes from the Foundation for the MBNQA. The National Institute of Standards and Technology and the American Society for Quality Control collaborate in the management and administration of the Award.

MBNQA is an award for quality in general, not for software quality in particular. It is unlikely, however, that software quality will play no part in the overall evaluation; and many winners (such as AT&T, Cadillac, Federal Express, IBM, Motorola, Texas Instruments, and Xerox) have had substantial software activities. Certainly the seven evaluation criteria (in effect a quality model) are as relevant in the software domain as any other; they are:

- Leadership (the senior executives' success in creating and sustaining a quality culture)
- Information and analysis (the effectiveness of information collection and analysis to maintain a customer focus, drive quality excellence, and improve performance)
- strategic quality planning (the effectiveness of integrating quality requirements into business plans)
- Human resource development and management (the success of efforts to realise the full potential of the work force to meet a company's quality and performance objectives)
- Management of process quality (the effectiveness of systems and processes for assuring the quality of products and services)
- Quality and operational results (the improvement of quality and operational performance and supplier quality, demonstrated through quantitative measures)
- Customer focus and satisfaction (the effectiveness of systems to determine customer requirements and satisfaction and the demonstrated success in meeting customers' expectations)

Companies initially submit an application. Applications are reviewed against the evaluation criteria by teams of trained examiners, and all applicants receive written feedback reports identifying strengths and areas for improvement. Finalists receive site visits, with final award decisions being made by a panel of judges. Awards are normally presented by the president of the United States in Washington, D.C. Final contenders receive more than 400 hours of evaluation.

The primary value of the MBNQA quality model is for self–assessment and internal improvement. Management would be mistaken to make the winning of an award a primary and overt objective.

This information draws mainly on tutorial notes by David Kitson of the SEI, to whom acknowledgement is gratefully given.

The Information Technology Association of America (ITAA) Quality Awards

These awards are specifically for software quality. They were introduced in 1992 and modelled on the MBNQA. They are open to all companies in the U.S. software industry. An award may be made annually in each of three categories (total quality, documentation/training materials quality, and customer support quality).

The European Quality Award (EQA)

The EQA [40] is also derived from the MBNQA. Principal support comes from the European Foundation for Quality Management (EFQM). Awards have been made since 1992.

The EQA is based on the European Model for Total Quality Management, which has nine criteria (compare with the seven of MBNQA). The model defines nine criteria for quality, grouped under two main headings. Together with the weightings currently allocated to each, they are:

- enablers (50%)
  - leadership (10%)
  - people management (9%)
  - policy and strategy (8%)
  - resources (9%)
  - processes (14%)
- results (50%)
  - people satisfaction (9%)
  - customer satisfaction (20%)
  - impact on society (6%)
  - business results (15%)

As with the MBNQA, the primary value of the European Model for TQM is for self–assessment and internal improvement, rather than as a definition of how to compete for an award. Other benefits come from its use in benchmarking and for internal training.

More detail on the EQA is given in the next section.

Commercial Proprietary

Compita, UK: Software Technology Diagnostic (STD)

STD was developed by the Scottish Development Agency, who were aware of the importance of software development within the economy of Scotland and wished to encourage competitiveness through improvements in practice. Its original purpose was to enable the Agency to evaluate the performance of Scottish software companies, compare that performance with international good practice, build up a database of results, identify opportunities for improvement, and encourage improvement.

In recognition that most Scottish software development is carried out by small and medium-size enterprises (SMEs), an important objective of STD was that it should be appropriate to, and affordable by, SMEs.

The development responsibility and exploitation rights for STD have since passed to a commercial company, Compita Ltd. STD has a significant share of the (as yet small) UK market, but has achieved little if any penetration overseas.

More detail on the STD is given in the next section.

Software Productivity Research (U.S.A., UK): Software Quality and Productivity Analysis (SQPA)

Software Productivity Research (SPR) is a specialist service provider, active in the eastern United States and the UK, which markets a method of software process benchmarking and improvement, based on the SQPA method developed by Capers Jones in the mid-1980s for

Hewlett–Packard. The SPR (commercial) method stresses the derivation of improvement priorities from business goals, emphasises the value of benchmarking, and focuses on the collection of data from projects rather than from the organisation as a whole. The measurement approach is heavily based on function points.

Corporate In–House

Bell Canada, Northern Telecom, and Bell–Northern Research: Trillium

Trillium is used worldwide within the above-mentioned group of companies, both for self–assessment and for the assessment of existing and prospective suppliers. The model is, however, in the public domain. It has passed through nine drafts, from Version 1.0 (August 1991) to Version 3.0 (December 1994).

The Trillium model has a telecommunications orientation. It incorporates material from ISO 9001, the Malcolm Baldrige National Quality Award, IEC 300, IEEE software engineering standards, and internal Bellcore standards. In addition to process maturity, it offers the ability to assess the appropriateness of the technology used in the process.

It has a wide scope, taking a systems rather than a more limited software view, and covering "all functions that contribute to the customer's perception of the product . . . including engineering, marketing, customer support, and quality assurance." It is still under active development: a major extension is planned to cover Management Information Systems, and others may include hardware development, and manufacture and service.

More detail on Trillium is given in the next section.

British Telecom (UK): Software Supplier Assessment (SSA) and Health Check

BT have two separate in–house methods. SSA is used for second–party capability evaluation. Health Check is used for internal assessment–driven improvement. Little or no information is available in the public domain.

Siemens (Germany): Siemens Assessment Methodology and Optimised Processes and Architectural Leadership (OPAL)

Siemens worldwide assessment and improvement programmes in systems and software [26] are driven from the Application Centre Software in Munich (part of Siemens Corporate Research and Development). The Centre has 30 employees in two departments: Software Development Process, and Software Quality.

Siemens Assessment Methodology is a combination of the SEI's SW–CMM, BOOTSTRAP and ISO 9001, with other inputs from sources such as Trillium, and further adaptations to suit company–specific requirements. Its focus is the achievement of goal–oriented process improvement, and it is thus embedded within the OPAL programme. Assessments produce both SEI–style levels and BOOTSTRAP–style profiles.

The company–specific adaptations were of two main kinds. The first were to fit the method to the circumstances of smaller software groups (up to about 50). The second comprised enhancements to cover systems engineering, configuration engineering, and interfaces to marketing, product definition, and service and other business processes.

The Improvement Program OPAL was developed in response to the recognition that the development of complex software systems is a critical core competence for competitiveness, and one in which Siemens must be world class. It is part of a wider initiative for improving the competitiveness of all divisions of the company.

Improvement in OPAL is performed through improvement projects, undertaken by Process Improvement Teams (PITs). An improvement project will be defined on the basis of a set of recommendations (typically around 100 in number) from an assessment, which are then grouped into action clusters and prioritised. The results of improvement projects are tracked, and measured by a goal–oriented metrics system.

Siemens's experience with these models is the subject of Chapter 8.

IBM Europe: Software Development Benchmark

This benchmark was developed under the leadership of Peter Goodhew, at the Paris offices of IBM Europe, as a result of requests from IBM customers, for the purpose of conducting a survey of software development in European industry.

The benchmark is based on a set of 64 parameters, partitioned into two groups: a group of practice parameters (factors defining how organisations go about developing software), and a group of performance parameters (factors defining the effects of software development on organisational performance). Each parameter can be measured on a five–point scale, very much in the style of the Crosby Grid, except that only points 1, 3, and 5 are explicitly defined for each parameter (intermediate points 2 and 4 may be awarded "by interpolation"). That is illustrated in Figure 4.4, which shows the point definitions for the first of the 64 parameters.

The parameters are grouped under seven headings:

- organisation and culture,
- process,
- quality,
- methods and tools,
- technology and innovation,
- planning and estimating, and
- measurements.

At the time of writing, self–assessments are known to have been received from 358 software development organisations. Preliminary correlation studies have been carried out between the practice parameters and the performance parameters, to investigate how the former influence the latter. To the writers' knowledge, this is the first time that a detailed cause–effect statistical analysis has been attempted. The results must be treated with caution, because so many parameters are involved and the cause–effect relationships are likely to be very complex and difficult to unravel. It is nevertheless a highly significant and innovative initiative.

More detail on the IBM Europe Benchmark is given in the next section.

Parameters	Points				
	1	2	3	4	5
Vision	Maximise development output; managers dicate direction; cost reduction key goal		User or customer service emphasis; employee involvement; quality and cycle time are key drivers		Leadership in quality and service

Figure 4.4. Extract from the IBM Software Development Benchmark.

CLASSIFICATION OF MEASUREMENT MODELS

In this section we select some of the models catalogued in the previous section, and look at them in more detail. The models selected are ones which offer the ability to measure either the software (or some related) process or some broader set of factors in an organisation. We may call models of that kind *appraisal models*. We will study the *architecture* of appraisal models, and group them into different *architectural types*.

The architecture of any appraisal model AM will be defined in terms of six major properties:

- a set of features {F} to be measured;
- a feature scale FS, against which the features are measured;
- a set of conditions {C}, used to define points on the feature scale;
- a condition scale CS, against which the conditions are measured;
- an appraisal result AR; and
- supplementary information SI.

Thus (only for those who like a formal shorthand)

AM = [{F}, FS, {C}, CS, AR, SI].

The meaning of each of these terms will now be explained, and illustrated by reference to the simple example of the Crosby Maturity Grid (Figure 4.1).

Appraisal models AM fall into two classes. First there are process models, such as the Software CMM; all process models break the total process down first into process areas and then into practices. Second there are general models, such as the Crosby Maturity Grid, which embrace a wider range of factors than just process factors.

The set of features {F} are those things which an appraisal model allows to be measured. (In process models, the features are the process areas.) In many models, the features are organised into higher–level groups (ranging from three to nine in number). In the Crosby Grid, the features are the six measurement categories which label the horizontal rows.

The feature scale FS is the measurement scale which is applied to the members of the feature set. Three types of scales are found in the models studied: a yes/no scale, a graded scale, and a continuous scale. A yes/no scale indicates that the model only recognises the presence or absence of a feature; improvement of a feature, beyond movement from absent to present, cannot be measured. Either a graded scale or a continuous scale indicates that the model allows improvement in a feature to be recognised and measured. In the Crosby Grid, the five stages which label the columns constitute a graded feature scale.

The set of conditions {C} comprise the definitions of what it means for each feature to be at any point on the feature scale. (In process models, conditions are the practices which make up the process areas.) Conditions may be of two kinds: specific or generic. Specific conditions are those which are unique to a single feature. Generic conditions are those which commonly apply to a range of features. A model may use only specific conditions, or only generic ones, or a mixture. In the Crosby Grid, the conditions (which are specific) are the definitions which populate the grid, one for each row/column intersection.

The condition scale CS is the measurement scale which is applied to each condition, to indicate the extent to which it is satisfied. In the models studied, two types of scale appear: a yes/no scale and a graded scale. As with the feature scale, yes/no indicates simple presence or absence of a condition, whereas a graded scale makes it possible to recognise and measure improvement in the extent to which a condition is satisfied. The conditions in the Crosby Grid are measured on a yes/no scale: each condition is either satisfied or not satisfied.

The appraisal result AR is the final result derived from measuring whether the conditions for each of the features are satisfied. In the models studied, there are two types of appraisal result, either a *profile* (showing the achievement level for each feature separately) or a *single–value measure* (showing the achievement level for the whole organisation across all features). The Crosby Grid yields a maturity profile, a stage (from 1 to 5) for each of the six measurement categories.

The supplementary information SI is any additional information which is necessary or helpful in order to describe and understand the model.

Each of the models described in this section, using the above architecture of appraisal models, is a theory or hypothesis about how it may be useful to understand reality so as to manage it better. The architectural framework itself is a theory or hypothesis about how it may be useful to understand appraisal models so as to use them better. If all that sounds too abstract, remember two wise sayings.

- There is nothing so useful as a good theory.
- All models are wrong. Some are useful.

So it has proved. Based on these models are improvement methods and practices which have achieved practical results of major importance in the real world.

With that, let us turn to the appraisal models and their architectures. Eleven models have been analysed to date, and five main architectures have been identified. The architectures are distinguished according to a combination of two characteristics.

The first characteristic is whether (and, if so, how) a model allows the improvement of features to be recognised and measured. If both the feature scale and the condition scale are simple yes/no scales, then improvement (beyond movement from absent to present) is not measurable. If the feature scale and/or the condition scale are multi-point (graded or continuous), then improvement is measurable.

The second characteristic is whether the conditions in the model are specific, generic, or a mixture of both.

Of the 18 architecture types made possible by combinations of those two characteristics, five have been observed in the 11 models that are analysed here. The five architecture types are shown in Figure 4.5. The figure also shows the appraisal models which have been included within each type, and partitions them between general quality models and process models.

Each of the eleven selected appraisal models will now be shown in a series of diagrams, in terms of the architectural properties already set out:

AM = [{F}, FS, {C}, CS, AR, SI].

Each diagram indicates the architectural type of the model. Each property is explicitly labelled in the diagrams, except for the condition set CS, which is shown by a shaded area.

In addition to comparing the architectural properties of the eleven models, it is interesting also to compare their feature sets. These represent different views of what is important in achieving software excellence. It would be an interesting, though difficult, exercise to attempt their unification.

The diagrams (Figures 4.6 to 4.15) appear on the following pages. For some of the larger models, diagrams extend over more than one page.

Counting (Figure 4.6) the number of conditions per guideline in ISO 9000-3 is an imprecise art. The principle used here has been to count the lowest–level conditions which can be exactly referenced (e.g., "5.4.2.1.d" or "6.9" in ISO 9000-3).

Architecture Type	Characteristics		Appraisal Models	
	Measurement of Feature Improvement	Conditions	General Quality Models	Process Models
Type 1	NO (yes/no feature scale, yes/no condition scale)	Specific	• ISO 9001/9000-3	• Software CMM
Type 2	YES (graded feature scale, yes/no condition scale)	Specific	• Crosby Maturity Grid • IBM European Benchmark	• Trillium • INCOSE SECAM
Type 3	YES (graded feature scale, yes/no condition scale)	Mixed (specific and generic)		• S/W Tech Diagnostic • SPICE • EPIC SE-CMM
Type 4	YES (continuous feature scale, yes/no condition scale)	Generic	• European Model for TQM	
Type 5	YES (graded feature scale, graded condition scale)	Specific		• BOOTSTRAP

Figure 4.5. Architecture types for appraisal models.

The reader should be aware that Figure 4.7 is not a standard way of representing the Software CMM. It is, however, the most appropriate way within the architectural conventions adopted in this chapter, and it has the virtue of highlighting the CMM's differences with other models. Defining goals for KPAs is a valuable feature, not provided by most models.

The number of conditions in each cell is counted (subjectively) as the number of distinct statements. For example, "A stronger quality leader is appointed but main emphasis is still on appraisal and moving the product. Still part of manufacturing or other" is counted as comprising three conditions.

The Crosby model in Figure 4.8 (and others that have followed it more or less closely) is a powerful one, in that it offers clear definitions of improvement (quantitative or qualitative) for each feature across all stages.

The number of conditions in each cell is counted (subjectively) as the number of distinct statements. For example, "Quality and productivity measured. Function points (or equivalent metric) used. Size of applications portfolio known" is counted as comprising four conditions.

The IBM model illustrated in Figure 4.9 is very close to the Crosby original. The main differences are its size (64 parameters against six measurement categories) and the fact that intermediate points 2 and 4 are undefined. Its 64 parameters provide a more comprehensive overview of the factors defining practice and performance than any other model.

Like the Software CMM, Trillium (Figure 4.10) leaves Level 1 (the domain ruled over by primeval chaos!) undefined. Unlike the Software CMM, it allows each process area (roadmap) to improve by the accretion of process–specific practices (in just the same way that

TYPE 1	ISO 9000-3 GUIDELINES FOR APPLYING ISO 9001 TO SOFTWARE
FEATURE SET: **23 Quality Guidelines**	**FEATURE SCALE:** **Yes/no**
Framework	
Management responsibility	22 conditions
Quality system	3 conditions
Internal quality system audits	1 condition
Corrective action	5 conditions
Lifecycle activities	
General	1 condition
Contract review	16 conditions
Purchaser's requirements specification	5 conditions
Development planning	33 conditions
Quality planning	6 conditions
Design and implementation	8 conditions
Testing and validation	18 conditions
Acceptance	5 conditions
Replication, delivery and installation	13 conditions
Maintenance	25 conditions
Supporting activities	
Configuration management	19 conditions
Document control	11 conditions
Quality records	1 condition
Measurement	8 conditions
Rules, practices and conventions	1 condition
Tools and techniques	1 condition
Purchasing	3 conditions
Included software product	1 condition
Training	1 condition

CONDITION SCALE: Yes/no (conditions are satisfied/not satisfied)
APPRAISAL RESULT: Certification/noncertification
SUPPLEMENTARY INFORMATION
1 Certification/noncertification is to the ISO 9001 standard as interpreted by the guidelines.

Figure 4.6.   ISO 9000-3 guidelines for software.

improvement is achieved in Crosby and the IBM Benchmark by the accretion of feature–specific conditions).

Of all the process models analysed in this section, SECAM (see Figure 4.11) is unique in having process–specific practices defined for each process at each level.

It shares with the Software CMM the important property of specifying goals for each KFA.

The "common key practices" in Figure 4.12 showing the Software Technology Diagnostic (STD) model arise from common wording used for certain practices across all KPAs. SPICE's "generic practices" are clustered into "common key attributes."

SPICE (Figure 4.13) was the first model to use a six–level architecture. It was also the first model to use the term "generic practices," though the concept had arguably been introduced in the Software Technology Diagnostic. In SPICE, however, the levels beyond level 1 are wholly dependent on generic practices, whereas in STD they are in general a combination of generic and specific practices.

TYPE 1		SEI CMM FOR SOFTWARE (SOFTWARE CMM) (version 1.1)
FEATURE SET: 18 Key Process Areas (KPAs)		**FEATURE SCALE:** Yes/no
Level 2: Repeatable	Requirements management	12 key practices
	Software project planning	25 key practices
	Software project tracking and oversight	24 key practices
	Software subcontract management	22 key practices
	Software quality assurance	17 key practices
	Software configuration management	21 key practices
Level 3: Defined	Organisation process focus	16 key practices
	Organisation process definition	11 key practices
	Training programme	16 key practices
	Integrated software management	19 key practices
	Software product engineering	20 key practices
	Intergroup coordination	17 key practices
	Peer reviews	9 key practices
Level 4: Managed	Quantitative process management	18 key practices
	Software quality management	13 key practices
Level 5: Optimising	Defect prevention	18 key practices
	Technology change management	19 key practices
	Process change management	19 key practices

CONDITION SCALE: Yes/no (key practices are present/absent)

APPRAISAL RESULT: Maturity level

SUPPLEMENTARY INFORMATION

1 The maturity level is the highest level for which all KPAs are satisfactory, provided that all KPAs at lower levels are also satisfactory. Default is level 1 (for which no KPAs are defined).

2 Key practices for each KPA are structured under 5 headings (common features): commitment to perform, ability to perform, activities performed, measurement and analysis, and verifying implementation.

3 A set of goals (2 to 4 in number) is defined for each KPA.

Figure 4.7. Software CMM.

TYPE 2	CROSBY QUALITY MANAGEMENT MATURITY GRID				
FEATURE SET: **6 Measurement** **Categories**	**FEATURE SCALE: Graded**				
	STAGE 1 **Uncertainty**	**STAGE 2** **Awakening**	**STAGE 3** **Enlightenment**	**STAGE 4** **Wisdom**	**STAGE 5** **Certainty**
Management understanding and attitude	2 conditions	2 conditions	2 conditions	3 conditions	1 condition
Quality organisation status	3 conditions	3 conditions	3 conditions	3 conditions	3 conditions
Problem handling	4 conditions	2 conditions	2 conditions	2 conditions	1 condition
Cost of quality as percentage of sales	2 conditions	2 conditions	2 conditions	2 conditions	2 conditions
Quality improvement actions	2 conditions	1 condition	1 condition	1 condition	1 condition
Summation of company quality posture	1 condition	1 condition	1 condition	1 condition	1 condition

CONDITION SCALE: Yes/no (conditions are satisfied/not satisfied)
APPRAISAL RESULT: Profile of maturity stages
SUPPLEMENTARY INFORMATION
1 The maturity stage for a measurement category is the highest stage for which the condition is satisfied, provided that the conditions for lower stages are also satisfied.

Figure 4.8. Crosby Quality Management Maturity Grid.

TYPE 2	IBM EUROPEAN SOFTWARE DEVELOPMENT BENCHMARK				
FEATURE SET: **64 Parameters**	**FEATURE SCALE: Graded**				
	POINT 1	**PT 2**	**POINT 3**	**PT 4**	**POINT 5**
Vision	3 conditions		3 conditions		1 condition
Shared vision, mission, goals	3 conditions		3 conditions		3 conditions
Development strategy	2 conditions		2 conditions		2 conditions
Management style	4 conditions		4 conditions		3 conditions
Employee involvement	1 condition		4 conditions		3 conditions
Job flexibility	1 condition		2 conditions		3 conditions
Benchmarking	1 condition		1 condition		1 condition
Training and education	1 condition		1 condition		2 conditions
Skills	2 conditions		2 conditions		5 conditions
User/customer orientation	3 conditions		3 conditions		4 conditions
Problem solving	3 conditions		3 conditions		2 conditions
Project goals	1 condition		1 condition		1 condition

Organisation and culture

Figure 4.9. *Continued*

Process	Development/ maintenance process	2 conditions	2 conditions	2 conditions
	Process Improvement	1 condition	2 conditions	2 conditions
	Project management	1 condition	2 conditions	3 conditions
	Standards and guidelines	1 condition	2 conditions	3 conditions
	Systems assurance	1 condition	1 condition	3 conditions
	User relationships	1 condition	1 condition	3 conditions
	Design for operation	1 condition	1 condition	2 conditions
	Delivery on schedule	2 conditions	2 conditions	2 conditions
	Delivery within budget	2 conditions	2 conditions	2 conditions
	Project cycle time	2 conditions	2 conditions	2 conditions
	Scope creep	1 condition	1 condition	1 condition
	Maintenance effort compared to new devt.	1 condition	1 condition	1 condition
Quality	Quality vision	3 conditions	3 conditions	3 conditions
	Quality processes	2 conditions	3 conditions	2 conditions
	Quality assurance	1 condition	1 condition	1 condition
	Quality measurements	1 condition	1 condition	3 conditions
	Defect prevention	2 conditions	1 condition	2 conditions
	Inspections or walkthroughs	1 condition	2 conditions	1 condition
	Testing	1 condition	1 condition	2 conditions
	Defect removal efficiency	1 condition	1 condition	1 condition
	Defect density of delivered software	1 condition	1 condition	1 condition
	Defect prevention effort	1 condition	1 condition	1 condition
	Testing effort	1 condition	1 condition	1 condition
	First year defect correction costs	1 condition	1 condition	1 condition
Methods and Tools	User requirements	1 condition	1 condition	2 conditions
	Design	1 condition	1 condition	5 conditions
	Testing	1 condition	1 condition	4 conditions
	Usability	2 conditions	2 conditions	2 conditions
	Reuse	1 condition	1 condition	2 conditions
	CASE and development tools	1 condition	4 conditions	3 conditions
	Methods and tools maintenance support	1 condition	1 condition	3 conditions
	Development/ environment	3 conditions	4 conditions	4 conditions
	Programming language	1 condition	1 condition	1 condition
	Project planning and tracking	1 condition	1 condition	3 conditions
Technology & Innovation	Exploitation of innovation & creativity	1 condition	2 conditions	2 conditions
	Technology strategy	2 conditions	1 condition	3 conditions
	Innovation	1 condition	1 condition	2 conditions
	New applications (last 2 years)	1 condition	1 condition	1 condition

Figure 4.9.   *Continued*

Planning & Estimating	Estimating tools	1 condition	1 condition	2 conditions
	Estimating approach	1 condition	1 condition	2 conditions
	Estimating accuracy	1 condition	1 condition	1 condition
	Planning	1 condition	1 condition	2 conditions
	User/customer confidence	1 condition	1 condition	1 condition
Measurements	Satisfaction survey	1 condition	2 conditions	4 conditions
	User/customer satisfaction	1 condition	3 conditions	2 conditions
	Employee morale	3 conditions	2 conditions	4 conditions
	Software metrics	3 conditions	4 conditions	5 conditions
	Use of measurements	1 condition	2 conditions	4 conditions
	Historical measurements data	1 condition	1 condition	1 condition
	Development productivity	3 conditions	3 conditions	3 conditions
	Maintenance assignment scope	1 condition	1 condition	1 condition
	Cancelled projects	1 condition	1 condition	1 condition

CONDITION SCALE: Yes/no (conditions are satisfied/not satisfied)
APPRAISAL RESULT: Profile of points achieved
SUPPLEMENTARY INFORMATION
1 The scale point for a factor is the highest point for which the condition is satisfied.
2 Points 2 and 4 are undefined, but may be awarded by interpolation.

Figure 4.9.   IBM European Benchmark.

TYPE 2	**TRILLIUM (version 3.0)**				
FEATURE SET: 27 Roadmaps	**FEATURE SCALE: Graded**				
	LEVEL 1	LEVEL 2 Repeatable &	LEVEL 3 Defined &	LEVEL 4 Managed &	LEVEL 5 Fully
	Unstructured	project orntd	process orntd	integrated	integrated
OPQ — Quality management		6 practices	16 practices		
Business process engineering		4 practices	4 practices	OPQ = Organisational process quality	
HRDM — Human resource devt and management		9 practices	42 practices		
Process — Process definition		2 practices	15 practices	1 practice	
Technology management		1 practice	4 practices	6 practices	2 practices
Process improvement and engineering		2 practices	19 practices	13 practices	1 practice
Measurements		11 practices	16 practices	4 practices	1 practice

Figure 4.10.   *Continued*

Management	Project management		42 practices	15 practices	3 practices	
	Subcontractor management		14 practices	4 practices		
	Customer-supplier relationship		4 practices	4 practices		
	Requirements management		11 practices	2 practices	1 practice	
	Estimation		14 practices	4 practices		
QS	Quality system	14 practices	15 practices	2 practices	2 practices	2 practices
Development Practices	Development process		2 practices	7 practices	2 practices	3 practices
	Development techniques		3 practices	6 practices	4 practices	
	Internal documentation		4 practices	9 practices		
	Verification and validation		6 practices	9 practices	4 practices	
	Configuration management		18 practices	3 practices		1 practice
	Reuse		3 practices	9 practices	4 practices	1 practice
	Reliability management		5 practices	6 practices	1 practice	
DE	Development environment		4 practices	6 practices	2 practices	1 practice
Customer Support	Problem response system		9 practices	3 practices		
	Usability engineering		4 practices	10 practices	2 practices	
	Lifecycle cost modelling		1 practice	3 practices	1 practice	
	User documentation		1 practice	7 practices	2 practices	
	Customer engineering		8 practices	5 practices		
	User training		2 practices	2 practices		

CONDITION SCALE: Yes/no (practices are present/absent)
APPRAISAL RESULT: Profile of maturity levels
SUPPLEMENTARY INFORMATION

1 The maturity level for a roadmap is the highest level for which the requisite number of practices are present, provided that the requisite number at lower levels are also present. Default is level 1 (for which no practices are defined).

Figure 4.10.   Trillium.

TYPE 2	INCOSE/CAWG SECAM INTERIM MODEL (version 1.40)				
FEATURE SET: 18 Key Focus Areas (KFAs)	**FEATURE SCALE: Graded**				
	LEVEL 1 Performed	**LEVEL 2** Managed	**LEVEL 3** Defined	**LEVEL 4** Measured	**LEVEL 5** Optimising
Management Planning	6 practices	15 practices	24 practices	10 practices	7 practices
Tracking & oversight	7 practices	9 practices	25 practices	9 practices	5 practices
Subcontract mgmt	3 practices	5 practices	18 practices	3 practices	4 practices
Intergroup coordination	6 practices	10 practices	11 practices	2 practices	4 practices
Configuration mgmt	4 practices	6 practices	19 practices	2 practices	6 practices
Quality assurance	6 practices	3 practices	10 practices	4 practices	7 practices
Risk management	4 practices	12 practices	24 practices	4 practices	5 practices
Organisation Process management and improvement	8 practices	11 practices	8 practices	8 practices	5 practices
Training	3 practices	15 practices	15 practices	5 practices	6 practices
Technology mgmt	3 practices	9 practices	15 practices	2 practices	5 practices
Envt & tool support	5 practices	10 practices	14 practices	6 practices	5 practices
Systems Engineering System concept def	5 practices	15 practices	15 practices	5 practices	7 practices
System requirements	3 practices	9 practices	26 practices	3 practices	5 practices
System design	3 practices	16 practices	15 practices	4 practices	4 practices
Integrated engineering analysis	4 practices	11 practices	21 practices	4 practices	7 practices
System integration	5 practices	13 practices	13 practices	3 practices	6 practices
System verification	6 practices	15 practices	9 practices	5 practices	5 practices
System validation	6 practices	11 practices	9 practices	3 practices	4 practices

CONDITION SCALE: Yes/no (practices are present/absent)
APPRAISAL RESULT: Profile of maturity levels
SUPPLEMENTARY INFORMATION
1 The maturity level for a KFA is the highest level for which the requisite number of practices are present, provided that the requisite number at lower levels are also present.
2 A set of goals (2 to 5 in number) is defined for each KFA.

Figure 4.11.   INCOSE CAWG SECAM.

TYPE 3	SOFTWARE TECHNOLOGY DIAGNOSTIC (version 2.2)			
FEATURE SET: 20 Key Process Areas (KPAs)	**FEATURE SCALE: Graded**			
	LEVEL 1 Initial	**LEVEL 2** Repeatable	**LEVEL 3** Defined	**LEVEL 4** Managed
Change management				
Configuration management		7 key practs	1 key pract	
Contract management		7 key practs	2 key practs	
Contract staff management		7 key practs	1 key pract	
Development process		9 key practs	3 key practs	
Documentation process		3 key practs	1 key pract	
Maintenance process		3 key practs	1 key pract	
Operations management		4 key practs		
Organisation management			5 key practs	
Problem management				
Process management		3 key practs	2 key practs	1 key pract
Procurement		4 key practs	1 key pract	
Product management		4 key practs	1 key pract	
Project management		12 key practs	4 key practs	2 key practs
Quality management		6 key practs		1 key pract
Requirements specification		7 key practs	2 key practs	
Security management		3 key practs	2 key practs	
Staff performance mgmt		6 key practs		
Technology management		2 key practs	1 key pract	
3rd-party subcontract mgmt		6 key practs	1 key pract	

(Vertical column labels: LEVEL 1 — 6 Common key practices; between LEVEL 2 and LEVEL 3 — 7 Common key practices; between LEVEL 3 and LEVEL 4 — 7 Common key practices)

CONDITION SCALE: Yes/no (key practices are present/absent)
APPRAISAL RESULT: Profile of maturity levels
SUPPLEMENTARY INFORMATION

1 The maturity level for a KPA is the highest level for which the requisite number of key practices are present, provided that the requisite number at lower levels are also present. Default is level 1 (for which no key practices are defined).

2 Common key practices are structured under a number of standard headings, as follows: process management (abilities, process goals, process measures, process definition, process verification); process audit (output audit); process instantiation (abilities, product measurement, additional definition, output verification).

Figure 4.12. Software technology diagnostic.

At the time of writing, SPICE has moved to a substantially new version 2.0 which uses the ISO 12207 Standard for Software Life Cycle Processes as a reference model.

EPIC SE–CMM (Figure 4.14) adopted the SPICE architecture unchanged. At present there is no indication whether it will respond to the changes in SPICE.

Figure 4.15 illustrates the European Foundation for Quality Management (EFQM) Model or the European Quality Award (EQA) Model. It is the only model, among those shown here, which uses a continuous scale for assessing features.

The set of Criterion Parts is partitioned into "enablers" (compare the practice factors in the IBM Benchmark, Figure 4.9) and "results" (compare the IBM performance factors). The two conditions for all the "enablers" are their degree of excellence and their degree of deployment.

TYPE 3	SPICE (version 1.0)					
FEATURE SET: 35 Process Areas (PAs)	**FEATURE SCALE: Graded**					
	LEVEL 0 Not Performed	LEVEL 1 Performed Initially	LEVEL 2 Planned and Tracked	LEVEL 3 Well Defined	LEVEL 4 Quantitatively Controlled	LEVEL 5 Continuously Improving
Customer-Supplier Acquire software product/service		5 base practs				
Establish contract		4 base practs				
Identify customer needs		3 base practs				
Perform joint audit and reviews		6 base practs				
Package, deliver and install s/w		7 base practs				
Support operation of software		7 base practs				
Provide customer service		4 base practs				
Assess customer satisfaction		4 base practs				
Engineering Develop system reqts & design		4 base practs				
Develop software requirements		5 base practs	6 Common key practices	7 Common key practices	7 Common key practices	7 Common key practices
Develop software design		4 base practs				
Implement software design		3 base practs				
Integrate and test software		6 base practs				
Integrate and test system		6 base practs				
Maintain system and software		5 base practs				
Project Plan project life cycle		6 base practs				
Establish project plan		10 base practs				
Build teams		3 base practs				
Manage requirements		5 base practs				
Manage quality		6 base practs				
Manage risks		8 base practs				
Manage project resources		5 base practs				
Manage subcontractors		5 base practs				

Figure 4.13 Continued

			12 generic practices	5 generic practices	3 generic practices	5 generic practices
Support	Develop documentation	5 base practs				
	Perform configuration mgmt	8 base practs				
	Perform quality assurance	5 base practs				
	Perform problem resolution	6 base practs				
	Perform peer reviews	8 base practs				
Organisation	Engineer the business	6 base practs				
	Define the process	13 base practs				
	Improve the process	9 base practs				
	Training	4 base practs				
	Enable reuse	7 base practs				
	Provide software engineering environment	5 base practs				
	Provide work facilities	5 base practs				

CONDITION SCALE: Yes/no (practices are present/absent)
APPRAISAL RESULT: Profile of maturity levels
SUPPLEMENTARY INFORMATION
1 The maturity level for a PA is the highest level for which the requisite number of practices are present, provided that the requisite number at lower levels are also present. Default is level 0 (which is defined as the absence of base practices).
2 Generic practices are structured under a number of common features. At level 2 they are: planning performance, disciplined performance, verifying performance, tracking performance. At level 3: defining a standard process, perform the defined process. At level 4: establishing measurable quality goals, objectively managing performance. At level 5: improving organisational capability, improving process effectiveness.

Figure 4.13.   SPICE.

The two conditions for all the "results" are their degree of excellence and their scope. Definitions for these conditions are given corresponding to the 0 percent, 25 percent, 50 percent, 75 percent, and 100 precent points.

A number of variants of the model are offered, depending on the different purposes for which it may be used. The variant shown above is the one used for formal award assessments.

BOOTSTRAP (Figure 4.16) is unique in that it does not apply a yes/no scale to the measurement of the practices for each feature. It instead applies a four–point scale (absent/weak/fair/complete, absent/weak/fair/strong, absent/weak/fair/extensive, absent/basic/significant/extensive, scarce/fair/good extensive, etc.).

Its other main characteristic is that it is intermediate between what we have called in this section "general quality models," which measure a wide range of features, and "process models," which measure only the component areas of the software process. BOOTSTRAP measures process and technology, though its measurement of technology is rather weak. It is considered, however, to be in spirit nearer to being a process model than a general quality model.

TYPE 3	EPIC SYSTEMS ENGINEERING CMM (SE-CMM) (version 1.1)					
FEATURE SET: **18 Process Areas (PAs)**	**FEATURE SCALE: Graded**					
	LEVEL 0 Not Performed	LEVEL 1 Performed Initially	LEVEL 2 Planned and Tracked	LEVEL 3 Well Defined	LEVEL 4 Quantitatively Controlled	LEVEL 5 Continuously Improving
Engineering Analyse candidate solutions		6 base practs				
Derive and allocate requirements		9 base practs				
Evolve system architecture		8 base practs				
Integrate disciplines		6 base practs				
Integrate system		8 base practs				
Understand customer needs and expectations		5 base practs				
Verify and validate system		6 base practs				
Project Ensure quality		7 base practs	12 generic practices	5 generic practices	3 generic practices	5 generic practices
Manage configurations		5 base practs				
Manage risk		6 base practs				
Monitor/control technical effort		6 base practs				
Plan technical effort		10 base practs				
Organisational Define SE process		4 base practs				
Improve SE process		4 base practs				
Manage product line evolution		5 base practs				
Manage SE support environment		7 base practs				
provide knowledge and skills		8 base practs				
Coordinate with suppliers		5 base practs				

CONDITION SCALE: Yes/no (practices are present/absent)
APPRAISAL RESULT: Profile of maturity levels
SUPPLEMENTARY INFORMATION
1 The maturity level for a PA is the highest level for which the requisite number of practices are present, provided that the requisite number at lower levels are also present. Default is level 0 (which is defined as the absence of base practices).
2 Generic practices are structured under a number of common features. At level 2 they are: planning performance, disciplined performance, verifying performance, tracking performance. At level 3: defining a standard process, perform the defined process. At level 4: establishing measurable quality goals, objectively managing performance. At level 5: improving organisational capability, improving process effectiveness.

Figure 4.14.   EPIC SE-CMM.

	TYPE 4	EUROPEAN MODEL FOR TQM (EFQM 1996)				
	FEATURE SET: **32 Criterion Parts**	**FEATURE SCALE: Continuous**				
		0%	25%	50%	75%	100%
Leadership	Visible TQ leadership Consistent TQ culture Recognising/appreciating . . . efforts Resourcing and supporting TQ Customer/supplier involvement Promoting TQ externally	2 conditions (enabler s)	2 conditions (enabler s)	2 conditions (enabler s)	2 conditions (enabler s)	2 conditions (enabler s)
Policy and strategy	Based on TQ concept Based on relevant and comprehensive info Implemented organisation-wide Communicated internally/externally Regularly updated and improved					
People management	People Resources planned/improved Skills and capabilities developed . . . People and teams agree targets . . . People involved . . . and empowered Effective . . . communication					
Resources	Financial resources Information resources Suppliers, materials, buildings, equipment Application of technology					
Processes	Quality vision Quality processes Quality assurance Quality measurements Defect prevention					
Customer satisfaction	Inspections or walkthroughs Testing	2 conditions (results)	2 conditions (results)	2 conditions (results)	2 conditions (results)	2 conditions (results)
People satisfaction	Defect removal efficiency Defect density of delivered software					
Impact on society	Defect prevention effort Testing effort					
Business results	First year defect correction costs User requirements					

CONDITION SCALE: Yes/no (conditions are satisfied/not satisfied)
APPRAISAL RESULT: Profile of percentages achieved
SUPPLEMENTARY INFORMATION
1 The percentage for a criterion part can be determined in one of two ways. It may be the percentage corresponding to the highest condition satisfied, provided that the lower conditions are also satisfied. Alternatively, it may be an interpolation between the percentage corresponding to the highest condition satisfied and the percentage corresponding to the next higher condition.
2 All the "enabler" criterion parts share a common set of conditions. Similarly all the "results" criterion parts share a common set of criteria (different from those of the "enablers").

Figure 4.15.   European Model for TQM.

TYPE 4	BOOTSTRAP (early version)				
FEATURE SET: **12 Process** **Factors**	**FEATURE SCALE: Graded**				
	LEVEL 1 Initial	**LEVEL 2** Repeatable	**LEVEL 3** Defined	**LEVEL 4** Managed	**LEVEL 5** Optimising
Global orgm					
Quality system		3 practices	6 practices		
Resource management		4 practices	3 practices		
Global methodology					
Process-related functions		4 practices	4 practices	1 practice	
Lifecycle-independent functions		8 practices	17 practices	13 practices	5 practices
Lifecycle functions		8 practices	24 practices	5 practices	
Project organization					
Coordination			1 practice		
Development		1 practice			
Testing, verification, validation		1 practice			
Support		1 practice			
Project methodology					
Process-related functions		5 practices	7 practices	12 practices	2 practices
Lifecycle-independent functions		7 practices	12 practices	3 practices	
Lifecycle functions		9 practices	21 practices	3 practices	

CONDITION SCALE: Graded (4-point scale)
APPRAISAL RESULT: Maturity level and/or profile of maturity levels
SUPPLEMENTARY INFORMATION
1 The maturity level for a process factor is the highest level for which the requisite number of practices are present, provided that the requisite number at lower levels are also present. Default is level 1 (for which no practices are defined).
2 The overall process maturity level is given by an algorithm designed to yield a result equivalent to the SEI CMM for Software maturity level.

Figure 4.16.   BOOTSTRAP.

FEATURE SET: 7 Technology Factors	FEATURE SCALE: Yes/no
Global technology Technology innovation	4 practices
Technology for lifecycle-indep't functions	11 practices
Technology for lifecycle functions	27 practices
Tool integration	5 practices
Project tech'logy Technology for lifecycle-indep't functions	8 practices
Technology for lifecycle functions	18 practices
Tool integration	5 practices

CONDITION SCALE: Graded (4-point scale)
APPRAISAL RESULT: Profile of maturity levels
SUPPLEMENTARY INFORMATION
1 the maturity level for a technology factor is satisfactory or unsatisfactory, depending on whether the requisite number of practices are present.

Figure 4.16.   BOOTSTRAP, *concluded*

Table 4.1.   Terminology Used in SPICE Compared with that Used in the Previous Part of Chapter 4

SPICE Terminology			
Functionality	*Scoring*	*Rating*	*Capability*
Functional Process Architecture	Guidelines for scoring the base practices	Guidelines for rating scores to calculate capability profiles	Capability Level Architecture

Terminology Used in the Previously Discussed Catalogue					
Features (F)	Feature Scale (FS)	Condition Scale (CS)	Algorithm	Appraisal Result (AR)	Capability Levels

DETAILED COMPARISON OF BOOTSTRAP, CMM AND SPICE

In this part of the chapter BOOTSTRAP is compared with CMM and SPICE concerning the process architecture, capability evaluation, and improvement planning. Table 4.1 shows how the SPICE terminology relates to the previously defined one.

Each software process assessment and improvement model has two dimensions which are functionality and capability. The functionality dimension contains the processes to be evaluated and the capability dimension the capability or maturity levels against which the processes will be evaluated.

The Original BOOTSTRAP Process Model

The Functionality Dimension

The functionality dimension was formed enhancing the processes of the SEI model (formed according to DoD 2167A standard (DOD-STD-2167A, 1988) with processes aligned with

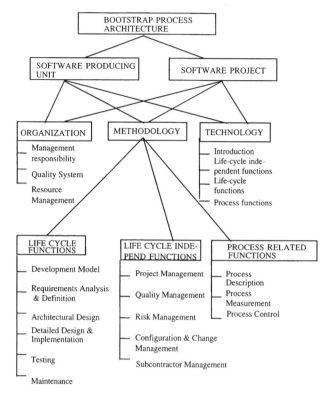

Figure 4.17. The BOOTSTRAP process model version 2.3—the functionality dimension.

the ISO 9001 and ISO 9000-3 requirements, the processes of the ESA life-cycle model, and general TQM principles. This resulted in a tree based architecture of process clusters and processes as outlined in Figure 4.17.

The Capability Dimension

The capability dimension of the original BOOTSTRAP process model was formed by adopting the maturity levels as defined generally in the SEI model [12]. The maturity scale includes five capability stages known as maturity levels: initial level, repeatable level, defined level, managed level, and optimising level. In principle, when a Software Producing Unit (SPU) undergoes improvement, it passes through the levels in this order, and its capability is determined as the last satisfied maturity level. The BOOTSTRAP methodology enhanced the traditional SEI maturity levels by dividing each of them into four quartiles and started to measure the process capability using this quartile scale accordingly within each of the five maturity levels.

In addition the BOOTSTRAP methodology is able to evaluate each attribute of the functionality dimension separately on a five-point maturity scale (Figure 4.18), identify weaknesses and strengths, and establish attribute based improvement plans. This is based on the fact that the attributes of the BOOTSTRAP process model can span several maturity levels. That means that an attribute (a process) may have practices of different maturity levels. Therefore, the key process areas and key practices of the CM Model were not applied as such in the BOOTSTRAP methodology (Figure 4.18).

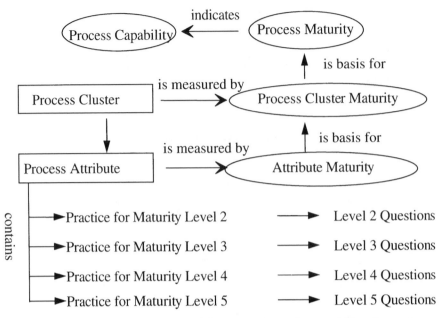

Figure 4.18. BOOTSTRAP process model Version 2.3—the capability dimension.

The SPICE Process Model

The SPICE process model defines software development processes and practices that may be implemented to establish and improve an organisation's software acquisition, development, maintenance, operation, and support capabilities. Practices in this model are organised using an architecture that will help software personnel to understand how to continuously improve their software processes. The architecture of the SPICE process model contains two hierarchies (Figure 4.19) formed from different viewpoints. The hierarchy on the left is based on grouping by type of activity, that contains the functionality dimension, while the hierarchy on the right is based on grouping by type of implementation or institutionalisation activity, which forms the capability dimension of the SPICE process model.

The Functionality Dimension

The functionality dimension of the SPICE process model is composed pf process categories,[1] processes,[2] and base practices.[3] Each process in the model is described in terms of base practices, which are its unique software engineering or management activities. Processes in turn are grouped into five process categories, that contain five to seven processes each.

The processes as defined in the SPICE process model are not processes in the sense of being complete process models or descriptions. The definitions contain descriptions of essential practices, but they do not determine how to perform the process. Therefore, the functionality dimension of SPICE process model is rather descriptive than prescriptive in nature.

The functionality dimension of the SPICE process model is quite similar to the BOOTSTRAP process architecture, where the process clusters (organisation, life cycle functions,

---

[1]A *process category* is a set of processes adressing the same general area of activity.
[2]A *process* is a set of activities that achieves a purpose.
[3]A *base practice* is a software engineering or management activity that addresses the purpose of a particular process.

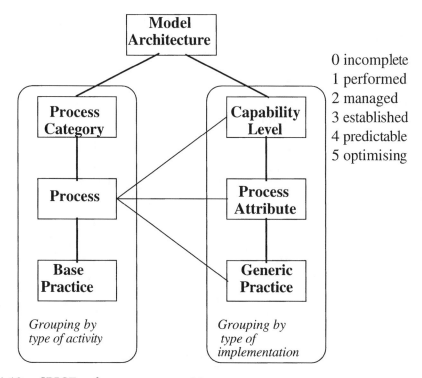

Figure 4.19.   SPICE software process architecture.

etc.) represent the process categories, the process attributes (project management, quality management, requirements analysis, etc.) represent the processes, and the questions are related to the base practices (Figure 4.20).

The Capability Dimension

The capability dimension of the SPICE process model defines evolving capability of the implemented or institutionalised processes in terms of capability levels,[4] process attributes (former common features),[5] and generic practices.[6] The decomposition was derived based on grouping by type of implementation or institutionalised activity.

There are six capability levels in the SPICE process model, that are: Incomplete (0), Performed (1), Managed (2), Established (3), Predictable (4), and Optimising (5).

In the SPICE capability dimension each process of the functionality dimension may have features in its implementation that address on each of the capability levels. In the CMM each key process area is only valid within one maturity level which means that each process is mapped onto a single capability level. In the BOOTSTRAP process model each base practice is assigned to one capability level (see dotted lines in Figure 4.20), but a process may include base practices from two to three different capability levels and may, therefore, span over many

---

[4]A *capability level* is a set of process attributes (former common features) that work together to provide a major enhancement in the capability to perform a process.

[5]A *process attribute* (former common feature) is a set of practices that address an aspect of process implementation or institutionalisation.

[6]A *generic practice* is an implementation or institutionalisation practice that enhances the capability to perform any process.

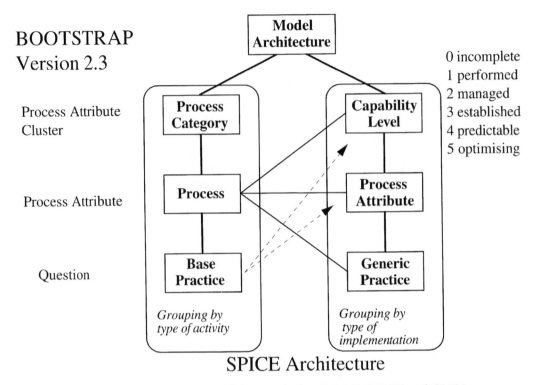

Figure 4.20. The SPICE process model compared to BOOTSTRAP and CMM.

capability levels which enables the BOOTSTRAP methodology to evaluate each process separately on the capability scale, providing the basis for the calculation of capability profiles (Figure 4.20).

Scoring and Rating

When performing an assessment, the processes of the functionality dimension are evaluated according to scoring principles, and rating and measurement models describe how the scores are aggregated into capability measures.

The BOOTSTRAP Principles

The BOOTSTRAP methodology includes guidelines for scoring and the BOOTSTRAP algorithm for rating. The BOOTSTRAP algorithm was needed for two reasons. First, the number of practices and corresponding questions in the questionnaires vary between different capability levels. Second, in the BOOTSTRAP capability dimension processes may span several maturity levels.

Scoring Principles

Individual practices of the BOOTSTRAP process model are scored by using a score of five values, represented most commonly with such adjectives as: absent, weak, fair, extensive, and non-applicable. Thus, the "yes" answer is divided into three different intensity levels [23], [24]. This allows to define more precisely the attribute profiles and helps in evaluating the practice implementation that may be of various degrees of "yes." The practices that cannot be applied in the organisation or project can be left out as nonapplicable practices. The evaluation is done using questionnaires, where each practice is presented with one or more questions.

The BOOTSTRAP Algorithm

Each question of the BOOTSTRAP questionnaire represents a base practice that is understood as a step [11], [28] on the way to improved capability. Each question is answered on a linguistic scale: complete (1 step), fair (0.66 steps), basic (0.33 steps), absent (0 steps). Three questions answered, for instance, by absent, basic, and complete represent $0 + 0.33 + 1 = 1.33$ steps. Each question is assigned to a single maturity level, that offers the basis for counting the number of steps for each maturity level. The total number of steps represents all steps achieved on all levels.

Counting of steps implies that there are different distances between the maturity levels. The distance d2 between maturity level 1 and 2 is defined by the number of steps (applicable questions) on level 2. The distance d3 between maturity level 2 and 3 is defined by the number of steps (applicable questions) on level 3, etc. This is very different from a scale where only satisfaction percentages per level are calculated leading to a scale with equal distances between the levels. In the BOOTSTRAP methodology as well as in the CMM the number of questions on each maturity level differs considerably. For example, in the BOOTSTRAP questionnaire version 2.22 (that resulted from the BOOTSTRAP project) there were: 28 questions on level 2, 54 on level 3, 19 on level 4, and only 5 on level 5.

Steps also imply that satisfaction percentages are weighted by statistical significance. If you calculate pc2 (average satisfaction percentage on level 2) and d2 (number of applicable questions on level 2) and multiply pc2 × d2 you obtain the number of the steps achieved on level 2 (the simple adding procedure described at the beginning of this section). This means that steps are obtained by multiplying the satisfaction percentage with the number of questions on which the calculation is based. This means that 50 percent on level 4 (d4 = 19 in Figure 4.5) represent a distance of 19 × 0.5 on the step scale, whereas 50 percent on level 3 (d3 = 54) represent a distance of 54 × 0.5 on the step scale which is about three times more significant.

The example presented in Figure 4.21 shows a case where maturity level 2 is fully satisfied, level 3 is satisfied by 25 percent, and level 4 by 50 percent. Using the percentage-based scale a

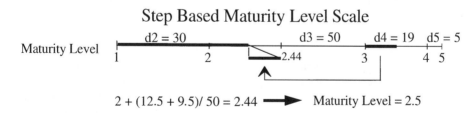

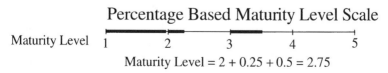

Figure 4.21. An example comparing step-based and percentage-based maturity level scales with each other.

maturity level of $2.25 + 0.5 = 2.75$ is obtained. If the statistical significance is taken into account, 50 percent on level 4 represent $(19 \times 0.5) = 9.5$ steps on the scale, 25 percent on level 3 represent $(50 \times 0.25) = 12.5$ steps on the scale, which means a maturity level of $2 + (9.5 + 12.5) / 50 = 2.44 = 2.5$. As long as the questions are not equally distributed (the same number of questions per level for each attribute) a step-based maturity scale is statistically more reliable.

When counting the steps for each process attribute the BOOTSTRAP algorithm takes into account scores which the SPU or project gained on the next highest level. In a basic rating all steps achieved on all levels are mapped onto the maturity level scale. In a refined rating only those steps count which are achieved up to the next highest level. (Figure 4.22)

In the example presented in Figure 4.22 the steps on levels 2 and 3 are only partially satisfied, whereas on level 4, 50 percent of the practices are fulfilled.

This way of counting ensures (1) that innovations on level 3—the next highest level—are taken into account, and (2) avoids taking into consideration extreme cases such as the satisfaction of level 4 (too many basic practices are missing).

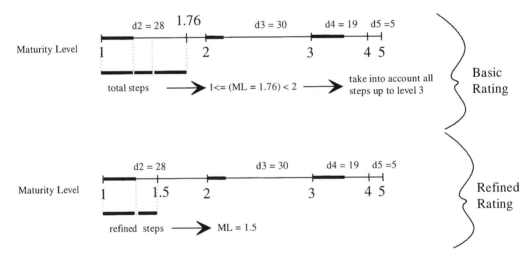

Figure 4.22. Using the innovation rule. (ML = maturity level.)

When calculating the maturity level of the entire SPU or a project the BOOTSTRAP methodology uses a key attribute rule to ensure that the maturity level of the entire organisation depends on the lowest key attribute levels in the profile [10]. The BOOTSTRAP methodology uses selected clusters of practices (*key attributes*), like, for example, Quality Management. A threshold level T_{max} is calculated by the lowest maturity level by which one of the key attributes is satisfied by less than 50 percent. For the SPU or project level only the steps achieved on levels 2 to T_{max} are taken into account.

In Figure 4.23, for example, the application of the key attribute rule leads to a reduction of project maturity to only 1.5 (see corrective mark in Figure 4.23) because basic key attributes like quality system are fairly weak so that only scores up to level 2 have been taken into account for the calculation of the overall project maturity. This means that the lowest key attribute levels determine the overall SPU/PRJ maturity. Nevertheless through the innovation rule they take into account innovative scores for attributes, thus obtaining a profile with higher and lower values.

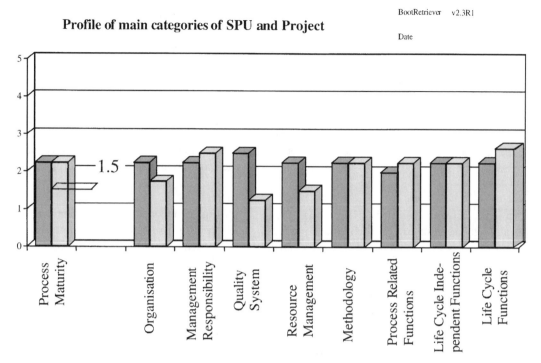

Figure 4.23.   Sample part of a BOOTSTRAP maturity profile.

Scoring and Rating with SPICE

The practices in the SPICE process model form the criteria against which the assessment is performed. At least one process instance of each process defined in the assessment scope must be included. The assessment is supported with an assessment instrument, that is, a data gathering tool (or set of tools) supporting the evaluation of SPICE profiles (further requirements are described in the Assessment Instrument Standard of SPICE).

Scoring

A process is considered to be at capability level 0 (Incomplete) when none of its base practices is existent. If the process exists, then the assessment team may try to understand whether all its base practices are adequately performed (at capability level 1) using the following four-point scoring scale:

Not adequate:	The base practice is either not implemented or does not to any degree contribute to satisfying the process purpose.
Partially adequate:	The implemented base practice does little to contribute to satisfying the process purpose.
Largely adequate:	The implemented base practice largely contributes to satisfying the process purpose.
Fully adequate:	The implemented base practice fully contributes to satisfying the process purpose.

From level 2 to 5 the assessors will try to judge whether the process is managed and institutionalised in terms of being planned, tracked, defined, measured, and continuously improved. The assessor's scores at each these levels is based on the process attribute (former common feature) or generic practice adequacy rating defined as a judgment, within the process context, of the extent to which an implemented common feature or generic practice satisfies the purpose of the process. The scoring scale used for the adequacy rating of the common features or generic practices has also four discrete values as follows:

Not adequate:	The generic practice is either not implemented or does not to any degree satisfy its purpose.
Partially adequate:	The implemented generic practice does little to contribute to satisfy its purpose.
Largely adequate:	The implemented generic practice largely satisfies its purpose.
Fully adequate:	The implemented generic practice fully satisfies its purpose.

Rating

Using the scoring scale, the assessment team examines all process occurrences, within the scope of the assessment, and scores adequacy for each common feature or generic practice in each capability level. The result for each capability level (except level 0), is derived based on the scores and using equal weight for each score and applying a percentage scale. The resulted capability level rating of each process is defined as a matrix: $CLn = [\%N, \%P, \%L, \%F]$, where CLn = capability level (n =1 ... 5)[7],

$\%N$ = percentage of generic practices judged as not adequate,
$\%P$ = percentage of generic practices judged as partially adequate,
$\%L$ = percentage of generic practices judged as largely adequate,
$\%F$ = percentage of generic practices judged as fully adequate, and where
$\%N + \%P + \%L + \%F = 100\%$.

A typical output from a SPICE assessment for a process X, may therefore be (Figure 4.24):

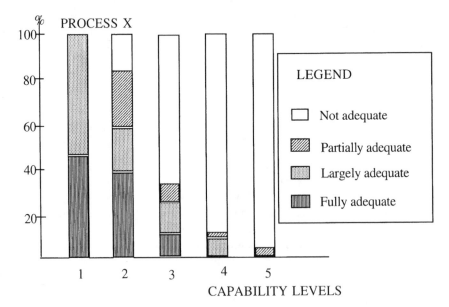

Figure 4.24. Example of a SPICE process profile.

[7]The special case is level 1 where there is only one generic practice. Therefore the initial score and the rating are equal on that level.

Conclusions: The SPICE Conformant BOOTSTRAP Methodology

In order to be SPICE conformant an assessment and improvement methodology should

- be conducted by qualified assessors;
- fulfill requirements of a SPICE assessment process;
- be based on the SPICE process model;
- use an assessment instrument;
- provide SPICE-like process profiles.

The New BOOTSTRAP Process Model

Meanwhile a SPICE-compliant Version 3 of the BOOTSTRAP process architecture has been field tested in the SPICE phase 2 trials. This architecture has not been published so far and takes the following aspects into account.

The Functionality Dimension

BOOTSTRAP Version 3 bases on the ISO 12207 (Figure 4.25) life cycle processes standard which formed the basis for the SPICE architecture. This process standard contains three process categories (comparable to the process clusters in Version 2.3) consisting of a number of processes (comparable to the process attributes in Version 2.3) each of which contains a checklist if practices are performed (comparable to the list of base practices defined in SPICE).

The Capability Dimension

The new BOOTSTRAP process model adopts the SPICE capability levels with their detailed contents as such in principle. Common features are redefined in order to make them better applicable in the practical assessment resulting in only two process attributes (common features) on each capability level.

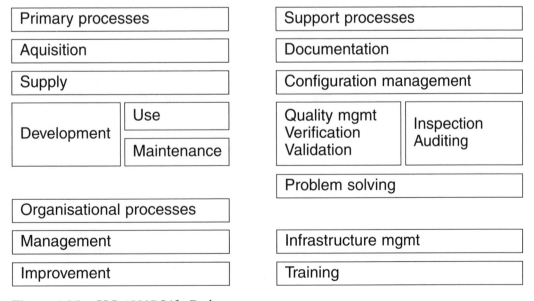

Figure 4.25. ISO 12207 Life Cycle processes.

Scoring Principles

As the BOOTSTRAP scoring principles include one no answer, and three progressive yes answers, they were technically quite easy to align with the SPICE adequacy scores: Not adequate, Partially Adequate, Largely Adequate and Fully Adequate. The only difference is that in the BOOTSRAP approach you are able to omit a practice by scoring it Nonapplicable. In SPICE the same mechanism is included by allowing to tailor the process.

Rating Principles

The SPICE way of rating a process is to produce an adequacy vector for each capability level including the percentage of the occurrences of the different adequacy scores addressed to the base practices against the common features. The output vector is:

$$\{(\%F,\%L,\%P)_1,(\%F,\%L,\%P)_2, (\%F,\%L,\%P)_3, (\%F,\%L,\%P)_4, (\%F,\%L,\%P)_5\}$$
with $(\%F,\%L,\%P)_i$ representing the adequacy rate for capability level i
         for $i = 1. . . 5.$

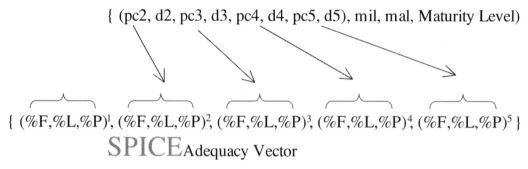

Figure 4.26.   Relationships between the SPICE and the BOOTSTRAP result vectors.

     The BOOTSTRAP way of calculating a capability level is simply to count the number of steps per level (multiply the average satisfaction percentage by the number of questions on each maturity level) and to map the number of steps onto the capability level scale.

     The SPICE adequacy vector refines the satisfaction percentage values of the BOOTSTRAP vector—for example, pc2 is refined by the adequacy rate $(\%F,\%L,\%P)_2$. However, the SPICE vector does not take into account the statistical significance of the adequacy ratings as it is done in the BOOTSTRAP vector through the values d2, d3, d4, and d5. The adequacy rate (100,0,0) could be the answer to one question or the answer to 20 questions, the adequacy vectors would not tell you.

Future BOOTSTRAP Results

BOOTSTRAP Version 3 provides both profiles: capability level profiles calculating a maturity level per process, an adequacy profile per process explaining in more detail (with adequacy vectors) why this maturity level was calculated (Figure 4.27).

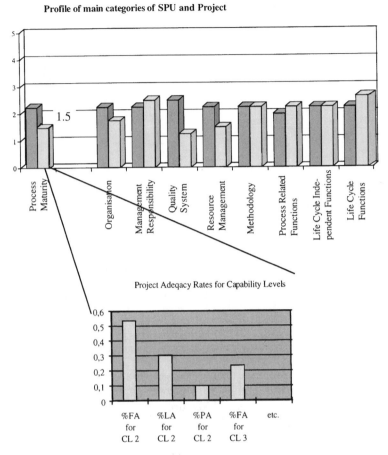

Figure 4.27. Combining the SPICE and BOOTSTRAP way of presenting the assessment results.

PROCESS IMPROVEMENT PLANNING

The SPICE PIG (Process Improvement Guide, Figure 4.28) describes procedures and necessary steps to plan improvement taking into account:

1. The capability profiles as assessment output
2. Typical profiles of industry in the same sector (benchmarking)
3. The practices of the Baseline Practice Guide (BPG) as a guideline about which practices should be in place
4. Target profiles describing the improvement goals in terms of capability profiles to be achieved
5. Improvement plans including a measurement plan for collecting records to analyse cost benefit, return on investment, and success or failure

to finally achieve the improvements in the organisational unit's software process.

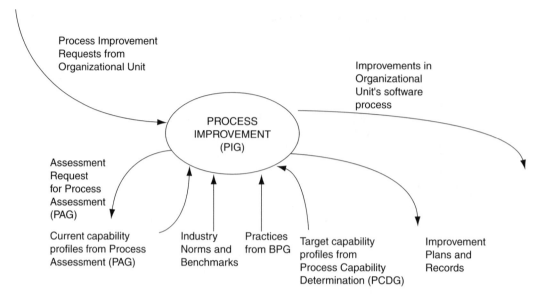

Figure 4.28. Factors necessary to have a SPICE-compliant improvement planning process.

BOOTSTRAP version 2.3 largely covered most of these topics by

1. providing BOOTSTRAP maturity profiles as assessment output;
2. running a European-wide BOOTSTRAP database supporting benchmarking;
3. providing a BOOTSTRAP process architecture with a set of practices;
4. providing a standard template for assessment reports and action plans including the definition of business goals, priorities, and target profiles; and
5. including in the template for action plans a framework for improvement projects which requires to define measurable goals to identify the return on investment (ROI) and if and how the goals have been achieved.

BOOTSTRAP Version 3 is fully SPICE compliant and

- Covers all base practices from the BPG;
- Uses the six capability levels defined in SPICE;
- Calculates adequacy vectors for each process in addition to the maturity level profiles.

SOFTWARE PROCESS IMPROVEMENT MODELS IN THE CONTEXT OF BUSINESS PERFORMANCE

Most of the models we have discussed (CMM, BOOTSTRAP, etc.) are assessment models (see classification in Chapter 3) and create the architecture of an ideal organisation onto which industry is mapped. However, most of these models have been established from very technical viewpoints and miss links back to the business viewpoint.

An example is the strategy of some Japanese firms to enter the European market, as it is perceived by the European competitors. A European firm (a radio manufacturer, also developing the software for radios) was always confirmed to produce radios which are running through extensive tests and thus have to be sold at a certain minimum price. The Japanese competitor realised that there is a market demand for different radios (at different price and quality levels) and also started to develop and distribute radios at low cost (with lower quality and functionality). However, it was not the quality of the system but the *perceived quality* from the different levels of the customers that was deciding the market success, so that many customers bought the low-price radios and the European radio sales became smaller. This does not mean that the Japanese firm was not offering quality, it rather means that they offered different systems with different quality levels (of course, also including systems of the same high standard as the ones offered by the European firm).

This discussion highlights the importance of new success factors like flexibility, and configurability, which have to be combined with the standardisation approaches underlying the assessment models.

Thus, in a typical business scenario, a division could produce 100 percent quality and achieve high maturity grades, but it still could fail in business due, for instance, missing flexibility and system configurability.

Another example is the Microsoft and Apple story. A major reason why the quality of a MacIntosh computer is perceived (by the customers) as higher than that of a personal computer (PC) is the fact that a Mac (once bought) remained stable over years, whereas due to an upgrade philosophy of rapidly changing versions with exponentially increasing resource demands the PCs are just stable for about 1.5 years and then either have to be largely upgraded or exchanged.

Now imagine a situation in which the same game starts with the Mac, where due to largely increasing resource demands the Mac also has to be upgraded every 1.5 years. This would lead to a disappearance of the stability argument and the customers would perceive the quality of PC and Mac as the same, and would therefore buy the lower price PCs in the future.

Of course, this is just a story, but it shows some ideas of typical business strategies, which at the end correlates not only with defect rates but also with how customers perceive quality.

In general, a system comprises production factors that are the causes of the actual process and, as a direct consequence, the software product. But what happens on the far side, as it were: what are the effects of the actual process and the product which it generates? Those effects may be called the performance measures of the actual process.

Finally, in order to determine where improvement effort should be targeted among the factors of production, it is necessary to understand how changes in the production factors bring about changes in the performance measures, so as to achieve (to the greatest degree possible) measurement–based and feedback–controlled improvement (Figure 4.29).

The eight production factors and seven performance measures in Figure 4.29 constitute only a first–level decomposition of the total system—they are only the highest–level components.

In the case of the box labelled "established process," we are accustomed to a far more detailed decomposition (provided by all the process maturity models), through process categories, to process areas and ultimately to base practices. A similar kind of decomposition can be provided for other (though not all) boxes.

For instance, among the production factors a first–level decomposition of "organisational factors" might be as follows.

- Leadership (including culture, management style)
- Internal communication
- Strategy (including goals, vision, policy)
- Innovativeness (including change management)
- Decision making (decision quality, implementation)
- Organisational structure

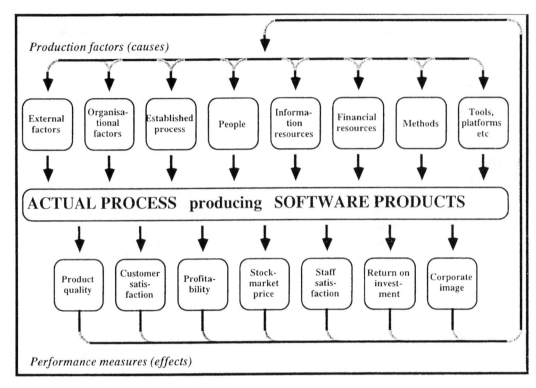

Figure 4.29. The model of production factors and performance measures.

Similarly, among the performance measures a first–level decomposition of product quality, following [18], would be as follows.

- Functionality
- Reliability
- Usability
- Efficiency
- Maintainability
- Portability

In seeking to understand systemic relationships in the system, it is necessary to deal with these decompositions of the main components. Understanding the interactions among the factors of production, for instance, means understanding the relationships among their lower–level components.

One relationship between "established process" and "methods" is the "use's" relationship: a particular base practice, for example, uses one or more specific methods (which may be alternatives or may be used together). That relationship could be represented in a matrix of the following form (Figure 4.30).

A different kind of relationship, which might be called "boosters/inhibitors to change" might exist between "established process" and "organisational factors," where specific organisational subfactors might boost (positive) or inhibit (negative) attempts to improve specific base practices. Boosters might be things such as "clear corporate strategy communicated to software practitioners." Inhibitors might be things such as "corporate fear culture." That relationship could be represented in a matrix of the following form (Figure 4.31).

	Method A	Method B	Method C			
Base practice 1	x					
Base practice 2		x	x			
Base practice 3				x		
		x				
					x	

Figure 4.30. Matrix showing "uses" relationship between practices and methods.

	Booster A	Booster B	Booster C	Inhibitor X	Inhibitor Y	Inhibitor Z	
Base practice 1				D		D	
Base practice 2		+			D		
Base practice 3	+			+			D
						D	
		+					

Figure 4.31. Matrix showing "boosters/inhibitors to change" relationship.

Such matrices are just one example of simple modelling tools which could be used to investigate relationships of various kinds operating within the system modelled in Figure 4.31. Other tools would include, for instance, cause–effect diagrams of the kind shown in [41].

A BACKWARD LOOK AT PROCESS MATURITY MODELS

From the systems perspective given by the discussion in the previous sections, let us take a concluding look back at process maturity models as they stand at present. A number of points can be made.

- Process maturity models measure one attribute (maturity) of one factor of production (established process). They take no account of other possible process attributes (such as fitness, flexibility, etc.). By emphasising process, they de–emphasise the other production factors.
- This narrow focus has both a strength and a weakness. The strength is the strength that lies in simplicity: they are simple models which, because they abstract massively from reality, are easily understood. The weakness comes precisely from that massive simplification, if their use is not accompanied by a balanced understanding of how process interacts with other production factors to impact overall performance measures [9].
- Process maturity models measure maturity by counting the presence or absence of standard practices. This is a very simple means of measurement. One interesting feature is that, by their very nature, such models are unable to measure the maturity of individual practices: they can only provide indicators but not exact metrics. It also cannot fairly cope with organisations whose set of practices, for good and deliberate reasons, varies from the standard set.
- Process maturity models are unconcerned with cause–effect relationships. They are based on a very simple proposition, that software product quality is a function of software process quality. Such a statement of a static equality can be vastly misleading, because it ignores the real–world chains of events which are interposed between a process change and a product change, the speed at which they unfold, and the extent to which they are affected by other causes.
- Process maturity models generally aim to create a step-by-step self learning and improvement cycle as outlined in the *Kaizen* philosophy [20].

Chapter 5 discusses a goal-based strategy to align technical improvement plans with business goals, thus achieving a better understanding of the cause-effect relationships.

REFERENCES

1. R. Bache and G. Bazzana. *Software Metrics for Product Assessment*, McGraw Hill, 1994.
2. V. Basili, "An Experience Factory," *Proceedings of the International Conference on Lean Software Development*, Stuttgart, Germany, Oct. 1992.
3. G. Bazzana, O. Andersen, and T. Jokela, "ISO 9126 and ISO 9000—Friends or Foes?" *Proceedings of the Software Engineering Standards Symposium 1993*, IEEE Computer Soc. Press, Los Alamitos, Calif., 1993, pp. 79–88.
4. P. B. Crosby, *Quality is Free—The Art of Making Quality Certain*, McGraw-Hill, New York, 1979.
5. W.E. Deming, *Out of the Crisis*, MIT Press, 1982.
6. DoD 2167A, *Military Standard. Defence System Software Development*, DOD-STD-2167A (February 29, 1988).
7. A. Dorling, "SPICE—Software Process Improvement and Capability dEtermination," *Software Quality Journal*, Vol. 2, 1993, pp. 209–224.
8. *ESA Software Engineering Standards ESA PSS-05-0. Issue 2*. ESA Board for Software Standardisation and Control, European Space Agency, Paris, Feb. 1991.
9. N. Fenton, *Software Metrics: A Rigorous Approach*, Chapman & Hall, 1991.

10. V. Haase et al., "BOOTSTRAP: Fine Tuning Process Assessment," *IEEE Software*, July 1994, pp. 25–35.

11. V. Haase, R. Messnarz, and R.M. Cachia, "Software Process Improvement by Measurement," *Shifting Paradigms in Software Engineering*, R. Mittermeir, ed., Springer Verlag, Vienna, New York, Sept. 1992.

12. W.S. Humphrey and W.L. Sweet, *A Method for Assessing the Software Engineering Capability of Contractors*, Software Engineering Institute, CMU, Technical Report CMU/SEI-87-TR-23, 1987.

13. W.S. Humphrey, ed., *Managing the Software Process*, Software Engineering Institute (USA), Addison-Wesley Publishing Company, New York, Wokingham, Amsterdam, Bonn, Madrid, Tokyo, 1989.

14. W.S. Humphrey, "The Personal Process in Software Engineering," *Proceedings of the 3rd International Conference on the Software Process*, 1994, pp. 69–77.

15. W.S. Humphrey, "Introducing the Personal Software Process," *Annals of Software Engineering*, Vol. 1, 1995, pp. 311–325.

16. ISO 9000-3, *Quality Management and Quality Assurance Standards, International Standard, Part 3: Guidelines for the Application of ISO 9001 to the Development, Supply and Maintenance of Software*, ISO, 1990.

17. ISO 9001, *Quality Systems, Model for Quality Assurance in Design/Development, Production, Installation and Servicing, International Organisation for Standardisation*, Geneva, 1987.

18. ISO 9126, *Information Technology—Software Product Evaluation—Quality Characteristics and Guidelines for Their Use*, 1991.

19. ISO/IEC 12207, *Information Technology—Software Life Cycle Processes*, 1st ed., Aug. 95.

20. Imai, M., *Kaizen: The Key to Japan's Competitive Success*, Random House, New York, 1986.

21. J.M. Juran, *Juran's Quality Control Handbook*, 4th ed., McGraw-Hill, New York, 1988.

22. B. Kitchenham, L. Pickard, and S.L. Pfleeger, "Case Studies for Method and Tool Evaluation," July 1995, pp. 52–62; correction, Sept. 95, pp. 98–99.

23. P. Kuvaja and A. Bicego, "BOOTSTRAP: Europe's assessment method," *IEEE Software*, Vol. 10, No. 3, May 1993, pp. 93–95.

24. P. Kuvaja et al., *Software Process Assessment and Improvement, The BOOTSTRAP Approach*, Blackwell Business, Oxford, UK, 1994.

25. P. Kuvaja and R. Messnarz, "BOOTSTRAP—A Modern Software Process Assessment and Improvement Methodology," *Proceedings of the 5th European Conference on Software Quality*, September 17–20, Dublin, Ireland, 1996.

26. T. Mehner, "Siemens Process Improvement Approach," *Practical Improvement of Software Processes and Products: Proceedings of the ESI–ISCN 95 Conference on Measurement and Training Based Process Improvement*, Vienna, Sept. 1995.

27. R. Messnarz and H.J. Kugler, "BOOTSTRAP and ISO 9001: From the Software Process to Software Quality," *Proceedings of the APSEC'94 Conference*, Computer Soc. Press of IEEE, Tokyo, Japan, 1994.

28. R. Messnarz and H. Scherzer, "The Evolution of a Quantitative Analysis—the BOOTSTRAP—Approach," *Proceedings of the Interdisciplinary Information Talks 95*, G. Ghroust and P. Doucek, eds., Oldenbourg, Vienna, Munich, 1995, pp. 198–213.

29. R. Messnarz, "A Comparison of BOOTSTRAP and SPICE," *Software Process Newsletter*, No. 8, Khaled El Emam, ed., IEEE Computer Soc. TCSE, Winter 1996/1997.

30. M.C. Paulk, B. Curtis, and M.B. Chrissis, eds., *Capability Maturity Model for Software*, Software Engineering Institute (U.S.A.), Technical Report CMU/SEI-91-TR-24, Carnegie Mellon University, Pittsburgh, Pa., 1991.

31. M.C. Paulk and M.D. Konrad, "An Overview of ISO's SPICE project," *American Programmer*, February 1994.

32. M. Paulk et al., *Capability Maturity Model for Software, Version 1.1*, CMU/SEI-93-TR-24, February 1993.

33. M.C. Paulk et al., *Key Practices of the Capability Maturity Model*, Version 1.1, Technical Report CMU/SEI-93-TR-25, Software Engineering Institute, Pittsburgh, 1993.

34. M.C. Paulk, M.D. Konrad, and S.M. Garcia, "CMM Versus SPICE Architectures," *Software Process Newsletter*, No. 3, IEEE Computer Soc. TCSE, Spring 1995, pp. 7–11.

35. M.C. Paulk, C.V. Weber, and M.B. Chrissis, *The Capability Maturity Model: Guidelines for Improving the Software Process*, Addison-Wesley, Reading, Mass., 1995.

36. M.C. Paulk, "The Evolution of the SEI's Capability Maturity Model for Software," *Software Process Improvement and Practice*, Vo'l. 1, Pilot Issue, Spring 1995, pp. 3–15.

37. K. Pulford, A. Kuntzmann-Combelles, and S. Shirlaw, *A Quantitative Approach to Software Management*, Addison-Wesley, 1995.

38. C.W. Reimann, "The Malcolm Baldrige Quality Award and ISO 9000 Registration, Understanding Their Many Important Differences," Standardisation News, Nov. 1993.

39. TickIT, *Guide to Software Quality Management System Construction and Certification Using ISO 9001, Issue 2.0*, DISC TickIT Office, 1992.

40. G. Waldner, "Total Quality Management and the European Quality Award," *Practical Improvement of Software Processes and Products: Proceedings of the ESI–ISCN 95 Conference on Measurement and Training Based Process Improvement*, Vienna, Sept. 1995.

41. G. M. Weinberg, *Quality Software Management, Vol. 1, Systems Thinking*, Dorset House, 1992.

Chapter 5

Goal-Based Software Process Improvement Planning

Christophe Debou

ami®[1] User Group c/o Q-Labs GmbH, Germany

INTRODUCTION

"Two-thirds of the US Software Process Improvement (SPI) initiatives did fail so far." This statement was unofficially spread in recent SPI forums although official SEI investigation [23] gives more optimistic figures. To my mind an initiative fails when no or low impact has been achieved on project practices and business performance through process changes. With this definition, the 2/3 figures may still be optimistic. So far, there exist no statistics in Europe so far due to the much lower number of organisations committing to such initiative. But one would probably come to the conclusion that at least two-thirds of the initiatives do not come to the end properly even if they do not fail. The two main reasons for nonsuccess are the changes of business situation (basically, reorganisation, organisation bought by another, merge between two groups, . . .) for one third and the lack of management sustain for another one third. This lack of senior management support is mainly due to a lack of visibility toward potential benefits and actual return on investment in industry but also to an inadequate way of handling such initiatives which are viewed more as a theoretical exercise than a critical item for the business. Furthermore, the link between process improvement and product improvement, for instance, CMM-based, is far from being validated. Other reasons mentioned for the nonsuccess are:

- Midmanagement resistance to change; on the one hand, they are asked by their boss to improve productivity and on the other hand, from project to obtain more resources to

[1]ami is a registered trademark of the ami user group.

reduce delays: so "what the hell do we have to do with SPI." Their career development is mainly linked to the margin observed on projects and not to the SPI effort.
- SEPG not having the right skills—another consequence that the management does not take the initiative seriously.
- SPI not treated as a project (one of the most important) with clear objectives.
- Late action plan: momentum is lost both at management and practitioner level.
- Wrong scope that is trying to produce organisational-wide processes as a whole whereas at level 2, project requirements for improvement should be first looked at.
- No real relationships between improvement actions and business objectives.

In fact, to our mind, the latter issue causes most of the troubles: SPI is not perceived as a business issue.

Whose fault? It is not our role to blame anybody, but whatever is stepwise applied for certification purposes can only lead to misuse. There is usually an overemphasis on the assessment process, maturity questionnaire, maturity profile and the Capability Maturity Level (CMM). The ISO 9001 Syndrome (to document a posteriori processes/procedures for sake of certification) starts to apply for the Software Engineering Institute (SEI) CMM/Maturity level. This hurts the whole SPI community. For chance, there exist some organisations, respectively, senior managers who do perform right, who do understand the concepts (actually the same what was called some years ago Total Quality Management) and do apply it effectively and not "literally." There exist ISO 9001-certified organisations that are living it everyday (refer to Chapter 12, the second Alcatel case study). When a CMM-based assessment is performed, the purpose is quickly well understood (organisational structure for improvement already exists), people expresses their satisfaction with their quality system, management has to admit that the investment upfront was high but worthwhile (they measured it). There also exist ISO 9001- or even TickIT-certified organisations that perform crash actions just before the certification to clean up their quality system. A software process assessment reveals the "cheating" immediately while interviewing practitioners: *"just an overhead activity, shelfware procedures and instructions, . . ."* And one of their main concerns relates to the commitment of management for the starting SPI initiative: *"Yet another initiative."*

The history of SPI is also symptomatic of the current state of the practice. In 1987, the first software development maturity questionnaire [26] was produced, followed in 1989 by the reference book of Watts Humphrey [25] *Managing the Software Process.* Then, the essential software practices described in Humphrey's book were structured (also shortcut from some necessary details) in a way to be used as a model for assessment and as a roadmap for the improvement action plan: the Capability Maturity Level [8, 9] (CMM). Some clones of the CMM and the related assessment method were designed to fit to given industry sector, for example, Trillium for Telecommunications, or a given geographical sector, for example, BOOTSTRAP for Europe (including ISO 9001 and ESA-PSS 005 requirements) [24]. Tools for assessing the capacity of the software development force became quite sophisticated with the new Software Process Improvement and Capability Determination (SPICE project) whose aims become an ISO standard by 1998 [27, 34]. The scope has been extended to border activities of software development, for example, customer-supplier process. Overall strategy for performing a self-improvement initiative has been missing for a long time. This history may remind us how object-oriented technology became popular. First languages were designed, then one started to think how to do object-oriented (OO) design, then object-oriented analysis and then finally, how to integrate OO in a full life cycle.

Some strategies for software process improvement covering the full picture have recently come up, that is, the SPICE Process Improvement Guide [32], the SEI IDEAL model [28], and the ami approach [2, 3]. Most of them have the particularity to be goal-driven, with ami adding the necessary details to set-up goals and manage metrics.

Adequate process improvement planning has been one of the main bottlenecks for the majority of organisational software process improvement programs. How should one translate assessment results into concrete actions that management can buy into? And this exercise is much tricky than trying to cover nonexisting or deficient CMM practices. This is what we will address in this chapter, that is, how to structure improvement program based on the initial process analysis. First major goal-oriented improvement framework will be introduced. Emphasis will be put on the ami approach, which has already proven its efficiency in several industrial environments. Then, the process of building goal trees, linking business goals, software process goals, improvement actions, and follow-up indicators, will be introduced. Finally, guidelines on how to build goal-trees from several process analysis methods (CMM, BOOT-STRAP, SPICE, TickIT) will be given and illustrated with industrial case studies. But, first, let's identify the necessary components for a successful SPI program.

THE NECESSARY COMPONENTS FOR A SUCCESSFUL SOFTWARE PROCESS IMPROVEMENT APPROACH

The author's personal experiences in SPI and the analysis of successful existing software process improvement approaches led to the determination of an empirical set of necessary components:

Assessing
The current development process has to be assessed to point out the problems and areas to be improved. The assessment can be conducted against a written organisational process model or a universal process maturity model, the most used one being the SEI Capability Maturity Model [8, 9]). An assessment procedure (including rating rules) and optionally an evolutionary maturity model or a best practices list or a generic software development model (any local standard) are needed.

Modelling
Process improvement requires a basis for defining and analysing processes. In that context, process Modelling can fulfil many roles [10] such as the detection of problem areas, estimation of impact of potential changes to the software process (simulation), comparison of alternative software processes. A process Modelling formalism is necessary.

Improving
All steps from initialising the program, setting goals and actions based on assessment, implementing and monitoring them continuously until sustaining and deployment activities should be described in an improvement framework.

Measuring
Measurement is considered as a monitoring or controlling tool on the one hand and as a support for decision making with respect to process improvement on the other hand. A measurement framework (guidelines for quantitative definition and evaluation of improvement goals, measurement plan production, and implementation) is required.

Beside these components, an improvement organisation should be put in place for sponsoring, coordinating, implementing, and promoting the improvement initiative. All those components are shown in Figure 5.1 to build the Modelling/Assessing/Measuring/Improving paradigm.

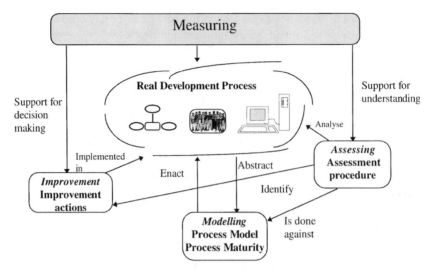

Figure 5.1. The Modelling/Assessing/Measuring/Improving paradigm.

GOAL-ORIENTED IMPROVEMENT FRAMEWORK

Taxonomy of Software Process Improvement Strategies

Card [7] identified two basic approaches to process improvement, namely, the analytic approach and the benchmarking approach.

1. The *analytic* (or bottom-up) approach relies on quantitative evidence to determine where improvements are needed and whether improvement initiative has been successful, for example, Shewhart cycle [21] or the Software Engineering Laboratory (SEL) approach [29]. The SEL combines a quality improvement paradigm with a measurement framework, namely, the Goal/Question/Metric (GQM) paradigm [4]. In addition, the concept of experience factory covers the reuse of experience and collective learning. Improvement means are determined through controlled experiments.
2. The *benchmarking* approach (or top-down) depends on identifying an "excellent" organisation and documenting its practices and tools. The most famous benchmarking approach is the Software Engineering Institute (SEI) Capability Maturity Model [8, 9]. It works under the assumption that an organisation who will adopt these practices and tools will become also excellent: "Learn from the best." The full improvement strategy has been illustrated in the IDEAL model [28, 30].

To this taxonomy, a mixed approach (e.g., the ami approach [3]; see SPICE Process Improvement Guide [32]) can be added considering explicitly measurement as the basis for improvement but relying on an evolutionary model of development process capability for the assessment phase. The main goal-oriented improvement strategies will be presented next, namely, the PDCA cycle, the SEL approach, ami, IDEAL and SPICE PIG.

The Shewhart Cycle: The Basis of Process Improvement

The Shewhart approach (see Figure 5.2) made popular by Deming [21] is now referenced by almost all improvement initiatives.

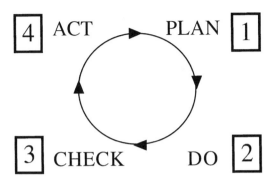

Figure 5.2.   The Shewhart improvement cycle.

1. **Plan**
   - Define the problem
   - Establish improvement objectives
2. **Do**
   - Identify possible problem causes
   - Establish baselines
   - Test change
3. **Check**
   - Collect data
   - Evaluate data
4. **Act**
   - Implement system change
   - Determine effectiveness

The goal of this approach is to optimise and improve a single process mode/production line. It uses such techniques as feedback loops and statistical quality control to experiment with methods for improvement and build predictive models of the product.

The cycle begins with the definition of a plan for improving an activity. Once the improvement plan is implemented (do), results are checked, and actions taken to correct deviations. The cycle is then repeated.

The Shewhart approach was broadly adapted by Japanese industry in the 1950s and 1960s for the identification of areas of improvement. This philosophy known as *Kaizen* developed (*Kaizen* means "continuous improvement programmes" in Japanese) which consists of gradually changing an organisation by changing the management. *Kaizen* is the Japanese concept that describes the continuous, never-ending improvement of process-management, software development, and software evolution. *Kaizen* is the "process oriented way if thinking versus the west's innovation and results-oriented thinking."

The starting point for *Kaizen* is the recognition that a problem exists; the ultimate goal is to make gradual changes. *Kaizen* should be implemented as a policy that involves all company personnel where management should be the driving force behind the change. The concept of *Kaizen* has been introduced as an umbrella which encompasses a wide range of activities: Suggestions systems, quality circles, Total Quality Control, customer orientation, automation, discipline, and quality improvement. Attention is focused on the process rather than the results. by getting the process under control, results should improve automatically because of the good work practices, employee motivation and the value of individual contribution will become inherent in company philosophy.

Software Engineering Laboratory Process Improvement Strategy

The Software Engineering Laboratory (SEL) was established in 1976 for the purpose of studying and measuring software processes with the intent of identifying improvements that could be applied to the production of ground support software within the Flight Dynamics Division (FDD) at the NASA/Goddard Space Flight Centre (GSFC) [29]. The SEL has a three-member corporation:

- NASA GSFC, the user and manager of the software systems
- The University of Maryland, investigating advanced concepts in software process and experimentation
- The Computer Sciences Corporation (CSC), major contractor for building and maintaining the software

The original plan of the SEL was to apply evolving software technologies during development and evaluate the impact of these technologies on the products being created (cost, reliability, etc.). In this way, the most beneficial approaches could be identified through empirical studies and then captured once improvements were identified. They rapidly came to the conclusion that attributes of the development organisation (type of software, goals of the organisation, development constraints, environment characteristics, etc.) were significant drivers for the overall definition of process change. The most important step in process improvement is to develop a baseline understanding of the local software process, products and goals.

Their resulting process improvement paradigm is a three-phase model (Figure 5.3) also called Quality Improvement Paradigm (QIP):

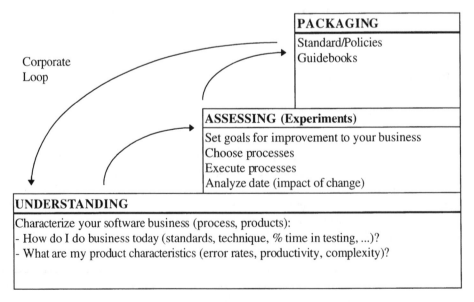

Figure 5.3. SEL process improvement paradigm.

- *Understanding.* Improve insight into the software process and its products by character-ising the development environment, including types of software, problems defined, process and product characteristics.
- *Assessing.* Measure the impact of available technologies and process change on the prod-ucts developed. Determine which technologies are beneficial and appropriate to a par-ticular environment and more importantly how the technologies or processes must be refined to best match the process with the environment. The GQM paradigm [4] is being applied for defining and evaluating a set of operational goals, using measurement. It represents a systematic approach for tailoring and integrating goals with models of the software processes, products and quality perspectives based upon the specific needs of the project and the organisation.
- *Packaging.* When process improvements are identified, technologies are packaged for application in the whole organisation, that is, standards, training; policies, etc.

Their process improvement strategy is based on the following principles:

- Although it is called process improvement, the actual goal of the organisation is to improve the software product.
- Changes must be driven by local goals, characteristics and product attributes. For exam-ple, an organisation whose primary goal is to shorten time to market will take different approaches to process change than organisation whose primary goal is to produce defect-free software.
- Measurement is a vital component of the approach for measuring process and products attributes at the beginning, the effect of process changes on the product, product improvement against the organisational goals.
- To capitalise on experiences gained from completed projects (Packaging), a separate organisational infrastructure (not the development organisation) must be built. This is called the Experience Factory.

The SEL also emphasises that the bottom-up approach would benefit from using some model for selecting process changes (e.g., CMM) and that both approaches may be comple-mentary [29].

The SEL has conducted at the NASA/Goddard Space Flight Centre successful experi-ments during the last 17 years evaluating promising technologies like Ada, Cleanroom, OO. Those valuable achievements and contributions in software engineering were rewarded by the first IEEE Computer Society Software Process Achievement Award in 1994 [29].

In conclusion, the concept of process improvement within SEL focuses on the continuous understanding of both process and product as well as goal-driven experimentation and analy-sis of process change within a development environment. The new Fraunhofer Institute for Experimental Software Engineering (IESE) located in Kaiserslautern, Germany and led by D. Rombach, is aiming at transferring the SEL principles to the European scene, looking at shortening time needed for transferring research technologies into industrial practice [33]. Detailed guidelines for applying goal-oriented measurement (GQM templates, sample GQM plan) are available [6].

Guidelines for putting the QIP in place have been proposed in An Inductive Software Process Improvement method (AINSI) [5]. This method integrates many complementary techniques to CMM-based assessment, such as qualitative analysis, methods for data collection (the GQM approach), and quantitative evaluation. Their focus is to first understand what exists in an organisation and determine what causes significant problems. Then solutions could be devised and evaluated in pilot studies or even controlled experiments. Only after a solution has been found to be effective and efficient, then it should be integrated into the existing process. The high-level steps are:

1. Set up the process improvement team
2. Model the existing process
3. Conduct qualitative analysis
4. Define and document an action plan
5. Set up a measurement program
6. Perform a pilot project
7. Change the process and the organisation

ami: A Quantitative Approach to Process Improvement

Application of Metrics in Industry (ami) is a 2-year program which started in December 1990 under sponsorship of DG XIII of the Commission of the European Communities through the ESPRIT program promoting the use of measurement in software development. The ami consortium comprises: GEC Marconi Software Systems (UK), Alcatel Austria Forschungszentrum (Austria), Bull AG (Germany), Objectif Technologie (France), GEC Alsthom (France), ITS (Spain), Olivetti Group (Italy), RWTÜV (Germany), and South Bank University (UK). The goal of the project was to develop a practical approach and to validate it on a variety of projects all over Europe. This approach is described in the so-called ami handbook [3]. ami was not a purely theoretical work but reused and adapted existing technologies such as the SEI CMM [8, 9, 25] and the GQM paradigm from Basili and Rombach [4] to build the ami paradigm: Assess–Analyse–Metricate–Improve. The ami approach is similar to the Shewhart cycle (Plan–Do–Check–Act) for process improvement. ami has taken this cycle, based on common-sense principles, and developed it for software measurement.

The ami method of introducing and conducting a software measurement program [11, 18] is a 12-step, iterative, incremental, goal-oriented procedure, coupling together a model-based process assessment technique with a quantitative approach to software development issues from the viewpoints of process, products, and resources. The twelve steps are grouped by three in activities. A schematic description of the ami paradigm is given on Figure 5.4 and all steps are described later on.

Why should we consider ami as a process improvement paradigm? ami can be applied for many purposes when measurement is used for management or decision making and therefore also for process improvement. The whole approach offers a complete framework for process improvement while fulfilling the main requirements for such approach: iterative (continuous), goal-oriented, quantitative, involvement of everyone in the organisation, and necessary management commitment.

The ami paradigm is a combination of a software process definition in terms of entities of the process, product, and resources and their related attributes, and an improvement framework originally illustrated by the SEI CMM and the GQM paradigm. ami attempts to cover the whole improvement cycle. It is slightly different from the SEL approach described above since a maturity model is advised for validating the feasibility of a goal.

The relationships between ami and other process improvement approaches are twofold:

- ami integrates and enhances to its purpose existing approaches (SEI CMM, GQM paradigm). ami extends the area covered by the CMM ("what is to be done") by a stepwise procedure covering the methodological viewpoint of the process improvement ("how to

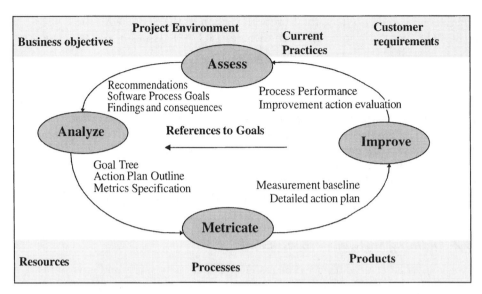

Figure 5.4.   ami activities in SPI context.

do it"). Whereas the key idea of the CMM is to identify improvement areas, ami makes the improvement resolvable as a result of metrics feedback indicating success or failure of process activities. The cooperation of both methods appears as a kind of symbiosis: the SEI CMM provides a good snapshot of the process but not provide a strategy for change; ami provides a reasonable change strategy, but is worthless without an objective and a stable assessment procedure.

- ami is a "tool" for controlling (and improving afterward) the conduct of process model techniques, that is, a given phase, the passage from a maturity level to another (SEI CMM) or the introduction of ISO 9000.
- ami is not competing with any other SPI initiatives such as CMM, BOOTSTRAP, and SPICE. They all can be integrated into the ami framework.

The 12 steps will be described hereafter, illustrated with a continuous case study. This project is one of the 20 validation projects performed during the ami project [19]. This is a real-time embedded software project in a maintenance phase.

"Assess" Activity: Assessing the Project Environment

Step 1: Assessing the Project Environment

The aim of this step is to point out weak areas—critical and problematic parts of the development process. The ami® consortium advises the use of Capability Maturity Model [8, 9] defined by the SEI. The outcome of this particular procedure is not only the scaled result of the assessment in terms of a maturity level (from 1 to 5), but a set of weak areas that serves as input for defining the software process goal together with business objective set up by management. Although recommended, the assessment is not restricted to the SEI CMM procedure. A quality audit (ISO 9001 or TickIT) or similar investigation is valid as long as there is a guarantee of getting an objective and sufficiently exhaustive view of the development process.

Alternatives are, among others, the European version of the SEI CMM, the ESPRIT project 5441 BOOTSTRAP (Chapter 4) which includes ISO 9001 issues in the assessment method, and the future ISO SPICE (see Chapter 4).

Case study

The project is a real-time embedded software project in the maintenance phase. The management perceived a number of risk areas that the use of metrics would aid in controlling and monitoring, for example, productivity, estimating, and software quality. According to those areas, a budget was agreed with the project manager and a senior engineer was allocated to the task of metrics promoter. The SEI CMM was used to assess the project involving the project manager, the project quality manager and the department quality manager. The results of the assessment confirmed the underlying feeling of where the weak areas of the project lay. The assessment also indicated other weak areas like training but these were in fact to be addressed at a higher level of management.

Step 2: Defining Software Process Goals

The weak areas detected during the assessment as well as business and environment specific objectives will serve as a basis for the definition of software process goals. At the beginning a reasonable number is one or two per project.

Step 3: Validating Software Process Goals

This is a very important and sensitive step which may result in the success or failure of the entire improvement program. Goals established in the previous step are to be validated in order to ensure their consistency in terms of:

- Consistency between goals and your assessment conclusions
- Consistency between selected goals and time scales
- Consistency between goals and budget

The degree of ambition of the goals should also be checked in two ways:

- Check the difficulty of the goal against the ability of the development environment to fulfil it. From this viewpoint, there are two classes of goals: *knowledge goals* (to evaluate, to monitor, to understand, to predict, e.g. to support estimation process with historical data) and *change goals* (to increase, to reduce, to achieve, to change, to improve, e.g., to improve productivity while maintaining quality). The first class is applicable from maturity level 2 upward, the other requires at least maturity level 3. Therefore, metrication has to be first supported by knowledge goals before making use of improvement goals.
- Check the timeliness (short- /mid/long-term) of the goals resolving inconsistencies and giving priorities based on agreement of all participants.

Case study

Interviews with the main project actors allowed the identification of primary goals. At the start, there was a great temptation to go straight for improvement goals. But, it became apparent that one need first to establish baselines against which improvement could be measured. This was reinforced by the level of maturity. From an initial set of 10 goals, 6 were selected from project members at different levels and areas of interest. In examining them, certain goals were identified as being subgoals of other goals. So a goal tree could be produced in anticipation. We will focus on the following goal:

G1 To Gain a Better Understanding of Project Software Quality

"Analyse" Activity: Defining Goals and Metrics

Step 4: Breakdown of Goals into Subgoals

This step is a simplified adaptation of Basili's Goal/Question/Metric paradigm [88], a flexible method for refining goals of any level to metrics using process- and product-related questions. The thinking process for decomposing goals into subgoals is documented with a table of questions and a list of related entity-attribute pairs. The decomposition process runs as follow:

```
goal_level = primary

  Repeat

          Define Who (actors in the organisation) may contribute
          to current goal

          Define the list of entities related for each goal of
          goal_level from the point of view of the selected actors

          For each entity of the list

                  Ask questions related to the goal

          Decomposition in sub-goals

          decrement goal_level

  Until quantifiable sub-goals are attained
```

The goal tree visualises the relationships between business objectives, software process goals, high-level improvement activities, and related follow-up metrics. When software process goals are defined (e.g., make reliable estimates, achieve full trace-ability), one should try to identify viewpoints (who is playing a role in achieving this goal, e.g., senior management, project managers; software engineers, Quality Assurance, etc.) and entities they manage in this context (e.g., estimation process, estimation review). For each viewpoint, questions on the entities in the context of this goal will be set (e.g., How accurate is the estimation process? Are concurrent estimates performed?). Then subgoals (in fact, improvement actions) can be broken down. To support this process an entity attribute table can be produced (Table 5.1). The entities can be products, processes, or resources that are part of the activity connected to the viewpoint. The

Table 5.1.   Entity-Attribute Table

Entity	Attribute	Viewpoint
Software product	Size Reliability	Project manager
Testing process	Duration Effectiveness	Integration manager
Staff	Experience	Human resources

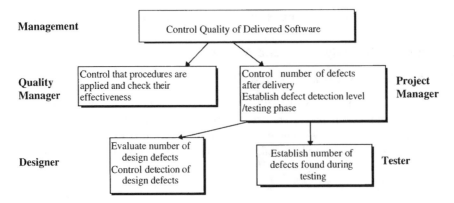

Figure 5.5.   Example of goal tree with link to organisational roles.

attributes are a characteristics or property of an entity. The link between the goal and the entity is formulated by the participants or viewpoint (equivalent to a decision maker).

Figure 5.5 shows a goal tree outlining, for each level, who is responsible for achieving the goal. With this view all levels of the organisation are able to understand how they do personally contribute to the management objectives.

There are several possible structures for the goaltree depending on the context and how the brainstorming is performed. In this chapter several possibilities are highlighted. As a minimum it is essential to show the relationships between high-level goals (business goals), lower-level goals (typically contribution to the business goal from all organisational levels from senior management to practitioners), improvement actions (provide rationale for actions), and/or indicators for following-up (both obtained through the questioning process).

Case study
The metrics promoter collected a lot of information on goals at a number of levels in the organisation. The project perceived that there were three areas that one needed to consider in the context of quality:

1. *Where did the errors occur in the code? Did some software parts cause more errors than others?*
2. *What about test coverage? Were some code parts missed during testing?*
3. *What sort of turnaround was given to report software errors?*

Other issues could have been raised to gain further insight into this goal, for example, to measure the complexity of each module. However, it was decided to restrict these three subgoals because they could be achieved with little change to the project organisation and little additional load. One subgoal is considered for our purpose:

  G1.1 Provide Information on the Location of Software Errors

Step 5: Verifying the Goal Tree

The verification includes checks of:

- homogeneity of levels of detail in each branch of the tree;
- the internal consistency of the tree, that is, is there a contradiction between goals and subgoals; and

- the external consistency of the tree, that is, the relevance of the goal tree to software process goals.

Step 6: Identification of Metrics by Questions

An additional questioning procedure with the aim of describing subgoals in a quantitative way is applied on a validated goal tree with elementary subgoals (expressible with metrics) at the leaf level. The outcome is a set of metrics covering the goals selected in the appropriate step of the measurement program. ami offers a so-called *basic metrics set* which has been proved as useful as starting a measurement program for the first time.

Case study

The questions derived from the subgoal G1.1 are:

Q1.1.1 In which modules are software errors located and what type are they?
Q1.1.2 In which functions are software errors located and what type are they?

The derivation of the metrics was quite simple:

M1: Software error location function and module reference.
M2: Software error classification

"Metricate" Activity: Implementing the Measurement Plan

Step 7: Writing the Measurement Plan

The measurement plan should contain all information of interest for the metric data collection procedure as objectives of the measurement plan, metrics definitions, metrics analysis procedures, responsibilities, timescales, references, and a logbook for recording measurement activities. In addition of being a plan for the collection of data, the measurement plan records information of the software development environment, the software development process, the strengths and weaknesses of the environment and process, and a standard for communication between the participants. The handbook includes detailed templates for the measurement plan and metrics definition.

Two types of metrics can be considered:

- Performance metrics to establish the measurement baseline.
- Metrics to be used for root-cause analysis of problems identified in the assessment phase.

In the context of an SPI program, a detailed action plan will be produced at that stage.

Step 8: Collecting Primitive Data

Collection is performed manually (e.g., using collection forms) or automatically by support of tools for static analysis (size, structure of code, documents, etc.), by dynamic analysis (statement coverage during testing, etc.), configuration management (number of faults, run times, change requests, etc.), project management (schedule, costs, etc.), and data management (measurement data). A metrics database (or simple spreadsheet) belongs to the kernel of the system.

Case study

The majority of data was collected manually and drawn from existing sources within the projects such as library systems, quality assurance reports, and configuration control. Overall, there was a feeling that using tools to automate the collection process would have reduced the collection effort and increase the data accuracy.

Step 9: Verifying the Primitive Data

The metrics data should be verified as it becomes available in order to allow corrections and additions. Furthermore, the accuracy of the data collection process may be quantified. Motivating feedback to the data collectors can be provided. During data verification any obviously unusual data (outliers) should be detected and the reasons should be identified.

"Improve" Activity: Exploiting the Measures

Step 10: Data Presentation and Utilisation

Any controlling, changing, and/or improvement activity starts with an appropriate presentation of the measurement data. Advantages of graphical presentation aids against statistical techniques are robustness (because of no underlying statistical assumptions) and their user-friendliness as information is conveyed in a more clear way.

Step 11: Validating Metrics

Validation of metrics means showing that they are adequate for the purpose required for them. This can be done through a procedure that is either objective or subjective. For an objective validation we compare the measurement data with an expected trend or with an expected correlation to other data. In a subjective validation people who are involved in the process give an opinion as to whether the metrics correspond to the subgoal.

Step 12: Relating the Data to Goals

Goals for metrics within the knowledge class are categorised between evaluation (understanding) and prediction goals. When dealing with prediction goals, the interpretation of data may require a model (e.g., cost, reliability, quality models) to relate an inherent property of the software (metrics) and the final performance of the product. By relating data to goals, the objective is to determine if goals are fulfilled, how quickly they are fulfilled, and if they are not fulfilled, then why. This last step involves producing an action plan based on the collected data which can involve improvements to the development process. From this action plan, this step will also include a modification of the software process goals. In the case of improvement actions, new goals will cover the monitoring of those actions.

Case study

The metrics promoter assembled the results and presented them to the project manager using a combination of tabular and graphical diagrams. This was prepared 6 months after the start of the initiative when results were sufficient to show trends. At this early stage, the members of the project realised from the reports that some of the metrics were not as valuable as initially thought. Some of them were dropped while others were collected in a modified form. This number could have been greater if the verification steps had not been carried out. A simple example of interpretation is given on the charts below. Figure 5.6 provides the distribution of errors (logical and algorithmic) within modules (a significant sample). It shows which parts of the system are particularly error-prone and the types of errors and therefore give insights for the goal G1.1. This can be also related with another goal dealing with the identification of well-tested parts of the software. A comparison can then be made to see if the more poorly tested parts of

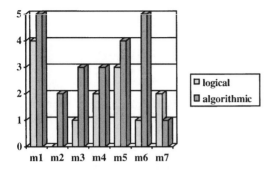

Figure 5.6. Number of errors found during integration.

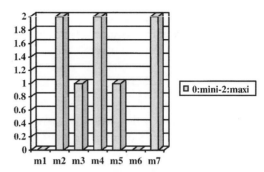

Figure 5.7. Degree of module testing.

the software are the parts where the most errors are found. Figure 5.7 gives per module the degree of module test (0 means minimum testing, 1 average testing, and 2 maximum testing). It appears that more errors, essentially algorithmic, occurred in less-tested modules.

Finally, a better view of the software in terms of error-proneness and testing was provided and will drive the implementation of improvement actions, mainly concerning the module test phase.

After stepping through the loop, it is worth quantifying the initial benefits of the improvement program. The iterative aspect of the method permits either, by reassessment, the refinement of goals and metrics set, but also the improvement of the metrication process (data collection, storage, analysis, etc.). Having elicited an appropriate degree of experience and an appropriate amount of information from the measurement process, improvement action can be taken, depending on the goals fulfilled.

The ami approach has been perceived to be an excellent means for selling software measurement and its necessity for process improvement. This goal-oriented approach is rather straightforward to apply and self-contained. The efficient use of measurement is demonstrated through a wide range of examples and case studies [19]. Several experiences have already been published in the telecommunications [13, 14, 20] and defence [31] areas.

The scope of applying ami was not only the measurement aspect but also the software project management issues and internal decision making. As an approach for introducing measurement, ami has the following advantages against other approaches, like a bottom-up approach (first collect data then think what you can do with the data!):

- Ease of implementation of a measurement program (easy-to-use and pragmatic approach described in a structured sequence of necessary actions)
- Minimal cost impact, predictable costs with a limited variance (selection of the appropriate metrics for the appropriate goals with a clear link to decision making)
- Motivation of the project staff (address directly the user's needs by providing a goal-oriented and customised set of metrics)

ami has also been successfully applied for driving improvement programs in the telecommunication and Defence areas [1, 12, 16]. ami has provided support for:

- Understanding the contribution of software development to business goals
- Setting quantitative goals for process improvement

- Preparing detailed action plans
- Monitoring improvement programs
- Sustaining the deployment phase

SEI IDEAL Approach

IDEAL (*Initiating* phase, *Diagnosing* phase, *Establishing* phase, *Acting* phase, *Leveraging* phase) is a software process improvement model recently developed by the SEI [28, 30]. It provides a sequence of recommended steps for initiating and managing SPI programs. This is the most recent attempt to describe a strategy for SPI, based on lessons learnt of SEI clients and internal SPI activities at Hewlett-Packard. The model is composed of five main phases:

- *Initiating phase*: This covers setting up the initiative, obtaining management sponsorship, establishing the infrastructure (management steering committee, SEPG), and the global SPI plan.
- *Diagnosing phase*: An assessment is performed to establish the baseline of the organisation's current state. The results and first recommendations will be integrated with existing and/or planned improvement efforts for further elaborating the SPI action plan. This is where the CMM plays its major role as software development process reference model.
- *Establishing phase:* Strategies and priorities for improvement are set up. The SPI action plan will be completed in accordance with organisation's vision, lessons learned from past improvement, and key business issues and long-term goals. Teams for implementing improvements are established and actions are planned. We will return later to this phase.
- *Acting phase:* New processes are defined, piloted, measured, and deployed across the organisation.
- *Leveraging phase:* At that time, a lot of experiences, data (metrics) have been gathered and should be made available to the whole organisation. Those information should be used to revise the SPI strategy.

Let's concentrate on the establishing phase, the gap between the process analysis and the implementation. The major steps are shown in Figure 5.8. The link to business visions, goals, and issues is emphasised as well as the necessity to set SPI goals in a quantitative way. Although those steps are rather detailed, there is no real clue how to concretely set up the goals or how to transform findings and recommendations into improvement actions. Only a rather heavy but exhaustive framework is given.

SPICE PROCESS IMPROVEMENT GUIDE

The ISO Software process assessment initiative has grown out of an initial UK Ministry of Defense "The sister of DoD in UK." effort called ImproveIT. ISO/JTC1/SC7/WG10 is developing an international standard for software process assessment (refer to Chapter 4).

The objective of Software Process Improvement and Capability Determination (SPICE) is to provide a common approach and framework for assessment and improvement

We will concentrate on the so-called Process Improvement Guide [32] which describes the steps to perform within a complete improvement cycle based on the SPICE assessment technology. Figure 5.9 describes the basic steps.

The phase of analysing assessment results and deriving an action plan is described in terms of inputs and outputs in Figure 5.10. Basically the approach advocated is emphasising the definition of goals and the usage of measurement to show quantitatively the current status of

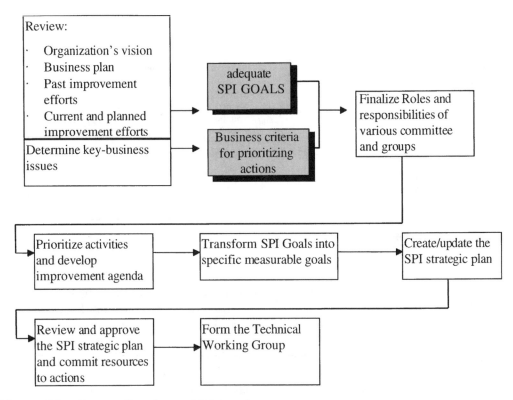

Figure 5.8. Process flow for establishing phases.

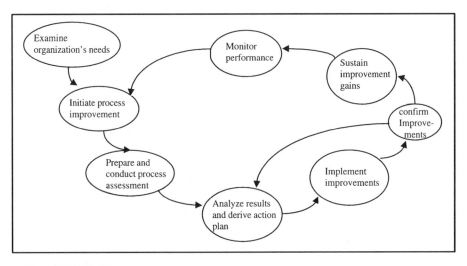

Figure 5.9. SPICE SPI steps.

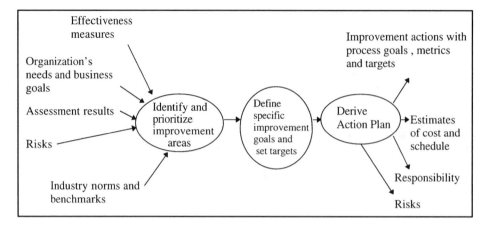

Figure 5.10. Detailed steps for the action plan production phase.

processes and practices against a general understanding of software engineering best practices (the Reference Model for Processes and Process Capability), and to show to what extent software processes are effective in achieving the organisation's needs and business goals.

Goals definition starts during the first step when analysing organisation's needs and business goals. The objectives of process improvement should be identified in terms of product quality, development cost or time to markets (external driver) or prediction ability.

The phase of action plan production is broken down into three steps (Figure 5.10):

- Identify areas for improvement based on the assessment outputs, the organisation's improvement goals, effectiveness measures if available, risk factors, and any industry norms or benchmarks that provide a basic comparison framework for assessment results. This will result in a list of improvement areas.
- For each of these areas, a target for improvement should be defined either in terms of process effectiveness (e.g., percentage of project with an accuracy of ± 10 percent of effort estimates) and/or target process capability profiles as defined by SPICE (capability level for given process). This involves defining goals, devising the right metrics to measure their achievement, and setting appropriate target values.
- Finally, an action plan should be derived covering improvement actions with associated process goals and improvement targets, responsibilities, initial estimates of effort, benefits and schedule, and risks to products and to the organisation if actions are taken or not taken.

We will come back to SPICE in the Case Studies section, with a concrete example of how to develop a goal tree based on the initial SPICE-conformant assessment.

CONCLUSIONS ON SOFTWARE PROCESS IMPROVEMENT STRATEGIES

From the historical point of view, the analytic approach from the SEL has been at the root of the first large-scale and documented process improvement experiments. But some of the drawbacks may relate to the relative high cost of building such an improvement organisation and the relative complexity of the concepts although perfectly sound from the engineering point of view. The management of the SEL [29] recently admitted that their approach would be perfectly complemented with a CMM-based approach for initially selecting the processes to improve based on a kind of model of best practices. This is what ami did, integrating GQM and CMM-based assessment, looking in depth at the measurement aspects of SPI.

The SPICE Process Improvement Guide uses those principles for the action planning phase of its process improvement loop. As a matter of fact, some members of the initial ami design team were strong contributors to the PIG. Nevertheless, SPICE remains rather vague on how to come up with the goals, the actions, and the metrics. This is what ami is concretely addressing.

Finally IDEAL is one level of abstraction higher compared to the SPICE PIG, mentioning the necessity for measuring goals but without illustrating it.

In conclusion, the author's recommendation, based on current industry feedback and concerns, is to adopt a mixed approach integrating a best-practices model for the assessment phase with a goal-oriented method supporting the initiation of the program, the definition of improvement actions, and their follow-up. In the next section, a proposal for steps to bridge the gap between the assessment and the improvement actions will be outlined, using as a basis the goal tree concepts from ami and following the main principles previously described.

BUILDING GOAL TREE TO STRUCTURE IMPROVEMENT PROGRAMS

Introduction to the Proposed Approach

In Chapter 4, major process improvement strategies were introduced and compared. An ideal approach based on the combination of the existing ones would fulfil some basic principles like business-driven, goal-oriented, iterative, and supported by measurement. As discussed in the Introduction, the critical phase in any SPI initiative relates to the translation of process assessment results into improvement actions, including obtaining commitment from management. In this chapter, a technique will be proposed based on some of the ami concepts as well as the ideas developed in the SPICE Process Improvement Guide. We will attempt to keep the steps generic, that is, independent from any process analysis method. The instantiation will be performed in the next section with some major process assessment approaches and best practices models like CMM, SPICE, BOOTSTRAP, and ISO 9001/TickIT audits. Basically SPI programs will be structured using the so-called goal tree, a visual means to provide the whole organisation with the link between business goals, SPI goals, high-level actions, and metrics to monitor changes.

Critical Role of Measurement in Any SPI Program

"There is no possible improvement or even technology assessment if one does not know current quality and productivity baseline." This statement [5] summarises why measurement is a necessary item in any improvement program; an organisation must use measures to generate the baseline understanding of processes and products that will form the basis of improvement program. Actually successful SPI programs have had a strong measurement program in place, for example, Motorola, Hewlett-Packard, McDonnell, Douglas Aerospace, Hughes, TRW.

The use of measurement in SPI is threefold [5, 6, 7]:

- To provide a quantitative basis of comparison for future process changes
- To better understand the issues that may or may not have been identified in the qualitative analysis (assessment), for example, the high cost of certain activities may make them the priority improvement targets, nonproductive activities analysis, etc.
- To make the decision making less risky when selecting new technologies/processes/practices

What types of metrics are necessary? There are several levels of indicators that are to be taken into account:

- "Business performance" (indirect measures of the benefits of the SPI program): those indicators are the one visible outside the product development organisation. Having this definition, one can differentiate between:
    - Visibility to the customer with related business goals; that is, time to market, customer satisfaction in terms of quality (number of customer complaints after delivery, schedule (estimation accuracy) and/or functionality, average repair time in support and maintenance;
    - Visibility to business management more related to organisational product and process improvement goals, for example, productivity, lower costs, etc. Examples of metrics are costs of servicing customer complaints, number of projects cancelled and associated costs, and personnel turnover.
- Software development performance: these indicators are typically related to the software process goals. Examples of them are defect density per phase, effort distribution, accuracy of estimates of project size/effort, effort due to rework, stability of requirements, etc.
- Activity/process/pilot measurement: these metrics are typical action plan progress metrics. This can be the follow-up of a pilot project (definition of objective criteria of success) or the deployment of new practices across the organisation:
    - Conformance measures (percentage of projects that are applying the processes)
    - Efficiency measures of this new processes
    - Cost/benefits analysis for the introduction of a new software technology or practices

One of the difficulties of such cost/benefits analysis is to link them to the usual factors: Productivity, Predictability, Quality (PRQ). This is quite an easy task for life cycle activities (efficiency of testing, etc.) but much more tricky for support processes like estimating, planning, requirements management, configuration management or risk management. Some examples follow:

- Estimation process: combination of how efficient is the estimation technique and how stable and complete the requirements inputs are
- Requirements management: completeness, traceability, rework due to requirements
- Configuration management: full traceability, integrity of product
- Risk management: did I anticipate risks early enough and what did I gain/lose?

For all these metrics, a measurement framework should be defined based on goal definition. This is what will be presented next. Another important measurement item is the selection of a general model for determining the overall ROI of the program. The Raython quality model is certainly the most complete one (Figure 5.11). They found out that their cost of nonconformance dropped from 42 percent of the whole project cost (1989) to 11 percent in 1993 [17].

Upfront Activities with Regards to Business Goals

In order to better prepare the action planning phase, some actions shall be taken beforehand (before and during the assessment) towards improving management understanding. Management should start to investigate upfront how important to their business, software is, identify business goals and critical areas. Our experience is that typically the "ideal" talk from SPI sup-

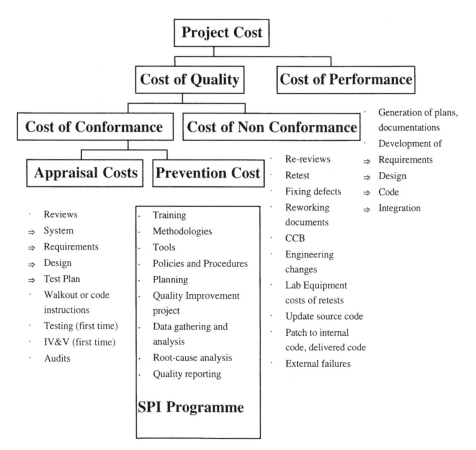

Figure 5.11.   Quality model.

pliers did not bring managers to think in terms of business objectives, critical areas (SPI customer projects). If the last project failed to deliver the product on time due to a deficient configuration management system, this should drive the forthcoming actions toward the current release. If a platform development starting up now is critical for the survival of the organisation as basis for all future products, then the emphasis should be first in requirements engineering of this project!! SPI should not be viewed as an ivory tower, far from development reality, as the ISO 9001 team were often viewed as. This can be achieved by:

1. organising the SEPG [22] with both a central team and members within the projects and
2. having improvement teams concentrate on critical project improvement needs first.

So management should be prepared to provide some information that is of very high value for the SPI program:

- Their business goals, new challenges, evolution of the role of software in the business, objectives in terms of time to market or development lead time, quality level, cost and productivity, customer initiatives (assessment of suppliers' capacity, visibility program toward supplier's product development).

• Their priority in terms of projects or areas within the organisation in the short- and mid-term as well as their goals on these projects (priority toward schedule, quality, or features?). Basically, who may be the first customer(s) of the SPI initiative. Here different criteria may be used, that is, importance of customer, reusability, willingness of project leader, current level of practices. The assessment has given the big picture on the organisation capability but the objective is to first improve project practices. We have to remember that at level two, the focus should be on project, not on the organisation. So it is worthless to define organisationwide working groups to write down processes. It is more efficient to try to transfer best practices from some projects to others and cover concrete project improvement requirements.

Three major steps have been identified for building a goal tree:

1. Defining of SPI goals based on senior management inputs (Figure 5.12)
2. Refining those goals into high-level improvement actions to build a goal tree (Figure 5.13)
3. Attaching metrics at each level of the goal tree (Figure 5.14)

A continuous example will be followed along the three steps (refer to the full goal tree in Figure 5.15).

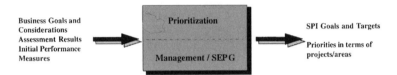

Figure 5.12.   SPI goal definition.

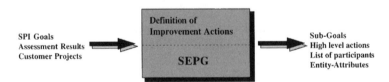

Figure 5.13.   Definition of high, level improvement actions.

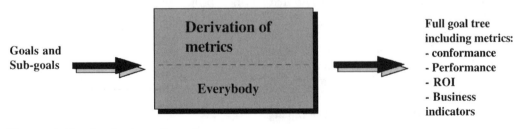

Figure 5.14.   Derivation of metrics.

Step 1: Define SPI Goals

Business management has provided the business goals and future orientations of the organisation. It is now up to the technical management to translate those business goals into software process goals, basically answering the question, "In which area should we improve the software development process to achieve the business objectives?" The approach will be different whether the business goal is "time to market" or zero defect.

It may be difficult to differentiate what is a business goal and what is an SPI goal. A simple answer would be that business goals are the ones that have a direct relationship with the customer (external or internal like marketing) whereas SPI goals are linked to the internal development processes. A business goal can be linked to a given project that is critical for the future of the organisation which would make this project the first customer of the SPI program in the short term.

The second input to the SPI goals definition is the result of the assessment. It should help in prioritising which area should be improved first. Capability model like the CMM emphasised getting management practices under control first before looking at more technological issues. Those models are providing a road map for improvement. They should not be used as checklists, to be used in deriving the improvement as the gap between the model and the reality.

Another important source of information is the quantitative data that is available in the organisation. This data typically complements the qualitative results of an assessment. When such "reliable" performance data is available, it can be used to set quantitative targets for the

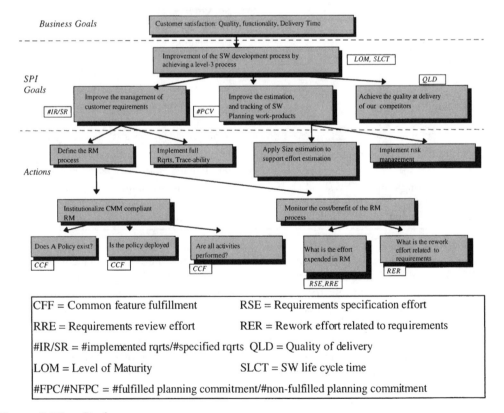

Figure 5.15. Goal tree.

SPI goals. But at a lower maturity level, the data is usually inconsistent across projects. One's first actions should then be to collect baseline performance measurements per project.

So, basically with this information, the potential goal contributors will be brought together to define what is their role in achieving this goal. The contributors can be middle-management, project managers, quality engineers and developers. After some rounds of brain-storming and collaborative work across the organisation, a hierarchy of SPI goals is produced according to the roles and responsibilities of those people (the arrangement may also be flat instead of hierarchical).

As soon as short- and long-term SPI goals are defined covering priority areas and projects, they should be checked against available budget, the given timeframe, and the "level of maturity of the organisation" or whether the goals are not too much ambitious compared to current situation. At the prioritisation meeting, it is typical to see management emphasising technical issues ("what about checklists for code reading"), the main reason being to escape from their responsibility since the issues are mostly addressing their practices.

Table 5.2 shows some example of business goals and related SPI goals:

Table 5.2. V & V, Example of Business Goals and SPI Goals.

Business Goals/First Level of SPI Goals	SPI Goals
Decrease development costs by X%	Adapt Verification and Validation effort according to the criticality of the system and subsystems Manage stability of requirements Understand costs
Decrease project delays	Improve effort estimation by using historical database, expert opinions, and upfront size estimates
Decrease project lead time	Reduce testing phase from 12 to 6 months through automatic testing and archive test sentences for re-tests at a later stage.
Improve visibility on project status	Have risks detected earlier Have requirements traceable across the life cycle
Ensure that starting Project XYZ should have a complete requirements basis to achieve customer satisfaction	Ensure feasibility of marketing requirements Ensure feasibility and testability of technical requirements

In our continuous example, the business goal was rather general: improve customer satisfaction in terms of quality, functionality, and time. The next level of goals may be due to a customer requirement: to continue to do business with the customer, the organisation has to achieve an equivalent to level 3 process on the CMM ladder. This should actually only be an SPI goal per se when specifically required by the customer. Now organisations like Boeing are not asking formally for a level of maturity but want their supplier to make a plan and implement essential practices that forms the level 2 and later level 3. The three characteristics from the business goal are found at the next level of SPI goals: improvement of management of requirements, achievement of level of quality of our competitors after delivery, and improvement of project management processes.

Step 2: Define High-Level Improvement Actions

In the second step, high-level improvement actions are defined and linked to the SPI goals. One way to select those improvement actions is to:

- Define who in the organisation may contribute to the SPI goal, the so-called viewpoints
- For all those viewpoints, investigate what entities they do manage in the context of the goal

Derive a list of questions about the entities with regards to the goals.

- Based on the response to the question (sometimes after some small investigation or data gathering), define improvement actions. Some first metrics may be collected to narrow the scope of some actions.
- Continue for the new set of actions/subgoals until you reach the lowest level of actions necessary for your management to make decisions regarding which one to prioritise.

The more you derive actions, the lower in the organisation you are, finally reaching developers.

The current goal tree will be presented to management for first approval and therefore has to be complemented with cost and time information (short-, mid-, or long-term, low-, mid-, and high-cost). With such a representation, the rationale for the actions is immediately visible, including how they contribute to the overall objectives.

An important set of goals/actions that should be established upfront relates to the need for investigating deeper, and if possible quantitatively, issues that have been brought up during the assessment but without the necessary details. For instance:

- What are the error-prone or inefficient activities?
- What are the low-quality work products, and bottlenecks for subsequent activities?
- What is the origin of defects usually found by the customer (root-cause analysis)?

Another critical type of goals should look at how product quality is affected by process changes, an assumption at the base of any SPI trend which has never been validated in each environment.

How the goal tree was built up should be also documented, specially the rationale behind goals (relationships to assessment results and/or management issues) and actions (relationships to any recommendations, metric, etc.).

Step 3: Derive Metrics

To complete the goal tree, metrics shall be attached to each level of goals and actions. The same process described above for breaking down into subgoals can be applied here as well: ask questions, that is, how will I be able to monitor quantitatively the achievement of the goal. Different types of metrics can be considered:

- Business indicators
- Conformance metrics
- Performance metrics
- Return on investment metrics or cost/benefits

In our example in Figure 5.15, at the bottom of the tree, for requirements management conformance metrics dealing with the implementation of a standard requirement process and

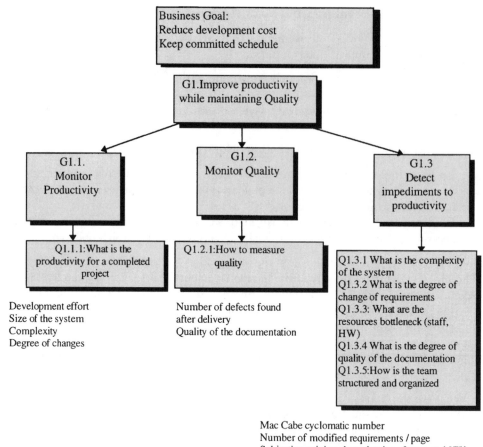

Figure 5.16. Goal tree for driving improvement actions selection.

cost/benefits metrics (looking at the rework effort linked to bad requirements management) will be collected. Some example of metrics can be found in Chapter 6.

Another full goal tree from the ami validation projects [19] is shown in Figure 5.16. The metrics attached to each question (for G3) have allowed to detect after a short data collection and analysis phase what are the main bottlenecks to productivity and consequently define some actions.

Next Steps: Build Initial Action Plan and Get Commitment

As soon as the goal tree is built up, the production of the action plan can start. An example of contents for such action plan is given below.

- Background/history
- Organisational infrastructure for SPI including rules and responsibilities

- Action plan management
  - Reporting mechanism
  - Review and approval mechanism
  - Tracking data
  - Risk management
  - Escalation procedure
  - Configuration management
- Overview of assessment
- Documented goal tree (business goals, SPI goals, etc.)
- Improvement actions (to be repeated for each action)
  - Rationale
  - Inputs
  - Results expected
  - Dependencies with other actions
  - Resources
  - Time schedule and effort (Gantt chart)
  - Subtasks
  - follow-up metrics
  - Pilot project
  - Mechanism for deployment
  - Training needs

Appendix: Gantt chart
                 Summary of effort

Finally, reaching management commitment may be an easy matter if they are continuously involved from the beginning of the initiative and consulted at the critical milestones. However, the management presentation of the action plan should be handled with care, avoiding technical details of the action. Typical concerns of management are:

- What is the overall effort?
- Does cost includes training, project effort?
- What are the main deliverables/milestones?
- From which point in time are we able to decide whether to pilot or deploy a practice and by which mechanism?
- Can we trace back actions to assessment findings or any other business considerations? (goal tree)
- Investment needed in tools, PCs, etc.?
- How will the feasibility of a new technology be analysed?
- Has the impact of SPI on projects with regard to resources and delays been evaluated?

CASE STUDIES

Introduction

So far, the building of a goal tree in the context of an SPI program was presented independently from any assessment methods. In the following part of this chapter, we will look how to concretely build up such goal trees from the results of four major process analysis approaches, namely, CMM-based assessment, BOOTSTRAP, SPICE, and ISO 9001 audits [15]. Each subchapter will be split into two parts: guidelines for tailoring and a case study from industry. The case studies may cover not only the action planning phase but also the full improvement cycle.

Application to CMM-Based Assessment

Goal Tree Tailoring Guidelines

CMM-based assessment's outputs are a list of strengths, weaknesses, and consequences of those weaknesses structured by so-called key process areas (KPAs). Those statements based on various interviews describe in a rather undetailed way what the issues are. No detailed conformance ratings are usually available except some high level KPA profile.

So, the definition of software process goals may need an additional more quantitative investigation on the root-cause analysis of the issues. A straight KPA-oriented goal setting would hide any cross-KPA problems like traceability that cover requirements management, product engineering, and configuration management.

Findings (but not KPAs) should be prioritised according to their level of contribution to business goals (when improvement would occur in that area) and the criticality of their consequences. Then, software process goals can be derived through aggregation of those critical findings and consequences, so that each goal covers a set of problems.

The corresponding consequences of the findings may provide hints on what metrics may be used to monitor improvements. For example one major consequence of the lack of discipline in requirements management was customer complaints due to missing features and high rework effort caused by noncontrolled requirements changes and weak requirements traceability.

The third level of goals corresponds to high-level definition of improvement actions. Here the KPA-related goals as described in the CMM may be useful for devising those actions. Those goal statements leave a certain flexibility for the implementation. Typical actions are: building a historical database to support the estimation process, introducing the notion of criticality of subsystems to better manage resources, implementing traceability across the life cycle, and formalising requirements management process (numbering, exit criteria, validation test, inspections, etc.

At the fourth level, two branches may be envisaged, one for each of the management's main concerns. The first can cover pilot/implementation/institutionalisation of new practices. The first customer project of the new practices should be mentioned at that level. We would not recommend using straightforward CMM key practices/subpractices by just filling in the gap between the current practice and the CMM model. Those practices can serve as a checklist for completeness. A better approach is to derive from the goals (about three per KPA are defined) what improvements should be implemented in the context of the business and software process goals. The final target is not certification but improvement of daily performance.

The other path may relate to monitoring the costs and benefits of the new process element.

Case Study

This example coming from the telecommunication field will cover the assessment and action planning phase with the application of a goal-oriented approach, that is, ami. The company (2500 employees with 300 software engineers) is developing and manufacturing various telecommunication network systems (network management systems, protocols, etc.). The software function in such systems had been growing by about 20 percent per year since 1985. The first discussions with senior management revealed a strong commitment to software process improvement and a pilot initiative was started during the second quarter of 1993 which Objectif Technologie, a services company, member of the original ami consortium, and a major SPI actor in Europe, was invited to support and coordinate.

Preparation Phase

Before performing the assessment, it was deemed necessary to clarify business goals for software improvement. This was achieved through several brainstorming sessions with management. First, the impact of software on the whole business has been evaluated as well as the main difficulties or weaknesses observed during the development process. These observations taken from existing audit results and from a further audit carried out by the consultants were summarised as a list of potential risks for future business. Along with them, three main business goals have been defined for the next three years:

G1: Reduce time to market
G2: Reduce number of remaining bugs after installation
G3: Get homogeneous software maturity

Assessment Phase

The assessment was carried out over a relatively short period (3 months). Two pairs of people conducted various audits on the basis of questionnaires and on documents collected for some projects. A total of 150 person-days was needed for completion of the assessment (100 Interviews, 18 projects) and for drawing up the first conclusions based on the key process areas of the CMM. Key observations reported during this period included the excellent framework and strong cooperation with the software teams. This was largely due to two factors: initial presentation of the top management goals and the organisation of preparatory meetings. Findings were identified and linked to business goals. The main findings were:

- KPA Project Planning: project planning unreliable due to the lack of past data, incomplete list of tasks and the lack of flexibility in resource allocation: to be linked to G1 and G2.
- KPA Project Tracking and Oversight: project tracking and predictability insufficient, meaning that reestimates are not done; there is no real visibility on the projects; and necessary decisions are not taken in time: to be linked to G1 and G2.
- KPA Software Configuration Management: configuration management not properly done due to missing work-products definition, missing CM activities, lack of tool support: to be linked with G2 (product quality)

KPA Software Quality Assurance: SQA generally not performed: linked to G1 because a lot of rework was done due to late bugs, and linked to G2 because essential Quality Assurance (QA) activities were not performed and a lot of bugs remained after delivery.

Action Phase

We will concentrate next on the goal "time to market." The first step was to identify the participants that are the major contributors to this goal as well as the entities they are managing in this context. The four main key players, the managed entities and the actions on those entities are summarised in Table 5.3.

The final goal tree is shown in Figure 5.17, including as well the main improvement actions.

The next step deals with the definition of metrics attached to each goal. First metrics will be used to better understand the current issues. The assessment has produced rather high-level statements on the practices. This need to be complemented with data looking at the root cause

Table 5.3.   Participants and Entities They Manage

Participants	Entities	Action
Project manager	Tasks Estimates Risks/deviations to plan Budget	Check the list of tasks and activities Consolidate Analyse Allocate
Development team	Estimates, reestimates Completed task	Provide for individual tasks Provide effort spent
Quality engineer	Risks Defects Issues (non-conformance of product and process)	Identify Analyse origin with developers Raise to upper management
Verification team	Tests Test phase	Define testing strategies and organise tests Evaluate testing coverage

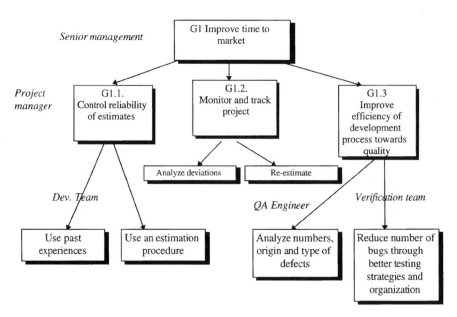

Figure 5.17.   Goal tree.

of problems. For instance, the goal "make reliable estimates" involves several processes, that is, estimation process, requirements management and review process, and several related products, that is, effort estimation, planning, and requirements definition document. A list of questions and the corresponding metrics had been produced to help in refining the problems and hence drive better the action plan:

Estimation Process:

Q1.1:	Does a policy exist? Is it followed?	% projects applying policy
Q1.2:	Are concurrent estimations achieved and compared?	% projects concurrent estimations
Q1.3:	Does the policy use past data?	
Q1.4:	Is past data validated?	Volume of validated data
Q1.5	Is the volume and quality of past data sufficient?	
Q1.6:	Is a margin evaluated?	% projects with margin
Q1.7:	What is the effort spent to estimate?	% of total effort
Q1.8:	How many times is reestimation conducted?	Number of reestimations

Requirements Management:

Q2.1:	Do adequate requirements exist?	% complete requirements
Q2.2:	Is interpretation needed?	% of ambiguities
Q2.3:	How many changes may occur after project start?	Number of requirements changes
Q2.4:	Are the changes mandatory (driven by customer)?	
Q2.5:	Is the impact of a change assessed prior to decision?	% impact evaluated

Estimation review process:

Q3.1:	Does a review policy exist? Is it followed?	% projects applying policy
Q3.2:	What is the frequency of rework of the estimation?	
Q3.3:	What is the effort dedicated to review?	Review effort

Now while looking at other branches of the tree, metrics will be needed to support the goals itself during the action plan implementation. Concerning the "use past experiences" sub-goal, the metrics to be regularly collected for building historical database were:

- Effort spent for each task per person/effort estimated
- Extra effort spent for completion of tasks
- Effort spent on unplanned work: meetings, illness, maintenance of old product
- Effort spent on correction of errors introduced in earlier phases (after corresponding review)
- KLOC estimated and final KLOCs (Kils Lines of Code Kils stays for thousand)
- Number of defects/type/phase of detection

For the goal "analyse deviations," additional metrics were collected like availability of resources, number of versions in parallel, number of components per version, frequency of evolutions, and number of changes of resource allocation.

The following indicators have been calculated by the project management tool as being the measurement baseline for monitoring improvements.

- Percentage of unavailability per person for a department: 15 percent was the average figure

- Average slippage between estimates and reality per category of task: the time when slippage is mentioned is also recorded, that is, after 50 percent of task completion or after 70 percent of task completion
- The rework ratio: effort spent for correction of errors introduced in a phase/effort spent to develop this phase

Thus, metrics were extremely useful in supporting improvement for the analysis of weaknesses, the decisions for adequate actions, and the follow-up of those actions.

The following improvement actions were implemented:

- Install a database and collection mechanism (refer to previous list of metrics)
- Review the estimation procedure
- Organise systematic reviews of estimation
- Claim for margin calculation
- Define a process—adapted to the customer—to resist requirements changes

Before the improvement actions, the effort overrun was between 15 and 20 percent for 70 percent of projects. After 1 year; the overrun dropped to 10 percent for about 40 percent of projects and to less than 10 percent for the others with a quarterly estimation for all projects. From senior management to practitioners, applying a goal-oriented approach like ami has led to greater confidence in the ROI of the improvement program. Senior and middle management were satisfied with receiving quantitative feedback from projects on regular basis: they were able to follow the impact of software on business and to analyse problems and weaknesses in greater depth. The software engineers were satisfied with understanding how they would contribute to the overall strategy.

Application to BOOTSTRAP

Goal Tree Tailoring Guidelines

Like ami, the BOOTSTRAP project [24] was performed within the framework of the ESPRIT program. Its goal was to develop a method for software process assessment, quantitative measurement, and improvement. BOOTSTRAP enhanced and refined the SEI's process assessment method and adapted it to the needs of the European software industry, that is, including ISO 9000-3 (guidelines for software quality assurance) attributes and the ESA's PSS-05 software engineering standards (refer to Chapter 4 for further details).

The BOOTSTRAP method covers the assessment activity. A maturity level is calculated for each attribute of the process quality through questionnaire-guided interviews. This model takes into account three main dimensions in the process: organisation, technology, and methodology issues, methodology being broken down into life cycle independent functions, life cycle functions, and process-related functions. A detailed profiling technique is also provided giving individual process attributes ratings. But there is no goal-oriented approach to map the maturity profile onto improvement activities and goals. All those measurements are calculated for each assessed project and for the organisation (SPU or Software Producing Unit)

How Can You Build the Goal Tree?

An analysis of project maturity profile (the SPU profile will be left out in a level 1 organisation where the emphasis should be on individual project improvement) will allow the easy detection of weak quality attributes.

Those will be prioritised according to business goals and translated into software process goals. For instance, on Figure 5.18, the weaknesses are quality management, quality assurance, and risk management for organisation and engineering support areas.

The next steps to identify improvement actions are in a similar way as described in the CMM guidelines for building a goal tree. What is useful is the easy visualisation of pockets of excellence projects, and determining which transfer of practices to other critical projects needs to be considered first.

Contrary to the CMM, there is no reference model describing practices. Those deficient practices are visible at the level of questions used for interviews.

As general guidelines, those measures of capability profile should be used very carefully. They should be a minor impact in driving the action planning. A lower percentage for a given set of practices should be analysed carefully in terms of cost/benefits implementation trade-off together with business considerations. Fulfilling the X percent missing for achieving full coverage should not be the objective per se.

Assessment

A real case study has been derived from a BOOTSTRAP article in *IEEE Software* of July 1994. The derivation of the goal tree was approached a bit differently than in the above guidelines [24].

The assessed organisation is developing a control system to visualise industrial processes. The project being assessed is currently in the maintenance phase, and the project is continued with development of a larger system in which the assessed system is integrated. An improvement project was started and run in parallel with the development introducing software engineering

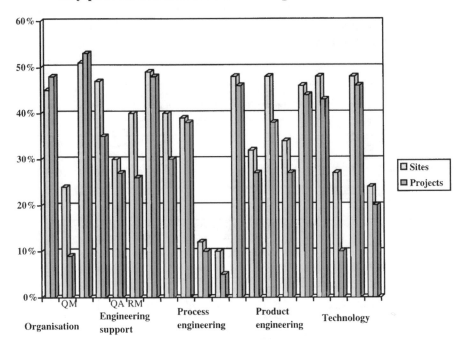

Figure 5.18. Average BOOTSTRAP attribute profiles for both organisations and individual projects.

practices based on the findings of the BOOTSTRAP assessment. The BOOTSTRAP profile showed significant weaknesses in project management and design. Detailed investigations on those two issues highlighted the following facts:

Design   Twelve person-days were needed to correct an error during maintenance because there were no graphical or textual representations of the module structure and of the links among modules and the product interfaces

Project management   No detailed workflow charts and cost and effort based on sound histori-cal data were available despite the fact that a project-management tool has been purchased. But since no training had been performed, it is never been used properly.

Based on that data, the following software process goals were defined together with the priority high-level actions.

G1: To reduce effort for maintenance
A1: Introducing a case tool based on structured design

G2: To produce reliable estimates
A2: To implement a project management methodology based on the existing tool.

Analyse

From the analysis of the top software process goals and related actions, a framework for action plan and measurement is built (Figure 5.19)

The goal tree merges main improvement actions and related goals. The leafs define the necessary metrics to monitor the achievement of the goals.

With regards to G1, a redesign of software will be performed. The benefits will be evalu-ated on the next maintenance activities. With regards to G2, the existing project management methodology shall be applied and supported with the definition of a historical and tracking database for estimation purposes.

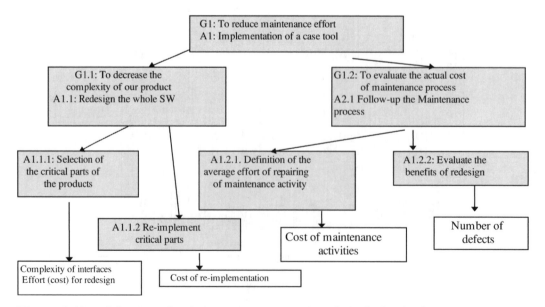

Figure 5.19a.   Merging of main improvement action with goals for Goal G1.

Metricate

For supporting and evaluating the benefits of the redesign, the following metrics were collected:

- Interface complexity metrics to select critical parts of the software.
- Cost of redesign and reimplementation for the forthcoming cost/benefits analysis.
- Cost of maintenance activities after redesign
- Number of defects as an indicator of quality for the redesigned product.

For project management, typical project progress metrics from completed projects were collected for feeding the historical database (effort, size, time) and facilitating the estimation for new projects. The same data was collected for project tracking purposes.

Improve

The data analysis revealed the following facts after having implemented the necessary improvement actions:

G1.1.1   The redesign took only 4 person-months. The redesign was not really important but the effect of design on the maintenance seemed to be important.

After redesign of parts of the system and the use of professional design techniques in a further project, a reduced meaningful effort per maintenance activity (about 4 person-days) was achieved, which was about one-third of the previous effort. Moreover the redesign effort was amortised in about 6 months of maintenance activities. The quality of the product significantly increases.

G1.2.1   The implementation time was reduced by half with the same amount of effort. As a matter of fact, the graphical and textual design facilitated the decomposition of the product into different units that could be developed in parallel.

G2.1   The main benefits were the clear breakdown of a project into work packages together with a more reliable resource estimation. In the requirements phase resources were estimated

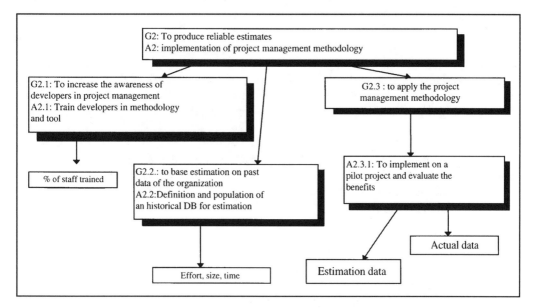

Figure 5.19b.   Merging main improvement actions with goals for Goal G2.

within 30 percent and after analysis and design within 10 percent. Repeating the BOOT-STRAP assessment will check whether the weak process quality attributes detected at the first reassessment have been improved.

Application to ISO 9000-3

Background

In the last years ISO 9000 series became more and more the quality standard. Never before a standard has got such a broad acceptance all over the world.

As ISO 9000 is independent from the industry segment, IT industry has some problems with the application. The 1991 *ISO 9000-3 Guidelines* for the application of ISO 9001 to the development, supply, and maintenance of software attacked this problem but was only a guideline. TickIT is an initiative to take ISO 9000-3 as a baseline and uses it for certification purposes. This is not a standard but a UK-based certification scheme toward the ISO 9001 application in IT.

To demonstrate a quality management system according to ISO 9000-3 (or ISO 9001) internal audits have to be performed regularly. The nonconformities are handled through so-called corrective actions. Corrective actions aim at either improving a specific process or improving the way a process is followed.

In the following we show how ami and a goal tree and the ISO 9001 standard can be applied to use this mechanism of internal audits for starting a process improvement cycle. The tracking of corrective actions is required by ISO 9000-3, nevertheless there are no guidelines how to do it. We will see how a goal tree can be used for tracking and visualisation of the improvements.

Assess

In our example the assessment can be done through an internal audit. ISO 9000-3 requires a checklist. This checklist and the documented quality system, as well as how far daily life differs from the written procedures, is assessed. The weaknesses are described in corrective actions describing the nonconformities. The next step is to define goals as a baseline for the analysis phase. In our example TickIT certification is used as business goal.

Analyse

In the analysis phase the results of the internal audit are analysed in order to define improvement actions. How the example is decomposed can be seen in Figure 5.20. The goals are broken down until quantifiable goals are reached. In this case all the bottom goals are either metrics concerning the definition or concerning the deployment.

Metricate

The Measurement plan for these very simple metrics has to be defined here. There are different kinds of metrics: level of definition and percentage of institutionalisation.

For the definition metrics (DF = definition factor) three categories are used:

–	Redefinition necessary
0	Minor weaknesses
+	O.K.

For the institutionalisation metrics (IF) five categories are used:

0%	Little effective usage
25%	Applied to about one-quarter of the potential
50%	Applied to about half the potential

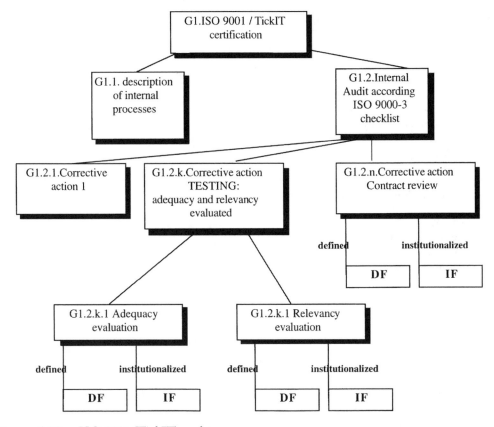

Figure 5.20.   ISO 9001/TickIT goal tree.

75%   Applied to about three-quarters of the potential
100%   Applied to full potential in all relevant areas and activities.

Improve

Through follow-up audits an assessment of the actual status of the progress can be made. The following diagram (Table 5.4) can be used for monitoring. After closing all corrective actions the next higher-level goal is reached.

Application to SPICE

Goal Tree Tailoring Guidelines

SPICE produces the following results [27]:

- A four-point rating scale (N for not achieved, P for partially achieved, L for largely achieved, and F for fully achieved) for each process capability attribute of each process instance.

    CUS.3 [instance of project] CL.PA = N/P/L/F

- An aggregate process attribute rating for the organisation represented by several projects.

    CUS.3 [number of instances] CL.PA = [% fully, % largely, % partially, % not]

- An aggregate capability level

Table 5.4.   A Sample Audit Approach to Follow-Up Improvements

Element	Definition			Institutionalisation				
	–	0	+	0	25	50	75	100
Quality System Framework								
Management responsibility		X				X		
Quality system	X						X	
Internal quality system audits		X					X	
Corrective actions			X					X
Life Cycle Activities								
Contract review			X					X
Purchaser's requirements specification		X						X
Development planning			X					X
Quality planning	X					X		
Design & implementation			X				X	
Testing & Validation		X					X	
Acceptance		X					X	
Replication, delivery, & installation	X				X			
Maintenance			X				X	
Support Activities								
Configuration management	X						X	
Document control			X			X		
Quality records			X		X			
Measurement			X			X		
Rules, practices, & conventions			X					X

$$\text{CUS.3 [number of instances] (CL1 to CLn)} = [\%\text{CL1}; \%\text{CL2}, \ldots]$$

where   CUS process category
CUS.3 = process within category
CL = capability level
PA = process attributes
CL1 to Cln = capability level range

As pointed out for BOOTSTRAP, the value of such ratings is rather subjective and is one of many drivers of the action planning phase.

SPICE advocates the early definition of software process goals, metrics and targets. The SPICE process measurement framework is illustrated in Figure 5.21 and compare with ami's measurement structure using an example coming from the PIG.

Software process goals are split between conformance objectives, to reach a certain capability level for a given process or achieving ISO9001 compliance and effectiveness goals, a more business-oriented expression of process performance.

Those goals can represent the second level of the goal tree. The aggregate capability level for all process attributes and process attribute ratings can help with selecting which process

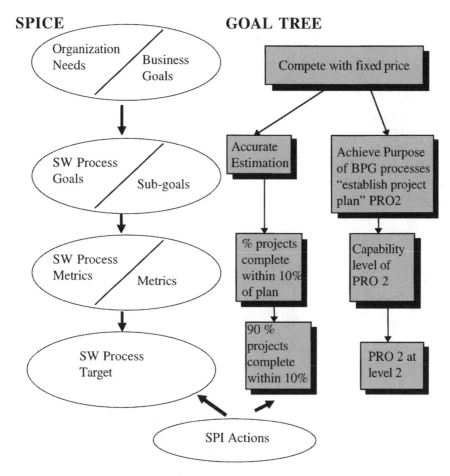

Figure 5.21. SPICE measurement framework.

should be improved and towards which capability level. Other types of goals need a thorough investigation of issues and their criticality toward the business. The ratings are of poor help for this purpose.

For the actions, the single process attribute rating for each process should be used to identify best practices or pockets of excellence in the organisation that could be transferred elsewhere. Apart from transfer actions necessary to achieve a certain level of process capability as described in the SPICE model, one should check that those actions should contribute to the effectiveness goals as well. Other specific actions linked to the effectiveness goals will cover collection and evaluation of performance date.

Case study

This case study has been built using the example from the appendix of the SPICE Process Improvement Guide [32]. The company develops interactive multimedia software for PCs. Although quality assurance personnel provides independent review of all products, defective products have been distributed and unhappy customers have called the company to report problems.

The top-level management of the company defined as a business goal: To improve our ways of developing software products with fewer defects at no higher cost or length of time to market.

Before the assessment, since product quality had been identified as a serious problem, each software engineer was encouraged to keep track of time spent:

- On correction of problems identified by customers
- For requirement analysis, design, and documentation before coding
- On corrections of problems identified by the developer

Those measurements shall be used to raise awareness of how much time was being spent correcting problems and how much of this time might be spent better in upfront activities to prevent those problems from happening.

When starting a SPICE assessment, the scope, that is, what processes to assess, shall be defined. It was decided to evaluate:

Customer-Supplier Process Category (CUS)

CUS.3 Identify customer needs

CUS.6 Support operation of software

CUS.8 Assess customer satisfaction

Engineering Process Category (ENG): All processes

Project Process Category (PRO): All processes

Support Process Category (SUP): All processes

The result of the assessment showed a satisfactory situation in PRO, most of the processes being at capability level 2 and some at three. Most of the design activities (ENG) were as well at level 2.

The problem areas were related to requirements definition (CUS.3: identify customer needs; ENG.1: develop system requirements and design; ENG.2: develop software requirements), and system testing (ENG.6: integrate and test system). Here is an example of ratings for the process "identify customer needs":

CUS.3[P1,P2,P3];1.1 = [0, 25,25,50]	⇨ process performance
CUS.3[P1,P2,P3];2.1 = [0,0,40,60]	⇨ performance management
CUS.3[P1,P2,P3];2.2 = [0,0,0,100]	⇨ work product management
CUS.3[P1,P2,P3];3.1 = [0, 0,0,100]	⇨ process definition
CUS.3[P1,P2,P3];3.2 = [0, 0,0,100]	⇨ process resources

Those processes should be improved in priority to achieve capability level 2. But one needed to ensure that conformance to SPICE processes would affect positively the product quality. So a program of measurement of defects was put in place to provide visibility of measurement.

So the resulting goal tree would be split into two types of branches, one type dealing with achieving a certain SPICE capability level for deficient critical processes, another type dealing with monitoring how process performance quantitatively evolves. The final goal tree would look like that in Figure 5.22.

Some targets have been established based on the initial measurements like rework time less than 5 percent, percent of time spent on new projects > 50 percent, no single product with more than one open problem report/100 KLOC (Kils Lines of Code).

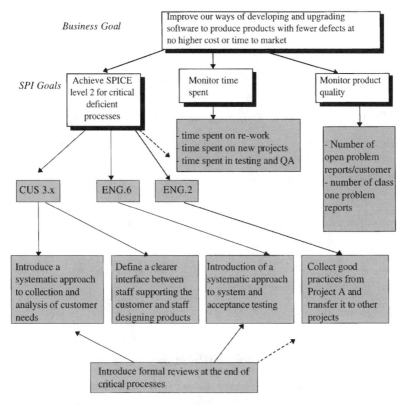

Figure 5.22.   Goal tree based on SPICE process analysis.

CONCLUSION

As conclusion, instead of general sentences, a checklist will recap the main recommendations and issues to be followed during the action planning phase:

1. The management team (not only research and development [R&D] but also business, financial, etc.) has defined business goals for the organisation to initiate the SPI initiative.

   ❐ Yes with quantitative target   ❐ Yes without target   ❐ No

2. At the completion of the assessment, business and R&D management have provided their priority in terms of business goals and areas to be improved (projects, teams, process domains)

   ❐ Yes   ❐ Yes partly   ❐ No

3. A task force composed of full-time SEPG, a few experts in priority domain and representative (if possible project leader) of customer projects has been set up to produce the action plan

   ❐ Yes   ❐ Yes but not fully staffed and part-time   ❐ No

4. A goal tree has been established and agreed after several brainstorming meeting with management and experts

   ❐ Yes   ❐ Yes but incomplete   ❐ No

5. Based on questions documenting the goal tree, data has been collected to understand the root-cause analysis of problems before devising the action plan.

   ❐ Yes   ❐ Some   ❐ No went to action planning from assessment findings

6. Based on metrics in the goal tree, a measurement plan is set up to establish a quantitative baseline of project performance.

   ❐ Yes   ❐ Partly   ❐ No

7. The action plan integrates short- and long-term goals and actions; the short-term goals (2 to 3 months) will show visibility of the initiative to everybody in the organisation.

   ❐ Yes   ❐ Yes but few short term   ❐ No

8. The whole organisation has been presented as soon as possible with the action plan with visible commitment of management.

   ❐ Yes   ❐ Yes but later   ❐ No

REFERENCES

1. A. Kuntzmann-Combelles, "From Assessment to Improvement Actions: Compared Experiences with CMM and SPICE," *Proceedings of the 5th European Conference on Software Quality*, Dublin, Sept. 1996.

2. *Esprit II 5494 ami:ami Handbook*, Published version, March 1992.

3. K. Pulford, A. Kuntzmann-Combelles, and S. Shirlaw, *A Quantitative Approach to Software Management*, Addison-Wesley, 1995.

4. V. Basili and H. Rombach, "The TAME Project: Towards Improvement-Oriented Software Environments," *IEEE Transactions on Software Engineering*, Vol. 14, No. 6, June 1988.

5. L. Briand, K. El Eman, and W. Melo, "AINSI: an Inductive Method for Software Process Improvement: Concrete Steps and Guidelines," *Proceedings of the Second ISCN Seminar*, Vienna, Sept. 1995.

6. L. Briand, C. Differding, and D. Rombach: *Practical Guidelines for Measurement-Based Process Improvement*, Technical Report of the International Software Engineering Network, ISERN-96-05, 1996.

7. D. Card, "Understanding Process Improvement," *IEEE Software*, July 1991.

8. M.C. Paulk, B. Curtis, and M.B. Chrissis: *Capability Maturity Model for Software, Version 1.1*, CMU/SEI-93-TR-24, Feb. 1993.

9. M. Paulk et al., *Key Practices of the Capability Maturity Model, Version 1.1*, CMU/SEI-93-TR-25, Feb. 1993.

10. B. Curtis, M. Kellner, and J. Over, "Process Modelling," *Communication of the ACM*, Vol. 35, No. 9, Sept. 1992.

11. C. Debou, "ami: a New Paradigm for Software Process Improvement," *Proceedings of the First ISCN Seminar*, Dublin, May 1994.

12. C. Debou and A.M. Kuntzmann-Combelles, "From Business Goals to Improvement Planning: Practical Use of ami," *Proceedings of the SPI96/ISCN96 Conference*, Brighton, Dec. 1996.

13. C. Debou and S. Stainer, "Improving the Maintenance Process: A Quantitative Approach," *Proceedings of the 6th International Conference on Software Engineering and Its Application*, Paris, Nov. 1993.

14. C. Debou, N. Fuchs, and H. Saria, "Selling Believable Technology," *IEEE Software*, Nov. 1993.

15. C. Debou, N. Fuchs, and M. Haux, "ami: a Taylorable Framework for Software Process Improvement," *Proceedings of the Second ISCN Seminar*, Vienna, Sept. 1995.

16. C. Debou, A. Kuntzmann-Combelles, and A. Rowe, "A Quantitative Approach to Software Process," *Proceedings of the 2nd International Symposium on Software Metrics*, London, Oct. 1994.

17. R. Dion, "Process Improvement and the Corporate Balance Sheet," *IEEE Software*, July 1993.

18. C. Debou, J. Lipták, and L. Pescoller, "Managing Software Process by Applying ami," *Proceedings of the MSP-92 IFAC—Annual Review in Automatic Programming*, Vol. 16, Graz, May 1992.

19. C. Debou, J. Lipták, and H. Shippers, "Decision Making for Software Process Improvement: a Quantitative Approach," *Proceedings of the 2nd International Conference on "Achieving Quality in Software," ACQUIS 93*, Venice, Italy, Oct. 1993, pp. 363–377. Also in: *The Journal of Systems and Software*, Vol. 26, 1994, pp. 43–52.

20. C. Debou, L. Pescoller, and N. Fuchs, "Software Measurements on Telecom Systems— Success Stories?" *Proceedings of the 33rd European Conference on Software Quality*, Madrid, Nov. 1992.

21. W.E. Deming, *Out of the Crisis*, MIT Press, 1982.

22. P. Fowler and S. Rifkin, *Software Engineering Process Group Guide*, CMU/SEI-90-TR-24, Sept. 1990.

23. D. Goldenson and J. Herbsleb, *After the Appraisal: a Systematic Survey of Process Improvement, its Benefits, and Factors that Influence Success*, CMU/SEI-95-TR-009, Aug. 1995.

24. V. Haase et al., "BOOTSTRAP: Fine-Tuning Process Assessment," *IEEE Software* July 1994, pp. 25–35.

25. W. Humphrey, *Managing the Software Process*, Addison-Wesley, Reading, Mass., 1989.

26. W. S. Humphrey and W.L. Sweet, *A Method for Assessing the Software Engineering Capability of Contractors*, Software Engineering Institute, Sept. 1987.

27. D. Kitson, "An Emerging International Standard for Software Process Assessment," *Proceedings of the European SEPG Conference*, Amsterdam, June 1996.

28. B. McFeeley, *IDEAL: A User's Guide for Software Process Improvement*, CM/SEI-96-HB-001, Software Engineering Institute, Feb. 1996.

29. F. McGarry et al, *Software Process Improvement in the NASA Software Engineering Laboratory*, CMU/SEI-94-TR22, Dec. 1994.

30. B. Peterson and R. Radice, *"IDEAL: an Integrated Approach to Software Process Improvement (SPI),"* SEI Symposium, Pittsburgh, Pa., Aug. 1994.

31. I. Perez, P. Ferrer, and A. Fernandez, "Application of Metrics in Industry" *Proceedings of the 3rd European Conference on Software Quality*, Madrid, Nov. 1992.

32. SPICE Consortium, *Guide for Use in Process Improvement*, Working Draft 1.0, 1995.

33. D. Rombach, "New Institute for Applied Software Engineering Research," *Software Process Newsletter*, No. 7, IEEE Computer Soc. TCSE, Fall 1996.

34. SPICE project team, *Product Specification for a Software Process Assessment Standard*, ISO/IEC JTC1/SC7/WG10 NO 16, 1993.

RECOMMENDED READINGS

ami Handbook [2]
The *ami Handbook* describes in easy terms a 12-step approach for quantitative software management. Concrete guidelines on how to set up and implement a goal-oriented measurement programme are given. The approach for devising goals and metrics is been particularly applicable for SPI initiative.

Software Process Improvement in the NASA Software Engineering Laboratory [29]
This report summarised the achievement of the Software Engineering Laboratory over the past 20 years. This report was the reference document when the SEL was rewarded by receiving the first IEEE Computer Society Software Process Achievement in 1994.

Software Engineering Process Group Guide [22]
This SEI technical report describes in details the role of the Software Engineering Process during an SPI initiative as well as the several committees and groups that need to be established. Several layers of actions plans are presented. Although useful for understanding how the initiative performs after the assessment, the report gives the wrong impression that SPI is a heavy and bureaucratic business. All the guidelines have to be tailored to each organisation.

SPICE Guide for Use in Process Improvement [32]
The *SPICE Guide for Use in Process Improvement* gives an overview in process, and describes an eight-step model covering the full improvement cycle, cultural issues, and management issues. Annexes cover very useful and innovative date like the use of the goal-oriented process measurement framework and an illustrative case study of application of the guide: a good piece of work.

IDEAL: A User's Guide for Software Process Improvement [28]
This is the most recent guide from the SEI that describes a stepwise approach to process Improvement based on experiences gathered by companies that worked with the SEI. However, "how to do things," for example, how to devise an action plan is not explained; only inputs, main actions, and outputs for each step are given.

Chapter 6

Process and Product Measurement

Gualtiero Bazzana
Marino Piotti
Onion S.p.A., Italy

INTRODUCTION

All models must be validated before we start to reuse the best practice in other projects and environments.

In the previous chapters of the book the assessment methods, experimental approaches, the Application of Metrics in Industry (ami) framework, goal trees, and the assignment of metrics to the subgoals have been discussed. In this chapter different ways of measurement are discussed, namely:

- Product measurement
- Process measurement

For both, cost benefit analysis will be of central importance.

Guidelines for the establishment of data collection plans, measurement and validation guidelines, and the establishment of a metrics database will also be given.

The chapter will emphasise that measurement is the foundation of effective process/product improvement and is, therefore, capable of being related to business needs.

Similarly, there will be reference to the "environment" in which the improvement measurement is taking place—namely, SPICE/CMM for process improvement as well as the more measurement focused projects (such as SCOPE [*Software Certification Program in Europe*]).

Thus, both the process and product metrics will provide "management" measures.

MEASUREMENT IN SOFTWARE ENGINEERING

Software Metrics: A Long History

The metrics used in the measurement of software development processes are commonly considered as also evidence of the product's characteristics. The role of the quantitative measures of the software processes/products covers a fundamental importance in all improvement paradigms.

In particular, the collection and the quantitative analysis of objective data constitutes one of the milestones of Total Quality Management programs; for instance the (Plan–Do–Check–Act) PDCA paradigm [1] devotes a complete step of the cyclic approach to process improvement (namely the "Check" step) to the quantitative analysis of the results obtained from the introduction of modifications to the processes in order to validate the effectiveness and the appropriateness of improvements before deploying the new practices within the Company Quality Management System.

All this is inserted in a context of increasing awareness of the need to verify experimentally and objectively the effectiveness of the processes, to which the various approaches followed by international quality award schemes (above all the Deming Prize, the Malcolm Baldrige [2], and the European Foundation for Quality Management (EFQMA) [3]) have significantly contributed.

This simply means that Process Improvement and Total Quality Management approaches are putting increasing importance to an experimental approach (in adherence to the Galileo scientific scheme) against the dogmatism of not substantiated "best practices"; in this light, the slogan of a major IT company is very nice: "In God we trust, all others must bring data."

Also, the ISO 9000 series set an increasing emphasis to the collection of objective data and the use of quantitative methods, although they do not embody completely the approach to continuous processes improvement.

In the second release (dated 1994) of ISO 9001[4], concerning Clause 4.20, "Statistic Techniques," it is required that both measurement needs be identified and data collection procedures be defined. Moreover, the specific norm for software (ISO 9000-3 [5]) foresees the need to use measures of both product and process to manage and check the process of development and delivery.

But what is the state of the art on software measures? As recognised also by ISO 9000-3, there are no universally agreed measures of software quality. In fact, while in the past research was focused on the definition of quality models and metrics applicable in a way independent from the context (refer to the plethora of software quality models, among which the most known are probably those by Boehm [6], Arthur [7], and Bowen [8]), in the last years it has become clear the need to characterise few and simple measures dependent from the application context and from the goals that have to be monitored.

In the meanwhile, the approach to the definition of the measures has become more rigorous (see Fenton [9]), as well as the demonstration of their statistic validity (see Schneidewind [10]) and their interpretation (refer to Hetzel [11]).

Definition of "Management by Metrics"

Management by metrics is considered as one of the most important features for the monitoring and the improvement of the software development process. But what really is management by metrics?

By management by metrics we mean "the approach to measurement in which indicators are collected as part of the process of managing software development. Metrics are seen as a standard way of measuring attributes of the software development process, such as: size, cost, defects, timeliness" [12].

The principle underlying such definition is that the only way to control a process is to measure it; it follows that the collection and interpretation of properly defined measures is the key point for the assessment of the current status of a process, the definition of the improvement actions, and the evaluation of their results (continuous improvement).

With reference to a specific software quality system and following a total quality approach, the Companywide Software Measurement System will monitor the various aspects of the software development process (contract acquisition, development cycle, subcontractors' management, maintenance, etc.), collecting measures on each project according to the criteria that directly affect the customer satisfaction (quality and timeliness of the product/service delivered) and the economic results of the business (cycle time and efficiency/productivity).

The measures collected have to be presented in graphical form, so that the management can easily control both the overall picture at a specific point, and the trend over time at various levels of detail (activity, project, customer, product line, business unit, overall process).

To sum up, the management by metrics approach is characterised by the following distinguishing features:

- Metrics are related to the company (or business unit) strategy and business
- Metrics are oriented toward managers, whose commitment is essential for the success of the initiative
- Metrics are focused on subjects like: costs, timeliness, and defects
- Data is collected at a very coarse level of granularity
- Metrics are used to monitor and drive process improvement in order to substantiate changes in an objective and quantitative way

The last point is of paramount importance; it means that the main goals of a management by metrics program are:

- To provide the quantitative information essential to single out the opportunities for improvements
- To verify the advantages of the implemented changes to the development process

It derives that a management by metrics program must be composed of two parts: the former is devoted to the identification of behavioural rules of the software producing unit, whereas the latter monitors the application of the derived rules.

The former is experimental and tries to find out meaningful correlation: we can thus compare it to physics; the latter guides quality planning and the monitoring of results: it can thus be likened to engineering.

Usage of Software Metrics

In general, software metrics can be effectively adopted in the followings four fields (for a more detailed discussion, refer to Grady [13]):

- *Support to the control of the development plans and to progress control.* In this case the used metrics are typically: resources utilization, distribution of the resources across phases, degree of completion, anticipated and consolidated product size (in lines of code, Function Points, features or other means). The usage of this kind of metrics is of paramount importance for the project leaders to monitor the status and progress of development. In case historic company indicators are available (typically relating to indicators of productivity, defect density, timeliness), the usage of this type of metrics becomes the fundamental tool to undertake the decisions that will influence the project success, for example: allocation of the resources, definition of planning milestones, planning of the start of integration of the developed components, reliability of the product for the release to the market, etc.

- *Evaluation of the quality of a software product.* In this case the measures are directly applied to the software product (code and documentation) independently from the development process in use. The objective is to attain an evaluation of the quality level of the most important product characteristics that, coherently with the standard ISO 9126 [14], can be identified as follows: functionality, reliability, efficiency, usability, maintainability, and portability. For each of such characteristics it is possible to identify sub-characteristics oriented to technical issues, for each of which one or more quantitative measures are available, often dependent from the technology and from the development process. In this field the work of international standardization bodies is very active also in the definition of the evaluation process [15]. Such measures are the basis for software product certification schemes, which, according to a specific survey [16], could constitute a complement to the certification of quality systems.

- *Quantitative evaluation of improvement opportunities.* In this case the measures constitute a classification of the original causes for the problems found in the development of a software project and/or in the exercise of a software product. Normally, these activities (commonly known as Root Cause Analysis [RCA]) are applied to the errors find in field, with the goal to understand the causes for fault insertion and for missed error detection. Consolidated techniques allow to characterise all the possible causes, to collect them, to analyse and report them (normally in the form of Ishikawa diagrams), to stratify them (typically by process phase and/or by type) and, above all, to identify (according to the Pareto principle) the set of causes of most recurrent problems, whose solution guarantees a significant improvement, thus optimising the cost/benefit ratio. For its nature, RCA is not limited to the analysis of the errors in field but can be applied in a natural way also to other types of problems, for example: scheduling slippage, low productivity, etc.

- *Validation of the effectiveness of the improvement actions.* In this case the measures are used to ascertain whether the changes inserted at organisational/methodological/technological levels had a positive impact on the quality of processes and products. To this extent, a small set of measures have to be collected and analysed along time and across various projects that are comparable.

Existing Guidelines to Set Up a Management by Metrics Program

The definition of a set of reference measures is fairly complex, owing to the large number of defined quantitative methods and, above all, the awareness that the metrics must be decided at the company level in accordance with the business goals and the peculiarities of the specific market.

In this sense it is much more important to learn and apply a sensible approach to the definition of individual metrics rather than to look for the optimal solution in the scientific literature.

The more consolidated and applied methodology for the definition of metrics is probably the Goal Question Metric technique (GQM) [17], (which is extremely effective as well as simple.

It is structured in the following steps:

- Define your goals.
- Ask the questions that you need to answer in order to give evidence of the goals.
- Define the metrics that allow you to give quantitative data for each question.

To get an overview of the metrics defined in literature, it is possible to have a look at several bibliographic references, among which the following ones are certainly very interesting:

- The methodology of ami [18] that, starting from the GQM technique, allows the application of an improvement scheme very similar in its essence to PDCA scheme, also giving at the same time a set of basic core measures.
- Metrics defined by the Software Engineering Institute in adherence to the Capability Maturity Model (CMM) [19]; it is interesting to note that the metrics have been subdivided both with respect to the company goals and with respect to the maturity levels.
- The suggested metrics from the Software Engineering Laboratory (SEL) [20]; this is a very interesting set of metrics defined in adherence to a pragmatic and bottom-up approach to processes improvement, in which quantitative measures play a central role.
- The Hewlett-Packard (HP) Company-Wide Quality Control Scheme [21, 22]: in this case very few simple metrics applied in several sites have allowed the derivation of several rules that are now declared to be adopted in all starting projects.
- The Bellcore guidelines to monitor the Quality of Service [23]: in this case a set of indicators related to a specific application domain (i.e., telecommunications) has become a de facto standard way to report the quality of delivered products and of the related service.
- The Pyramid Best-practices [24]: these show several examples of successful applications of the homonymous approach throughout Europe.
- The set of indicators proposed for covering the ISO 9126 product quality characteristics [25]: this is the first attempt to relate quantitative indicators to software product quality standard characteristics (i.e., functionality, reliability, efficiency, usability, maintainability, and portability); no quantitative feedback is available so far.

How to Set Up, Feed, and Care for a Management by Metrics Program

In order to make a metrics program of practical usefulness, a set of activities have been defined:

- Data collection
- Data integration
- Data analysis
- Reporting
- Interpretation for product and process improvement
- Interpretation for the tuning of the metrics program

In the following such aspects are briefly explained.

Data Collection

Data must be collected on a regular basis by the people responsible for the activity they refer to; this means that various bodies have to be involved (e.g.: software development, planning, configuration management, testing, etc.). It is important that basic data are collected at a fine granularity level, in order to allow several views and analysis in following steps.

Data Integration

Due to the fact that data is collected at a fine granularity level by several organisational units, the data has to be integrated at a coarser granularity (project, sub-project or functional level) to allow the research for correlation among them and subsequent interpretations.

Data Analysis

Data has to be analysed through the search for correlation among the collected indicators. The main goal is to verify that the more the activities are conducted according to what is defined in the Quality Management System and the more the indicators that refer to duration, reliability, and productivity are enhanced.

Reporting

The aim of reporting is to produce structured and easily interpretable documents to spread the information among the organisational units.
The advantages in using a well-structured reporting system are several:

- it contributes to spreading the meaning and the objectives of the metrics program to every interested organisational unit;
- it guides the collection of only useful data;
- it guarantees the visibility of the work done; and
- it constitutes the foundations upon which to base the analysis of the process and the improvement activities.

There normally are two different types of reports:

- the former is delivered quite often (e.g., on a monthly basis) and constitutes a collection of data without any interpretation;
- the latter contains the interpretation of data and is discussed with/delivered to management (e.g., on a yearly basis).

Interpretation for Product and Process Improvement

The goal of this activity is to analyse the collected data in order to derive indications both for project and process level.
   Interpretation has to be done by teams in which both Quality Representatives, Project Leaders, and Senior Management are involved.

Interpretation for Tuning the Metrics Program

The analysis of quantitative data is useful also for fine-tuning the metrics program, defining new metrics, analysing data at different granularity levels, building an historical data base, and so on.

PRODUCT MEASUREMENT

Specifying and Measuring Software Quality

The ISO 9126 Standard

The ISO/IEC 9126 is the result of the joint committee of ISO and International Electrotechnical Commission (IEC) and is published under the title *Information Technology—Software Product Evaluation—Quality Characteristics and Guidelines for Their Use* [14].
   This standard gives a definition of software quality in terms of factors and ought to represent the end of a long lasting discussion on this subject [6–8, 22, 26–29]. Its main content is the

representation of quality of software as seen by software users. Six characteristics are defined in the standard as the building blocks of software product quality. They are (see Figure 6.1):

- *Functionality:* "a set of attributes that bears on the existence of a set of functions and their specified properties. The functions are those that satisfy stated or implied needs."
- *Reliability:* "a set of attributes that bear on the capability of software to maintain its level of performance under stated conditions for a stated period of time."
- *Usability:* "a set of attributes that bear on the effort needed for use, and on the individual evaluation of such use, by stated or implied set of users."

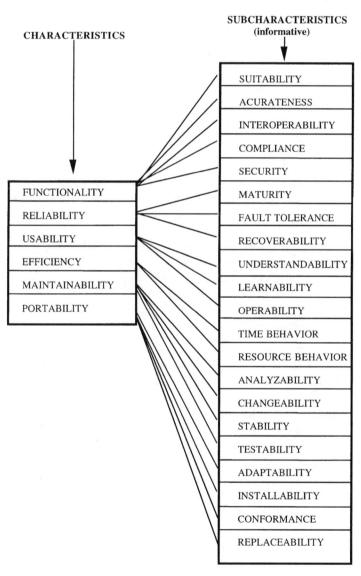

Figure 6.1.   The ISO 9126 quality model.

- *Efficiency:* "a set of attributes that bear on the relationship between the level of performance of the software and the amount of resources used, under stated conditions."
- *Maintainability:* "a set of attributes that bear on the effort needed to make specified modifications."
- *Portability:* "a set of attributes that bear on the ability of software to be transferred from one environment to another."

In addition, a short description of an "evaluation process model" is given in an informative appendix, that also defines a set of subcharacteristics that details the concepts of the above-mentioned six characteristics.

Evaluating Software Product Quality

The evaluation process model proposed by ISO 9126 has been designed so that it may in principle be applied to any phase of the development life cycle for each component of the software product.

It consists of three main stages:

- Quality Requirement Definition,
- Evaluation Preparation, and
- Evaluation Procedure.

It must be noted that the process relies on the existence of a pool of (undeclared) techniques and metrics; as a consequence, a number of detailed activities are not present. In particular, analysis and validation of metrics are considered as feeding this pool, and thus not being part of the main process. In the following, a short explanation of the three stages of the evaluation process is given.

The purpose of the initial stage (Quality Requirement Definition) is to specify requirements in terms of quality characteristics (and possibly subcharacteristics). Since a software product is composed of different components, the requirements may differ for the various components.

The purpose of the second stage (Evaluation Preparation) is to set up evaluation and to prepare its basis. It is broken down into three steps:

- *Quality metrics selection.* Here metrics that correlate to the characteristics of the software product and allow direct measurement are established. Possible metrics are numberless: every quantifiable feature of software or interaction with its environment is a candidate metric.
- *Rating level definition.* The purpose of this activity is to define the scales onto which measured values will be mapped. Moreover, scale values must be divided into ranges corresponding to the levels of satisfaction of the requirements. Another time, no general values are possible; rather, they must be defined for each specific evaluation.
- *Assessment criteria definition.* This activity must prepare a procedure for summarising the results of the evaluation of the different characteristics. For instance, decision tables or weighted averages might be used. Managerial aspects such as time and costs may also be included in the procedure.

The last stage (Evaluation Procedure) is where the evaluation is actually performed in terms of:

- *Measurement.* The selected metrics are applied to the software product, obtaining values distributed on the defined scales.

- *Rating.* For each measured level, the rating level (i.e., satisfaction) is determined.
- *Assessment.* The final step of the software evaluation process implies the summary of rated levels. By using the assessment criteria defined, a global result on the quality of the product is derived and then compared with managerial aspects (time, costs and so on) in order to take a decision.

The major evolution of the ISO 9126 are being accomplished through a number of guidelines for its usage, among which the one dedicated to the list of metrics and indicators is of particular interest [25].

PRODUCT MEASURES: A REFERENCE

A thorough overview of product metrics, both from a theoretical and pragmatic point of view is given in [30].

Such a book covers the topic in full length, including:

- An analysis of approaches to software product assessment
- The ISO 9126 model
- The underlying principles of software product measurement
- The available assessment techniques
- Metrics analysis approaches
- Tools for data collection
- Case study experiences
- Management issues in software product evaluation

In the following paragraphs, some case studies are reported in order to give a snapshot of pragmatic experiences.

An Example: Reliability Evaluation and Prediction

Despite the fact that reliability is one of the characteristics of ISO 9126 and that information technology (IT) people judge it as the most important feature for software, there exist more techniques [31] and models [32, 33] in theory than reported experiences in practice.

In the following an experience matured at Italtel Linea UT is reported [34], whose objectives can be summarised as follows:

- to try on field the pragmatic applicability of software reliability models to big industrial products;
- to test the predictive capability of such models;
- to start a software reliability measurement program; and
- to develop an integrated environment for the automatic support of time-consuming data collection and analysis activities.

Even if a large quantity of high-quality failure data was stored carefully in a fault-log system and we also had reliability tools at our disposal, we found out that applying reliability growth models in the large is not a trivial matter; through a number of trial and error experiments we came to a reference scheme that was found to be effective. As shown in Figure 6.2, the analysis strategy is composed of three main steps:

- Data analysis
- Selection of the best models and
- Analysis of the predictive capability

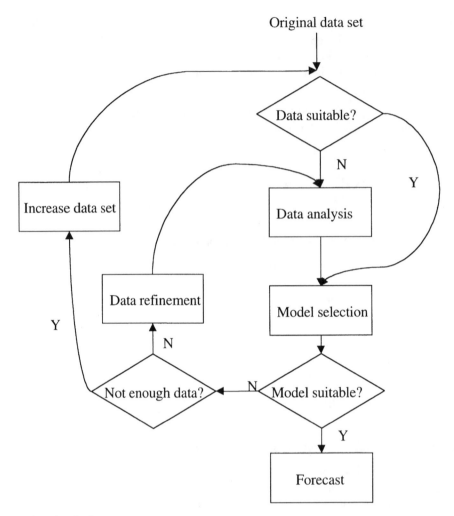

Figure 6.2. Analysis strategy.

We think that the scheme is of general validity and needs slight modifications in case the objectives to assess are a bit different from the ones of the specific experience.

Data analysis was needed on the original data set in order to cope with underlying hypotheses of models, in particular:

- there must be a growth in reliability,
- faults should be of "similar size" (i.e., they ought to cause failures at similar rates),
- failure times shall be bias-free, and
- interfailure intervals should be expressed in processor time.

Such preconditions lead both to a reduction of the data set and to changes in inter-failure times.

Concerning selection of the best model, it is known that there is no model that is best for any data set; rather, the fitness of the model must be checked for the specific data set [35]. In accordance to [36], after estimating model parameters with support of a tool [37], four selection criteria were used (accuracy, deviation, tendency, noise) to rank the most widespread reliability growth models. The results of the application of the selection criteria for the phases of Internal Validation, Qualification with the Customer and Operation showed that there was no one model that performed best for all the phases. Such conclusions could not have been reached in case the choice was made on the grounds of models assumptions. You have to use quantitative analysis based on experimental results.

The most challenging part of the work consisted in deriving expected failures and then checking with actual failures; this meant cross-checking evaluations with real results. Results were pretty good, with an average discrepancy in the range of 10 percent for all the phases. Such results are comparable to other similar reported experiences [38, 39] and give momentum to the pragmatic applicability and usefulness of reliability growth models.

The first experience was quite successful; nevertheless, it was felt that the maturity of the methods used was not sufficient to plan an application of the models within running projects. In particular, the following areas were considered critical for the success of the initiative:

- fine-tuning of the methods adopted for initial data manipulation
- validation of those software reliability models that proved to be best during the first experience onto another data set
- trial usage of models that are less stringent on the assumption of reliability growth (since this precondition prevents the application of models in the early steps of testing)

A second case study was therefore performed [40], focusing the attention on the behaviour of a whole software release of the system, that is, the whole set of software equipping the various processors of the system. The choice of considering the whole system rather than a subsystem was determined by the interest which both the provider and the customer expressed on the system reliability. A critical look at the first experience revealed some potential weaknesses in the initial phase of data manipulation, that is crucial for the overall success of a reliability program. In particular, the following areas of improvements were addressed:

- application of quantitative statistical methods (e.g., Laplace test) for detecting the point where reliability grows steadily, and
- refinement of the approach for transforming interfailure times from calendar intervals to processor times.

During the first experience one of the major drawbacks was also the time needed to make accurate predictions. These considerations suggested the adoption of S-shaped models [41]. As a matter of fact, in order to apply the models in the industrial domain, it is felt that a crucial condition is represented by the time needed to collect valid data for beginning to make accurate predictions.

In particular, an interesting point is the amount of calendar time needed for data collection before making accurate predictions. The following tables summarise, for each phase of experience 1 and 2, the following information: the time corresponding to failures excluded due to absence of reliability growth, the time needed for obtaining accurate predictions, and the time to which predictions applied. All times are expressed in calendar months.

The adoption of the S-shaped model allowed a better predictive capability as well as a contraction of the time needed to obtain good predictions as shown in the following table; this is due to the fact that the assumptions on the reliability growth trend were relaxed. In this way, time needed for getting accurate predictions can be considered almost acceptable for a fully fruitful industrial application, in particular, using the S-shaped model allowing a considerable reduction of "lost" time.

Table 6.1. Time Needed for Predictions During the First Experience

	Total Time	Time Excluded	Time Needed	Time Predicted
Validation	7	2	2	3
Qualification	7	1	2	4
Operation	20	4	8	8

Table 6.2. Time Needed for Predictions During the Second Experience

	Total Time	Time Excluded	Time Needed	Time Predicted
Qualification	6	—	2	4
Operation	13	—	6	7
Qualification & Operation	19	—	10	9

An Example: Maintainability Evaluation

Maintainability evaluation is one of the simplest product evaluation activities thanks to the availability of automatic tools (static analysers) that allow the derivation of complexity metrics that can be analysed and integrated in order to derive indications about the maintainability aspects of the software product.

Detailed experience reports are given in this book in Chapters 9 and 10.

It is very important not to also make the mistake of adopting such measures for assessing other characteristics of the software product, likewise functionality and reliability, that in the authors' experiences are scarcely correlated with the internal structure of the programs.

Complexity analysis was probably the first approach to software measurement [42]; nowadays this approach is losing part of its appeal due to the lack of evidence between software complexity and reliability and to the growth of new programming paradigms that are very difficult to measure with the classic approach, which is fit mainly for the purpose of third-generation procedural languages.

An Example: Usability Evaluation

In the following an experience report of usability evaluation is reported, matured at Italtel Linea UT. The goal consisted in the statistical evaluation of alarm logs produced by operating switching in field in order to:

- improve the usability for operators, by reducing the number and typology of alarms (that are often too many or too verbose, thus resulting in excessive documentation that cannot be analysed thoroughly);
- single out software failures not notified by users but in any case detected by Operation and Maintenance procedures; and
- collect quantitative data describing the operational profile of the product in field.

The analysis started from the collection of alarm logs produced during 1 month by eight major switches operating in field, characterised by varying size and typology.

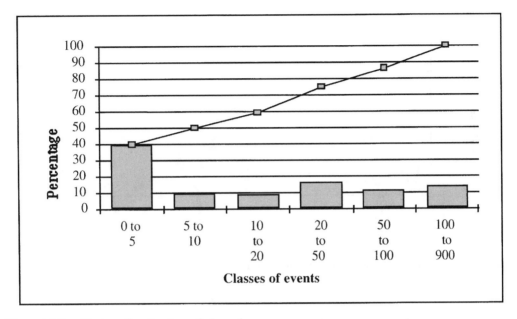

Figure 6.3.   Pareto distribution of alarm logs.

Data was then statistically analysed, paying attention, in particular, to the following aspects:

- number of alarms notified
- stratification by typology of alarm
- stratification by class of switching
- distribution within the day

A first interesting thing to note was the fact that, among 900 types of events, a group of only 5 contributed to about the 40 percent of alarms notified, as shown in Figure 6.3.

Moreover, among the first 20 events more frequently notified, it is noteworthy to distinguish that only one was pertinent to software failures, whereas the others were related to periodic audits or to anomalies in the network.

The distribution of events during the day was also very helpful to discriminate the events that caused the biggest overhead (Figure 6.4).

Figure 6.5 shows the optimization in operability (in terms of number of printed pages per month) that could be obtained simply by removing a very limited number of alarms that provided no major contribution in the monitoring of the status of the equipment.

It is possible to say that the adoption of the techniques described proved to be at the same time very simple and very useful since it provided valuable insights at both organisational and technical levels at a very low cost.

As a consequence, activities were subsequently pursued with the following aims:

- application of such analysis in a systematic way,
- introduction of the technical mechanisms needed to better the operability, and
- analysis of feedback on failures with RCA analysis activities.

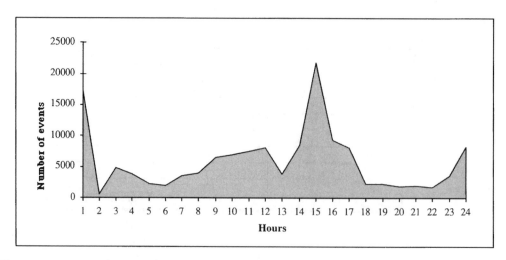

Figure 6.4.   Distribution of events during the day.

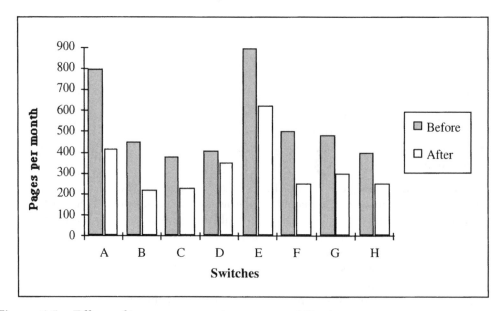

Figure 6.5.   Effects of improvement actions on operability issues.

ISO 9126 and ISO 9000: Friends or Foes?

The relationship between product and process evaluation/improvement is somewhat contro-versial [43]: Which one gives the highest return on investment? Are both necessary? Is one the precondition for the other?

The feeling of IT representatives is traced by a European-wide awareness survey (reported in [16]), that had the following goals:

Do you think that certification against ISO9000 is enough to guarantee the quality of software products?

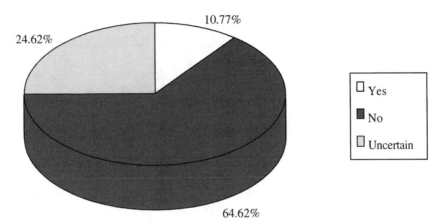

Figure 6.6.   Appraisal of ISO 9000 certification with regard to the quality of delivered products.

- To evaluate the current situation of software product evaluation and certification and, more generally, of the sensibility about software quality problems.
- To identify the needs and demands for software product evaluation and certification.
- To understand which factors and agents can influence the dissemination of this software engineering practice.
- To get a feeling about the expected relationship between product and process certification.
- To study the level of knowledge of relevant standards in this field.
- To understand how potential users would expect an evaluation service to be carried out.

In particular, a critical look at the results concerning the relationship between product and process quality reveals the following interesting aspects:

- Process certification according to ISO 9001 is felt as not enough to guarantee the quality of a specific software product (Figure 6.6).
- Software product evaluation alone is felt as not enough to understand the maturity of the development environment and thus it is better to accompany it with a process assessment (Figure 6.7), for instance, by means of the SEI CMM or BOOTSTRAP approach [44].

This concept is heavily underlined when ISO 9000 certification was considered: a very low percentage of the interviewed declared that such certification can give a sufficient guarantee of the quality of the delivered products. Product and process are closely linked and cannot be separated when quality is analysed: this is confirmed by Figure 6.7, showing that most people ask for a combined assessment (both process and product).

We stress the tight relationship that is perceived by all interviewed people, considering that no major difference in the judgement is evident looking at different roles or application domains or country (indeed, where ISO 9000 registration is more widespread—e.g., in the UK—the awareness of the need to combine it with product evaluation is particularly strong).

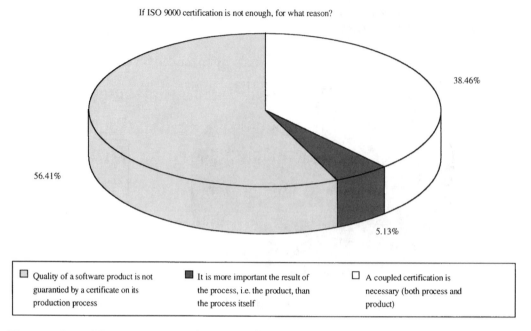

If ISO 9000 certification is not enough, for what reason?

38.46%

56.41%

5.13%

| Quality of a software product is not guarantied by a certificate on its production process | It is more important the result of the process, i.e. the product, than the process itself | A coupled certification is necessary (both process and product) |

Figure 6.7. ISO 9000 necessary but not sufficient for software product quality.

PROCESS MEASUREMENT

Measurement for Project Control and Process Management

Quoting Trodd [45], one of the key objectives of effective process management is to ensure that the results of any changes made can be measured to verify that they have resulted in improvements to performance and quality. This requires the establishment of a set of key performance indicators which are related to business goals as well as an associated set of project performance measures which provide the quantitative information from which the indicators are determined. Such indicators can then be used to help identify improvement opportunities and to quantify the improvements achieved.

An approach to implement a measurement programme to support software process management was developed by the METKIT Project; it developed a set of 20 training modules on process improvement and "Measurement as a Management Tool" [46]. A "Measurement Starter Kit" [47] was also developed to provide assistance to organisations wanting to setup a software measurement programme.

To establish an effective measurement programme a number of problems ands barriers have to be tackled, such as:

- lack of management commitment,
- imprecise or inappropriate objectives,
- unclear linkage to business and management goals,
- differing management and staff expectations,
- undefined assessment criteria,
- lack of feedback,

Table 6.3. Example of Key Performance Indicators Attached to Business Goals

Productivity	Function points (or Lines of Code) per person-month
	Cost per Function Point Count
Quality	Percentage effort spent on rework
	Percentage effort spent on reviews
	Effectiveness of reviews
	Effectiveness of system testing
	Average effort to correct defect found in development
	Percentage of bad fixes during development
Estimates	Estimated versus actual effort (variance)
	Estimated versus actual timescale (variance)

- concerns about misuse of information,
- need for cultural change, and
- long-term engagement.

Any of such problems and barriers can cause the programme to fail; ensuring that the programme and its objective are clearly linked to business and management goals is the key barrier to be tackled.

In order to overcome such problems, in [45] an Iterative approach to measurement programmes is proposed and explained in detail, consisting of steps that represent an evolution of the GQM approach, namely:

1. appoint an executive sponsor;
2. establish scope and goals;
3. define indicators, measures, and models;
4. setup a data collection infrastructure;
5. explain the programme;
6. devise success criteria;
7. set baselines and targets for indicators; and
8. develop a feedback mechanism.

In the following, it is shown the derivation process used in [45] for extracting a core basic set of metrics useful both for project management and for controlling process improvement.

First of all, key performance indicators have to be defined clearly, attached to the business goals of the software producing unit (Table 6.3).

Based on such indicators, it is possible to assess the current performance of projects by means of a set of questions (Table 6.4).

Such questions can also be complemented with other aspects used to analyse the need for improvement based on current and recent performances; for example: What factors affect productivity? Which modules cause most operational failures? What factors affect the accuracy of estimates?, etc.

Quantitative answers to the questions (and hence to the indicators) can be provided by combining a number of simple metrics, as shown in Table 6.5.

In this way we derive a set of metrics to collect to reply to all questions and thus reporting a value attached to business goals. Additional guidelines for setting up a successful measurement program can be found in [48].

Table 6.4.   Example Questions for Tracking Project Effectiveness

Productivity	Q1.1—What is the productivity of the projects? Q1.2—What is the cost of productivity?
Quality	Q1.3—What percentage of effort is spent on rework? Q1.4—What percentage of effort is spent in reviews? Q1.5—How effective are reviews? Q1.6—How effective is system testing? Q1.7—What is the avg. effort to correct defect found in development. Q1.8—What is the percentage of bad fixes during development?
Estimates	Q1.9—How accurate are project effort estimates? Q1.10—How accurate are project time-scale estimates?

Table 6.5.   Example Questions for Tracking Project Effectiveness

Productivity	Q1.1=>Size/ Actual effort Q1.2=>Size/ Development Cost
Quality	Q1.3=>Rework effort/ Total effort Q1.4=>Review effort/ Total effort Q1.5=>No. Defects detected/ (No. Defects introduced + No. Defects from earlier phases) Q1.6=>No. Defects found in system test/ Total number of defects (system test + operation) Q1.7=>Rework effort/ No. Defects corrected Q1.8=>Defects caused by bad fixes/ Defects corrected
Estimates	Q1.9=>(Actual effort - Estimated effort)/ Actual effort Q1.10=>(Actual time - Estimated time)/ Actual time

Of particular interest for those organisations that closely follow the CMM in their process improvement effort is the definition of indicators attached to the maturity levels; as a matter of fact, in [19] indicators are defined for the various maturity levels, with respect to the following categories:

- Progress
- Effort
- Cost
- Quality
- Stability
- Computer resource usage
- Training

Measurement for Tracking the Effectiveness of Process Improvement

Process improvement is sometimes advocated as the new silver bullet for software engineering. Indeed many companies are devoting a great deal of effort and investment in order to set up quality systems and raise the maturity of the software development process [49]. These efforts are based on the assumption that the best practices of software development have a positive impact on the ultimate goals of a software producing unit, namely, timeliness, productivity, and quality. We feel that a slight problem might exist: it is very difficult to quantify the gains and make them tangible; moreover, it is even harder to find out quantitative relationships between process maturity level and the achievements at a companywide level. This is a problem for the widespread adoption of process improvement.

Several experiences (e.g., [12, 20, 49–51]) report the impacts in timeliness, productivity, and quality due to the adoption of best software engineering practices. The reader is, however, always a bit sceptical since the effects are indirectly inferred: there is no quantitative evidence that the good results were in fact a consequence of process improvement. One wonders if they might be due to a change of project manager, or to good luck, or whatever. What is meant is that the software engineering community needs quantitative data showing evidence of positive correlation between process maturity levels and project results. This would be much more effective than any theoretical assumptions about good engineering practices. The reader will suddenly recognize that this approach has an intrinsic problem: we find it difficult to assign quantitative values to process maturity and to stability of the development process, in order to track improvements and their effects on final goals. This might be due to the following reasons:

- Management by-metrics schemes (see, e.g., [17, 18, 52]) which usually start from company goals; thus they derive indicators that are related to business but are not directly related to the development process.
- Standards related to quality management systems (such as ISO 9000-3 [5]) scarcely take into account process stability and maturity. All you can know is whether a company is certified or not. This could allow you to have a correlation in which the results of several companies (some of which are already certified, some not yet certified) are compared and we might analyse whether clusters exist. This sort of chart, even if utterly interesting, is very difficult to draw since no two companies use the same set of indicators and thus their results are not comparable. Even if they were, such a diagram would not help a specific company to understand whether its own QMS is working well.
- Maturity level grading ([53]), even if extremely useful, is characterised by levels that are a bit too far one from another. In order to successfully shift from one level to the following (and thus having two points on the desired diagram) you have to wait no less than 2 years. This time interval is often too long for a company to monitor whether the right path has been chosen.

It is notable that almost all improvement programs warn you about making more than one change at a time to your process, otherwise you will not be able to assess its efficacy. This is due to our limited ability to assess the effects of changes in the software development process. Unfortunately, this imposes unrealistic constraints: making one change at a time every 2 years will not advance the capabilities of software producing units to the level required by the market. As a consequence, current process assessment and improvement schemes are open to criticism with respect to their sparse data collection techniques [54] or to the small step-by-step insufficient improvement which is not aligned with total quality management.

Bringing improvements to the development process of a complex software producing unit is a time consuming, trial-and-error activity. Unless the organisation is very rigid, process improvements will not become consolidated in a short time interval; rather, different attitudes will coexist for quite a long time. Thus, some projects might fully adopt new practices (these are commonly known as 'pilot projects'), some others might incorporate new issues to a limited extent, while others will keep on with the old practices. This can be due to various reasons, such as: conclusion of a big project, severe schedule pressure, psychological resistance, etc.

As mentioned above, the SEI has proposed a set of software measures [19] that are compatible with the measurement practices of the CMM. Within this set there are two very interesting process related indicators which provide information on the stability of the process by monitoring the number of requests to change the process and the number of waivers to the process. Such indicators are "Process Change Requests" and "Waivers from Process Standards," and their interpretation is as follows:

- "Process Change Requests": a large number of requests may indicate that the defined processes are not as efficient as believed or may not be appropriate to a particular project,
- "Waivers from Process Standards": a large number of waivers granted may indicate that the processes are actually undergoing ad hoc revisions and are not as stable as believed.

The idea of defining indicators aimed at keeping track of process stability is extremely worthy and should be expanded toward statistical process control techniques. In the following, a proposal is made for a process indicator, named "Process Standardization," aimed at providing more insights within the stability of the development process and the effects of process improvements. The "Process Standardization" indicator measures the level of adherence to what is defined in the Quality Management System (QMS). In order to do so, for each activity of the development life cycle, waivers to the QMS are taken into account by means of the definition of typical "behaviours." Behaviours represent the possible attitudes through which an activity can be exploited. Such behaviours are specific for each software producing unit (SPU). It is felt that four or five behaviours are normally sufficient: one corresponding to the thorough application of the QMS principles and of the latest process improvement actions, the others attached to typical predefined waivers. Waivers can embrace all aspects of the development process but are most likely to be directed toward: the presence/absence of documentation; the way documents are written; the bounds among activities; the adoption of specific techniques, etc. At Italtel SIT BUCT, for instance, all behaviours are defined within an Operating Procedure. An example of the different behaviours defined for the system test activities is sketched in Table 6.6.

Table 6.6.   Behaviours and Waivers—an Example

Behaviour	Testing activity
1	No constraint has to be respected and no document has to be produced
2	The only constraint for starting test execution is the completion of conditioning tests.
	Test reports can be produced in a simplified way.
3	The constraints for starting test execution are: • completion of conditioning tests; • completion of coding and integration testing activities. Test reports have to be produced in accordance to QMS
4	According to the QMS (integral adoption of all standard operating procedures)
5	Fully accordance to the QMS and automation of test-suites for non-regression

Based on the aforementioned assumptions, the "Process Standardization" indicator is computed as follows:

$$PS = Sum \ ((Wi * Ci)/ \ Maxw)$$

where:

> Wi = weight associated to the adopted behaviour (Behaviours 1 to 5) Table 6.6;
> Ci = number of exploited activities; and
> $Maxw$ = weight corresponding to the full adherence to QMS and process improvement (the value 5 in Table 6.6).

Process Standardization ranges between 0 and 1, where 1 represents a situation of complete adherence to the QMS and 0 corresponds to complete deregulation, while intermediate values provide the difference between what defined into the QMS and what is actually applied. The indicator can be computed at various levels of granularity. For the purpose of keeping track of process improvement effects, it is felt that it is useful to compute it for each project both a global level and for each of the major phases of the development process. The approach has proven to be very fruitful for the following reasons:

- it provides unambiguous and quantitative evidence of the level of adoption of the QMS rules;
- the definition of expected behaviours during the planning phase allows a careful oversight of quality issues within projects, and
- the correlation between Process Standardization and indicators of the measurement system (e.g., reliability, timeliness, productivity, etc.) can be used to derive a quantitative indication of the impact of process improvement on business goals.

For details on the application of such a scheme, the interested reader is referred to [50].

Case Studies from Industrial Experiences

Experiences in metrics collection are numerous; to quote but a few we can list:

- detailed presentation of RCA activities and of the associated results [56], reported also in a subsequent chapter of this book;
- the experiences in collecting process metrics matured in the Pyramid Project [57], ranging among various application domains;
- experiences in various industrial companies in Italy [12];
- the experiences matured at Siemens worldwide [58];
- the experiences matured at Hewlett-Packard worldwide [22];
- the experiences matured at Schlumberger worldwide [59];
- the experiences matured at Bull Arizona [60];
- the experiences matured at NASA's Mission Operations Directorate [61];
- the experiences matured at Italtel RM [62]; and so forth.

Cost Benefit Analysis

Despite the many approaches to software metrication and process improvement, quantitative cost-benefit analysis for software process improvement is still a difficult area.

A cornerstone in this field consists of the analysis conducted by the SEI with results from process improvement activities conducted by a set of American companies (among which are: GTE, Hughes Aircraft, IBM, Lockheed, Motorola, Schlumberger, Siemens, Texas Instruments), with analysis of quantitative Return On Investment [63].

Table. 6.7.   Summary of the Results for 13 Organisations

Measure Category	Range	Median
Yearly cost of SPI per software engineer	$490–$2004	$1375
Productivity gain per year	9%–67%	35%
Early detection gain per year	6%–25%	22%
Yearly reduction in time to market	15%–23%	19%
Yearly reduction in postrelease defect reports	10%–94%	39%
Business value (ROI – saving/cost of SPI)	4.0–8.8	5.0

Table 6.7 summarises the results, which in any case, in the author's opinion, are scarcely reliable due to the scarce data set upon which they are based. In any case they should be taken as examples of what can be achieved when investing on SPI with constancy of purpose.

When looking for analysis of cost/benefits for single improvement actions, it is felt that the approach used in [21] could probably be the most useful.

Concerning European experiences of quantitative return on investment from Process Improvement, many expectations are put in the European Strategic Program for Research in Information Technology (ESPRIT) European Systems and Software Initiative (ESSI) Program of the European Commission, which is supporting some hundreds of Process Improvement Experiments throughout Europe and is aiming at setting up a Best-Practice Library, inclusive of quantitative data and cost/benefit analysis.

LESSONS LEARNED FROM THE APPLICATION OF METRICS PROGRAMS

Some conclusions can be stated about the usefulness and effectiveness of metrics programs

- The good
  - Metrics are able to furnish quantitative data about indicators directly connected to the goals of the software producing unit.
  - The analysis of data makes it possible to derive rules that can afterward be used in a predictive way.
  - The availability of quantitative data allows one to make knowledgeable decisions both at project level and at the level of software producing unit development process.
  - Feedback on the quality management system is copious and fruitful.
  - Programmers are mainly cooperative, since they do not perceive the metrics program as a way to measure their performance.
  - The analysis brings an increased awareness about the complexity of the processes in terms of activities and responsibilities.
- The bad
  - Tool support was underestimated and usually is bigger than expected for data collection and evaluation. If you want your data to be collected within a reasonable time interval, and if you want data granularity at a finer level than the overall project data, the additionally needed effort is high. On the contrary, it seems that tool support is negligible in some of the project work steps, such as data integration, analysis, and presentation if they are mainly based on spreadsheets.

- Time constraints sometimes prevent the right people from carefully taking part in data analysis; this results in insufficient feedback considering the impressive amount of data collected.
- Sometimes "bad" results are difficult to accept or tend to be interpreted as personal judgments.
- The ugly
  - Comparability of data across differing companies is almost impossible, due to the differing goals, cultures, and organisational structures, in addition to the differing assumptions that are behind the definition of both indicators (e.g., we have been faced with several different interpretations of "defects density" and "re-use") and raw data (e.g., what is a Line of Code [LOC]).
  - The time needed to derive useful guidelines is extremely long: a couple of years are needed to begin seeing the first correlation come out, and more time is expected before a whole set of rules will be available which pertain to software.

REFERENCES

1. L. J. Arthur, *Improving Software Quality—An Insider's Guide to TQM*, Wiley, 1992.

2. ASQC, Malcolm Baldrige—National Quality Award—Award Criteria, American Society for Quality Control.

3. European Organisation for Quality—AICQ, "The Use of Quality Award Criteria and Models for Self-assessment Purposes," *Proceedings of 1st European Forum on Quality Self-Assessment*, Milan, Mar. 1994.

4. *ISO 9001, Quality Systems—Model for Quality Assurance in Design, Development, Production, Installation and Servicing*, 2nd ed., ISO, 1994.

5. *ISO 9000-3, Quality Management and Quality Assurance Standards—Part 3: Guidelines for the Application of ISO 9001 to the Development, Supply and Maintenance of Software*, ISO, Sept. 1990.

6. B.W. Boehm et al., *Characteristics of Software Quality*, TRW Series of Software Technologies, Vol. 1, North Holland, 1978.

7. L. J. Arthur, *Measuring Programmer Quality*, John Wiley and Sons, 1985.

8. T. P. Bowen, G.B. Wigle, and J.T. Tsai, *Specification of Software Quality Attributes*, Vols. I, II, and III Rome Air Development Centre, RADC-TR-85-37, 1985.

9. N. Fenton, *Software Metrics—A Rigorous Approach*, Chapman & Hall, 1991.

10. N. Schneidewind, "Methodology for Validating Software Metrics," *IEEE Transactions on Software Engineering*, Vol. 18, No. 5, May 1992, pp. 410–422.

11. B. Hetzel, "The sorry state of the art of software measurement," *Software Quality Assurance and Measurement—A Worldwide Perspective*, N. Fenton, R. Whitty, and Y. Iizuka, eds., Thomson Computer Press, 1995.

12. G. Bazzana et al., "Software management-by-metrics: experiences in Italy," Invited paper, *Proceedings of CSR 10th Annual Conference*, Amsterdam, Oct. 1993.

13. R.B. Grady, "Successfully applying software metrics," *IEEE Software*, Vol. 27, No. 9, Sept. 1994.

14. ISO/IEC 9126, *Information Technology—Software Evaluation—Quality Characteristics and Guidelines for Their Use*, ISO, Dec. 1991.

15. ISO/ IEC JTC1/ SC7 N1317, *ISO/ IEC CD 14598—5.2 Information Technology—Evaluation of Software Product—Part 5: Evaluator's Guide.* P. Robert, ed., ISO Committee Draft, Jan. 1995.

16. G. Bazzana, et al., "ISO 9000 and ISO 9126: Friends or Foes" *Proceedings of IEEE Software Engineering Standards Symposium*, Brighton, Sept. 1993.

17. V. Basili and D. Weiss, "A Methodology for Collecting Valid Software Engineering Data," *IEEE Trans. on Software Engineering*, Vol. SE-10, Nov. 1981.

18. A. Kuntzman-Combelles et al., *Metrics Users' Handbook*, AMI Project, Cambridge, 1992.

19. J.H. Baumert and M.S. McWhinney, *Software Measures and the Capability Maturity Model*, CMU/SEI-92-TR-25, Sept. 1992.

20. SEL, NASA Goddard Space Flight Center, *Software Engineering Laboratory Relationships, Models and Management Rules*, SEL-91-001, Feb. 1991.

21. R.B. Grady and D.L. Caswell, *Software Metrics: Establishing a Company-wide Program*, Prentice-Hall, 1987.

22. R.B. Grady, *Practical Software Metrics for Project Management and Process Improvement*, Prentice-Hall, 1992.

23. Bellcore—Bell Communication Research, *Reliability and Quality Measurements for Telecommunications Systems (RQMS)*, Technical Reference: TR-TSY-000929, June 1990.

24. Pyramid Consortium, *Quantitative Management: Get a Grip on Software!* Technical Reference: EP-5425 Y 91100-4, Dec. 1991.

25. M. Azuma, *Information Technology—Software Product Evaluation—Indicators and Metrics*, ISO/JTC1/SC7/WG6 Project 7.13.3, Working Draft, Mar. 1993.

26. A.C. Gillies, *Software Quality—Theory and Management*, Chapman & Hall Computing, 1992.

27. M.S. Deutsch and R.R. Willis, *Software Quality Engineering*, Prentice Hall, 1988.

28. T. Forse, *Qualimetrie des systèmes complexes*, Les Editions d'Organisation, 1989.

29. A.Von Maryhauser, *Software Engineering Methods and Management* Academic Press, 1990.

30. R. Bache and G. Bazzana, *Product Metrics for Software Assessment*, McGraw-Hill, London, 1994.

31. G.Bazzana et al., "Assessing the Reliability of Software Products," *ESREL Conference*, Munich, May 1993.

32. J.D. Musa, A. Iannino, and K. Okumoto, *Software Reliability—Measurement, Prediction, Application*, McGraw-Hill, 1987.

33. M. Xie, *Software Reliability Modelling*, World Scientific, 1992.

34. G. Bazzana et al., "Applying Software Reliability Models to a Large Industrial Dataset," *Information and Software Technology*, Nov./Dec. 1993.

35. R. Troy and R. Moawad, "Assessment of Software Reliability Models," *IEEE Transactions on Software Engineering*, Vol. SE-11-6, No. 9, Sept. 1985.

36. S. Brockelhurst and B. Littlewood, "New Ways to Get Accurate Reliability Measures," *IEEE Software*, July 1992.

37. Reliability and Statistical Consultants, Ltd., "Software Reliability Modelling Programs," May 1988.

38. D.A. Christenson, "Using Software Reliability Models to Predict Field Failure Rates in Electronic Switching Systems," *Proceedings National Security Industrial Association Annual Joint Conference on Software Quality and Reliability*, Washington, D.C., 1988.

39. B. Lennselius and L. Rydström, "Software Fault Content and Reliability Estimation for Telecommunications Systems," *IEEE Journal on Selected Areas in Communications*, Vol. 8, No. 2, Feb. 1990.

40. G. Bazzana et al., "An Industrial Approach to Software Reliability and Security through Testing," *AFCEA Conference*, Rome, 1994.

41. S. Yamada, Ohba, M., and Osaki, "S-Shaped Reliability Growth Modelling for Software Error Detection," *IEEE Transaction on Reliability*, Vol. R-32, No. 5, 1983.

42. T.J. McCabe, "A Complexity Measure," *IEEE Transactions on Software Engineering*, 1976.

43. T.E. Vollman, "Software Quality Assessment and Standards," *IEEE Computer*, June 1993.

44. P. Kuvaia et al., *Software Process Assessment & Improvement: The Bootstrap Approach*, Blackwell, 1994.

45. E. Trodd, *A Minimum Set of Metrics for Effective Process Management*, Proceeding of SP-ISCN 96 Conference, Brighton, Dec. 1996.

46. METKIT Consortium and BRAMEUR Ltd., METKIT Industrial Package, 1994.

47. Brameur Ltd., A Starter Kit for Setting up a Measurement Programme, 1994.

48. L.C. Briand, C.M. Differding, and H.D. Rombach, "Practical Guidelines for Measurement Based Process Improvement," *Proceeding of SP-ISCN 96 Conference*, Brighton, December 1996.

49. J. Herbsleb et al., "Benefits of CMM-Based Software Process Improvement: Initial Results," *SEI Technical Report*, Aug. 1994.

50. G. Damele et al., "Quantifying the Benefits of Software Process Improvement in Italtel Linea UT Exchange," *International Switching Symposium 95*, Berlin, April 1995.

51. M.A. Cusumano, "Japan's Software Factories," Oxford University Press, 1991.

52. AT&T, *Process Quality Management and Improvement Guidelines*, AT&T Quality Steering Committee, Issue 1.1, 1988.

53. M.C. Paulk et al., *Capability Maturity Model for Software*, CMU/SEI-91-TR-24, ADA240603, SEI, Carnegie Mellon University, Pittsburgh, Pa, 1991.

54. T.B. Bollinger and C. McGowan, "A Critical Look at Software Capability Evaluations," *IEEE Software*, July 1992.

55. H. Kumi, "Quality Management by ISO-9000 and by TQM," *Proceedings of EOQ 93*, Helsinki, Finland.

56. G. Damele et al., "Process Improvement through Root Cause Analysis," *AQUIS '96*, Florence, Jan. 1996.

57. K.H. Moeller and D.J. Paulish, *Software Metrics: a Practitioner's Approach to Improved Software Development*, Chapman & Hall, 1992.

58. D.J. Paulish, *Case Studies of Software Process Improvement Methods*, SEI Technical Report, CMU/SEI-93-TR-26 ESC-TR-93-200, Dec. 1993.

59. H.Wohlwend and S. Rosenbaum, "Software Improvements in an International Company," *Proceedings of the 15th ICSE*, IEEE Computer Soc. Press, 1993.

60. E.F. Weller, "Using Metrics to Manage Software Projects," *IEEE Computer,* Vol. 27, No. 9, Sept. 1994.

61. G. Stark, R.C. Durst, and C.W. Vowell, "Using Metrics in Management Decision Making," *IEEE Computer,* Vol. 27, No. 9, Sept. 1994.

62. G. Bazzana et al., "Quantifying the Benefits of Software Testing: an Experience Report from the GSM Application Domain," *Proceedings of Objective Quality Conference,* Florence, 1995.

63. J. Herbsleb et al., "Software Process Improvement—State of the Pay-Off," *American Programmer,* Vol. 7, No. 9, Sept. 1994.

Chapter 7

Costs and Benefits of Software Process Improvement

Khaled El Emam and Lionel Briand

Fraunhofer—Institute for Experimental Software Engineering, Germany

INTRODUCTION

In recent years a substantial number of organisations have gained experience in software process improvement (SPI). Furthermore, some researchers have studied such organisations by collecting and analysing costs and benefits data on their SPI efforts. The objective of this chapter is to review and summarise the empirical evidence thus far on the costs and benefits of SPI. The intention is that this review would be utilised to support the business case for initiating and continuing SPI programs, to aid in the selection amongst the alternative improvement paradigms, to make more accurate estimates of the costs and benefits of such efforts, and to help set and manage the expectations of technical staff and management.

The need for such a review is supported by the results of two recent surveys that were conducted by the SEI. The first survey was administered to individuals at the National SEPG Conference in 1993 and at an SPI tutorial during the Software Engineering Symposium in 1993 [25]. The respondents represented organisations that had mature SPI programs. More than 70 percent stated that they need information on the benefits of SPI (by choosing the "very high" or "high" response category in terms of characterising their needs), which was also ranked as the highest need of the respondents. This indicates a need for consolidation of the evidence on the benefits of SPI. The second survey solicited information from organisations that had conducted software process assessments, published in 1995 [26]. The results indicate that 77 percent of the respondents "Strongly Agree" or "Agree" that SPI has taken longer than expected and 68 percent stated that SPI has cost more than expected. This indicates a need for information to help estimate the costs of SPI and to set and manage expectations from SPI.

Two general paradigms to SPI have emerged, as described by Card [10]. The first is the analytic paradigm. This is characterised as relying on "quantitative evidence to determine where improvements are needed and whether an improvement initiative has been successful." The second, the benchmarking paradigm, "depends on identifying an 'excellent' organisation in a field and documenting its practices and tools." Benchmarking assumes that if a less-proficient organisation adopts the practices of the excellent organisation, it will also become excellent. These SPI paradigms are covered in this chapter. Readers can select the data that is most applicable to the SPI paradigm that they intend to use or are using.

Empirical studies that have been conducted do not answer all of the questions about SPI; those that have been answered are not to the level of detail that some may wish. However, the available data do provide us with credible guidance in our SPI efforts, which is undoubtedly preferable to no guidance.

As the title suggests, the chapter is divided into two main parts. The first presents data on the costs of SPI, and the second on the benefits of SPI. In the second part we also use results from the empirical research literature to provide some guidelines to help attain the promised benefits of SPI. Subsequently, we discuss some methodological issues pertinent to benefits studies in order to give the reader an appreciation of the issues involved in doing this kind of work and also to help interpret future benefits data.

THE COSTS OF SOFTWARE PROCESS IMPROVEMENT

The most common and interpretable measures of the costs of SPI are in terms of dollars and/or effort. A recent study sponsored by the U.S. Air Force [6] found that government organisations tend to characterise investments in process improvement in terms of costs, whereas industry tends to characterise it in terms of effort expended on SPI activities. In some cases, cost measures such as calendar months have also been used. The studies that we summarise below show the costs of SPI using different analytical and benchmarking approaches. The amount of detail that we can present is directly a function of the amount of publicly available information.

Costs of Assessment and Improvement Based on the CMM

A number of companies have published the cost details of their process improvement efforts based on the CMM. Some of these are summarised in Table 7.1. Another study conducted at the SEI determined the amount of time it takes organisations to increase their maturity levels on the CMM for the first three levels [28]. The distribution of assessments that used the original SPA method and the replacement CBA-IPI method in the data set is not clear however, and whether any differences in method would have had any effect on the time it takes to move up one maturity level.

Two groups of organisations were identified: those that moved from level 1 to level 2, and those that moved from level 2 to level 3. On average, it takes organisations 30 months to move from level 1 to level 2. Those organisations, however, varied quite dramatically in the amount of time it takes to move up one maturity level. A more reliable measure would be the median. In this case, the median was 25 months. Organisations that moved from level 2 to level 3 took on average 25 months (the median was also 25 months).

It is expected that the size of the organisation would have a significant impact on the number of months it takes to move from one maturity level to another. The variation in the size of the organisational units that were assessed was not given in the report, however. Therefore,

Table 7.1.   Verification & Validation, Organisational Experiences Illustrating the Costs and Benefits of SPI

Ref.	Organisation & SPI Program	Costs	Benefits
[30]	• SPI effort at the Software Engineering Division of Hughes Aircraft • The division had 500 professional employees at the time	• The assessment itself cost U.S. $45,000 • Cost of a 2-year SPI program was U.S. $400,000 • Implementation of the action plan to move from ML1 to ML2 was 18 calendar months	• Achieved annual savings of U.S. $2M • Benefits were calculated to be five times the improvement expenditures • Quality of work life had improved (e.g., fewer overtime hours by the software engineers)
[44]	• SPI effort led by the Schlumberger Laboratory for Computer Science	• Large engineering centres (120–180 engineers) have 1–5 full-time staff on SPI Smaller centres (50–120 engineers) have up to 3 full-time staff on SPI	• Improved project communication • Customer reports confirm that product quality has improved • Improved time to market by reducing requirements validation cycles to 15 from 34 • More than double previous productivity • Increased percentage of projects completed on schedule from 51% to 94% • Halved the defect density in the products
[6] [7]	• Data was collected from 33 companies using questionnaires and/or interviews	• The authors present examples of data on the costs of activities related to SPI • For example, some organisations increased from 7% to 8% of total effort on data collection, and increase up to 2% of project costs on fixing design defects	• Some organisations witnessed increased productivity, reduced defect levels, reduced rework effort, reduction in costs and greater within estimate project completions • In particular, some organisations achieved a ROI of 10:1 • Other benefits included less overtime and employee turnover, and increased cooperation between functional groups

Continued

Table 7.1.   *(Continued)*

Ref.	Organisation & SPI Program	Costs	Benefits
[8]	• Corporatewide SPI effort at AlliedSignal Aerospace starting in 1992	• Using data on SEPG investment measured in full-time equivalent headcount for eight sites, the maximum was 4%	• A 7:1 productivity increase in the calendar time to generate documents over 1000 pages with a 50% reduction in the cost per page • Independent V&V deficiency reports on the documentation have decreased to approximately zero • LOC maintained per person has increased by 50% and testing time has decreased by 60% with no evident increase in delivered defects
[14]	• Organisation is the Software Systems Laboratory in Raytheon, employing 400 software engineers • SPI initiative started in 1988; results reported after five years • Organisation has progressed from Level 1 to Level 3 during that period	• U.S. $1 million invested every year	• A 7.7:1 return on every dollar invested • Rework costs reduced from 41% of overall project costs to 11% • More projects finish ahead of or on schedule and under or on budget • Productivity increases by a factor of 2.3 in 4.5 years • Software engineers spend fewer late nights and weekends on the job and improved general morale

these results should be taken as general guidelines to check an organisation's own estimates of the time it takes to move up the maturity ladder.

Another study of U.S. companies found results that are consistent with those mentioned above [6]. It was found that organisations at level 2 spend between 12 to 36 months at level 1 with an average of 21 months, and organisations at level 3 had spent 22-24 months at level 1 with an average of 23 months. Organisations at level 3 spent from 12 to 20 months at level 2 with an average of 17.5 months. This is corroborated with data from the improvement efforts at AlliedSignal [8] where advancement from Level 1 to 2 and from Level 2 to Level 3 took 12 to 14 months across different sites.

Effort to Rate A Process Instance

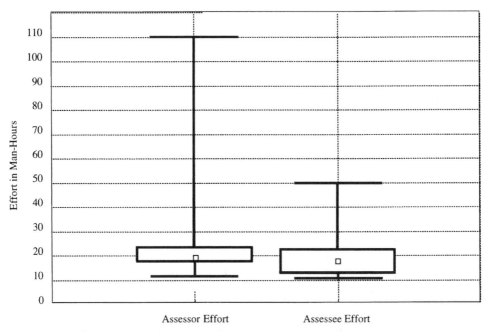

Figure 7.1.   Effort in person-hours to judge and rate the adequacy of a process instance for each of the five SPICE process categories.

Costs of Assessments Based on SPICE

During the SPICE trials (see Chapter 12 for more details), data was collected on the amount of effort it takes to conduct an assessment. The median value for an assessment was found to be 110 person hours. This was based on data collected from the ratings of 324 process instances during the SPICE trials. Variation, however, was quite substantial ranging from approximately 33 person-hours to 824 person-hours. These numbers include total assessor and assessee effort. Of course, one explanation for this is the fact that some assessments rated much more process instances than others.

The box-plots for the assessor and assessee effort per process instance rated are shown in Figure 7.1. The median total effort spent by the assessment team members per process instance is 8.3 person hours. This number excludes the effort to fill up the forms and questionnaire that were required by participants in the SPICE trials. However, the overall variation is very large. The minimum value is 1.4 person-hours per process instance and the maximum was 100 person hours. The median total effort spent by the employees of the assessed organisational unit per process instance was 7.6 person-hours. The variation again was large, ranging from a minimum of 0.7 person-hours per process instance to a maximum of 40 person-hours.

Ongoing work by the SPICE trials team focuses on explaining the variation that was seen in this data. However, the current results can still be utilized as an aid in estimating assessment effort.

Why is there so much variation among assessors than among assessees? A possible explanation is the fact that assessees are invited to predefined sessions according to an interview plan, while the assessors have to deal with many such interviews. Thus all delays per interview might largely sum up over the number of interviews.

Costs of Registration to ISO 9001

A multiple regression model has recently been constructed to estimate the effort it would take an organisation to meet the requirements of ISO 9001 [40]. Data was collected from 28 software organisations that were registered to ISO 9001 in Canada and the United States. There are two inputs to the model: (1) the size of the organisation in number of employees, and (2) the degree of noncompliance to ISO 9001 clauses. Noncompliance is a comparison of the fulfilled points with the total number of ISO 9001 checkpoints. Both sets of data were collected by questionnaire and a sample of responses were verified with the respondents to increase confidence in the reliability of the responses. The model to predict effort in person-months is:

$$\text{Ln (effort)} = -2.793 + 0.692 * \text{Ln } (x_1) + 0.74 * \text{Ln } (x_2)$$

where:

x_1 = number of employees within the scope of registration
x_2 = degree of compliance of the organisation to the ISO 9001 clauses prior to the improvement effort

The model was validated using data collected from five organisations that were not included in the model development sample. A brief comparison of the model prediction versus the actual effort is given in Table 7.2.

Costs of Measurement-Based Process Improvement

Measurement-based process improvement relies on the acquisition of data and factual information in order to suggest process improvement actions. As opposed to the models presented above, it does not rely on a generic model of software development and predefined improvement steps (an overview of this approach to SPI is given in [4]). In the context of measurement-based process improvement, another advantage is that precise cost information is usually readily available and can therefore be used for computing quantitative and objective cost estimates. However, it is difficult to determine to which extent the cost figures below are comparable to the ones presented for CMM, SPICE, and ISO-9001. The cost of measurement implies a con-

Table 7.2.   Comparison of Actual Versus Predicted Effort for ISO 9001 Registration

Org. #	Size	Non-compliance (%)	Predicted	Actual	Residual
1	175	35	30.3	31.2	0.9
2	108	15	11.6	13	1.4
3	170	30	26.5	27	0.5
4	45	100	25.8	36	10.2
5	100	70	34.4	37	2.6

tinuous support to projects and not just a one-time snapshot of the software processes in an organisation. In addition, the benefits of measurement-based process improvement also include a better manageability of projects as well as supporting process improvement activities. It also provides a much more detailed characterisation of processes and, more importantly, provides insight into the products of these processes.

In order to assess the cost of measurement-based process improvement, we will use four main sources for which data are in the public domain: NASA GSFC Software Engineering Laboratory (SEL) [2], Motorola [12], Hewlett-Packard [27], and Philips Sound & Vision [41]. The results seem to be consistent across these four organisations. They all seem to indicate that the cost of measurement itself (collecting, checking, storing, and analysing data) should not exceed 1 or 2 percent of the project resources. However, additional effort has to be planned for technology transfer if an organisation wants to make improvement possible. A careful introduction and tailoring of new technologies will take substantial effort but we do not believe there is any other alternative for improvement.

At the NASA GSFC SEL, about 10 percent of the cost of development is invested in SPI activities including research (designing studies and analysing results), technology transfer (producing standards and policies), and data processing (collecting forms and maintaining databases), the latter accounting for less than 2 percent of the cost. At Motorola, data collection activities represent roughly 1 percent of project resources. Philips Sound & Vision reports a cost of approximately 1 percent, including both data collection and the introduction of inspections. The discrepancy between these figures is in part due to the strong involvement of the NASA GSFC SEL in research activities related to measurement-based SPI and to the fact that these four organisations did not report cost in a consistent manner.

THE BENEFITS OF SOFTWARE PROCESS IMPROVEMENT

The types of studies that document the benefits of SPI include organisations that have used the CMM, organisations that have used ISO 9001, and organisations that have followed other models. Benefits data is also available for organisations that have followed measurement-based improvement programs.

Benefits of Improvement Based on the CMM

Examples of organisations that have documented the benefits of improvement based on the CMM are summarised in Table 7.1. Studies that have investigated the benefits of higher maturity level scales on the CMM based on a statistical analysis of data from a larger number of organisations are summarised in Table 7.3.

Benefits of Registration to ISO 9001

Many software organisations are being audited against the clauses of ISO 9001. A number of surveys have been conducted that evaluate the benefits of ISO 9001 registration in industry. Some of the results of these surveys have been presented in [43] and are summarised in Table 7.4.

With respect to registration to ISO 9001, the few studies that have been conducted seem consistent in their findings that it can bring benefits. However, many of these studies were not specific to software organisations. Therefore, more research specifically with software organisations would help the community better understand the effects of registration.

Table 7.3.   Summaries of the Benefits of Higher Maturity Level Scores on the CMM

Ref.	Description of Study	Results
[26]	• Survey of individuals whose organisations have been assessed against the CMM • The authors tested the relationship between maturity levels and subjective measures of effectiveness	For the first three maturity levels, organisations at higher maturity levels tend to perform better on the following dimensions (respondents chose either the "excellent" or "good" response categories when asked to characterise their organisation's performance on these dimensions): • ability to meet schedule, • product quality • staff productivity • customer satisfaction, and • staff morale. The relationship with the ability to meet budget commitments was not found to be statistically significant.
[35]	• Correlation study that investigated the benefits of moving up the maturity levels of the CMM • They obtained data from historic U.S. Air Force contracts; two measures were considered: (1) cost performance index which evaluates deviations in actual vs. planned project cost, and (2) schedule performance index which evaluates the extent to which schedule has been over/under-run	• generally, higher-maturity projects approach on target cost • generally, higher-maturity projects approach on-target schedule
Chapter 8 of this book	• Implementation of a company wide improvement programme based on CMM like assessments and a methodology to estimate improvement potentials and priorities	They report the following experimental reductions in error costs based on maturity levels: • 17% from Level 1 to Level 2 • 22% from Level 2 to Level 3 • 19% from Level 3 to Level 4 • 44% from Level 4 to Level 5
Chapter 9 of this book	• Implementation of a companywide improvement program based on BOOTSTRAP assessments and a metrics driven action plan	• *Efficacy* and *Productivity* show a significant growth • *Timeliness for the Customer* tends to decrease, resulting in about a maximum of 10% scheduling deviation • *Fault density in operation*, after a decisive improvement, shows stability on values which are felt as satisfactory.

Table 7.4.   Surveys of the Benefits of Registration to ISO 9001

Description of Survey	Overview of Some Relevant Findings
A survey conducted in 1993 had 292 responses with almost 80% of the responding organisations being registered to ISO 9001	• 74% felt that the benefits of registration outweighed the costs • 54% received favourable feedback from their customers after registration
A survey of companies in the UK had 340 responses from companies that were registered	• It was found that 75% of the respondents felt that registration to ISO 9001 improved their product and/or service.
A survey of companies that were registered in the U.S.A. and Canada with 620 responses	• The most important internal benefits to the organisation included: better documentation (32.4%), greater quality awareness (25.6%), a positive cultural change (15%), and increased operational efficiency/productivity (9%); and • The most important external benefits to the organisation included: higher perceived quality (33.5%), improved customer satisfaction (26.6%), gaining a competitive edge (21.5%), and reduced customer quality audits (8.5%).
A survey of 45 software organisations in Europe and North America that have become ISO 9001 registered	• 26% reported maximum benefit from increased efficiency • 23% reported maximum benefit from increased product reliability • 22% reported maximum benefit from improved marketing activity • 14% reported maximum benefit from cost savings, and • 6% reported maximum benefit from increases exports

Source: [43].

Benefits of Improvement Using Other Models

Two studies have evaluated models that measure the maturity of software organisations. The two studies that we review are summarised in Table 7.5.

Benefits of Measurement-Based Improvement

With respect to measurement-based software process improvements, the benefits reported in the literature vary significantly. This is to be expected because the impact of measurement-based process improvement will depend on the initial level of maturity of the organisation, the complexity of the systems under development, and varying factors over the period of measurement. The results seem to suggest very significant improvements both in terms of productivity and quality. A summary of the benefits is given in Table 7.6. Such levels of improvement obviously outweigh costs such as those described earlier in this chapter and therefore

Table 7.5. Studies Investigating the Benefits of SPI Using Models and Methods Other than the CMM and ISO 9001

Ref.	Description of Study	Overview of Relevant Findings
[17]	A questionnaire was developed to measure the maturity of Management Information Systems (MIS) organisations along four orthogonal dimensions. These four dimensions were: (1) standardization, (2) project management, (3) tools, and (4) organisation. The authors investigate the relationship between maturity and the success of the requirements engineering process (RE success). Two dimensions of RE success were measured [18]: the quality of RE service, and the quality of RE products.	The relationship between the organisation dimension and the quality of service was found to be moderate (a Pearson correlation coefficient of 0.58) and was statistically significant. The relationships with the quality of RE products were all small or nonexistent and not statistically significant.
[32]	Jones presents the results of an analysis on the benefits of moving up the seven-level maturity scale of Software Productivity Research (SPR) Inc.'s proprietary model. This data was collected from SPR's clients.	His results indicate that as organisations move from Level 0 to Level 6 on the model they witness (compound totals): • 350% increase in productivity • 90% reduction in defects • 70% reduction in schedules

demonstrate the cost effectiveness of measurement-based process improvement. But measurement, like assessment, does not create improvement. It just makes it possible and supports it. For example, investing in measurement and neglecting technology transfer would not be likely to pay off as a process-improvement strategy. This is why these results should be interpreted with care since they do not imply that measurement in itself will lead to improvement.

ATTAINING THE BENEFITS FROM PROCESS IMPROVEMENT

Strong business interests by suppliers and users of software process improvement models and methods demand that there is empirical evidence demonstrating benefits. The above review of the empirical evidence supports the contention that software process does matter. The individual organisational experiences show that SPI can increase effectiveness, and the surveys show that on average organisations that do implement what are believed to be good software processes are better than those that do not or do less. However, attaining the benefits of SPI is not necessarily a simple matter of implementing a list of processes or process management practices. A detailed analysis of the empirical literature helps provide some guidelines to consider while pursuing an SPI effort.

Evidence for Customising Improvement Efforts

The surveys reviewed above seem to show that substantial benefits would be gained from SPI. But do organisations that focus on process always benefit? Existing evidence suggests that the extent to which an organisation's effectiveness improves due to the implementation of good software processes or software management practices is dependent on the characteristics of the

Table 7.6. Benefits of Measurement-Based Improvement

Description of Study	Overview of Relevant Findings
SPI efforts at NASA GSFC Scope: Flight Dynamics Division (FDD) Data that has been collected over a period of 20 years and 100 projects at the NASA GSFC SEL. The complexity of the flight dynamics software developed has tremendously increased over the years. Around 300 software engineers in the FDD Use the G/Q/M approach to measurement	• Cost to deliver decreased 58% in 5 years due mainly to an increase in reuse • Error rates per KSLOC decreased by 35% in 10 years (from 8.4 to 5.3 errors/KSLOC) • Improved ability to predict, control, and manage the cost and quality of software being produced.
SPI efforts at Hewlett-Packard Scope: Companywide initiative	• Three fold increase in productivity over 4 years • 80% reduction in defect density over 4 years • Reduction of the number of major defects during postrelease period • Predict testing completion within 10% of its actual duration and effort
SPI effort at Philips Sound & Vision Scope: data collected on three projects representing an effort of 60 staff-years Software for consumer electronics products CMM level 2 organisation	• Saved 10% of effort through early detection of defects • Reduced life cycle time
SPI effort at Motorola Scope: Companywide initiative 1 division of 350 software engineers 1 division of 70 engineers Use the Q/G/M approach to measurement	• One division achieved a 50 times reduction in defect density over 3.5 years. • Significant cost reduction due to improved quality • Better project management, e.g., Improved ship-acceptance criteria and schedule estimation accuracy • In general, the overall cost is acceptable and justified

project(s) and the organisation. However, the overall evidence remains equivocal as to which factors moderate the relationship between process and effectiveness.

For example, in [17] the relationship between some dimensions of maturity and the success of the requirements engineering process was investigated. As summarised in Table 7.5, it was found that only one dimension of maturity was related to success. This may indicate that the relationship is moderated (e.g., the magnitude of the relationship is different for large vs. small organisations). A number of possible moderating variables were considered.

A possible moderating variable is the size of the MIS organisation. For example, there have been some concerns that the implementation of some of the practices in the CMM, such as a separate Quality Assurance function and formal documentation of policies and procedures, would be too costly for small organisations [5]. Therefore, the implementation of certain processes or process management practices may not be as cost-effective for small organisations as for large ones. To investigate the possibility that benefits depend on the size of the organisation, the sample of MIS organisations was divided into those that were small (less than 100 employees) and those that were large (100 or more employees). Then the correlation between maturity and RE success was compared for the small and large MIS organisations. This analysis shows that there are no differences in the correlation between small and large organisations for all the dimensions of maturity. Therefore, MIS organisation size does not seem to moderate the relationship. This result is consistent with that found in [26] for organisation size and [13] for project size, but is at odds with the findings from [5].

To further confuse the issue, an earlier investigation [37] studied the relationship between the extent to which software development processes are standardized and MIS success. It was found that standardisation of life cycle processes was associated with MIS success in smaller organisations but not in large ones. This is in contrast to the findings cited above. Therefore, it is not clear how organisation size moderates the benefits of process and the implementation of process management practices.

Another possible moderating variable is the business sector of the organisation. A study on the benefits of higher CMM maturity did not find differences in terms of benefits for different industrial sectors [26]. Another study that investigated the effects of process implementation on meeting schedule and budget targets and on product quality did not, in general, find different effects for military versus nonmilitary projects [13]. An alternative differentiation is between government and non-government organisations. Using the data set in [17], the organisations were divided, but this time depending on whether they were government organisations or not. Then the correlation between maturity and RE success was compared for these two groups. This analysis indicates that there are no large differences in the correlation between government and non-government organisations for all the dimensions of maturity. Although, on the Project Management dimension, the difference does approach statistical significance (two-tailed $p = 0.07$), indicating that potentially the relationship between the Project Management maturity dimension and the quality of RE service is larger for government organisations. This indicates that business sector *may have* a small moderating effect on the maturity $\leftrightarrow$ RE success relationship.

Size and industrial sector are not the only factors that may have an effect on the benefits of process improvement. A study investigated the effects of user participation in the process and RE success [20]. It was found that the extent of uncertainty about information requirements had an impact on the degree to which user participation in the requirements engineering process was beneficial. Therefore, project uncertainty is another factor to consider when determining the benefits of implementing "good" practices.

The implication of the results presented above is that following stipulations about implementing certain processes or process management practices across the board (i.e., irrespective of the organisational and project characteristics) is ill advised. This is so until more consistent empirical evidence can be furnished. Meanwhile, one should evaluate the specific contexts of the organisation and projects before selecting process improvement actions and customise SPI efforts to local conditions.

Evidence for Considering Nonprocess Factors

None of the studies reviewed establishes a causal relationship, i.e., that process improvement is the cause of benefits that are witnessed. To establish causation one must at least rule out other possible causal factors that could have led to the benefits witnessed over the same period. Also, experience reports documenting benefits of SPI would have to rule out natural progress (i.e., if the organisation did not make any changes, would they have achieved the same benefits?).

It is clear that implementation of processes or process management practices are not the only factors that will influence effectiveness. Bach [1] has made the argument that individual software engineer capabilities constitute a critical factor having an impact on project and organisational effectiveness. He even goes further, stating "that the only basis for success of any kind is the 'heroic efforts of a dedicated team'." The importance of individual capability is supported by empirical research. For instance, a study found that the capabilities of the lead architect were related to the quality of requirements engineering products [16]. Another study found a relationship between the capability of users participating in the requirements engineering process and its success [21]. Other field studies of requirements and design processes also emphasized the importance of individual capabilities [11, 19].

The implementation of automated tools has been advocated as a factor that has an impact on effectiveness. This assertion is supported by empirical research. For instance, a study of the implementation of an Information Engineering toolset achieved increases in productivity and decreases in postrelease failures [24].

The best that can be attained with studies that focus only on process factors is strong evidence that SPI is associated with some benefits or that organisations *could* benefit from SPI activities. In order to improve our understanding of the influences of other factors on effectiveness more sophisticated empirical studies would have to be conducted. These would include building multivariate models that take the influence of nonprocess factors into account and investigate the interactions between process and nonprocess factors. Thus far, most studies have been limited to primarily bivariate analyses.

The message from current research, however, is that there are other nonprocess factors that do have an impact on organisational and project effectiveness. It would not be prudent to focus only on process and forget everything else. SPI should be part of an overall strategy that addresses, at least, weaknesses in people capabilities and the needs for tool support. Furthermore, the success of SPI is strongly influenced by the approach used for implementation of new practices. For example, a good practice may not provide anticipated benefits because the implementation was not performed properly.

Evidence for Goal-Directed Improvement

It has been shown that different processes have different impacts on the same measures of effectiveness. For example, a study that examined the effect of four dimensions of organisational maturity on the success of requirements engineering processes found that some maturity dimensions are related to success, while others were not [17]. In particular, the dimensions measuring standardisation, project management, and tools were found to be unrelated to success; but the organisation dimensions were related to success. Another study [13] investigated the relationship between seven software processes and measures of project performance. The results indicated that some processes and practices, such as project planning and cross functional teams, were related to product quality. However, practices such as user contact and prototyping were not related to quality.

Furthermore, it is not uncommon for studies that investigate the benefits of the implementation of processes to obtain different results depending on the measures of effectiveness that are used. For example, a study found that the use of cross-functional teams was related to the quality of products but not to meeting schedule and budget targets [13]. Another study [17] found a relationship between the organisation dimension of maturity and the quality of requirements engineering service, but not with the quality of requirements engineering products.

The message from this research is that an organisation should identify its business goals, identify measures for evaluating the attainment of its business goals, and then select to implement processes and process management practices that are most likely to have an impact on these measures that are important for the organisation. Off-the-shelf generic lists of processes to implement may not be as effective for all organisations.

There are organisations who are taking this assertion seriously in selecting the factors to focus their improvement efforts on. In an analysis of assessment data from 59 sites representing different business sectors (e.g., DoD contractor and commercial organisations) and different project sizes (from less than 9 peak staff to more than 100) available at the SEI [34], more than half of the sites reported findings that do not map into the key process areas (KPAs) of the CMM. This indicates that organisations are identifying issues to be addressed not covered by the CMM. Another implication of the above assertion is the right order which organisations should improve their processes. In a report of SPI based on the CMM [8] it is noted that "Business demands often necessitate improvements in an order which is counter to the CMM." In that particular case, the organisation initiated some process improvements that were not necessarily congruent with their next level of maturity, but were driven by their business objectives. Further evidence against following generic improvement paths comes from a study reported in [15]. The authors investigated whether the maturity path suggested by the process maturity framework of Humphrey and Sweet [31] follows a natural evolutionary progression. Their analysis was based on the basic idea that questions representing maturity levels already passed by organisations would be endorsed (i.e., scored yes) while items representing maturity levels not reached would fail. Their results did not support the original maturity path and led the authors to suggest that the original model seemed "arbitrary" in its ordering of practices and is "unsupported". The first five levels of the alternative maturity model that they empirically derived is shown in Figure 7.2. Of course, further studies are necessary to confirm this alternative model, but at least it enjoys some empirical support thus far. In addition, this study highlights that we, as a community, still do not know the "right" ordering of practices, and hence the importance of driving SPI along a path based on the organisation's objectives, and not necessarily by that of a generic model.

The empirical model continues further and should not be confused with the five CMM maturity levels. It is rather a bottom-up empirical approach which is different than the CMM assessment approach.

Success Factors for SPI

A survey reported in [26] investigated the factors that tended to characterise organisations that have had successful SPI programs, and the barriers that were faced. We summarise the key success factors and barriers in Figure 7.3. These should serve as initial guidelines for increasing the chances of obtaining benefits from SPI.

THREATS TO THE VALIDITY OF BENEFITS STUDIES

As shown above, there has been substantial empirical research to evaluate the benefits of software process improvement. Undoubtedly, there will be more such empirical research in the future. However, as well as demanding empirical evidence, consumers of empirical research must evaluate these works critically in order to determine how much confidence one should have in their results.

In this section we review a number of methodological issues that threaten the validity of conclusions that can be drawn from empirical studies of software process improvement. This review is intended to achieve two purposes. First, we will present guidelines for the consumers

Level 1: Reviews and Change Control

- Is a mechanism used for controlling changes to the code? (Who can make changes and under which circumstances?) (L2)
- Are internal software design reviews conducted? (L3)
- Are software code reviews conducted? (L3)
- Is a mechanism used for controlling changes to the software requirements? (L2)

Level 2: Standard Process and Project Management

- Is a mechanism used for controlling changes to the software design? (L3)
- Does the software organisation use a standardised and documented software development process on each project? (L3)
- Do software development first line managers sign off on their schedules and cost estimates? (L2)
- Is a formal procedure used in the management review of each software development prior to making contractual commitments? (L2)
- Is a formal procedure used to produce software development schedules? (L2)
- Are formal procedures applied to estimating software development cost? (L2)
- Is a mechanism used for managing and supporting the introduction of new technologies? (L4)

Level 3: Review Management and Configuration Control

- Are the action items resulting from code reviews tracked to closure? (L3)
- Are the actions items resulting from design reviews tracked to closure?(L3)
- Are the review data gathered during design reviews analysed? (L4)
- Is there a software configuration control function for each project that involves software development? (L2)
- Are code review standards applied? (L4)
- Is a formal procedure used to make estimates of software size? (L2)
- Is a mechanism used for periodically assessing the software engineering process and implementing indicated improvements? (L4)

Level 4: Software Process Improvement

- Are analyses of errors conducted to determine their process related causes? (L4)
- Is a mechanism used for ensuring compliance to software engineering standards? (L3)

Level 5: Management of Review and Test Coverage

- Are design and code review coverage measured and recorded? (L4)
- Is test coverage measured and recorded for each phase of functional testing? (L4)

Figure 7.2.   Empirically derived maturity model (first five levels only).

Key Success Factors

- Senior management monitoring of SPI
- Clear and compensated assignment of responsibilities for SPI
- Having well respected people within the organisation responsible for SPI
- The technical staff should be involved in the SPI effort
- Staff and resources are dedicated to SPI
- SPI goals are clearly stated and well understood in the organisation

Key Barriers to Successful SPI

- Excessive organisational politics and turf guarding
- Existence of discouragement and cynicism from previous experience
- The feeling among technical staff that SPI gets in the way of their "real" work
- SPI recommendations are too ambitious

Figure 7.3. Success factors and barriers to SPI.

of such works to help them evaluate the works. While some of the issues brought up may seem minor to nonspecialists, they do in fact have substantial impact on the conclusions that one can safely draw from the studies. Second, we will provide researchers in this area with a list of issues to note while conducting their research, and perhaps contribute to its improvement.

Biases of Particular Evaluation Methods

Two classes of empirical studies of the benefits of SPI have been conducted and reported: case studies and correlation studies. *Case studies* describe the experiences of a single organisation (or a small number of selected organisations) and the benefits it gained from increasing its maturity level. Examples of case studies are given in Table 7.1 as well as in [3, 9, 29, 36, 38]. Case studies are most useful for showing the potential benefits from the implementation of good processes. Given the substantial number of case studies documenting benefits from SPI, it is clear that it is possible to obtain considerable benefits from SPI. However, SPI case studies have a methodological disadvantage that makes it difficult to generalise their results. Case studies tend to suffer from a selection bias because organisations that have not shown any process improvement or have even regressed will be highly unlikely to publish their results, so published case studies tend to show mainly success stories (e.g., all the case studies referenced in this chapter are success stories). More worrisome is that we do not have an evaluation of how many case studies that are not success stories actually exist but were never published. Therefore, case studies do not demonstrate a general association between SPI and some benefits.

With correlation studies, one collects data from a number of organisations and investigates relationships between the implementation of good processes (e.g., maturity) and organisational and/or project effectiveness statistically. In correlation studies, data is usually collected through sample surveys, although this is not always the case. Correlation studies are useful for showing whether a general association exists between increased process implementation and effectiveness, and under what conditions. Examples of correlation studies are given in Table 7.3 and Table 7.6.

A problem is that the majority of organisations do not collect objective process and product data (e.g., on defect levels, or even keep accurate effort records). Organisations following the benchmarking paradigm do not necessarily have measurement programs in place to provide the necessary data. Primarily organisations that have made improvements and reached a reasonable level of maturity will have the actual objective data to demonstrate improvements (in productivity, quality, or return on investment). This assertion is supported by the results in [6] where, in general, it was found that organisations at lower CMM maturity levels are less likely to collect quality data (such as the number of development defects). Also, the same authors found that organisations tend to collect more data as their CMM maturity levels rise. Conversely, organisations following the analytic paradigm will tend to start measurement programs early in their SPI efforts, and therefore potentially have costs and benefits data. However, it was reported in another survey [42] that for 300 measurement programs started since 1980, less than 75 were considered successful in 1990, indicating a high mortality rate for measurement programs. This high mortality rate indicates that it may be difficult right now to find many organisations that have implemented measurement programs.

Therefore organisations that fail in their SPI efforts or who do not progress are less likely to be considered as viable case studies due to the lack of sufficient data. This enforces the case study selection bias alluded to earlier. Also, projects that have low implementation of processes or that do not have successful measurement programs may have to be excluded from a correlation study for the same reason. This would reduce the variation in the variables being measured, and thus reduce (artificially) the coefficients obtained from the correlation study.

This particular problem has been addressed in various ways in correlation studies however, but remains an issue for case studies. The study in [35] used data from contracts with the U.S. Air Force where schedule and budget data is regularly collected irrespective of the organisation's maturity. The study by Jones relies on the reconstruction of, at least, effort data from memory, as noted in [33]: "The SPR approach is to ask the project team to reconstruct the missing elements from memory." The rationale for that is stated as "the alternative is to have null data for many important topics, and that would be far worse." The general approach is to show staff a set of standard activities, and then ask them questions such as which ones they used and whether they put in any unpaid overtime during the performance of these activities. For defect levels, the general approach is to do a matching between companies that do not measure their defects with similar companies that do measure, and then extrapolate for those that don't measure. It should be noted that SPR does have a large data base of project and organisational data, which makes this kind of matching defensible. Other studies, such as [17 and 26] used subjective measures collected via questionnaires, therefore circumventing the difficulties of the collection of objective organisational and project data.

Appropriate Measurement

The manner in which variables are measured can have a nontrivial impact on the results of a study. Ideally, depending on the type of measure, appropriate measurement procedures should be followed. Below we discuss two common measurement problems in benefits evaluation studies.

Studies that utilize measures involving subjectivity should attempt to maximize and to evaluate their reliability. Reliability is concerned with random measurement error. For instance, it is known that single-item (or single question) measures in questionnaires tend to be highly unreliable [45]. Therefore, when measuring complex concepts such as maturity or success, one is strongly advised to develop multiple-item measures (where more than one question is used to measure the concept) when possible. Furthermore, minimal evaluations of the reliability of measurement should be performed. Some procedures for doing so have been introduced in [17]. Reliability evaluation for measures of process implementation is important because, according to current evidence, process assessments are not perfectly reliable (e.g., see [22, 23]).

The second problem concerns using coarse measures. For example, while the various dimensions of maturity have different effects on the process outcome, when combined into one dimension the overall effect may mask the dimensions that relate weakly to process outcomes, or vice versa. For instance, in a study [17] when four dimensions of maturity were summed up into one overall maturity dimension, the relationship between it and the quality of RE service was 0.33, which is statistically significant even though three of the dimensions are not individually related to RE service quality (i.e., the relationship was very small and not statistically significant). Therefore, this masking effect of coarse measures of process implementation distorts the effects of process implementation. Extreme caution should be taken when interpreting results from studies using coarse measures of process implementation. More reliable results would be obtained by considering individual dimensions separately.

Method of Data Analysis

The manner in which data is analysed can have a substantial impact on the results. In particular, the analysis method should match the unit of analysis that we want to draw conclusions about. For example, if we want to draw conclusions about the benefits to organisations from implementing software process management practices, then it is more appropriate to conduct an analysis where the unit of analysis is the organisation.

To illustrate this point, we consider the study reported in [26] and cited in [39] which found the relationships between CMM maturity levels and various measures of effectiveness to be statistically significant at the 0.05 alpha level. The reported data analysis pooled responses from 138 individuals representing 56 organisations (i.e., in many cases there was more than one respondent for each organisation). This pooling of data effectively makes the analysis at the individual unit of analysis rather than the organisation. This means that it is not appropriate to draw conclusions about the benefits of organisational maturity using this analysis approach. Another effect of this pooling is that it artificially increases the power of statistical tests and so increases the likelihood of finding statistically significant relationships. When the observations are not pooled and one response per organisation is used, the relationships are not statistically significant any more. Therefore, the strong conclusions drawn are not adequately supported by the results of the analyses. Of course, there are other ways of looking at this data. For example, all of the relationships were in the expected direction, and this is highly unlikely to occur by chance. But this conclusion is markedly different from the original one. Therefore, these results are not as compelling as they would originally seem, and so data analysis choices should be critically examined.

CONCLUDING REMARKS

In this chapter we have presented data that can be used to plan and manage software process improvement efforts. The costs and benefits data pertain to different approaches to process improvement. The reader can identify the approach that is most relevant to his/her environment and use this data as guidance.

The accumulation of empirical evidence can also give us some useful lessons to increase the chances of attaining the potential benefits of SPI. We have discussed a number of substantive issues that have been identified by empirical results thus far. These issues should at least be considered during an SPI effort.

We have also attempted to shed some light on the methodological issues pertinent to studies that evaluate the benefits of software process improvement. It is clear that further research on this topic is forthcoming, and thus one should be careful in interpreting the results of these studies. Also, the methodological weaknesses that we have identified should serve as a challenge to future empirical researchers.

ACKNOWLEDGMENTS

We wish to thank John Daly for reviewing an earlier version of this chapter.

REFERENCES

1. J. Bach, "Enough About Process: What We Need Are Heroes," *IEEE Software*, Vol. 12, No. 2, Feb. 1995.

2. V. Basili, et al., "The Software Engineering Laboratory—An Operational Software Experience Factory," *Proceedings of the 14th International Conference on Software Engineering*, 1992.

3. S. Benno and D. Frailey, "Software Process Improvement at DSEG: 1989-1995," *Texas Instruments Technical Journal*, Vol. 12, No. 2, Mar.–Apr. 1995, pp. 20–28.

4. L. Briand, C. Differding, and H.D. Rombach, "Practical Guidelines for Measurement-Based Process Improvement," *Proceedings of ISCN'96*, 1996.

5. J. Brodman and D. Johnson, "What Small Businesses and Small Organisations Say about the CMM," *Proceedings of the 16th International Conference on Software Engineering*, 1994, pp. 331–340.

6. J. Brodman and D. Johnson, "Return on Investment (ROI) from Software Process Improvement as Measured by US Industry," *Software Process: Improvement and Practice*, Pilot Issue, John Wiley, 1995.

7. J. Brodman and D. Johnson, "Return on Investment from Software Process Improvement as Measured by U.S. Industry," *Crosstalk*, Vol. 9, No. 4, Apr. 1996, pp. 23–29.

8. C. Buchman, "Software Process Improvement at AlliedSignal Aerospace," *Proceedings of the 29th Annual Hawaii International Conference on Systems Science, Vol. 1: Software Technology and Architecture*, 1996, pp. 673–680.

9. K. Butler, "The Economic Benefits of Software Process Improvement," *Crosstalk*, Vol. 8, No. 7, July 1995, pp. 14–17.

10. D. Card, "Understanding Process Improvement," *IEEE Software*, July 1991, pp. 102–103.

11. B. Curtis, H. Krasner, and N. Iscoe, "A Field Study of the Software Design Process for Large Systems," *Communications of the ACM*, Vol. 31, No. 11, Nov. 1988, pp. 1268–1286.

12. M. Daskalantonakis, "A Practical View of Software Measurement and Implementation Experiences within Motorola," *IEEE Transactions on Software Engineering*, et al., Nov. 1992, pp. 998–1010.

13. C. Deephouse, et al., "The Effects of Software Processes on Meeting Targets and Quality," *Proceedings of the Hawaiian International Conference on Systems Sciences*, Vol. 4, Jan. 1995, pp. 710–719.

14. R. Dion, "Process Improvement and the Corporate Balance Sheet," *IEEE Software*, July 1993, pp. 28–35.

15. D. Drehmer and S. Dekleva, "Measuring Software Engineering Maturity: A Rasch Calibration," *Proceedings of the International Conference on Information Systems*, 1993, pp. 191–202.

16. K. El Emam and N. H. Madhavji, "A Method for Instrumenting Software Evolution Processes and An Example Application," *Notes From The International Workshop on Software Evolution, Processes, and Measurements*, Technical Report #94-04 NT, Software Engineering Test Lab, Department of Computer Science, University of Idaho, 1994.

17. K. El Emam and N. H. Madhavji, "The Reliability of Measuring Organisational Maturity," *Software Process: Improvement and Practice*, Vol. 1, No. 1, 1995, pp. 3–25.

18. K. El Emam and N. H. Madhavji, "Measuring the Success of Requirements Engineering Processes," *Proceedings of the Second IEEE International Symposium on Requirements Engineering*, 1995, pp. 204–211.

19. K. El Emam and N. H. Madhavji, "A Field Study of Requirements Engineering Practices in Information Systems Development," *Proceedings of the Second IEEE International Symposium on Requirements Engineering*, 1995, pp. 68–80.

20. K. El Emam, S. Quintin, and N. H. Madhavji, "User Participation in the Requirements Engineering Process: An Empirical Study," *Requirements Engineering Journal*, Vol. 1, No. 4, 1996, pp. 4–26.

21. K. El Emam and N. H. Madhavji, "The Impact of User Capability on Requirements Engineering Success," submitted for publication.

22. K. El Emam, et al., "Interrater Agreement in SPICE-Based Assessments: Some Preliminary Results," *Proceedings of the 4th International Conference on the Software Process*, 1996.

23. K. El Emam, L. Briand, and R. Smith, "Assessor Agreement in Rating SPICE Processes," Technical Report ISERN-96-09, International Software Engineering Research Network, 1996.

24. P. Finlay and A. Mitchell, "Perceptions of the Benefits from the Introduction of CASE: An Empirical Study," *MIS Quarterly*, Dec. 1994, p. 353–370.

25. D. R. Goldenson, "Software Process Needs Analysis: Customer Perspectives," Presentation Slides, Software Engineering Institute, June 1994.

26. D. R. Goldenson and J. D. Herbsleb, *After the Appraisal: A Systematic Survey of Process Improvement, its Benefits, and Factors that Influence Success*, Technical Report, CMU/SEI-95-TR-009, Software Engineering Institute, 1995.

27. R. Grady and D. Caswell, *Software Metrics: Establishing a Company-wide Program*, Prentice Hall, 1987.

28. W. Hayes and D. Zubrow, *Moving On Up: Data and Experience Doing CMM-Based Process Improvement*," Technical Report CMU/SEI-95-TR-008, Software Engineering Institute, 1995.

29. J. Herbsleb et al., *Benefits of CMM-Based Software Process Improvement: Initial Results*, Technical Report, CMU-SEI-94-TR-13, Software Engineering Institute, 1994.

30. W. Humphrey, T. Snyder, and R. Willis, "Software Process Improvement at Hughes Aircraft," *IEEE Software*, July 1991, pp. 11–23.

31. W. Humphrey and W. Sweet, A Method for Assessing the Software Engineering Capability of Contractors, Technical Report CMU/SEI-87-TR-23, Software Engineering Institute, 1987.

32. C. Jones, "The Pragmatics of Software Process Improvements," *Software Process Newsletter*, IEEE Computer Soc. TCSE, No. 5, Winter 1996, pp. 1–4.

33. C. Jones, *Assessment and Control of Software Risks*, Prentice Hall, 1994.

34. D. Kitson and S. Masters, "An Analysis of SEI Software Process Assessment Results: 1987-1991," *Proceedings of the International Conference on Software Engineering*, 1993, pp. 68–77.

35. P. Lawlis, R. Flowe, and J. Thordahl, "A Correlational Study of the CMM and Software Development Performance," *Software Process Newsletter*, IEEE TCSE, No. 7, Fall 1996, pp. 1–5.

36. L. Lebsanft, "Bootstrap: Experiences with Europe's Software Process Assessment and Improvement Method," *Software Process Newsletter*, IEEE TCSE, No. 5, Winter 1996, pp. 6–10.

37. J. Lee and S. Kim, "The Relationship between Procedural Formalization in MIS Development and MIS Success," *Information and Management*, Vol. 222, 1992, pp. 89–111.

38. W. Lipke and K. Butler, "Software Process Improvement: A Success Story," *Crosstalk*, Vol. 5, No. 9, Sept. 1992, pp. 29–39.

39. B. Peterson, "Software Process Improvement Trends," *Proceedings of the European Software Engineering Process Group Conference*, 1996.

40. S. Rahhal, *An Effort Estimation Model for Implementing ISO 9001 in Software Organisations.* master's thesis, School of Computer Science, McGill University, Oct. 1995.

41. J. Rooijmans, H. Aerts, and M. van Genuchten, "Software Quality in Consumer Electronics Products," *IEEE Software*, Jan. 1996, pp. 55–64.

42. H. Rubin, "Software Process Maturity: Measuring its Impact on Productivity and Quality," *Proceedings of the International Conference on Software Engineering*, 1993, pp. 468–476.

43. Staff, "A Survey of the Surveys on the Benefits of ISO 9000," *Software Process, Quality & ISO 9000*, Vol. 3, No. 11, Nov. 1994, pp. 1–5.

44. H. Wohlwend and S. Rosenbaum, "Software Improvements in an International Company," *Proceedings of the International Conference on Software Engineering*, 1993, p. 212–220.

45. R. Zeller and E. Carmines, *Measurement in the Social Sciences: The Link Between Theory and Data*, Cambridge University Press, 1980.

Chapter 8

Siemens Process Assessment Approach

Thomas Mehner
Application Centre Software
Corporate Research and Development,
Siemens AG,

INTRODUCTION

The Application Centre Software is part of Siemens Corporate Research and Development. Our main task is the enhancement of the quality and productivity of Software (SW) and Systems Engineering within Siemens divisions and Siemens Operating Companies world-wide. The focus is on the underlying processes and quality management. Assessments are used for a first evaluation of the status of an organisation.

- The Siemens Software Process Assessment Approach is based on the Capability Maturity Model (CMM) of the Software Engineering Institute (SEI). Extensions have been made according to the BOOTSTRAP results and Siemens specific requirements targeting Process Improvement in industry. Enhancements in the assessment methodology have been made. New application fields can be covered by facultative add on questions (Systems Engineering, Configuration Engineering, reuse). A tailoring method for the Siemens assessment method was introduced to define a convenient scheme for differently sized organisations.
- Contents and goals of the Optimised Processes and Architectural Leadership (OPAL) program are described. For all Siemens divisions where SW is a relevant factor, an assessment with a following improvement program shall put the maturity level for SW development on a sound basis for industrial development.

- The phase of starting an improvement program begins with the final presentation of the assessment results. Procedure and the various possibilities for participation of the Application Centre Software are described.

    Experiences with improvement programs within Siemens AG in those programs are the final topic of discussion.

THE SIEMENS ASSESSMENT APPROACH

The Siemens Software Process Assessment is based on the SEI CMM and the BOOTSTRAP results. Furthermore, ISO 9000- and special company-aspects are considered [1–6] (Figure 8.1).

In this assessment an overall maturity level is computed for reasons of international comparability and for setting global goals. Additional information for improvement purposes is generated (Figure 8.2).

For each software development process defined for an organisation two categories of assessments are conducted:

- One Site Assessment—evaluates the maturity of the defined and documented process and further standards and rules to be used organisationwide. This includes development and quality handbooks as well as people's familiarity with the material.
- Two to three Project Assessments—evaluates the practiced software development and quality management for software based upon representative samples (projects). This assessment also covers project specific standards.

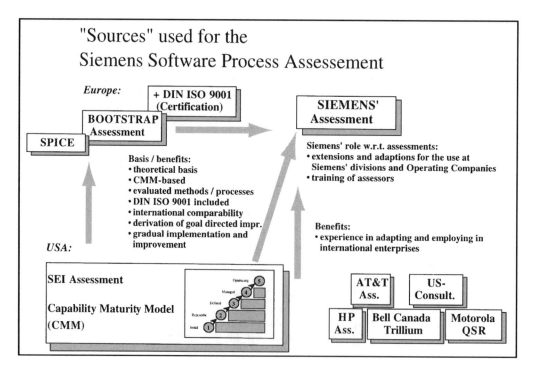

Figure 8.1.　Comparison of SEI and Siemens assessments.

The main effort is spent on:

- Detailed profiles and descriptions of strengths and weaknesses throughout 25 process-related areas (Figures 8.3 and 8.4). As illustrated in Figure 8.3, attributes are measured between a minimum of 1 and maximum levels between 3 and 5. Attributes span across different levels, but as in CMM (which is only valid on one level) they are valid in spans of two to three maturity levels. This explains the different maturity levels (MLs) reached by various attributes in Figure 8.3.

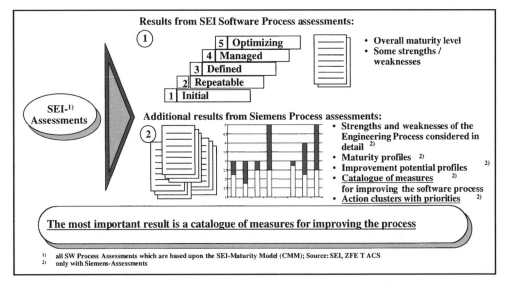

Figure 8.2. Comparison of SEI and Siemens assessments.

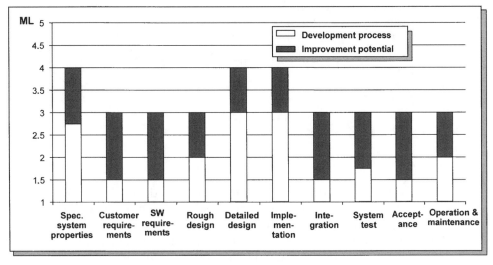

Figure 8.3. Development process, life cycle.

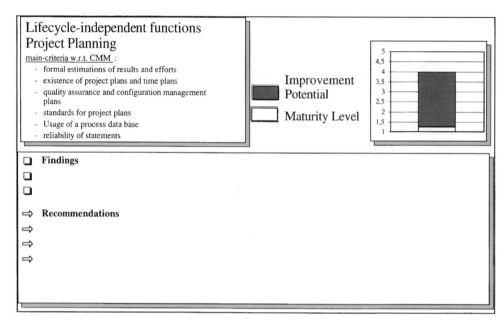

Figure 8.4.   Development process, life cycle.

Lfd.No	Page	Measure	Prio-rity	Criteria	Clu-ster
14	10	Develop key values and designate those responsible for them.	B		
15	10	Extensions to methods for registering and evaluating the quality and development costs for sub-contractors (e.g. phase expenses)	C		
16	10	Differentiated registration of quality costs (error prevention, testing, error correction).	B		
17	10	Correct and complete records of review data.	C		
18	10	Registration / evaluation of errors in all phases (integrated testing, early phases; simple procedures).	B C		
19	11	General tracking of all activities following reviews.			
20	11	Inclusion of review results in planning (includes revising deadlines).	B		
21	12	Examination of the primary data w.r.t. its relevance, efficiency, completeness, validity and evaluation value.	A		
22	12	Implementation of a metric system to measure processes and optimize them.	A		

Figure 8.5.   Catalogue of recommendations.

- The derivation of recommendations for improvement actions (Figure 8.5).
- The further processing of recommendations (clustering, prioritising, classification, timely structuring) to generate a stable basis for an improvement program. The action clusters are displayed in a portfolio according to their urgency (number of serious gaps) and to the importance of the topic for the specific business (Figure 8.6). This helps to allocate scarce resources for improvement to the most rewarding topic (upper right bullet!).

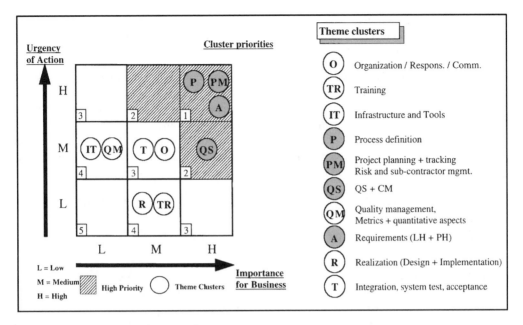

Figure 8.6. Portfolio of action clusters.

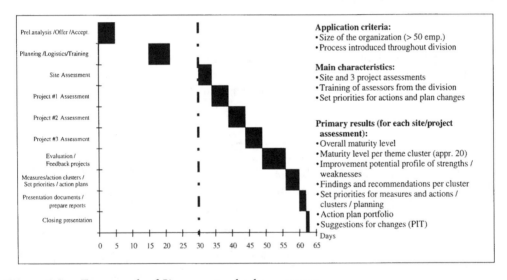

Figure 8.7. Framework of Siemens standard assessment.

Enhancements to the Siemens Assessment Methodology

Since our start at the end of 1992 the Siemens Assessment Methodology has been enhanced to make it appropriate for all application fields within Siemens. Figure 8.7 shows the scheme of our standard assessment, which is especially applicable for larger organisations with a standardized process. Here a separate result is generated for theory (defined process, quality management system, etc.) and for real life (a representative selection of two to five projects).

For small organisations with up to 50 software developers a different scheme had to be defined. In comparison to the method described above the following changes have been introduced and successfully applied (Figure 8.8):

- The separate assessment of site and projects was given up. Our experience is that in smaller organisations the difference of defined and documented process and procedures is smaller and the persons responsible are not strictly different. For this reason the site and project aspects are treated together in the assessment interviews and in the evaluation.
- The separate assessment of different projects (two to four) is done for large organisations to get a representative picture. For smaller organisations, members from different projects can be represented in the interview groups and the information can be gathered in one assessment.
- The participation of interview partners in the assessment was reduced to about half the amount.
- Time needed for the complete assessment from kickoff to final presentation was reduced to 4 weeks (from about 6 weeks for a standard assessment).

To complete our assessment application scope, we had to define one more type of assessment procedure (One Room Assessment) for very small organisations with about 10 software developers. Many Siemens business units mainly produce hardware. The products (e.g., dentist chair, vacuum cleaner) contain only small SW parts . Problems and role distribution (less specialization) in these areas are quite different from larger organisations. The effort (cost and human resources involvement) which can be spent for an assessment has to be reduced.

To comply with this different situation the following changes have been introduced and successfully applied (Figure 8.9):

- The separation of interviews with lower management and persons with specific roles on one side and practitioners on the other side was eliminated. In most cases persons have more than one role and hierarchical differences are not so important.

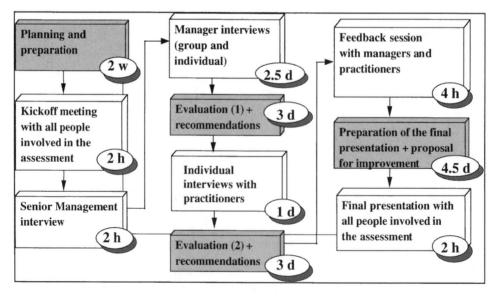

Figure 8.8.   Assessment scheme for small organisations.

- The participation of interview partners in the assessment was further reduced.
- Time needed for the complete assessment from kickoff to final presentation was reduced to 2 weeks.

In all three types of assessments we did not change the involvement of all levels of management and staff in the interviews. An executive briefing presents the three types of assessments and helps to select the right assessment approach based on the size and structure of the organisation.

In many of the assessments performed at Siemens it was realised that business processes (as core competence) were not covered by CMM like questionnaires [3]. CMM is rather technical and has a great improvement potential in including business aspects beside the technical management aspects. Therefore, major extensions had to be introduced:

- The interfaces at the beginning and at the end of the development process had to be included in more detail: marketing, product definition, and service.
- Most division's business is in systems engineering (building big software and embedded systems) up to complex engineering processes (ready to go plants and manufactories). This requires significant skills in configuration and architectural management with "(so called) streamlines" of many different versions and variants of the same products and systems. For this reason, facultative add-on questions had to be introduced for many theme clusters.

Figure 8.10 shows the structure of our questionnaire. White boxes are unchanged compared to the initial software engineering version. Grey boxes are completely new and the others have been supplemented.

CONTENTS AND GOALS OF OPAL

In 1994, Siemens AG started the "top-Initiative" (time optimized processes) for improving the competitiveness of all divisions of the company (Figure 8.11). The goal is to reach top positions in the global market.

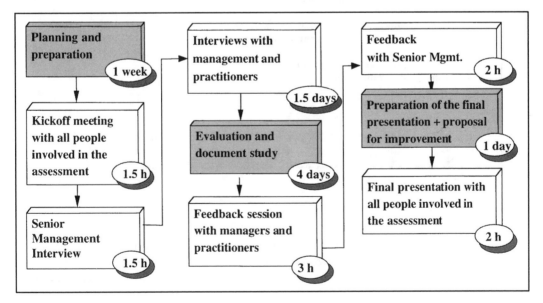

Figure 8.9.   Assessment scheme for very small organizations.

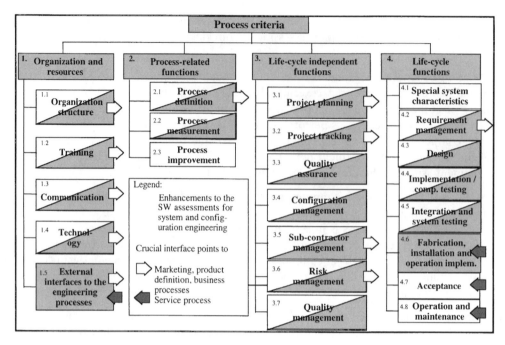

Figure 8.10. Structure of the new questionnaire.

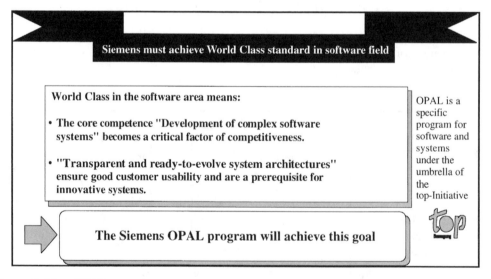

Figure 8.11. OPAL program.

The general impact of software at Siemens is steadily increasing. A considerable proportion of the returns are now software related. Software has strategic importance within a number of divisions. In some business areas there has been a shift from electromechanics towards electronics and thus toward software. Efforts for development and maintenance require billions of German marks. Some products require up to several thousand software developers. Development is often distributed over different sites and countries. Many systems are long lasting and evolutionary. Requirements with regard to quality, development time, and cost are more and more stringent.

The situation described above led to the creation of the strategic OPAL program which runs under the umbrella of the top-Initiative. The title "Optimized Processes and Architectural Leadership" describes the two focus points of the program:

- Assessment and Improvement of System Architectures (this aspect is not covered here)
- Assessment and Improvement of System Engineering and underlying processes

For all Siemens divisions where SW is a relevant factor, an assessment with a following improvement program shall put the maturity level for SW development on a sound basis for industrial development.

The main goal of OPAL is the fast and cost efficient development of good quality software. The focus is on software not only as a standalone product but by increasing impact as components of systems or a development instrument for systems.

The following approach is taken:

- Determination of strategic importance of software in all key business areas. Analysis of competitors with regard to efficiency improvements in software development.
- Execution of a process assessment in all key business areas where software is of strategic importance within 18 months. Classification of engineering processes according to the Capability Maturity Model (SEI) and identification of the potential for improvement by using the Siemens-uniform assessment methods for all Siemens Groups.
- Industrializing of the software and systems development, that is, achievement of at least maturity level 3 for all key business areas, where software is strategically extremely important within 3 years.
- This goal can be reached by:
  - Derivation of business specific efficiency programs which lead to the wide-spread introduction of measures based on the recommendations of the assessment.
  - Establishment of continuous improvement processes in all key business areas relevant for software development.
  - Both activities can be supported by the Application Centre Software.

IMPROVEMENT PROJECTS

Starting an Improvement Program

The results of an assessment are the main input for the improvement program:

A catalogue of recommendations (typically 60 to 120) lists all recommendations. For each, the following attributes are added:

- priority (three degrees);
- effort needed (rough estimation, three degrees);
- time frame (rough estimation, three degrees);
- action cluster (assignment of single recommendations to functional topics, which can be treated by a work group, the action clusters are prioritized in a portfolio matrix); and
- special criteria (depends on the assessed organisation; for example, relevance for ISO 9000, scope of recommendation (single group, whole organisation)).

This is a sound basis for developing an improvement project. As a management input, the goals of the organisation and the effort available must be given. With this information the recommendations can be selected and sequenced, so that the highest benefits (impact on improvement) can be expected for a given effort. Actions can be planned and responsible persons (e.g., work groups) can be assigned. The realisation can be done on a pilot basis for actions with complex implications or on broad basis when solutions are quite clear (Figure 8.12).

If an improvement program shall be successful, it must be a project. This means:

- a project organisation exists (e.g., Process Improvement Team [PIT] and work groups, responsibilities, budget, effort and time assigned);
- a goal-oriented planning for the realization of improvement actions exists;
- realization is tracked by PIT and senior management; and
- the results are measured by a metric system which has to be defined in accordance with the goals of the program and specific requirements of the organisation (e.g., reduction of cycle time, or error density in field).

There are three options for the participation of the Application Centre Software (ACS) in a business specific improvement program:

1. Especially large organisations with sufficient qualified resources are able to plan and implement a program without external help. In this case a deadline for reaching substantial improvement goals is fixed and a reassessment takes place after this time.
2. For other organisations there is a lack of knowledge about special topics, where weaknesses have been identified in the assessment. In this case the ACS has standard concepts available for some topics which can be adopted to organisation specific requirements and can be introduced quite fast (configuration management, formal inspections, risk management, Quality Assurance (QA) for external deliveries, defect prevention, project planing). This also includes training and coaching. For other topics, cooperation with technology labs within our central research division is available.

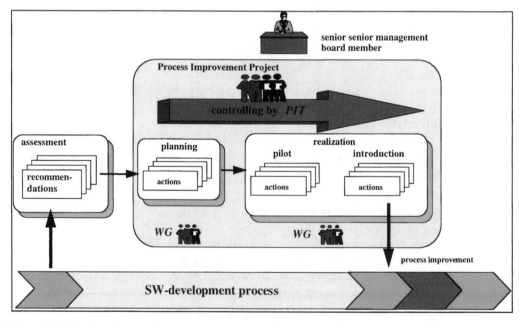

Figure 8.12.   Starting an improvement program.

3. For smaller organisations the availability of resources and know-how for an improvement program can be a problem. In this case the whole program is planned and managed by ACS.

Experience Data

Up to now more than 30 assessments (covering about 60 projects) have been finished. For most of them an improvement program started within reasonable time (which should not be longer than 2 months). We covered the following branches (Siemens divisions or associated companies):

- Telecommunications (switching, mobile networks) with very large systems; see for example, Chapter 9;
- power supply and power distribution;
- traffic systems with very high security requirements;
- automation;
- medical systems; and
- automobile technology.

The assessments have taken place at company sites in Austria, Brazil, France, Germany, Italy, Switzerland, UK, and the United States. We have amassed the following experiences:

Maturity Level

By our standard assessment we examine separately the defined process valid for organisations (site assessment) and the practices of two to five projects (project assessment). In the case of processes of organisations below level 2, projects are in most cases more mature than processes (site assessment). This means the globally defined process is not adequate and the projects have to add individual and local regulations and procedures to cope with their basic needs.

In the case of processes of organisations above level 2, the defined process is generally more mature than projects. Here procedures are well defined (e.g., by a central QA group) however the implementation in the daily life is only partly successful.

There have been processes with maturity level above 3, but up to now no project has reached level 3 (Figure 8.13).

Frequent Weaknesses

- *Insufficient QA.* In some cases QA is only formally defined with insufficient resources or roughly undefined by insufficient competencies. In such cases where QA cannot support the development, high test costs and/or low quality is the consequence.
- *Early Phases.* Development starts on an unstable basis. Interworking of development and marketing, sales, and service for specifying the requirements is insufficient. Improvement actions so far mostly focused on implementation and test.
- *Project Management.* Estimations are mostly done on an individual basis without defined method or tool support. Updating project plans is not sufficiently widespread. In many organisations progress tracking is based on accounting data (consumption of resources) instead of tracking of work products. As a consequence the missing of milestones is recognized rather late (firefighting instead of preventive action).
- *Metrics.* Basic data is often incorrect and incomplete. A clear connection to goals (general goals of the business or specific goals of an improvement program) and actions (threshold

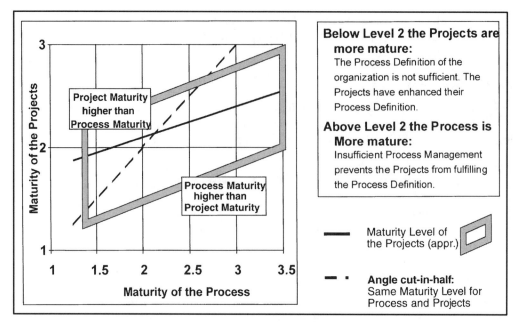

Figure 8.13. Maturity level distribution.

conditions with mandatory activities in case of deviations) is missing [7]. As a consequence it is difficult to define and track quantitative goals for an improvement program.

Typical Problems of Improvement Programs

If the start of an improvement program is postponed after an assessment ("Schedules and resources do not allow us to start now!"), the probability of a successful start later decreases significantly. After an assessment the staff members build up strong expectations for change. Problems described in the final presentation are well in mind. If this momentum is missed by waiting some months, the general opinion tends to be: nothing will happen.

Selection of PIT members is a critical task. Personality, technical knowledge, and sufficient competencies in the organisation are needed.

Senior management must show continuous interest in and support for the improvement program (sponsorship). This implies, for example,

- direct regular reporting based on project plan and the defined metric system with visible feedback,
- personal presence in all relevant meetings,
- introduction of special reward systems, and
- public announcement of a reassessment after 2 or 3 years.

All members of the organisation must have the impression that this is a project with high priority and that persons involved have the full support of senior management in case of conflicts.

The improvement must be a project with adequate resources. If those resources are not available in the organisation, external resources have to be added (e.g., improvement coaches from the ACS).

> *   increasing the maturity level by 0.75
>   during an 18 month improvement project

result: back to profit
- definition of product versions works (sales and development)
- precise estimations w.r.t. schedule and cost
- increased quality leads to higher acceptance in the market
- new product generation introduced in time at an important exhibition
- ISO 9001 certification passed

improvement key issues:
- process definition and process improvement
- project planning, project tracking, risk management
- requirements management, test phases

Figure 8.14.   Example of an OPAL result.

All employees should be periodically informed about what has just been done, what is planned, and what has already been reached (success stories) to keep attitudes open to change. This can be done by a regular newsletter and by information meetings which must provide a possibility for presenting and discussing problems frankly.

In some cases organisational structures (little kingdoms) prevent global solutions without very strong top management support.

Success in increasing efficiency can produce fear of losing human resources. We must always emphasize that this improvement enables the organisation to stay in the market and to develop more, or more complex, products with the same staff.

Cost/Benefit Calculation for OPAL

The experience of our work shows that the effort for an assessment-based improvement program consumes about 3 to 7 percent of the total development effort. This includes the assessment, the work done by a PIT and work groups, and the introduction of measures (training, investment, learning). According to our experience, the efficiency improvement of a successful program can be around 30 percent within 2 to 3 years. The measurement of the improvement has to be done according to the goals of an organisation. It can be a reduction of error density after delivery, development cost, or cycle time for development.

The program pays off very quickly. A specific result is shown in Figure 8.14. It shows the improvement of an organisation (medium size) from the automation field between first assessment and reassessment after 18 months.

REFERENCES

1. W. S. Humphrey, *Managing the Software Process*, Software Engineering Institute, Addison-Wesley, 1989.

2. SEI, *The Role of Assessment in Software Process Improvement*, CMU/SEI-89-TR-3, CMU, 1989.

3. SEI, *Capability Maturity Model*, CMU/SEI-91-TR-24, CMU, 1991.

4. SEI, *Software Engineering Process Group Guide*, CMU/SEI-90-TR-24, CMU, 1990.

5. *Software Process Unit Assessment Questionnaire*, *BOOTSTRAP*, 2i Industrial Informatics, Freiburg, 1991.

6. A. Völker, "Sortware Process Assessments at Siemens as a Basis for Process Improvement in Industry," *Proceedings of the ISCN'94* Conference, ISCN Ltd., Dublin, Ireland.

7. K. H. Möller and D. J.Paulish, *Sortware-Metriken in der Praxis, Handbuch der Informatik 5.4*, Oldenbourg Verlag, Munich, 1994.

Chapter 9

Quantifying the Benefit of a Long-Lasting Process Improvement Programme in Switching Applications

G. Damele, G. Caielli, D. Scrignaro
Italtel S.p.A., Italy

G. Bazzana, G. Rumi
Onion S.p.A., Italy

INTRODUCTION

Italtel is one of Europe's leading full-line manufacturers in the telecommunications field. Italtel designs, manufactures, markets, and installs systems and equipment for public and private applications. In Italy and abroad it implements systems and networks on a turnkey basis. The company is active, full-line, in every field of telecommunications, ranging from public switching to transmission, mobile telephony systems, private telecommunications, electronic interconnections, integrated IT-based systems for traffic and environmental monitoring, defence communications systems, modular metal structures, and electric panels.

Research and development is crucial to Italtel's competitiveness on the world markets; in the last years Italtel has invested in excess of 15 percent of sales in R&D in the most advanced sectors of telecommunications.

For more details on the company, the interested reader is referred to the Italtel World Wide Web (WWW) at the Uniform Resource Locator (URL) http://www.italtel.it

This chapter is divided into the following logical parts:

1. a general introduction, covering the Software Process Improvement (SPI) activities at Italtel, the reference development process and the adopted improvement model; and
2. a detailed technical and managerial analysis of SPI programs that have run at Italtel, focusing on particular switching systems.

A large proportion of the chapter is devoted to the second aspect, which gives a snapshot of a long-lasting SPI effort run at Italtel—the Business Unit Commutazione Pubblica (BUCT) focused on software development projects relevant to switching systems. Italtel experiences are also dealt with in Chapter 10, where we discuss an intensive Process Improvement Project, underway at Italtel RM (Business Unit Reti Mobili), focused on software development projects relevant to mobile communications systems.

For both experiences, the technical achievements, the quantitative results, and the major outcomes will be presented, focusing in particular on the following issues:

- high-level technical aspects of the developed system;
- high-level findings and recommendations from the initial assessment;
- the organisational issues of the SPI Project;
- the actions taken as part of the improvement program;
- the accompanying actions run to support the initiative;
- the measurement system adopted;
- an excerpt of the quantitative data collected from major projects, showing the trend of improvements;
- the procedures adopted to track the progress of the SPI Project;
- key findings and lessons learned; and
- the future goals.

In describing the SPI experiences, the emphasis will be on relationships between process assessment and improvement, impacts on designers' daily routine work, quantitative measures and pragmatic outcomes.

THE FOUNDATIONS FOR SPI AT ITALTEL

Software Process Improvement at Italtel

Concerning software process improvement, the following directions have been set at the company level:

- Software process improvement is deemed a strategic asset for continuously increasing the company capabilities in an extremely competitive worldwide market;
- For all Business Units, the following directions are valid:
  —SPI will be based on/combined with the attainment of ISO 9001 certification.
  —SPI will be based on an initial analysis of strengths and improvement opportunities.
  —SPI will be based on a reference model allowing the quantitative appraisal of achievements gained.
  —Quantitative measures from the major development projects of all business units have to be supplied on a quarterly basis to the central R&D Facilities for integration and reporting within a document intended for the top management of the company; to this end, a common set of basic metrics has been defined, to which all business units have to adhere.
  —SPI will be run under the responsibility of the R&D branch of the individual business units, in order to be as much as possible in touch with the needs and peculiarities of the addressed markets.
  —The central R&D and Quality branches shall act as catalysts for supporting the SPI initiatives of the business units, by means of organizing/conducting training, providing experts' advice, maintaining awareness on the international trends (Italtel actively participates in the SPICE initiatives and in many other international research projects),

circulating success stories at the company level, reporting the quantitative results in a coherent way, and—last but not least—giving pragmatic support in specific phases of an SPI Project (for instance: process assessment, modeling of new processes, alignment to ISO 9001 requirements, analysis/interpretation of measurement data, root cause analysis, etc.).

This "distributed" approach (which implies the absence of a centralized Software Engineering Process Group [SEPG]) so far has been felt to be successful in that it guarantees focus and effectiveness of the local initiatives, while keeping a sufficient level of control over directives and results. The "distributed" approach also implies that SPI programs run at different Business Units can adopt different technical/organisational choices, while keeping the same philosophy and approach.

The Reference Development Process

The software development and maintenance processes adopted at Italtel have been defined in agreement with ISO 9001 requirements (for which the company is certified). Software development has adopted a classic waterfall model and is characterised by heavy concurrent engineering and by very detailed impact analysis activities. This is because very seldom does the development of complex telecommunication systems starts from scratch, owing to the relatively long lifetime of these products on the market. Rather, the approach is normally feature-driven; that is, a new project focuses on additional features to be developed in an existing version of the system.

Seen from a high-level perspective, the reference development process includes the following activities:

- *Preanalysis*, including specification of user's requirements, listing of high-level requirements for the system (known as "features") and their packaging for the project
- *Analysis*, including impact analysis of various features and specification of functional requirements
- *Design*, including specification of system interfaces and specifications of design and test requirements
- *Coding*, including the development of source code units and their testing in simulated environments
- *Integration testing*, subdivided into various steps depending on the system architecture
- *System testing*, performed by a team independent of development, and subdivided into validation of new features, load and stress testing, and regression testing
- *Acceptance and operation*.

Moreover, the peculiarities of the developed products (big size and long life) have also led to well-founded and applied practices as far as supporting activities are concerned (especially configuration management, document control, planning, and tracking).

A Model for Process Improvement: PDCA

The setup and implementation of software process improvement at Italtel has been defined in accordance with a Plan-Do-Check-Act (PDCA) scheme and, in particular, with the PQMI guidelines [1]; this means that the process improvement program has been defined by the following steps:

- definition of the organisation and the responsibilities for the process (the "Process Owner" and the Process Management Team);

- definition of the development process (inputs, outputs, suppliers, customers and major activities/subprocesses);
- description of the metrics (if you cannot measure your results, then you cannot control your process and improve your performance);
- data collection and analysis;
- identification of the internal problems and the improvement opportunities for the process;
- selection of the best improvement opportunities (those expected to have the most positive impact); and
- implementation of the process improvements.

Figure 9.1 details, according to the PDCA cycle, the interactions between the metrics program, the quality system, and the software development process, following a total quality management approach [2].

The whole set of activities can be logically split into two different worlds: physics on the one hand, and engineering on the other hand. To the first group belong those activities aimed at identifying behavioural rules, whereas those activities aimed at the actual implementation and validation of the rules belong to the second group.

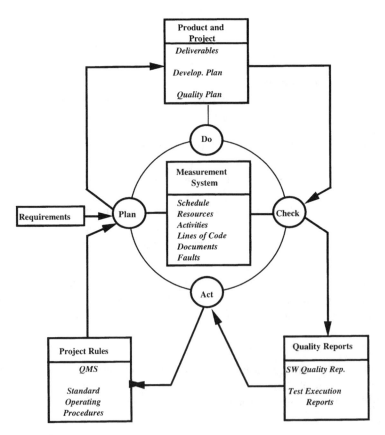

Figure 9.1.   PDCA at Italtel.

Figure 9.2 represents such a schema.

The presentation of both experiences is therefore arranged in accordance with the PDCA scheme.

QUANTIFYING THE BENEFITS OF A LONG-LASTING PI PROGRAM IN THE SWITCHING APPLICATION DOMAIN

The assessment of a long-lasting PI program was conducted in the software Laboratory of Italtel Digital Switching Business Unit (BUCT), near Milan. This Business Unit is committed, among other systems, to the development of the Linea UT telecommunication switching system. At the end of 1995, about 18 million Linea UT lines, more than 1000 exchanges, and 2000 Remote Subscriber Units (RSU) have been installed in about 20 countries worldwide.

Italtel Linea UT has been conducting a software process improvement program since 1991, following a Plan-Do-Check-Act scheme able to check and measure the products and the development processes in a quantitative way in order to single out, implement and monitor the improvement opportunities. The improvement program has its roots in the Quality Management System (QMS) that defines the organisation, its activities, and the techniques to be used during software development.

Architecture and Features of the Linea UT System

The Linea UT telecommunication switching system is quite a complex system (including several million lines of embedded code written in C and C-SDL) based on a modular approach, allowing various network configuration scenarios and to be supported facilitating a great variety of services, from Plain Old Telephone Service (POTS) to Broadband Integrated Services Digital Network (B-ISPN).

A typical configuration is composed of several modules interconnected through an internal network; each set of modules perform a specific function, for example,

- user interfaces to Plain Old Telephone Service, PBX, and Intergrated Services Digital Network subscribers;
- trunk interfaces and performance of signaling functions;
- application level of the OSI stack protocol; and
- interface between the operator and the system, for Operation and Management (O&M) functions.

From a technical point of view, signaling modules are based on proprietary solutions (both boards and real-time operating systems) whereas O&M runs on top of an UNIX-like platform.

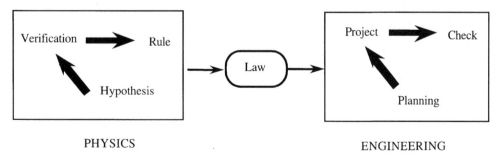

Figure 9.2. Application of the metrics program.

PLAN: Initiating SPI through Process Assessment at Italtel Linea UT

While achieving ISO 9001 [3] and ITQS [4] certification, Italtel Linea UT understood the importance of applying a continuous SPI program. In order to define priorities for the improvement program, in November 1991 a process assessment activity took place at Italtel Linea UT. The assessment adopted the BOOTSTRAP approach [5, 6], as described in this book. The assessment team concluded that, as of November 1991, Italtel was operating in a controlled way, corresponding to a maturity level at that date between the repeatable and the defined level both for the software producing unit (SPU) rules and for the project practices.

Many strengths were outlined by the assessment, in particular: the structure of the Quality Management System (QMS), the development model, and the practices adopted in project management, software maintenance, and configuration/ change management.

In order to boost process improvement with the aim of evolving toward a stable defined level, the following recommendations were made:

- strengthening of the impact of quality assurance (QA) practices at project level, together with the creation of a Software Engineering Process Group (SEPG);
- review of the QMS, in accordance with ISO 9000 standards;
- introduction of product quality planning and tracking (with validation of nonfunctional requirements toward the ISO 9126 model [7]);
- fine-tuning of standard operating procedures;
- strengthening of software testing practices, including the setup of automatic nonregression suites; and
- extension and broad application of the measurement system.

DO: Process Improvement Actions at Italtel Linea UT

With the beginning of 1992, Italtel Linea UT developed an action plan to implement the recommendations of the assessment. The improvement program was facilitated by several working groups dedicated to different work items. There was also a continuous training initiative at all levels, with the overall aim of integrating process changes into work practices within the smallest possible time frame.

In addition to the recommendations, it was decided to significantly increase the availability of documentation concerning the software product, and also to reengineer the backlog. Moreover, it was decided to define priorities among the suggested actions, with the aim of getting ISO 9000 certification as soon as possible.

The bulk of the improvement program took 2 years to complete, with a major review by management after the first year, which led to the decision to extend the scope of work, which also encompassed:

- the optimization of project management practices;
- the optimization of software requirements definition practices;
- the optimization of coding practices;
- root cause analysis on failures coming from the field;
- adoption of toolkits to check product quality; and
- quantitative estimation of failure trend based on reliability growth models (this gave good results, with a percentage error between estimates and actual data in the range from 5 to 10 percent [8]).

The overhead of the improvement program accounted for about 5 percent of the overall human resources of the Software Laboratory, including SEPG staff, ad hoc groups, work on standard operating procedures, data collection and analysis, and training of all staff but excluding adhoc improvement projects requiring a significant investment, namely:

- technical documentation reengineering,
- testing automation, and
- root cause analysis (RCA).

The following paragraphs are specifically dedicated to such issues, after a short overview of the tuning work performed on the QMS.

A Technical Insight: The QMS Tuning Initiative

The QMS plays a central role within the organisation and constitutes the place where the improvements which have shown positive results are deployed.

Within the QMS, the first step has been the specification of the software life cycle and the identification of roles and responsibilities. With respect to this life cycle structure, a set of Operating Procedures has been defined, also taking into account the requirements of the ISO 9000-3 International Standard. The Operating Procedures take into consideration both the development life cycle activities and the supporting activities.

As far as the development phases are concerned, the Procedures focus on the following topics:

- documentation guidelines,
- specification guidelines, and
- coding guidelines.

Referring to the supporting activities, the focus has been put on the improvement of the procedures concerning the following aspects:

- planning,
- configuration management,
- anomaly management, and
- measurement system.

The definition of the Operating Procedures has been driven by a bottom-up approach oriented pragmatically, in which a close connection with the Project and the usage of tools as an effective support can be seen as the most relevant and winning aspects.

The QMS is constantly kept aligned with the evolution of software development practices. Also, major activities currently in process are directed toward a stronger integration with the procedures of other organisational units whose work has tight relationships with software development, namely, Hardware Design and System Engineering.

A Technical Insight: Reengineering of the Technical Documentation

The documentation structure was defined in order to closely agree with the functional and structural organisation of the product. The description layers to which documentation was attached are summarised in Figure 9.3.

For each of the levels identified an appropriate documentation level was defined, in addition to the documentation of new features (impact analysis).

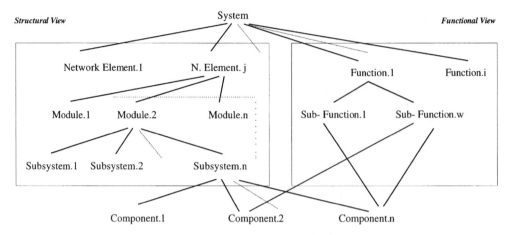

Figure 9.3. Documentation structure.

This allowed a description of the system to be maintained that would operate both from a functional and a structural point of view.

In order to keep track of the massive number of documents and software components, a traceability mechanism was built on top of the configuration management system, allowing us to:

- identify all product parts;
- relate product parts with technical documents (both specifications and test documents), for sake of traceability;
- relate product parts with software components;
- relate product parts with features, in order to perform impact analysis and plan regression testing; and
- relate product parts with the responsible level, allowing the automatic derivation of a skeleton of the development plan.

With respect to the highlighted document structure, the adopted approach for document reengineering was based on the following strategy:

- on the one hand, a decision was made to progressively correlate all the already produced documentation to the new defined rules;
- on the other hand, it was decided that all the new documentation had to be produced according to the new rules defined.

Table 9.1 gives quantitative data about the coverage of specification documents with respect to all the functions defined in the traceability tree.

Going into more detail, Table 9.2 gives the number of documents produced for each single type in Project C.

Two points are worth mentioning about documentation:

- Most of the produced documentation can be directly available to the Customer, which in this way can have a direct access to detailed technical information.
- The software producing unit is setting up a WWW access to the document repository, in order to facilitate browsing through the documentation. The website can be accessed by all the people involved in the project, with different levels of permission to access data.

Table 9.1. Number of Specification Documents for Three Successive Releases

Specification Documents	Project A	Project B	Project C
Degree of coverage	33%	46%	74%
Number of pages	~12,000	~24,000	~60,000

Table 9.2. Number of Documents Produced in Project C

Phase	Document	Produced
Requirements	Development Plan	1
	Quality Plan	1
	Product requirements	1
	Feature requirements	9
Specification	System specification	1
	Module specifications	7
	Subsystem specifications	193
	Function specifications	396
Coding/Implementation	Component design specifications	882
Test	Functional test specifications	270
Manuals	Project manuals	3

A Technical Insight: The Test Automation Initiative

The test automation initiative brought a rigorous definition of test levels, methods, and tools. The test levels identified are:

- Unit test
- Integration test
- System test

Tests are accomplished according to a black box approach, which ensures correctness and conformity to functional product requirements.

In addition, regression testing activities have been defined. Test automation has allowed, in particular, the thorough application of functional tests at each new load produced, thus succeeding in executing a huge number of tests (more than one thousand) in a couple of days. As a consequence, automation of regression testing has been one of the initiatives yielding the highest payoff at the product quality level.

Within this context, the following strategic topics were addressed:

- A systematic planning activity, which allows better management of time and resources.
- A test automatic execution which allows the whole set of test activities to be speeded up and controlled; in particular, test automation was very strong in the area of database management.
- Automatic execution of the regression tests, which allows improvement of test process effectiveness.
- Implementation of specific software development techniques in order to increase their testability (mainly by enforcing the standardisation of command syntax).

- Detailed metrics for evaluating the improvement opportunities of testing activities; such indicators were of course much more detailed than the basic ones defined in the measurement system (see discussion of this topic below).

In particular, collected metrics covered such aspects as:

- Test complexity (number of commands tested, number of parameters, etc.)
- Test size (number of test cases, number of test scripts, number of covered functions, etc.)
- Test execution (for all builds: number of tests executed, passed, failed)
- Number of failures discovered in all phases and broken down by subsystems, allowing us to compute testing effectiveness in the various phases and areas
- Test productivity (both in design and in execution)

The availability of such metrics allowed the analysis of test effectiveness broken down by subsystems/functional areas, thus focusing the available resources on the most critical and error-prone parts, in accordance with the Pareto principle (20 percent of software modules contribute to 80 percent of the system failures).

Moreover, the collection of detailed effort measurements singled out an improvement opportunity related to the test design activities: such activities proved to be the most effort consuming, especially for the update of test specifications as a consequence of small changes in the commands to be tested. Test specifications design and maintenance thus appeared to be an area of improvement that efforts should be focused on.

When analysing the guidelines for test design documents, it was easy to see that the main effort had to be spent in the description of the expected results. In most cases this was done in prose language, describing, for each test, all the updated tables, in detail down to the level of records and fields. Such information was felt essential but at the same time very effort consuming to maintain. As a consequence, a detailed technical analysis was conducted in order to define test patterns and to identify the specific information needed for the design of the various tests.

In some way this led to "object-oriented" testing, with classes of tests and tests treated as instances of a test class. A direct consequence of this approach was the definition of a formal language for test design, allowing semiautomatic test generation and maintenance starting from reference documentation. Indeed, a side effect was the improved readability of test documentation and the automation of test validation activities.

As originally foreseen, this technique allowed us to maintain and raise the high quality of test specifications while shifting the focus of testing activities from test design to test execution, which is well known to be the critical planning path for each software development project. Table 9.3 describes the percentage of effort breakdown of test activities before (Project C) and after the application of the enhanced technique (Project D). As a matter of fact, Project D exhibited improvement in fault density, and especially in the timeliness of testing, thus achieving a better time to market.

A detailed presentation of the test automation initiative can be found in [9].

A Technical Insight: The Application of Root Cause Analysis Techniques

As well described in [10], causal analysis (or, in other terms, Root Cause Analysis [RCA]) is a technique appropriate for identifying the causes and inner mechanisms that lead to costly or risky problems related to the quality of the delivered products or the efficiency of the development process. The goal of RCA is the formulation of recommendations to eliminate or reduce the incidence of the most recurrent and costly errors in subsequent development projects.

Table 9.3.   Variations in Testing Effort Breakdown

Effort Spent (%)	Project C	Project D
Analysis and test identification	25%	14%
Test specification	12%	15%
Test suite coding	11%	16%
Test execution	21%	32%
Test maintenance	31%	23%

RCA has been extensively used at Italtel BUCT for:

- Investigation of where and why problems have been introduced.
- Investigation of where the problems have been detected and why they were not detected earlier.
- Investigation of reasons for scheduling deviations.

The preliminary condition for the application of RCA is the traceability of the processes. In fact, for an objective approach, the processes shall be defined and described in order to perform analysis on the project documentation.

The RCA was first of all applied to a set of failures coming from the field and selected on the basis of their severity. The reasons for this choice were:

- The field failures are the most relevant aspect of the quality perceived by the customer.
- The field failures are the most important to analyse because they have not been captured neither by internal tests nor by validation tests with the customer.
- In accordance with an analysis performed specifically in the Linea UT environment, the cost to find, fix, and validate failures from the field was 70 times higher than the cost to find, fix, and validate failures found during system test.

On the basis of severity and of fair distribution across development areas, 98 failures out of a total of 311 were selected for analysis. The sample is thus considered to be fairly representative and of statistical validity.

The steps through which RCA was performed were:

1. Definition of the set of possible causes to investigate

In order to keep full control of the experiment, the analysis focused only on the processes internal to the Software Producing Unit, while processes mastered by external entities (such as technical assistance, system engineering, and field support) were not analysed. A team of experts in the different activities of the development process was set up with the aim of preparing a questionnaire including the possible causes of errors. In particular, a distinction was made between the causes for the fault injection and the causes for not detecting the error. A questionnaire was prepared for each phase of the development life cycle for a total of several hundreds of questions. It has to be underlined that, in order not to influence the subsequent collection of results, questions were not clustered in accordance with root causes but presented in a flat format.

2. Data collection

The data was collected by means of direct interviews with designers involved in development, testing, and fixing of the faulty features. Interviews adopted a backtracking strategy: each time a selected cause had roots in a previous phase of the development life cycle, the analysis jumped on that activity, starting a new interview with the appropriate questionnaire together with the people in charge of the activity under analysis. For this reason, starting from 98 failures, more than 300 interviews were done, involving 200 persons at varying responsibility levels. In order to select the right people to interview, the planning documents were taken into account.

3. Validation of collected data
Before analysing the data collected, a validation step was performed. The goal of validation was not to review the results in order to preprocess them but rather to allow the possibility of uncovering additional causes. For this reason the development area managers were asked to give their view of the causes onto which designers had already expressed their point of view. It was not seldom the case that opinions differed, sometimes utterly. In such cases, the analysis of inconsistencies between the different points of view proved invaluable in suggesting additional causes.

4. Analysis of data with usage of Ishikawa diagrams
The results of the interviews were stored into a database and then analysed using statistical analysis tools. In order to identify the root causes of the introduction and the missing detection of failures, "cause/effect" Ishikawa diagrams were adopted. Such diagrams are very useful for presenting RCA results since they show the relationships between the effects (that is to say, the symptoms observed) and the causes. They are also called fishbone diagrams owing to their resemblance to a fish's skeleton, with the head being the effect and the bones the causes at various levels of nesting.

Among the various outcomes, in Figures 9.4 to 9.6 three Ishikawa diagrams are reported.

- Error injection during coding (data from Project B)
- Missed error detection during system test (data from Project B)
- Scheduling deviation (data from Project C)

For the sake of clarity, the figures report causes only at the highest level of breakdown.

5. Alignment to RCA recommendations
The ultimate goal of RCA is process improvement. To accomplish this task an expert working group was set up to evaluate and propose a set of process improvement actions. Improvement actions were decided at three levels:

- Improvement to the development/testing process
- Improvement to specific technical aspects
- Improvement to the mechanics of RCA

As far as the development/testing processes were concerned, it was decided to implement the following improvement actions:

- More careful coordination between integration testing and system testing activities, in order to ensure the maximum synergy and the minimum overlap.
- Widening of test automation, in order to overcome scheduling problems during test execution and to force the application of standard rules instead of personal experiences.
- Controlled adoption of the risk management criteria used in deciding the accuracy of integration tests and in selecting system test cases, by means of the adoption of process waivers that have to be authorized by appropriate management levels.

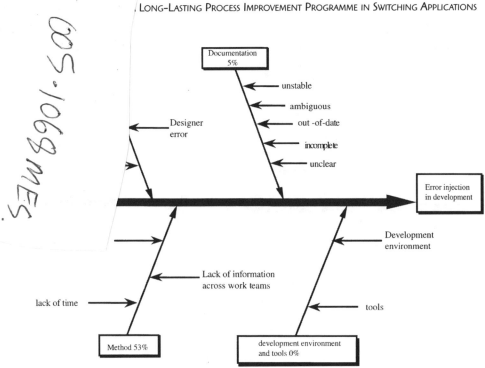

Figure 9.4. Categorisation of causes for error injection during coding.

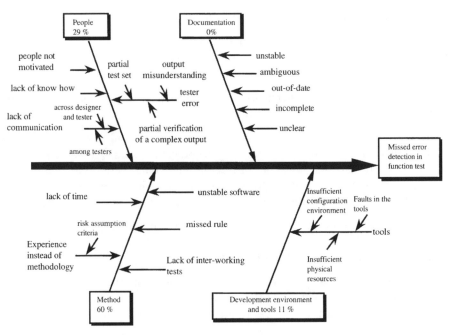

Figure 9.5. Categorisation of causes for missed error detection during system test.

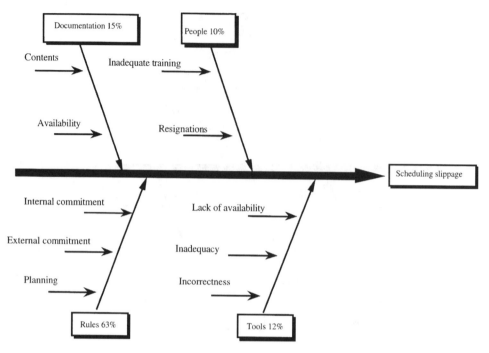

Figure 9.6. Scheduling slippage.

Concerning specific technical aspects, the following actions were agreed on:

- Extension of training on coding practices and testing guidelines.
- Review of system test documents in order to include additional non-regression tests aiming at covering the most frequently emerging issues.

As far as fine-tuning of RCA mechanisms is concerned, in order to improve its effectiveness and its pragmatic feasibility, the following actions were devised:

- Application of RCA as soon as the failure is detected, instead of project "postmortem" analysis; this is accomplished by enhancing the defect tracking system used, so that it will be possible to declare and store the "cause" chosen from a list of predefined motivations.
- Extension of RCA to the failures during integration testing, in order to benefit from the feedback before the release is shipped to First Office Application.

A detailed presentation of the RCA activities can be found in [11].

CHECK: The Impacts of SPI at Italtel Linea UT

The measurement system was a cornerstone of the improvement program; quoting from [12], we could say that "In God we trust, all others must bring data." Several actions were set up in order to track the effectiveness of Process Improvement actions, namely:

- collection of quantitative measures at the project level;
- analysis of measures across projects in order to analyse the impacts of Process Improvement; and
- process assessment.

Table 9.4.   Relationships between Goals and Indicators of the Metrics Program

Objectives	Indicators Relevant for the Customer	Indicators Relevant for the Project
Timeliness	• Timeliness for the customer	• Timeliness for the project • Efficacy
Reliability	• Failure rate in field • Test effectiveness	• Fault density
Documentation Resources	• Documentation for the customer	• Documentation for the project • Productivity

The various aspects are dealt with below.

The Measurement System

One of the key assets of the improvement program is the metrics initiative [13]. The main goals of the metrics program are:

- To provide the quantitative information essential to identify opportunities for improvements.
- To verify the advantages of the implemented changes to the development process.

In this context the main goal of the metrics program is measuring, in a quantitative way, the products and the development process in order to single out, implement, and monitor the corrective actions to improve both the process and the product.

The metrics have been defined in accordance with the goals of the SPU: timeliness, reliability, documentation, and resources. Indicators are collected and analysed from two different points of view: the customer and the project.

Table 9.4 summarises the indicators defined at customer and project levels and their relationships with the goals tracked by the metrics program. Indicators were defined following a Goal-Question-Metrics (GQM) approach.

These indicators rely on a core set of basic metrics (duration, failures, lines of code, activities, resources, documents) as detailed in Table 9.5.

Usage of the Metrics Program

As described in previous chapters, in order to make a metrics program of practical usefulness, a set of activities must be defined to help manage the information: data collection, data integration, data analysis, and reporting.

In the following discussion, such aspects are tailored to the Italtel Linea UT experience.

1. *Data collection.* Indicators are collected every 2 weeks by the different organisational units involved in the metrics program. Several organisational units contribute in collecting the metrics:

   - Planning Unit (for: Duration; Number of Activities; Resources)
   - Configuration Management Unit (for: Work; Size)
   - Software Producing Unit (for Number of produced documents)
   - Testing Unit (for: Number of failures)

Table 9.5.   Indicators of the Measurement System

Indicator	Meaning	Definition
Timeliness for the customer	Measures the delivering time of the product to the customer with respect to the initially agreed delivery date	T_{ec} / T_{cc}
Failure rate in operation	Measures the relation between the number of failures occurred during the operational phase and the duration of such phase	N_o / D_o
Test effectiveness	Measures the percentage of failures discovered during internal testing	$1 - (N_o / (N_e + N_o))$
Documentation for the customer	Measures the number of produced documents (limited to the layers visible to the Customer) with respect to the foreseeable ones (total coverage of the documentation tree)	Doc_{pc} / Doc_{ec}
Timeliness for the project	Measures the scheduling slippage from the detailed Development Plan	T_{ep} / T_{cp}
Efficacy	Measures the amount of work performed with respect to the elapsed time consumed	$DE = W_t / D_t$
Fault Density	Measures the number of faults occurred in field with respect to the afforded work	$DF = N_o / W_t$
Documentation for the project	Measures the total number of produced documents with respect to the foreseeable ones	Doc_{pp} / Doc_{pe}
Productivity	Measures the ability to produce work with respect to the resource profile	$DP = W_t / R_t$

Abbreviations: D_o, duration of the operational phase; Doc_{ec}, number of planned documents (limited to customer visibility); Doc_{pc}, number of documents produced (limited to customer visibility); Doc_{pe}, total number of foreseeable documents; Doc_{pp}, total number of documents produced; D_t, total duration of the project; N_e, number of failures of critical and major severity occurring during the organisational phase; N_o, number of failures of critical and major severity occurring during the operational phase; R_t, total number of person-years spent during the project; T_{cc}, total duration of the project; T_{cp}, actural duration of the project until the beginning of testing activities; T_{ec}, duration of the project according to the initial estimation; T_{ep}, duration of the project until the beginning of testing activities; W_t, total number of Delta Kilo Lines of Code (the delta takes into account changed, added, and deleted lines).

2. *Data integration.* Measures are collected with a very fine level of granularity; due to this fact they have to be integrated at a coarser granularity (project, subproject, or functional level) to allow the research for correlation among them and subsequent interpretations.
3. *Data analysis.* Measures are analysed through the inspection of trends in the collected indicators.

The main goal is to verify that the more the activities are conducted according to what is defined in the Process Improvement Plan and in the Quality System, the more the indicators that refer to Timeliness and Reliability are enhanced.

In this way, we search for correlation between aspects of duration and failure occurrence, on the one hand, and indicators strictly related to the development process on the other hand.

Table 9.6.   The Measurement System: Values Obtained from Three
Different Projects

	Unit	Initial Goal	Prj A Aug-92	Prj B Dec-93	Prj C Aug-95	Current Goals
Timeliness to customer	%	>90	100	98	93	100
Failure rate in field	F/Week	<10	4.02	5.98	6.88	<10
Testing effectiveness	%	>80	77	85	85	>80
Docum. for customer	%	>50	33	51	65.6	>60
Timeliness for project	%	>80	85	71	82	>80
Efficacy	Dkloc/Week	>18	18.5	34.6	41	>27
Fault density	F/Dkloc	<0.12	0.15	0.08	0.08	<0.05
Productivity	Dkloc/SY	>9	9.2	15.1	20.6	>14

4. *Reporting.* The aim of the reporting system is to produce structured and easily interpretable documents to spread the information among the organisational units. There were
several advantages to using a well-defined reporting system:

- it contributes to spreading the meaning and the objectives of the metrics program to
every interested organisational unit;
- it guides the collection of useful data and guarantees the visibility of the work done; and
- it constitutes the basis for analysis of the process and improvement activities.

At Italtel Linea UT, there are two different types of reports: the former is delivered
every 2 months and constitutes a collection of data without any analysis; the latter is delivered once a year and contains the interpretation of data.

Quantitative Data from Projects

Table 9.6 refers to the indicators for three major releases of the Linea UT switching system developed and delivered to the field during the period between 1990 and 1995. For
each indicator, the metrication unit is stated, together with the goal that was established at
the beginning of the program and the values for the three projects. The last column refers
to the new and challenging goals that have been defined for the projects currently under
development.

It has to be noted that comparability among the reported projects is possible owing to the
fact that the main difference among them is constituted by enhanced processes, whereas other
factors (e.g., size and staff experience) did not differ significantly.

Table 9.7 summarises the basic data for the three projects, showing that they are not toy exercises. Moreover, being three major releases of the same system (same application domain, same
technology, same development unit) it is possible to directly compare and cross-check them.

The following comments can be made:

- *Efficacy* and *Productivity* show a significant growth.
- *Timeliness for the Project* fluctuates around 80 percent, while *Timeliness for the Customer*
(100->98->93) tends to decrease, remaining in any case at a very high level (a result of
90 percent, that is to say, 10 percent scheduling deviation is considered an excellent
result by most software engineering surveys).

Table 9.7. Basic Data for the Three Reference Projects

Basic Data	Proj A	Proj B	Proj C
Duration in week	76	108	108
Number of failures in	685	1768	2283
Number of failures in field	209	311	350[1]
Delta KLOC	1406	3742	4428
Product size—KLOC	4058	6107	8865
Number of activities	888	3578	3132
Staff-Years	153	247	215

[1]: Value foreseen after 8 months from field installation.

- *Fault density in operation*, after a decisive improvement, shows stability on values that are felt as satisfactory. Despite this fact, the customer perceives in the field more failures per week (see the failure rate indicator) and thus might not be delighted by SPI results. This is because the size/complexity of products that are released has grown so much that improvement in fault density is overridden. This means that process improvement has to continue and even to accelerate in order to compensate for the unavoidable growth of applications released. Hence there is a need to understand where to focus the additional improvement efforts that should concentrate on bettering fault density up to the point that the fault rate becomes at least stable.

In general, the availability of quantitative data has allowed us to put an end to fruitless subjective discussions and to turn our focus to objective results. It is worth emphasizing that even if most of the time the data was shown to be aligned with subjective expectations, it was not seldom the case that data exhibited strong differences from the general consensus within the SPU.

Analysing the Net Contribution of Process Improvement

Knowledge of quantitative data is often much more convincing than any theoretical assumption about good practices; henceforth, an effort was made to find quantitative relationships between process maturity levels and the measurement data, in a way similar to what was reported in [14].

This shows that, after some data collection, one can really begin using the results in a true engineering approach. For these reasons such rules have been incorporated in an operating procedures of the QMS, in order for them to be publicly known and used within the SPU.

The net contribution from process improvement has been calculated, based on the differences between the current results and those predicted by a number of site-specific estimation procedures (based on data from past projects). Such rules are very important at Italtel Linea UT for the following reasons:

- They show that duration, resources, and failures are related to both the amount of delta KLOC and to a fixed base.
- They allow the prediction of the duration, effort, and failures of a project as soon as there is a sound estimate of the expected delta KLOC. This type of prediction is straightforward due to the existence of data sets upon which it is possible to derive estimates by analogy; thus such predictions are feasible very early in the life cycle.

Table 9.8.   Trend of the Process Standardisation Indicator

	Unit	Initial Goal	Prj A Aug-92	Prj B Dec-93	Prj C Aug-95	Current Goal
Process standardisation	%	>0.5	0.31	0.48	0.72	>0.8

Table 9.9.   Observed Relationships between PS and Business Goals

	Global PS
Timeliness	☺
Reliability (Failure rate in operation)	☺
Productivity	☺
Documentation for the customer	☺

The availability of predictive rules has been merged with the observation that the improvements in a medium-large organisation do not become consolidated in a short time interval; rather, different attitudes coexist for a long time. Thus, at Italtel Linea UT it was decided to define a new indicator, named "Process Standardisation" (PS), aimed at measuring the level of adherence to the QMS. To do so, for each activity of the development model, waivers from the QMS are taken into account by means of the definition of typical "behaviours," defined within a Standard Operating Procedure, and by the indication for each activity included in the development plan of the specific behaviour applied. PS is defined in such a way that it can yield values in the range between 0 and 1, where 1 represents the optimal situation. For the purpose of tracking process improvement effects, PS was computed both at the project level and for each major phase of the development process (specification, coding, test design, and test execution).

Table 9.8 shows the trend of the PS indicator for the three reference projects. Improvements are steady, showing a progressive alignment between QMS rules and project practices.

The correlation between Process Standardisation (PS) and business goals is summarised in Table 9.9 as a result of a quantitative study covering Projects A, B, and C. The "smiley face" ☺ means that a growth in PS has been shown to positively affect the results of the associated indicator.

For more details on the relationships between PS and business goals, the reader is referred to [16].

Interpretation of Quantitative Data

The indicators collected show that there have been several tangible improvements proven by quantitative data.

Considering each of the goals, improvements can be observed by both analysing differences between "before" and "after" metrics and by calculating the net benefits from process improvement (this last aspect has been performed using the technique defined in Chapter 5).

In the following, high-level results are summarised from a management point of view.

1. *Timeliness.* Timeliness for the Customer, though slightly decreasing, stays at a satisfactory level. This is notable, especially in the light of a recent survey carried out in Europe and Japan which showed that schedules are met only in a very small percentage of projects [15]; if we consider the net contribution of software improvement, it can be shown that timeliness capability has been improved by a factor of 30 percent (Figure 9.7).

2. *Documentation.* The availability of documentation both for the customer and for the project is quickly increasing and has reached its goals, without adversely affecting other indicators (in particular, timeliness issues).

3. *Reliability.* Fault density in operation (Figure 9.8) has dropped to less than one fault per 10 delta KLOC (by delta KLOC we mean the number of KLOC changed in a release with respect to the previous one), with an improvement from Project A to Project C of 54 percent, coupled by an increase of Testing Effectiveness. Positive results come mainly from the improvement action that automated nonregression test suites. To judge by a number of published studies, a fault found in the field costs 10 times more to correct than one found in testing; using this assumption, the improvement in testing effectiveness amounts to a savings of 27 percent in the effort to apply corrective maintenance.

4. *Productivity.* Our goals have been largely reached and we can observe significantly better performance along projects. Nevertheless, if we consider the difference between expected values and actual ones we arrive at the conclusion that this is the area where direct benefits from process improvement are less tangible.

Cross-Checking Process Improvement from an Assessment Perspective

In May 1994, 30 months after the first assessment, a second BOOTSTRAP assessment took place in order to monitor the effects of the improvement plan. The findings from the reassessment indicated that substantial improvements have been obtained. Italtel Linea UT has progressed to a maturity level between the defined and measurable levels for the SPU level and to a stable defined level for the project practices.

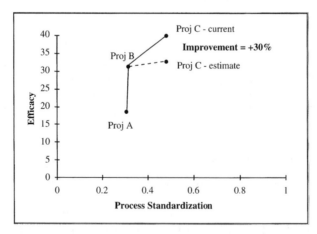

Figure 9.7. Timeliness versus process standardisation.

The assessment team concluded that the software team has established the foundation for continuous improvement, as was also officially recognized by ISO 9000 assessors during their last monitoring visit.

A detailed analysis of assessment profiles is reported in [16].

ACT: Deployment at Italtel BUCT

After several years of experience, there is tangible evidence that process improvement applied to software development provides good results.

In this context the role of the various improvement approaches is as follows:

- ISO 9000 is a prerequisite.
- PDCA and management by metrics are the driving factors.
- Periodic process assessments help in quantifying the status reached.

STEPS AHEAD

Given the good results obtained, the SPU is planning to widen the efforts devoted to continuous improvement. The following actions are planned:

- constant alignment between rules and project practices;
- stronger cohesion between unit and functional testing;
- more intensive usage of metrics and models within projects, for the sake of planning, tracking, and oversight;
- cross-checking of company-specific planning models versus more general ones; the first studies anticipate the possible adoption of Putnam-based rules [17];
- extension toward more extensive application of TQM techniques, with the adoption of the Malcolm Baldrige Award scheme;
- deepening of analysis of the effectiveness of QMS; and
- technological improvement combined with process improvement.

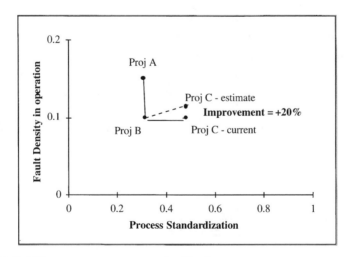

Figure 9.8.   Reliability versus process standardisation.

The following concluding section describes this last issue is some more detail.

A TECHNICAL INSIGHT: COMBINING PROCESS IMPROVEMENT WITH TECHNOLOGY EVOLUTION

In some cases we were aware of reaching a stage where the improvement of business goals became difficult. In such situations (which can be defined "improvement saturation"), technological innovations are needed that can help effect a breakthrough.

In such situations, SPI is valuable for improving both the process and the product. For this reason, Italtel Linea UT is pursuing a technology improvement effort with the goals of:

- reducing the amount of source code embedded in the systems, by means of appropriate techniques and the search for system solutions simplifying software development;
- adopting Object-Oriented paradigms;
- improving its software product with respect to the needs of the market (especially for ensuring flexibility and modularity when new features are released);
- enhancing the reusability and portability of software (focusing especially on runtime portability and reusability); and
- keeping up to date with technology innovation in the IT domain.

This challenging project, which is based on Object-Oriented methods and takes its direction from modern IT trends (e.g., Corba, Tina, Java, etc.), is likely to have a significant impact on software development processes and, as such, will have to be strictly coordinated with process improvement initiatives.

REFERENCES

1. AT&T, *Process Quality Management and Improvement Guidelines*, AT&T Quality Steering Committee, Issue 1.1, 1988.

2. G.G. Shulmeyer and J. I. McManus, *Total Quality Management for Software*, Van Nostrand Rheinold, 1992.

3. International Organisation for Standardization, *"Quality Management and Quality Assurance Standards—Part 3: Guidelines for the Application of ISO 9001 to the Development, Supply and Maintenance of Software*, ISO/IS 9000-3, Sept. 1990.

4. J.B. Souter and D.P. Cheney, "Information Technology Quality System Certification in Europe," *3rd European Conference on Software Quality*, Madrid, Nov. 3–6, 1992.

5. Members of the BOOTSTRAP Project Team, "BOOTSTRAP: Europe's Assessment Method," *IEEE Software*, May 1993.

6. P. Kuvaja et al., *Software Process Assessment and Improvement: The BOOTSTRAP Approach*, Blackwell, 1995.

7. International Organisation for Standardization, *Information Technology—Software Product Evaluation—Quality Characteristics and Guidelines for Their Use*, ISO/IEC IS 9126, Dec. 1991.

8. G. Bazzana et al., "Applying Software Reliability Models to a Large Industrial Data Set," *Information and Software Technology*, Dec. 1993.

9. S. Bassi, M. Crubellati, and S.M. Siciliano, "Test Process Management and Improvement," *Proceedings of Eurostar 95 Conference on Software Testing, Analysis and Review*, London, 1995.

10. L. Briand, K. El Emam, and W.L. Melo, "An Inductive Method for Process Improvement: Concrete Steps and Guidelines," *Proceedings of ISCN Conference*, Vienna.

11. G. Damele et al., "Process Improvement through Root Cause Analysis," *AQUIS 96 International Conference*, Florence, Jan. 1996.

12. L.J. Arthur, *Improving Software Quality—An Insider's Guide to TQM*, Wiley, 1992.

13. G. Damele et al., "Setting-up and Using a Metrics Program for Process Improvement." *Proceedings of AQUIS Conference*, Venice, Oct. 1993.

14. J. Herbsleb et al., *Benefit of CMM-Based Software-Process Improvement: Initial Results*, CMU/SEI-94-TR-13, SEI, Aug. 1994.

15. M. Azuma and D. Mole, "Software Management Practice and Metrics: EC and Japan— Some Results of Questionnaire Surveys," *Proceedings of AQUIS Conference*, Venice, Oct. 1993.

16. G. Damele et al., "Quantifying the Benefits of Software Process Improvement in Italtel Linea UT Exchange," *Proceedings of XV International Switching Symposium*, Berlin, May 1995.

17. L.H. Putnam, *Measures for Excellence*, Wiley, 1995.

Chapter 10

From Assessment to Improvement:

An Experience in the GSM Application Domain

R. Delmiglio, S. Di Muro, S. Humml, A. Lora
Italtel S.p.A., Italy

G. Bazzana, G. Rumi
Onion S.p.A., Italy

INTRODUCTION

The process improvement activities described here are being run at Italtel's Business Unit Reti Mobili (see description of Italtel's SPI programme in Chapter 9).

This Business Unit is committed to the development of global solutions for mobile communications in the worldwide market. A great deal of effort is currently invested in the GSM application domain (GSM 900, DCS 1800, PCS 1900, etc.) owing to the rapid market take-up, which is experiencing an unprecedented widespread growth rate.

Italtel RM is strongly committed to software process improvement that is felt to be a major leverage to increase the company capabilities. This is motivated by the high worldwide competitiveness in the target domain, the increasing complexity of the software embedded in the delivered systems, and the fact that projects are developed on an international multisite basis.

Also customers are more and more demanding regarding software process maturity and stability. With reference to this aspect, it is worth underlining the fact that one of the major customers took an active role in the process improvement program, by asking for process audits and by providing indications on the key process areas to be improved from their point of view. The "voice of the customer" proved to be a key factor in reinforcing the commitment and driving the improvement actions toward greater effectiveness.

ARCHITECTURE AND FEATURES OF GSM SYSTEMS

GSM is an European-born family of standards for the mobile telecommunication Digital Cellular Systems [1], allowing telephony services through mobile phones. Mobile telecommunications is not a very recent technology, but it is a rapidly evolving one. The main differences with wireline telecommunication access consist in:

- *Mobility management:* as a consequence of the fact that subscribers can continuously change their point of access to the network, routing of calls involves new concepts like: location management, handover (automatic transfer of a call in progress from one cell to another without speech disturbance), and roaming (free circulation of mobile stations across networks handled by different operators).
- *Radio resource management:* the link between the subscribers and the fixed infrastructure is not permanent and wave propagation limits and spectrum scarcity have to be taken into account.

From the architectural point of view, a GSM system is quite a complex object, since it has to deal with multiservices and with the peculiarities of cellular networks. Looking at the system from the outside, GSM is in direct contact with users, with other telecommunications networks and with the personnel of the service providers.

The internal GSM architecture distinguishes three parts: (the Base Station Subsystem (BSS), that is in charge of providing and managing transmission paths, the Network and Switching Subsystem (NSS), that is in charge of managing the communications, and the Operation and Maintenance Centre (OMC) which provides the interface to the system for the network operator.

Getting into details of the BSS, we can find the following Network Elements:

- A transmission equipment (the Base Transceiver Station [BTS];
- A managing equipment (Base Station Controller [BSC];
- A speech encoding/decoding equipment (Transcoder and Rate Adapter Unit [TRAU]) that performs also rate adaptation in case of data and, though considered a subpart of the BTS, is often sited away as a stand-alone equipment.

A simplified view of the architecture of a GSM system is provided in Figure 10.1, representing the various Network Elements as well as the standardised interfaces between them.

The goal of the RM projects referenced in this chapter is to develop the OMC, BSC, and TRAU Network Elements, together with a Local Maintenance Terminal (LMT) for controlling the Network Elements.

PLAN: INITIATING SPI THROUGH PROCESS ASSESSMENT AT ITALTEL RM

The Software Process Assessment Experience

Before the startup of a formal Improvement Program, SPI at Italtel RM was already an established practice, with a number of actions run between 1992 and 1995, namely:

- enforcement of Quality Assurance and Quality Control practices, with introduction of quality plans for each project;
- definition of guidelines for all the phases of the development life cycle;
- progressive strengthening of Configuration Management methods and tools;

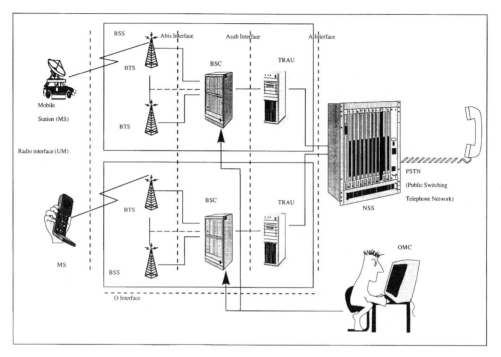

Figure 10.1.   Typical architecture of GSM systems.

- enhancement of planning and tracking practices, with introduction of Project Plans and Gantt charts;
- enhancement of test design and administration practices, with introduction of a separate team for testing within the development structure;
- enhancement of tool support for test execution;
- adoption of a Qualification Report accompanying load release to system test;
- introduction of tools for static analysis of the source code;
- definition of a measurement system and development of tools for data collection (Lines of Code [LOC], effort, etc.).

Such improvement actions allowed the Business Unit to attain very important results, both from a technical point of view and from the point of view of the Quality Management System (QMS) that was certified as ISO 9001 compliant. At that time it was felt that the improvement efforts had to be based on what already set up for the QMS and kept as a continuous activity monitored also by internal audits, in order to cope with an extremely competitive market; for this reason, software process assessment (SPA) activities were undertaken in order to focus the resources onto those areas that should provide the highest added value.

The Improvement Program started therefore with a Software Process Assessment conducted by Siemens Application Centre Software in accordance with the approach described in Chapter 8 of this book. In May–June 1995, some of the most important projects in the GSM area were subjected to a formal process assessment conducted by the Application Centre Software of the Central Research of Siemens AG. The activity was very broad and detailed, with interviews conducted with more than 35 people from the involved projects.

Results from the Assessment

The assessment highlighted a good maturity level for the software producing unit, singling out also some improvement opportunities that the management felt to be appropriate in order to raise the competitiveness in the global market.

The results of the assessment can be summarised as follows:

- the working practices were found to be in between the repeatable and the defined levels of the SEI CMM grading, depending on the projects. Even if such a result was felt as appropriate for the Business Unit at that time, the management understood the need for continuous improvement and strengthening of capabilities in order to face growing worldwide competition and to increase customers' satisfaction.
- Very positive aspects found were the cooperative attitude of the staff and the alignment between rules and practices. Such aspects were felt as very promising in the light of a SPI Project that would have impacted the existing behaviours.
- Considering the scope, relevance, and size of the impacted projects, it was decided to manage the improvements in a systematic way, setting up an ad hoc project to which an effort of about 5 percent of the R&D structure had to be devoted (including SPI Teams but excluding the deployment of actions with a large effort associated).
- The assessment resulted in a catalogue of about 100 detailed recommendations accompanied by a portfolio analysis of the action clusters: highlighting the areas that should be attacked first.

The top 10 recommendations for bettering cycle time and product quality are listed in the following (the order does not imply any priority among them):

- enforcement of handling of interdependencies across projects;
- systematic analysis of metrics and root cause analysis;
- improvement in change request procedure;
- improvement of preanalysis activities;
- improvement in design and interface specifications;
- enforcement in interworking tests;
- automation of target tests;
- better planning and managing of system test;
- technology innovation for the development environment; and
- strengthening of communication facilities across distributed development teams.

An Appraisal of the Assessment Experience

The Process Assessment was a very positive experience, and became the starting point and the invaluable source of recommendations for the Software Process Improvement Project.

Owing to the size of the organisations, the assessment was performed in adherence with the full standard approach, which proved to be balanced and effective. The evaluations given by the external assessor's representative were very much aligned with those of the internal representative, and the resulting picture was felt to be fair by both the technical staff and the management levels.

With respect to other assessment schemes, the following aspects were felt to be very valuable: the fitness with respect to the organisational structure and its goals, the adoption of clustering of actions, and, above all, the detailed recommendations together with their priority. This last output was very pragmatic and constructive, and thus became the true starting point for the improvement program.

During the running of the assessment a deviation from the interview-like style was tried, consisting in asking the staff to separately write down the best and worst aspects of the organisation and then collecting and publicly discussing the indications. This was extremely valuable both in singling out the improvement areas and in livening up the assessment atmosphere that can sometimes become gloomy or, at least, boring.

It has to be noted that for consistency with the assessment performed in BUCT, the results were also analysed by using the BOOTSTRAP algorithm. The results, seen in the light of a BOOTSTRAP grading, were generally more positive by a range of 0.25 to 0.5. In any case, the focus was on improvements rather than on maturity levels and thus this aspect was not explored in detail.

The Process Improvement Plan

The Process Improvement Plan was designed to meet the business goals of the company rather than to get to a predefined maturity level.

In some experiences reported in the literature, the process improvement team is formed with the mandate to help the organisation to become ISO 9001 certified within a specified timeframe. This type of strategy may be considered to be tied to business goals because it will help the organisation to get contracts or because it is demanded by a major customer. Similarly, some organisations consider achieving Level 3 on the Capability Maturity Model (CMM) to be important for business because it would help them to get contracts (especially in the United States). Progress is then measured by the proportion of Level 3 practices that have been implemented or the extent of compliance to ISO 9001 clauses. Success is measured by having all necessary practices implemented and ISO 9001 clauses adequately satisfied.

Strict adherence to an approach devoted only to the reaching of a formal status can have a number of disadvantages. When this approach is taken to its limit, the organisation does not need to actively measure important variables like product quality, productivity, and meeting budget and schedule targets, because these are not the main criteria used to evaluate progress and success. Therefore, the organisation may continue to put practices in place without knowing their effects on product quality, productivity, and predictability.

Even if ISO 9000 and CMM are precious sources of requirements and recommendations, putting practices in place on the faith that they are somehow "good" is of course not prudent. As noted in several studies, many of our intuitive ideas about software development may turn out to be incorrect once put to practice. In general, many practices that are in current use in software engineering have not been adequately empirically tested, and so we do not know if they really work, and under what conditions. It is therefore important not to confuse the difference between cause and effect: the goal is improving company goals through process improvement, not SPI in itself.

The result of this reasoning is that process improvement efforts ought to be driven by the desired effect, that is, it should be results driven. This is especially important for an organisation like Italtel RM which has already reached both ISO 9000 registration and a satisfactory maturity level and that has to deal with a competitive market requiring challenging capabilities in terms of delivery timeliness, product quality, and customer support.

Driven by such considerations, after the Process Assessment the Italtel RM management decided to start up a challenging Process Improvement Project, whose high-level objectives can be summarised as follows:

- to optimise the predictability of schedules [7] and the reaching of timeliness goals;
- to further enhance product quality;
- to raise the availability of documentation (both technical and user-oriented);

- to better the tool support to development activities; and
- to keep productivity levels at the current levels, while reaching the process improvement objectives of Italtel RM.

The analysis led to the setting up of an 18-month Process Improvement Project, focused on the following key aspects: planning, tracking, and oversight; requirements engineering; integration and system testing; and software development technology. The choice of a limited number of topics was made with the aim of avoiding the errors reported by other SPI programs that tried to solve all issues too rapidly. This is manifested in improvement programs with dozens of working groups and improvements being introduced concurrently. In practice, it is very difficult to have the capacity to change very rapidly without considerable disruption to ongoing projects. For each of the selected topics, a Working Group (WG) was established in order to propose, experiment with, validate, and apply those improvement actions showing the best return on investment. For each of the selected areas, the following rules were taken into account:

- One person shall be put in charge of the improvement area (this individual is normally referred as "the process owner").
- The Plan-Do-Check-Act paradigm shall be followed.
- A core set of basic metrics shall be defined at the beginning in order to collect data able to track and quantify the impact of the experienced improvements.
- Two lines of action shall be planned: the short-term implementation of those actions that require small overhead/elapsed time and the medium- to long-term planning of those actions involving a large amount of resources. This split is needed in order to focus both on quick solutions (that are very good for feeding and caring the enthusiasm about the improvement program) and on longer ones (these are the ones that are likely to have a greater impact on software engineering practices).
- Activities should be synchronised with project milestones, trying to define solutions just-in-time for their application within a (sub)project: this is extremely beneficial both for having timely feedback and for focusing on pragmatic issues and feasible solutions.

This last issue is particularly important considering the fact that it was dangerous to activate the biggest effort of all four areas in parallel: in this case the projects would have been overwhelmed and probably many improvement actions would have been rejected simply because of lack of time. As a consequence the high-level plan was defined in such a way that the improvement actions followed a just-in-time strategy and too many parallel streams in the "Do" step for the long-term actions was avoided.

The SPI Program is intended to be a continuous effort, handled with a management-by-objective approach with milestones and quantitative results. A very important verification point will be a new Process Assessment, which will be performed in order to track the extent of improvements gained.

DO: PROCESS IMPROVEMENT ACTIONS AT ITALTEL RM

In the following discussion an overview of the organisational structure for the SPI Program is given; afterward, for each of the four Working Groups, a summary is presented of the improvement actions designed and deployed. Finally, technical insights for some of the most important SPI actions are discussed.

Process Improvement Organisational Issues

In order to ensure the success of the Program, the SPI has been organised in the following way:

- A SPI Steering Committee (referred in the following discussion as PISC), chaired by the R&D Director and including all the managers reporting to him or her. The aim of this board (that meets regularly on a monthly basis, together with Process Improvement Program Office (PIPO) and Working Group (WG) Leaders) is to define priorities, assign resources, solve problems, and track the success of the initiative.
- A SPI Project Office (called PIPO and equivalent to a SEPG), composed of a few expert people, having the goal of planning/tracking the project, giving technical guidance, and harmonising/deploying the outcomes of the Working Groups.
- Four Working Groups, composed of technical representatives from the various projects involved and dealing with improvement actions; WGs were defined for the identified action clusters: planning and tracking (WG1), requirements engineering (WG2), integration and system testing (WG3), and technology (WG4).

Figure 10.2 gives an overview of the adopted organisational structure.

The process improvement steering committee has the role of driving the overall activities of the process improvement program by means of guiding, harmonising, and supporting the SPI activities.

Guidance is performed through defining the scope and boundaries of the SPI Program, approving the Improvement, and managing process assessment activities. Harmonisation is performed through coordinating SPI with the evolution of QMS; evaluating the SPI achievements with respect to the strategic goals of the Business Unit; and planning the widespread adoption of enhanced practices by other projects in the Business Unit.

Support is performed through approving actions involving a significant amount of resources and deciding the introduction of additional/changed practices within running projects, in cases where this has an impact either on the delivery date or on the resource profile.

The process improvement project office has the role of monitor, technical guide, and coordinator.

Monitoring is performed through tracking the detailed plans, coordinating the Working Groups, and collecting/analysing measurement data.

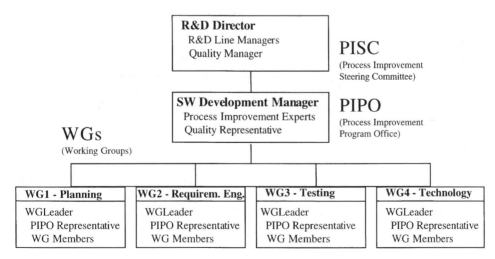

Figure 10.2.   Process improvement organisational structure.

Technical guidance is performed through: drafting the Process Improvement Plan and giving support to the Working Groups in the choice of most appropriate solutions.

Coordination is performed through addressing any issue that cannot be solved at Working Group level and organising training/dissemination actions.

The Working Groups have the role of implementing the process improvement actions by means of preparing and maintaining the detailed activity plans; collecting quantitative data; drafting new issues of software-related standard operating procedures; defining technical approaches for addressing the improvement actions; applying improvement actions onto pilot projects; and reporting the status of activities and any problem to the Project Office.

Process Improvement Actions

In the next paragraphs the technical details of the improvement efforts managed by the described SPI organisation are reported.

Actions are clustered in adherence with the topics managed by the four working groups and are clearly attached to the assessment recommendations.

After giving a minimal background, improvement actions are listed and commented. In order to give some flavour of the adopted approaches, for each Working Group one action is presented in more details, providing the technical insights.

Actions Related to Planning/Tracking/Oversight

Planning/tracking/oversight of big projects organised following a multisite development scheme is an inherently challenging job. In order to master the complexity of projects, planning is managed by a separate organisational unit that provides high level plans, checks project progress on a regular basis, reports the status to the management, and performs risk assessment and analysis, following up any decided action item.

Each phase is marked by a baseline, whose achievement has to be formally declared in accordance with prespecified quality criteria, concerning the completeness of documentation for the specific phase, the level of coverage for documentation of the following phase, test coverage, fault density, absence of operational restrictions, etc. Phases are in turn subdivided into activities associated with well defined milestones.

The Software Process Assessment singled out the following strengths concerning Planning/Tracking/Oversight: presence of accurate plans agreed at various levels, regular project tracking activities, collection of quantitative measurement, circulation of information about such data.

At the same time, the following improvement opportunities were identified: coordinated project management of parallel projects, extension of the usage of Root Cause Analysis (RCA) and adoption of planning/tracking tools purported for large projects.

As a consequence of such recommendations and of subsequent technical analysis, the following actions were designed and deployed:

- enforcement of handling of interdependencies across projects (see assessment recommendation 1);
- systematic analysis of metrics and root cause analysis (see assessment recommendation 2);
- adoption of more powerful planning/tracking tools;
- strengthening of oversight mechanisms through Progress Trend Analysis (PTA);
- collection and analysis of estimates and planning data from previous and current projects, with set-up of an Intranet-based repository for quantitative measures; and

• review of estimation procedures, basing them on analogy with previous projects as well as on models based on Lines of Code and Function Points.

In the following, some technical insights are given about the improvement in PTA-based oversight mechanisms.

A Technical Insight: Strengthening Oversight Mechanisms through Progress Trend Analysis (PTA)

Progress Trend Analysis is a technique that tracks the progress of activities with respect to a predefined quantitative trend, in order to single out as soon as possible any deviation and apply appropriate preventive and corrective actions.

PTAs can be applied at project level or, for sake of increased control, to each development phase. In order to apply PTA, for each phase a quantitative yardstick has to be defined (e.g., features for preanalysis, documents for analysis, lines of code for implementation, test cases for testing, etc.). Then an identification (or estimate) of the total number of items to be produced for that phase in that specific project has to be produced. The delivery dates of various items have then to be identified (usually deriving them from the development plans) and, as a consequence, a "Plan" curve can be determined constituted by the cumulative number of items which are planned to be delivered along time.

Such a "Plan" curve is the baseline against which the progress achievements are cross-checked, by means of periodic collection of project data and derivation of an "Actual" curve.

Figure 10.3 shows an example of a PTA graph (not referred specifically to any project) in which the "Plan" curve was designed as a straight line, whereas the "Actual" curve shows an S-shaped profile, which is by far the most frequent trend in software development projects.

The regular use of PTA is a major support to project management since it permits the detection of deviations from the expected trend very early, allowing the activation of countermeasures to prevent the impacts of these denation on the delivery deadline. Various techniques are available for analysing PTAs, as described in [2]. Sometimes just drafting the Plan curve is sufficient to point out unrealistic planning. In other circumstances, the need for additional resources becomes clear by observing a progressive distance between the two curves; sometimes the need

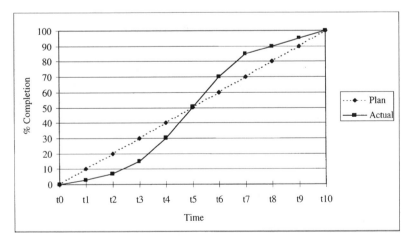

Figure 10.3. Example of Progress Trend Analysis (PTA) chart.

for replanning the number of items to be released or the shipping date becomes evident very early. After some experience, you are able to recognise typical patterns for the various development areas or for the various phases, which constitute a reference for subsequent projects.

As of this writing, PTA is extensively used in all project phases of all development projects. It is deemed a powerful technique both by development project leaders and by project management staff to perform quantitative tracking/oversight and to report the project status to the management.

Actions Related to Requirements Engineering

The Analysis and Design phases of the reference development projects are performed following a waterfall life cycle (with heavy concurrent engineering) that starts after the completion of Preanalysis activities. The development teams are put in charge of analysing the impacts on the existing system caused by the additional features; as an output, designers produce "Feature Sheet" documents, detailing the impacted subsystems, the technical activities to be performed and the effort estimates for analysis, design, implementation, and integration. After the review/approval of these Feature Sheets, analysis activities bring to the drafting of Functional Specifications documents (one for each functional area); such documents are the starting point for test design as well as for Customer Documentation drafting. After the review/approval of Functional Specifications, design activities now come to the drafting of Design Specifications Documents (DSD) (one for each subsystem) as well as Interface Specifications documents. Such documents are the starting point for coding.

Any modifications to approved specifications are handled through formal Change Requests. All documents are written in the English language in accordance with documentation standards.

The Software Process Assessment singled out the following strengths concerning Requirements Engineering: availability of well-defined standard operating procedures and guidelines for analysis/design; coverage of feature impacts; formalised interface documents.

At the same time, the following improvement opportunities were identified: enforcement of level of detail of DSDs and interface specifications; more controlled update activities in order to keep the documentation aligned with the implementation; adoption of the SDL specifications language and related CASE tools in order to increase the quality of documentation, perform consistency and completeness checks and generate code frames.

As a consequence of such recommendations and of subsequent technical analysis, the following actions were designed and deployed:

- improvement in change request procedure (see assessment recommendation number 3);
- enforcement of preanalysis activities (see assessment recommendation number 4);
- improvement in design and interface specifications (see assessment recommendation number 5);
- strengthening of traceability mechanisms;
- tuning of technical documentation guidelines;
- alignment of technical documentation to new guidelines for running projects in order to cover the whole documentation tree;
- reinforcement of code review procedures, combining tool driven checking with human inspections;
- introduction of formal specifications languages (namely, SDL)

In the following some technical insights are given about the improvement in interface specifications.

A Technical Insight: Improvement in Interface Specifications

Interface management is a very sensitive matter in architecturally complex systems being developed by different development teams. As a matter of fact, interfaces need to be described in extreme detail and frozen quite early in the development life cycle, in order to have a sound basis for design and coding activities. It happens that interfaces between system components developed by different teams change (although already frozen in a previously agreed version) because coding and detailed design show a need for such a change. If interfaces are changed at such a later stage of a project this leads to a great deal of effort to correct the changes and inform and agree with all involved teams. The matter is very important because the interface structure has big impacts also on the test procedures, the technical/customer documentation, and even the supporting tools.

Interface management was improved thanks to the development and adoption of a tool acting as a centralised repository (based on a relational data base) and as a filter for all the interface messages. Of course, the technical innovation had to be accompanied by organisational and methodological innovations, with the introduction of a Control Board and with the reengineering of the process flow covering all related activities.

Such an approach allowed better control of the design and maintenance of interfaces which led to improvements in product quality (no more possibility of misalignments between development teams) and in productivity (thanks to the automatic generation of message catalogues, interface documents, command manual skeletons, include files, configuration files, and support files for the target testing tools).

Actions Related to Testing

Besides review activities performed during the development phases, the validation of GSM systems involves several complex and effort-intensive tasks, that can be summarised as follows:

- Unit testing, focused on the single software module and performed in the development environment
- Host (offline) testing focused on the integration of different software modules in a simulated environment
- White-box testing focused on complete features in the target environment
- Black-box testing focused on a complete Network Element at the external interfaces in the target environment
- Integration testing focused on interconnected Network Elements in fully equipped configuration (complete BSS and OMC)
- System test: V&V of the global system in the final environment, with an end-user perspective
- Acceptance testing: trial of the system with the user in field environment.

At each step regression activities have to be performed with respect to features delivered in previous releases, features delivered in previous loads of the release under development, stability of the system after fixing of faults and/or implementation of Change Requests, changes in hardware/firmware/operating system/configurations, etc. As a consequence, regression testing has to be thorough, requiring considerable staffing. Moreover, regression testing is subjected to severe deadline pressures: testing is by definition on the critical path!

Besides the usual problem posed by big systems [3], the following aspects had to be taken into account:

- The equipment is quite complex.
- The development is subdivided among teams that are geographically distributed (multi-site development).

- The numberless possible configurations of the systems cause an exponential growth of situations to be considered.
- The test beds (environment and tools) need to be prepared ad hoc.
- The wide range of things to validate (firmware, operating systems, transmission protocols, application software dealing with call processing, application software dealing with operation and maintenance, etc.) requires utterly different approaches in test design and execution.
- The many relationships across physical objects (processors and executable processes) and features requires an accurate planning of deliveries and synchronisation points among the various development teams.

Early error detection and anticipation of test activities in an environment which offers easier testing and debugging facilities are therefore of paramount importance for both productivity and product quality.

The Software Process Assessment singled out the following strengths concerning testing: test design activities performed starting from analysis/design documents in parallel with development activities; existence of a well-defined test life cycle, with associated documentation and responsibilities; root cause analysis activities and collection of quantitative data about fault density, test effectiveness, etc.

At the same time, the following improvement opportunities were identified: strengthening of the testing across Network Elements, quality management of system test activities (planning/tracking, reviews, configuration management), adoption of test automation facilities, strengthening of the host testing phases in the development environment.

As a consequence of such recommendations and of subsequent technical analysis, the following actions were designed and deployed:

- enforcement in interworking tests (see assessment recommendation number 6);
- test automation [4] (see assessment recommendation number 7);
- better planning and managing of system test (see assessment recommendation number 8)
- strengthening of host (offline) testing;
- consolidation of regression testing suites; and
- improvement in object patch management.

In the following, some technical insights are given about the strengthening of host testing.

A Technical Insight: Strengthening of Host Testing

One of the goals of SPI was to fully deploy an improvement action already started before the startup of the SPI Program: strengthening of host testing, that is to say, the testing performed in a simulated, offline environment. The goal was to devise technical solutions allowing testing execution on host environment as soon as possible, without waiting for the availability of target prototypes; this was a major change to the development process, since it involved the strengthening of such activity from an organisational, methodological and technical point of view.

From a methodological point of view, several techniques were adopted for test design, depending on the peculiarities of the various areas, among which were: Finite State Machine techniques; input space partitioning techniques; command syntax, and boundary checks techniques.

Tests were not limited to functional aspects, but also included: negative cases (check of proper behaviour in presence of error conditions), stress testing (check of proper behaviour in limit conditions), endurance testing (check of proper behaviour for a long period of continu-

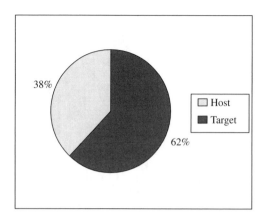

Figure 10.4. Distribution of failures versus environment.

ous functioning, for example, several days), interworking testing (check of proper behaviour of concurrent functioning of interleaved functions), conformance testing (check of proper behaviour of the system with respect to GSM specifications), interface testing (check of proper handling of the standard interfaces of the system, at various layers of functioning).

In order to follow a quantitative approach, a number of specific metrics were devised, distinguished in four major areas, in accordance with the taxonomy presented in Chapter 6: metrics used for project management, for product evaluation, for derivation of baselines and for assessment of best practices. For details on all metrics and results collected, the interested reader is referred to [5], whereas in the following the focus is put on the effectiveness of the achieved results.

Most failures were captured offline (Figure 10.4); moreover, the analysis of failures found on the target environment showed that only 17 percent of those were detectable on the host: most were in fact by their nature dependent on the physical configuration of test beds.

The following picture shows the test execution rates in host and target environments, exhibited by various areas characterised by varying complexity and different testing tools.

It is possible to note that host testing yielded a double productivity with respect to target testing (which was in any case more efficient than initially estimated, thanks to the fact that most faults had already been removed from builds). It has in any case to be noted that for some areas host testing was not feasible (e.g., A10) or proved to be effort consuming to set up (e.g., A2 and A5) and thus requiring additional improvement actions.

The test-fix-validate cycle was much quicker on host than on target, as reported by the following table, that shows an exponential growth of fixing effort (in person-hours) with respect to various testing phases (as taught by most software engineering textbooks!)

Actions Related to Technology Innovation

Technology innovation is of paramount importance for supporting the introduction of enhanced methods and procedures: as a matter of fact, if the new practices are not substantiated by gains in the daily routine work, it is very likely that they will be abandoned very soon and the whole SPI tends to be considered a bureaucratic exercise. A demonstration is easily recognisable even in the improvement actions of all Working Groups, that are heavily based on a technological support (e.g., planning tools, interface repositories, test automation mechanisms, etc.).

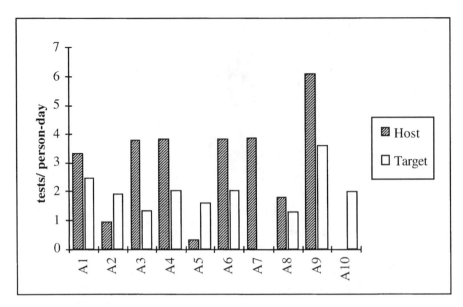

Figure 10.5. Test execution metrics.

Table 10.1. Maintenance Cost versus Fault Detection Phase

Testing Phase	Integration-Host	Integration-Target	System Test
Effort in bug-fixing (p-h)	1.34	3.73	21.55

The Software Process Assessment singled out the following strengths concerning Technology: robust configuration of the management environment, strong testing tools; safe evaluation and procurement procedures.

At the same time, the following improvement opportunities were identified: procedures for technology innovation, communication means; and CASE tools for the initial phases of the life cycle.

As a consequence of such recommendations and of subsequent technical analysis, the following actions were designed and deployed:

- Technology innovation for the development environment (see assessment recommendation 9)
- Strengthening of communication facilities across distributed development teams (see assessment recommendation 10)
- Tool support for cross-checking between plans and configuration management environments
- Enforcement of formal specifications languages and tool; [9]
- Setup of a Intranet infrastructure supporting project development activities.

In the following, some technical insights are given about the enforcement of formal specifications languages and tools.

A Technical Insight: Enforcement of Formal Specifications Languages and Tools

One of the goals of the improvement program was the widespread adoption of formal specifications languages and tools. Their usage was already present in the company, but was not consolidated in all software areas. The specific application domain (telecommunication) brought naturally to the extension in the adoption of the SDL language.

Specification and Description Language (SDL) is a formal specification language particularly suited for specifying and describing real-time systems (and thus for telecommunications software development projects). SDL has been developed and standardised by ITU in the recommendation Z.100. The latest version of the language (SDL-92) has expanded the language considerably and today SDL is a "complete" language also supporting object-oriented design by a type concept that allows specialisation and inheritance to be used for most of the SDL concepts. The basic theoretical model of an SDL system consists of extended Finite State Machines running in parallel, independent of each other and communicating with discrete signals. An SDL system consists of the following components: Structure (system, block, process, and procedure hierarchy), Communications (signals with optional signal parameters and channels, or signal routes), Behaviour (processes), Data (abstract data types), and Inheritance (relation and specialisation).

The distinguishing features of SDL can be summarised as follows:

- It is an international widely accepted standard, guaranteeing a long lifetime and controlled evolution as well as cross-project, cross-organisation validity.
- It is an industrially proven language.
- It is specifically designed for describing complex real-time systems, where parallel activities communicate with each other through discrete events.
- It is powerful in its capabilities and user-friendly in its graphical representation.
- It is formally specified and therefore possible to analyse, simulate, and translate.
- It is supported by powerful computer-based tools.

SDL specifications are usually complemented by Message Sequence Charts (defined by ITU in the recommendation Z.120, first published in 1992), a trace language for specification and description of the communication behaviour of real-time systems, in particular telecommunications equipment. A Message Sequence Chart shows, in graphical form, the sequence of messages sent between systems components and their environment and is intuitively easy to use and understand. As such, it offers a powerful support in describing the dynamic behaviour of an SDL system.

Other related techniques are Tree and Tabular Combine Notation (TTCN) and ASN.1 notations. They have emerged from the need of methods and tools that support verification and validation of both the standards and their actual implementation. TTCN, (standard ISO/IEC 9646-3, X.290) is a language for the specification of tests for communicating systems that introduces the concept of abstract test suites (consisting of abstract test cases). ASN.1 (Abstract Syntax Notation One; standard ISO/IEC 8824) is a generic notation for the specification of data types and values, particularly purported for the description of information that is independent of the transfer format.

The adoption of SDL supported by appropriate CASE tools covering modelling, simulation, and code generation, is expected to bring substantial benefits that are summarised in the following, with respect to the goals set for the process improvement program.

Timeliness. Designers will concentrate on problem-solving, reducing time spent for implementation; debugging and corrections of errors related to logic behaviour will be possible at the analysis and design level, saving a great deal of time; rapid prototyping will become easier, allowing the analysis and simulation of alternative solutions within a short time; follow-on products should have a reduced cycle time; more systematic code reuse should cut down on development time.

Product quality and reliability. Automatic code generation will result in consistent application code; simulation and testing can be anticipated and early error detection should result in higher product quality; the effectiveness of reviews should increase thanks to tool-supported validation and simulation; the availability of test suites supported by TTCN should better regression testing activities.

Technical documentation. Specifications and code will be automatically kept up to date and always describing the current application; technical documentation will be produced in a more formal and comprehensive way.

Productivity. Tool vendors claim for a 75 percent cost reduction in specifications/ implementation and even higher gains if the approach is also used in maintenance. While not fully believing in such figures (at least in the short to medium term), in the opinion of Italtel RM the adoption of SDL can bring to substantial benefits also at productivity level; another important aspect to be considered is staff motivation and morale that is raised by shifting from manually written specifications in natural language to CASE-supported specifications in formal language.

The adoption of SDL has been planned as a long-lasting effort made up of four main steps:

Step 1: Tool selection and procurement for evaluation
Step 2: Customisation for the specific environment and pilot application
Step 3: Introduction within one selected project
Step 4: Deployment and widespread adoption

At the time of this writing, Step 3 had started, after very intensive activities for Step 1 and 2. During Step 1, the requirements for tool procurement were identified (both from a technical and user's points of view) and summarised in an evaluation checklist (including more than 100 issues). This was afterward applied to the most promising CASE tools supporting SDL, coming to the procurement decision on the toolkit best matching with the needs of the impacted projects.

During Step 2, an evaluation copy of the CASE tool was procured and two standalone case studies were run (one involving brand new development, the other reuse of existing code) for experiencing modelling, simulation, validation, and code generation. At the same time, technical activities were undertaken with the tool provider for customising the code generator libraries to the peculiarities of the proprietary operating system. Step 2 was completed by performing host and target testing of the generated code, by deriving indications on memory allocation and real-time consumption, and by fully integrating the CASE tool with the software factory.

The introduction is not yet concluded and thus no quantitative measures can be derived. It is in any case felt that the widespread adoption of formalised languages and related CASE tool can be of great benefit for large-scale development projects, especially when developed on a multisite basis.

CHECK: THE IMPACTS OF SPI AT ITALTEL RM

Planning and Tracking the SPI Project

SPI was intended as a true project, thus adopting all mechanisms for planning/tracking and oversight.

In particular, an overall SPI Gantt Plan was developed, including all activities (with an average granularity of 2 weeks), as well as dependencies between activities and with external milestones. Plans were proposed by the Leaders of the Working Groups and harmonised by the PIPO, using an appropriate tool for project management. As soon as plans were defined and approved by the PISC, they constituted the baseline to be kept for comparison with progress during the SPI project.

Concerning progress tracking, on a monthly basis the PIPO provided the WG Leaders with the list of activities in progress, derived from the plan. On that, WG Leaders indicated the percentage of completion, changes in start or end date, and any additional notes required to comment the status of activities. This information constituted the basis for the production of the monthly Progress Reports and for changes to the SPI Plan. Cross-checking of actual completion versus planned was produced monthly by the PIPO and discussed during the PISC meetings.

In order to have quantitative data about the effort spent in the SPI Project (that is very important for computation of Return On Investment), the WG Leaders and the PIPO collected on a monthly basis the effort spent in the various groups. Effort accounted was differentiated among: definition of practices, attendance to meetings, production of ad hoc documentation, running of pilot projects, and measurements and application of enhanced practices in the project daily routine work. The PIPO also collected quantitative data about the effort spent by the technical staff in training and dissemination activities.

From a technical point of view, a specific configuration management environment was established to store and administer all the SPI outputs. In order to have an overview of the progress of activities with respect to the reaching of planned goals, a Progress Trend Analysis was also developed and maintained, showing the achievement of recommendations along time. To set it up, recommendations from the initial process assessment were mapped with activities in the Gantt Plan and were considered achieved when all the activities associated to one recommendation were successfully defined, experienced and deployed.

Figure 10.6 shows the Progress Trend Analysis for the SPI Program as of June 1996 (the PTA chart refers to the first formalised stage of the Process Improvement Program).

The Accompanying Actions

To feed and care for the SPI Program, three accompanying actions were defined, namely, training, dissemination, and measurement.

Concerning training, the following streams were felt as particularly relevant: training on process improvement methods and techniques; training on additional practices within pilot projects; widespread training on adopted practices; and analysis of training needs in the medium to long term.

Concerning dissemination, it has to be noted that SPI has major impacts on human factors and working practices; the success of the improvement program is thus severely dependent on the level of support offered by both the high management and the technical staff. Whereas the management was kept aligned by means of the monthly PISC meetings, the danger existed that the technical staff could be not aware of plans and achievements, especially in the first periods. As a consequence, an important issue to be addressed is the continuous feeding of enthusiasm about SPI, by means of evidence of the activities planned and of the beneficial results obtained. In order to support this aspect and to avoid the Not Invented Here syndrome, internal dissemination of SPI results, and circulation of know-how were performed on a regular basis.

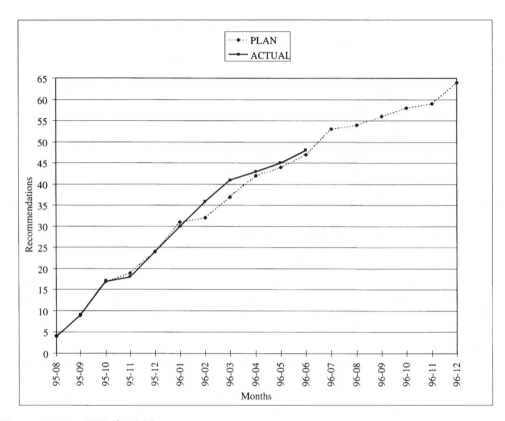

Figure 10.6. PTA for SPI.

Concerning measurement, the aim was twofold: to enhance the usage of quantitative indicators within projects and to provide quantitative indications about the effectiveness of the improvement program and its impact on business goals. For this reason, a number of detailed measures were defined and are being collected on several projects.

A Technical Insight: Measuring the Maintainability Index

In the following, the experiences matured in the measurement of product quality indicators are summarised (more details can be found in [5]). The goals of the product evaluation activity are:

- to define quantitative rules in order to master the complexity of a software product onto which corrective and evolutionary maintenance is foreseen for several years;
- to evaluate the current quality level of the application, especially for those parts that were error-prone in field and for those subsystems onto which major functional enhancements were planned (in both cases a decision had to be taken whether to restructure the existing software or to reengineer parts of it);
- to single out (by means of Pareto analysis) software parts that had to be subjected to Fagan code inspection;
- to provide designers with guidelines and rules for the development of easy-to-maintain code; and
- to derive baselines for cross-comparison at project level.

Table 10.2.   Static Analysis Metrics for Maintainability Tracking

Goal	Metric	Definition
Analysability	Statement size	Average number of operands and operator per statement
	Comment density	Percentage of comments versus number of statements
Testability	Cyclomatic number	As defined in McCabe [6] theory or, in other terms: number of decision points+1
Stability	Control Density	Percentage of control structures versus number of statements
	Number of statements	Number of statements in a function
Changeability	Nesting levels	Maximum depth of nesting of control structures
	Maximum distance	Maximum number of statements from the start to the end of a control structure

The activities undertaken are summarised with reference to the steps of the evaluation procedure proposed by ISO 9126 and described in detail in Chapter 6.

- Quality Requirement Definition
  In accordance with ISO 9126 and with the requirements expressed in the Quality Plan of the project, the target of evaluation was defined as the Maintainability characteristic, in terms of all its subcharacteristics: Analysability, Testability, Stability, and Changeability.
- Evaluation Preparation
  —Quality metrics selection
  A number of metrics were defined (largely based on source code structural complexity), as described in Table 10.2. Such metrics were related to coding rules and used as nonmandatory indications of which parts to reengineer when new features had to be developed. The association to subcharacteristics was done in such a way that the relationships are all 1:N.
  —Rating level definition
  As far as rating level definition is concerned, the following steps had to be performed: definition of lower and upper thresholds for metrics and backward integration of results: metrics --> subcharacteristics --> characteristics.
    The first aspect was accomplished starting from a set of reference threshold values and customising them by means of the derivation of metrics onto a statistical valid sample (about 30 KLOC) and their validation by means of code inspection.
    As far as integration algorithms are concerned, these were defined considering all possible combinations of values and defining a rating at characteristic level subdivided into five classes (as suggested by ISO 9126): poor, average, fair, good, excellent. In order to take into account the different importance of metrics, weighted composition methods were also used.
  —Assessment criteria definition (*Note:* assessment refers here to ISO 9126 evaluation procedure and not to process assessment activities.)
  The metrics (calculated for each function contributing to the source code of the product) were integrated using weighted composition algorithms in order to derive a single maintainability index at various levels of granularity (function, process, functional area, processor, network element, system).

Table 10.3. Thresholds for Static Analysis Metrics

Metric	Lower Bound	Upper Bound
Statement size	3	7
Comment density	0.2	0.65
Cyclomatic number	1	10
Control density	0	0.2
Number of statements	5	100
Nesting levels	1	6
Maximum distance	0	25

The maintainability index (MI) was defined in the following way: $MI = \text{Sum}_i (w_I * n_I)$, where w_i is the weight associated to each class (poor = 0, average = 0.25, fair = 0.5, good = 0.75, excellent = 1) and n_i is the percentage of functions falling in that class. In this way MI spans in the range [0. . . 1], with 0 meaning bad maintainability and 1 meaning optimal maintainability. Having defined as goal a target level for MI greater than 0.70, the Quality Plan of the project stated that subsystems with a MI below 0.6 had to be manually inspected in order to decide whether reverse engineering activities were needed.

- Evaluation Procedure
  —Measurement
  The selected metrics were automatically extracted from the software product, using a commercially available static analyser; in order to keep the human overhead to a minimum, several batch programs were developed to control the jobs and to produce the reports.
  —Rating
  In order to obtain outputs suitable for different types of users (middle management, designers, and QA team) the following reports were produced at different levels of granularity: overall quality report, list of functions subdivided by rating class, Kiviat graphs of average metric values, distribution of metrics, distribution of sub-characteristics, calling graphs among functions, and, for each function falling either in the poor or in the average classes, Kiviat graphs of metrics, and calling graph.
  —Assessment (*Note:* assessment refers here to ISO 9126 evaluation procedure and not to process assessment activities.)
  The final assessment stage involved several aspects: identification of critical components for which reengineering activities were needed, selection of the sample for manual code inspection, analysis of the MI with respect to the defined target, study of the variation of the maintainability index within and across the development of three projects (constituted by three successive releases), validation of metrics and models. Such aspects are dealt in more details in the following, where obtained results are summarised.

The analysis of data on the first release brought the following conclusions:

- The overall MI of the product was 0.73, thus largely meeting the target value defined at the beginning of the SPI.
- Despite this fact, some areas had maintainability problems, with values for MI sometimes below 0.65.
- Areas with a low MI were historically error-prone or quite difficult to maintain.

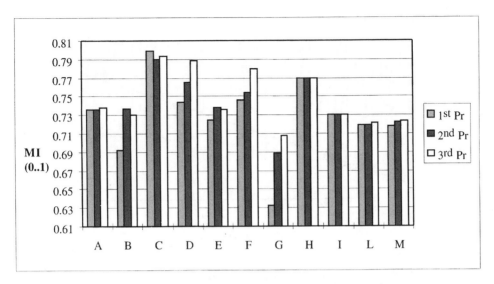

Figure 10.7. Maintainability index for some areas across various projects.

At the end of the third release, code maintainability had significantly improved, with a global MI greater than 0.76 and no areas below 0.7. Figure 10.7 shows the trend of the MI for a selected number of design areas.

The following aspects can be observed:

- Areas where a major reverse engineering was made had a substantial growth of the maintainability index (e.g., B, F)
- Areas where specific structural changes were made in accordance with suggestions from static analysis metrics, also showed a significant bettering (e.g., areas E, G)
- Areas based on existing code, where static analysis metrics were analysed during development (even if no specific actions were adopted) succeeded in controlling the impact of additional features within existing source code (e.g., areas A, H, I, L, M)
- Areas developing brand-new source code in adherence with the coding guidelines defined, exhibited a good MI, kept or even increased also after massive maintenance activities, which normally involve an increasing entropy (e.g., areas C, D)

The analysis of control graphs also provided useful feedback to designers, pointing out situations like: duplicated code that ought to be unified in appropriate modules; multiple-decision branches expanded too much; long modules that could have been easily broken down into submodules; questionable programming styles; usage of recursion in very complex functions; etc.

As far as metrics validation is concerned, the defined metrics and thresholds were felt as adequate, in the sense that they succeeded in maximising the return on investment from reengineering and code inspection activities, focusing the attention on the 20 percent of the modules that are likely to cause 80 percent of the maintenance troubles. Moreover, correlation and dependencies were sought in order to validate the model and to check the results with other indicators of the measurement system.

A strong correlation was found between the metric "Number of statements" and the metric "Cyclomatic number," thus demonstrating the multicollinearity of such metrics.

No statistical valid correlation was found between the Maintainability Index and, respectively, the Number of Statements (correlation coefficient = –0.58) and the 'Cyclomatic Number (correlation coefficient = –0.40), thus demonstrating the higher informative value of the

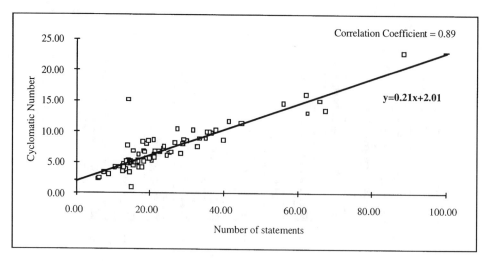

Figure 10.8. Multicollinearity of static analysis metrics.

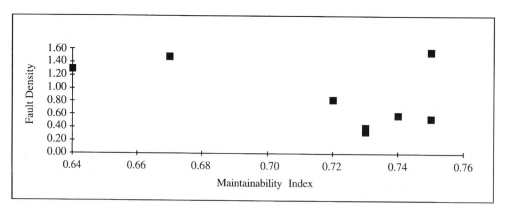

Figure 10.9. Correlation between Maintainability Index and Fault Density.

defined indicator with respect to the most widespread simple metrics normally used for tracking complexity and maintainability factors.

A significant correlation (correlation coefficient = +0,85) was found between the number of topological paths and the number of tests designed following a functional approach; this brought us to the idea that the testing coverage of the product (that was subjected to several thousand tests) was quite evenly distributed.

Correlation between MI and fault density Figure 10.9 was also analysed (see following figure) resulting in a weak inverse correlation, meaning that the higher the MI, the better the product in terms of reliability. This correlation is thought to be not fully statistically valid and thus it will have to be analysed in more detail in the future.

It is possible to say that the adoption of static analysis techniques was positive since designers focused their reverse engineering efforts on troublesome modules.

As a consequence of the results of the evaluation activities, a widespread adoption of the experienced techniques and the tools has been implemented, and currently the static analysis tools are available to all designers as part of the software factory; moreover, the following steps have been planned:

- usage of the approach for guiding code inspection and reverse engineering activities;
- extension of the usage of the static analysis tools in order to derive also testing paths assuring a topological coverage during early testing phases;
- tuning of the adopted quality model; and
- usage of dynamic code analysers allowing also the check of memory leaks, variables management, etc.

ACT: DEPLOYMENT AT ITALTEL RM

After the assessment, the kickoff of a SPI program and the definition of improvement activities, the defined recommendations have to be applied to the greatest possible extent to industrial products and projects within a given schedule.

If such step is missing, the overall SPI Program is fruitless and becomes merely an intellectual exercise.

But the deployment stage is also perhaps the most critical moment in a SPI Program, since the step from definition and pilot projects to application in the large can suffer from resistance, due both to budget/schedule limitations and to other barriers (including human factors).

In the following the typical problems to be overcome are analysed, followed by a set of solutions that proved to be valuable in the experienced SPI Program.

Problems to Overcome

At the time in which improvement actions are ready to be deployed in the daily routine work of major projects, the SPI program may be confronted with several arguments against the application, like:

- "the development in the current release has already reached a status in which the introduction of the new method or technology or tool is not possible," or
- "for the next release, the planning is frozen and there is neither personnel nor time available to introduce new or modified practices," or
- "in the current/next release there are no changes planned in this specific software area, henceforth the improvements cannot be introduced," or
- "the methodologies or tools that should be introduced are not sufficiently understood and thus the staff need to be thoroughly trained before using them," or
- "the tool or method does not fit completely to a our specific software application and is still a bit faulty/unstable; moreover, the case studies did not cover all application areas in full extent," or
- "there is no need to introduce improvements because there are no problems in our specific area: since the designers think they are doing things right, why should we impose on them to start playing with new, not so clear, rules?," and so on.

Some of these arguments are true; some are paradigms. In any case, to start the widespread introduction of process improvements, this nut has to be cracked. The bolt to be used to do it proved to be a combination of actions described in the below section.

Leverages to Overcome Barriers

The following leverages have to be combined in order to effectively switch from definition to deployment: contribution from management, detailed planning of deployment activities, case studies, review of plans with the middle management, training, measurement, and dissemination.

The driving force to direct the deployment has to be the SPI program office. The requirements are based on the previous agreed SPI Gantt Plan and have to be underlined by the senior management, accompanied by the offer of some help in terms of budget and/or additional personnel.

From a practical point of view, the SPI program office has to define and agree in cooperation with the affected middle management a detailed deployment plan of the improvement actions as part of the next version/release, deciding which improvements will be applied thoroughly, which improvements will be applied partially in specific software areas or in specific development teams and which improvements are not ready to be applied and have to be studied more (in this case the experimentation area has to be foreseen).

This plan must be realistic and pragmatic, that is to say it has to take into account the schedule and available personnel for the next release as well as the effort distribution across the different software areas and development teams. For those improvements which are felt still immature to be deployed in the large, a forecast for the completion of pilot applications has to be given.

This detailed deployment plan has to be discussed with the affected development supervisors and senior/key developers. Concerns have to be evaluated and, if necessary, the deployment plan has to be adjusted.

In the end, a common understanding on the objectives as well as on the deployment plan has to be reached and made official to the staff, by inserting new/enhanced practices in the Quality Plan as well as in the Development Plan of the new release.

In parallel to the definition of the deployment plan, a training plan for the staff heavily impacted by the changed or new methods and/or tools has to be defined in cooperation with the owner of the SPI activity and the middle management of the affected development department.

After the contents of the deployment actions have been distributed widespread within the designers community, the plan has to be followed up by the SPI program office. The actual progress status can be evaluated by combining the reports of the SPI activity owners (PI working groups) with those of the line managers of the affected development departments and can be controlled by accompanying measurements taken by the working groups and/or the SPI program office. Furthermore, the actual status of the SPI deployment has to be reported to the management as well as to the affected development teams. Unexpected results have to be analysed (root cause analysis) and discussed with the developers that were in charge of the specific activity.

At the end of the first release in which the activity has been applied a final evaluation is essential and a tuning of the development process for the next release has eventually to be performed, in agreement with the PDCA philosophy and the *Kaizen* continuous step-by-step improvement approach.

CONCLUSION

The outcomes of the first wave of Italtel RM SPI can be summarised as follows:

- Excellent results have been gained on:
  —strengthened planning/tracking practices and tooling,
  —documentation methodology and guidelines,
  —testing methodology,

—software factory evolution,
—harmonisation across projects,
—training dissemination,
* Good results have been gained on:
—deployment of practices in projects,
—interface management,
—coding guidelines and reviews,
—test tooling,
—communication facilities, and
—evolution of the Configuration Management environment.
* Improvement opportunities are still evident for:
—estimation practices, and
—systematic analysis of quantitative data.

The following additional aspects must be mentioned:

* Training and internal dissemination has been carried out on all the deployed topics in order to make all members of the technical staff able to profit from the innovations.
* External dissemination has been performed presenting various papers at different international events.
* Measurements have been used to keep control of the Process Improvement Program.
* Last but not least, management has played a central role in the overall initiative through a continuous and intensive commitment.

With respect to the goals set at the beginning of the SPI initiative, it is possible to say that the SPI first wave has been completed on time and within budget.

At the end of the SPI first wave, management decided that a good portion of the initially foreseen goals had been successfully attained, but that the deployment of results still needed additional work. Considering that projects are always confronted with new challenges, RM management gave the sign-off for new activities, having as foundations the following:

* the definition of new enhancements should be kept to a minimum in order to focus on the adoption of enhanced practices in the daily routine work of all projects;
* "long-runner" activities involving a big effort shall be managed as ad hoc projects;
* technology watch and innovation will continue, combining process improvement with product improvements;
* analysis of quantitative data shall be made more systematic.

From an organisational point of view, the following considerations were derived:

* the management layers PISC-PIPO-WG seems appropriate;
* planning/tracking of SPI is essential and thus PIPO staffing shall be kept;
* specific groups must be created for the various technical topics, resulting in more focused and smaller WGs (whose number has thus increased);
* management commitment ought not to diminish.

An SPI wave 2 was thus committed, covering 1997–1998 and embracing several topics that can be subdivided in three categories, in accordance with the taxonomy highlighted above:

* Deployment in projects
* Long runners
* New topics

Each of the above is briefly explained in the following.

1. *Deployment in projects.* The goal of this activity is to fully deploy the enhancements defined in the daily routine work of projects. To this end, it is essential to agree with the middle management a deployment plan for each department in which pragmatic and detailed activities for the next release are listed. Such a plan (which is part of the more general Quality Plan for a project) will have to include details such as: which new practices will be deployed in which software area/feature package; for each development team, the schedule for the deployment, including the provision of the required training and new hardware/software tools; an impact analysis, for each affected area, of the introduction of enhanced practices on the overall project staffing/schedule. This plan has to be agreed with the supervisors, Quality Management staff, and senior developers.

2. *Long runners.* This stream of actions covers those improvement opportunities that were identified and sketched in the SPI First Wave but that require a significant amount of effort and time and thus will be managed as ad hoc projects in the SPI Second Wave. They are briefly detailed in the following.

   - *Introduction of formal specifications languages and tools.* This activity has the aim of introducing the SDL language and related CASE tools in the development activities. It is covered by the SPECS Project which is financially supported by the European Commission under the European Systems and Software Initiative (ESSI) initiative.
   - *Test automation.* This activity, which is one of the most effort intensive of the whole SPI Program, has the following challenging goals: automated regression testing of embedded software on host environment (deploying experiences that showed to be best, through the harmonization of practices across the various groups); automated regression testing of embedded software on target environment (defining the best approach, setting up the environment and piloting test automation on a representative excerpt of test cases, in order to validate the approach and define the steps for test automation in the large); automated regression testing of Graphical User Interface (GUI) software (deploying the usage of commercial CAST tools, taking advantages of their advanced facilities for test automation); automated regression testing for fully equipped lines (defining the reference test-bed and the integration mechanisms across the tools as well as the mechanisms for ensuring reproducibility); automated regression testing for load/stress (using commercial CAST tools as well as developing proprietary solutions and defining technical means for automatic checking of results).
   - *Development environment and infrastructure.* The goal of this activity is the constant evolution of the development environment and infrastructure, with particular emphasis on: network infrastructure, new development environments, enhancements to configuration management environment, Intranet services, and software factory evolution.
   - *Quantitative measurement.* The goal of this activity is to strengthen quantitative measurement practices by means of: tuning of quality indicators and their application to all projects, strengthening of tools for data collection, piloting of project estimation tools (based on COCOMO, Function Points, and Putnam models) and setting up of a repository of historical data based on dynamic WWW structures.

3. *New topics*
   - *Customer documentation.* This activity has the aim to precisely define the processes and interfaces between development teams and customer documentation teams in order to produce customer documentation.

- *Object-Oriented (OO) development.* This activity has the aim of defining methodological approaches and supporting tools for the extensive adoption of OO practices in the software development projects.
- *System Improvements.* This activity has the aim of setting up a mechanism for channeling the experiences made by system test/field support staff in order to benefit of their hands-on experience to identify and prioritize improvement opportunities at product/system level that could result in competitive advantages with respect to the competitors.
- *Planning guidelines.* The goal of this activity is to package all experiences gained in SPI First Wave concerning planning, tracking and oversight in the form of a guideline to be part of the Quality Management System.

A detailed description of activities performed and achievements gained in the second SPI wave can be found in [8, 10, 11].

Lessons Learned from SPI at Italtel

It seems worthwhile to close the chapter with a list of the top twelve managerial recommendations that the authors think to have learned through running SPI Projects.

The following aspects have been crucial for the success of the initiative:

- The role of the improvement approaches
- The role of the assessment
- The role of the SPI organisation
- The role of senior management
- The role of measurements
- The role of case studies
- The role of the deployment plan
- The role of technology innovations
- The role of training and dissemination
- The role of the technical staff
- The role of product improvements
- The role of the customer

These aspects are dealt with below in more detail.

The role of the improvement approaches. SPI must be foreseen as a long term effort, since it takes several projects to define improvements, apply them, collect quantitative measures and deploy improvements in the large scale. In this context ISO 9000 is seen as a prerequisite, PDCA is the driving factor, management by metrics is essential to check improvements from a quantitative perspective, and assessments help in quantifying the status reached.

The role of the assessment. An assessment performed by an external, objective organisation is the best starting point for a SPI program. It is very important to select the most effective and applicable improvements and to group them in short-, medium-, and long-term activities. The short-term activities have to be started immediately to benefit of the momentum from the assessment.

The role of the SPI organisation. To keep the SPI program successful, a SPI program office, staffed with a few full time SPI experts and moderated by a senior manager, has the responsibility to drive the SPI program with constancy of purpose, to organise its activities, and to report the status. Middle management and staff from the affected development areas have to be involved in working groups to define specific actions. A steering committee, which is made up of the senior management, has to follow up, control, and drive the program, underlining its importance for the business goals of the company. Finally, the enthusiasm and influence of the WG leaders is of paramount importance for the success of the initiative.

The role of senior management. A 100 percent agreement with senior management has to be reached on objectives and actions. Senior management has to drive the program and to provide sufficient budget. Moreover, the senior management has to be the sponsor of the SPI program and has to make its sponsorship visible to all the affected staff.

The role of measurements. It is essential to report positive and negative results to the management as well as to the affected developers. The results from the WGs, and the applications completed by figures from accompanying measurements have to be reported by the SPI office, typically monthly. It would be far too easy to repeat here the much-abused sentence, "You cannot control what you cannot measure"—but it is true!

The role of case studies. Case studies are a necessity for big process and/or technology changes. On the one hand, they enable you to test the applicability of a theory to the concrete task and to provide the needed adjustment to the existing development environment. On the other hand, case studies help convince sceptical developers of the gain that can be obtained from the activity. Therefore the most affected and most hesitant developers should play an active role in performing the case studies; after experiencing the new practices, these previously doubtful staff members become often the best advocates of the activity.

The role of the deployment plan. It is very important to keep a constant alignment between the rules and the project practices, especially in large software producing units, where the deployment of improvement actions within the short term is rather difficult. To this end, it is essential to agree with the middle management on a deployment plan for each department in which pragmatic and detailed activities for the next release are listed. Such a plan will have to include details such as: which new practices will be deployed in which software area/feature package; for each development team, the schedule for the deployment, including the provision of the required training and new hardware/software tools; and an impact analysis, for each affected area, of the introduction of enhanced practices on the overall project staffing/schedule. This plan must be discussed with the supervisors and senior developers and has to be fine-tuned if necessary.

The role of technology innovations. A lot of the activities of a SPI program can only be effectively performed by introducing new technology and tool support both for the development activities (CASE tools, test tools, etc.) and for the supporting functions (planning tools, configuration management etc.) as well as for the technology infrastructure (communication facilities, software development workplaces, etc.). When these requirements are thoroughly elaborated and justified within a comprehensive strategy as an output of the SPI Program, it is also easier to get the investment approval from the senior management. In fact, without strong background on the expected gains, the investment proposals will have to go through the usual long questioning and will be most probably reduced or postponed due to budget restrictions and/or different priorities.

The role of training and dissemination. To introduce new methods, technologies, and tools on the large scale requires that a tailored accompanying training program be defined. This is important not only to teach the news but also to overcome doubts on the applicability of specific actions. A general dissemination and discussion with the affected development personnel has to be performed regularly.

The role of the technical staff. Software process improvement has to deal with processes mastered by technical staff members who are very proud of their work and are not willing to change or simply habits to follow an external guideline which would be felt as an unpleasant command and sometimes even an abuse of power. (If you look at a cornerstone of the software engineering literature like [7] you will discover that some cultural aspects of programmers have not changed that much in the last decades!). Henceforth, special care will be paid to sowing the seeds of process improvement in the software designer community and to breeding "fast followers." Middle management has to be involved in the definition of activities as well as in the definition of concrete deployment plans.

The role of product improvements. The increase in product size and complexity can often override the improvements made at project level, as seen for reliability indicators in one of the two experiences. To this end it is required that SPI run at a speed that is greater than the growth of the product. At the same time, actions must be taken to improve the product for the sake of simplifying software development and minimising source code.

The role of the customer. In one of the two experiences in chapters 9 and 10 a key customer contributed to SPI by performing his own audit and by following up our SPI activities. This was a big advantage since we got additional information about our customer's wishes. Also, we could increase the level of trust of our products by, in turn, informing the customer about our SPI activities. Moreover, focusing on the customer's wishes helps sustained management's commitment.

REFERENCES

1. M. Mouly, M. Pautet, *The GSM System for Mobile Communications,* Europe Media Publications, 1993.

2. SEL, NASA Goddard Space Flight Center, *"Software Engineering Laboratory Relationships, Models and Management Rules,"* SEL-91-001, Feb. 1991.

3. D.M. Marks, *Testing Very Big Systems,* McGraw-Hill, 1992.

4. G. Bazzana, et al., "Quantifying the Benefits of Software Testing: an Experience Report from the GSM Application Domain," *Proceedings of Objective Software Quality Conference,* Florence, May 1995. Published in *Lecture Notes in Computer Science,* No. 926.

5. G. Bazzana, et al., "Improving Software Quality through Quantitative Evaluation of Products and Processes," *ISCN Conference,* Vienna, Sept. 1995.

6. T. J. McCabe, "A Complexity Measure," *IEEE Transactions on Software Engineering,* 1976.

7. F. P. Brooks, Jr., *The Mythical Man-Month—Essays on Software Engineering,* Addison-Wesley, 1975.

8. R. Delmiglio, et al., "Test Automation in Telecommunication Systems," *Proceedings of EuroStar 97 Conference,* Edinburgh, Nov. 1997.

9. S. Scotto di Vettimo, et al., Usage of Formal Specifications Languages in the Development of GSM Telecommunications Systems, Genie-Logiciel, 1996.

10. S. Di Muro, et al., "SPI: an Experience report from GSM Development," *Proceedings of Aquis 98 Conference,* Venice, Jan. 1998.

11. S. Scotto di Vettimo, "Intranet as a Support to Process Improvement," *Proccedings of BEST 98 Conference,* Brescia, Nov. 1998.

Chapter 11

Process Improvement in Internet Service Providing

Gualtiero Bazzana

Enrico Fagnoni
Onion S.p.A., Italy

INTRODUCTION

This chapter presents the outcomes of a process improvement program, called PI³ (Process Improvement In Internet service providing), run at Onion. The PI³ Project is run under the auspices of the Commission of the European Communities (CEC) DG III within the scope of the European Systems and Software Initiative (ESSI) Initiative [1] of the European Strategic Programme for Research on Information Technology (ESPRIT) Fourth Framework. This support has proven to be extremely important in ensuring the overall success of the initiative, which lies in the mainstream of the company core business.

The chapter covers the following aspects:

- The status of software engineering practices at the beginning of the improvement program, in terms of: Onion development activities and weak/strong process areas singled out by a self-assessment
- The improvement plan defined to raise the maturity level and, above all, the development/maintenance capabilities of the software producing unit
- The steps in which the improvement program was organised, with emphasis on Testing and Configuration Management activities
- An innovative means for handling the Quality Management System with the support of a company Intranet
- Results achieved and lessons learned

ONION INVOLVEMENT IN SOFTWARE
DEVELOPMENT/USAGE

Onion is very committed in strengthening its business capabilities through software process improvement.

Onion is pursuing three business areas:

- *Communications.* Distributed Computing and Networking applications, Electronic Commerce, Internet/Intranet/Extranet Services, Multimedia Applications
- *Technologies.* Security Management, System Integration, Enterprise Resource Planning Systems, Custom Software Development
- *Consulting.* Business Process Re-engineering, ISO 9000 Quality Management Systems, Testing and Computer System Validation, Software Process Improvement.

More details can be found at the World Wide Web: http://net.onion.it/

Onion is intensively working in a technology environment that is evolving very rapidly. This IT revolution is fundamentally affecting the development paradigms and the key technical strengths for competition. As a consequence, at Onion software development is a key factor for communications and technologies services/products; software related activities can be classified into the following three classes:

- Software development for turnkey IT solutions: in this case software development follows a traditional waterfall life cycle with usage of C++ and Visual Basic as development languages.
- Service providing on Internet (e.g., Web server information publishing, support to customers' operations, setup of company Intranets, support to order processing and inventory management, etc.): in this case software is "embedded" within the provided service and is developed with innovative languages like ASP, Perl, VRML, and Java.
- Development of multimedia applications: in this case software development cannot follow a standard waterfall model, but has to face with fast prototyping, Rapid Application Development (RAD) and integration of software with multimedia assets.

Process Improvement started from the second application domain, in which a typical project is characterised by the following phases:

- Definition of service requirements with the customer
- Collection of assets to be included in the service
- Definition of the home page for the service
- Definition of search keywords
- Setup of the service structure
- Development of prototype
- Testing of prototype
- Review of the service prototype with the customer
- Completion of service development
- Testing
- Fixing of failures found
- Acceptance with the customer
- Insertion of service in production environment
- Linking of the service with most known search engines

PLAN: ANALYSIS OF THE INITIAL STATUS OF SOFTWARE ENGINEERING PRACTICES

Onion conducted a software process self-resulting in a maturity level assessed to be at level 1. Apart from the numerical grading, the assessment was very important in raising the consciousness about process improvement needs and key process areas that should be addressed first. In the following, the situation at the start of the improvement project is summarised from a technical, business, organisational, and cultural point of view.

- Technical issues
  The self-assessment, combined with a portfolio analysis of business needs, brought to the identification of the following areas for improvement, with reference to SEI CMM Level 2 Key Process Areas (KPAs), in decreasing order of impact onto business goals:
  —*Testing*. Testing was conducted by the developers, without adoption of any consolidated technique and with insufficient focus on user and service features; hence, testing effectiveness had room for improvement;
  —*Software configuration management*. There was provision neither for versioning, nor for change management; this caused low productivity, a high degree of regression testing, a general instability of released applications, and an insufficient reuse of artifacts; such issues applied to software code, technical deliverables, and also to published assets (pictures, photographs, films, forms, etc.).
  Strong key process areas at the start of the improvement program included Quality Assurance, with the presence of a Quality Manager committed to the enforcement of good engineering practices. Also requirements management was felt as satisfactory, especially in RAD, where the life cycle involves prototypes discussed with customers quite early and frequently. Project management also showed good beginnings.
- Business issues
  From a business point of view, PI³ assumed as pilot projects two of the most important developments under way in the company, in order to deploy the improvements as soon as possible in the core business areas, to take immediate advantage of the expected benefits. Concerning company capabilities, positive results from Process Improvement were expected in product reliability and development productivity/timeliness; such issues were tracked by a set of quantitative indicators.
- Organisational issues
  Organisational issues at the beginning of the experiment were marked by a focus on technology and on people-driven processes. Hence the processes might be defined as "ad hoc" or "chaotic" with the focus on short-term goals and several deficiencies in medium- to long-term issues. The assessment also highlighted the organisational strengths that would have constituted the basis for process improvement, in particular, attention paid to training; adoption of a rough measurement system to track projects; consciousness of the need for improvement and positive attitude toward it; competent and creative people, with a good mix of technical, managerial, and commercial profiles; state-of-the-art technology.
- Cultural issues
  The willingness to improve the whole development structure brought to the deployment of improvement actions in a positive framework, without resistance from the staff.

The Process Improvement Plan

After the assessment, an action plan was devised in order to increase the software development/ maintenance capabilities of the software producing unit.

The bulk of the improvement covered up to December 1998, accompanying the company from the incubation period, through takeoff and growth consolidation. The plan encompasses three main steps covering 3 years of elapsed time:

- Short-term improvement efforts (from June 1995 to December 1995)
  It was decided to strengthen training issues by means of the definition of a training plan (customised for various professional skills) and to enforce project management.
- Medium-term improvement efforts (from January 1996 to December 1996)
  This phase has as its goal to address configuration management and testing issues that both require significant investments in technology and time.
- Long-term improvement efforts (from January 1997 to December 1998)
  This phase will focus on the deployment of a complete Quality Management System, allowing for ISO 9000 registration and on the RAD development of medium and large projects (supported by another PIE Project, called RADIUM).

DO: THE PI³ PROJECT

As a consequence of the assessment, it was decided to focus on Process Improvement actions characterised by the following characteristics: highest payoff; relevance for all the business lines of the company; direct applicability and pragmatic feasibility in the medium term.

The KPAs exhibiting such characteristics were identified as being the following: configuration management (CM) and testing; for both of them, the PI³ project looked at both the definition of rules and the alignment of projects.

The phased work plan of the project was defined taking into account the following strategy:

- The Improvement Program shall be based on top of running pilot projects.
- To handle the average length of projects and to track the trends of results, the application of the PDCA scheme was planned on two projects.
- Each work-package of the PI³ Program was defined as a major subdivision of the project, ending with a verifiable end point.
- Project management was also clearly identified in terms of resources.
- Sufficient room was devoted to training and dissemination activities.
- Sufficient room was also devoted to quantitative measurement of results (in particular, effectiveness analysis and quantitative evaluation of Return On Investment [ROI]).

In accordance with the goals of the overall improvement plan, the required status of software processes at the end of the improvement program can be summarised as follows:

- Definition of processes and adoption of tools for the KPAs of testing and configuration management
- Adoption of the defined practices and of the tools in the daily routine work of projects
- Alignment of the staff to the defined methods, practices, and tools
- Increased maturity of the measurement system, tracking the most relevant indicators for the business of the company
- Beginning of formalisation of experiences gained by means of standard operating procedures constituting an initial kernel of the company QMS.

The maturity level of the company at the end of the Improvement Program was planned to be not too far from level 2; this would be a big success for the organisation because in this case we would have achieved a stable process with a repeatable management control level, by initiating rigorous project management of commitments, costs, schedules, and changes.

In particular, the improvement program was planned to bring the organisation close to level 2 for the KPAs directly affected by the improvement actions. In particular we expected significant improvements in the following practices: Life Cycle Functions: testing; Supporting Functions: configuration management; Process-Related Functions: process control; Technology: tools for CM and testing. Moreover, the Improvement Program was planned to also affect positively higher maturity-level key practices, like: process definition and process measurement.

What we felt to be most important in any case is not the fact of reaching a full level 2 for all practices but rather achieving full alignment between the defined practices and the daily routine work within the projects. In this case in fact it will be possible to improve company capabilities by means of a bottom-up continuous improvement suggested and enforced by the whole staff and not just a top-down effort driven by the management.

The goals clearly show that the Improvement Program represented a breakthrough in the status of software engineering practices of Onion.

Process Improvement Work Plan

The steps in which the improvement program has been organised can be summarised as follows:

1. Evaluation of the state of the art methods and tools
2. Procurement of the selected technology
3. Training on technology and underpinning methods
4. Definition of rules on how to apply the selected methods and tools to the pilot projects
5. Definition of quantitative measures to track the effectiveness of the improvement program
6. Application of the selected methods and tools to the pilot projects
7. Collection and analysis of quantitative data from the program experiment
8. Analysis of Return On Investment
9. Transfer of the lesson learnt to the whole staff
10. Transfer of the results into the standards operating procedures

Particularly important was the initial technology survey, that brought to:

- the evaluation and procurement of CM tooling (through selection of candidate toolkits, design of a checklist containing the most important aspects to be evaluated, comparative evaluation using the checklist, procurement);
- the evaluation and procurement of testing tooling (through the same approach described for CM);
- the drafting of a final report summarising the tools evaluated and giving a rationale for the final procurement decision.

The changes that were made to the technical environment in terms of equipment, tools, or other software introduced specifically for the process improvement activity are summarised in the following:

- Adoption of a WWW workbench including advanced authoring and testing features, as well as basic Configuration Management features

- Adoption of a WWW Test Product covering almost all the needs that were defined at the beginning of the technology survey
- Adoption of a CM environment particularly suited for document and asset management, also oriented towards ISO 9000 document and data control rules
- Set up of a WWW environment for the management of the Quality Management System

In the next section, we report technical details of the most substantial improvement efforts made.

Process Improvement Actions: Website Testing

Concerning testing, improvement actions included, among others: test design methods (reference documents, methods for extracting test cases, etc.), practices for unit test, practices for integration test, practices for system/acceptance test, methods for problem notification and tracking, and test reporting.

This resulted in much more detailed testing activities, introducing test design and reporting rules and clearly identifying the testing steps. Among the testing steps, the following were reckoned as particularly important: testing for service content and language; testing for hypertextual links; testing for hardware/software compatibility; testing for usability; testing for efficiency; regression testing.

As a consequence, the following test levels were defined depending on the application domain, either Programs (classic software development) or Websites (Table 11.1).

While we do not detail here the meaning of the testing levels associated with the Programs [2, 3], a short explanation is needed to clarify the test levels of websites.

The goal of syntactic tests is to check the basic correctness of Websites, from a syntactic point a view, a structural point of view (in particular, referring to "link resolution" aspects), and a performance point of view (in particular, looking at the number and size of pictures).

Security tests have as their goal the validation of security mechanisms and security enforcing functions, with particular emphasis on reserved and restricted areas; when looking for security of critical systems, using ITSEC [4] and ITSEM [5] guidelines can be extremely valuable.

Service tests have the goal of validating the resulting service from an user's point of view, thus adopting a black-box strategy without any assumptions about underlying architecture and implementation choices.

In addition, a standard test list was devised for all websites, to be applied both for acceptance purposes and for regression testing activities. Such a test list covers the following:

- Stylistic problems (spelling errors, particular tags, use of obsolete markup, particular content-free expression, empty container elements, etc.);
- Lexical problems (use of character sets, formatting-related problems, using white spaces around element tags, etc.);
- Syntax problems (illegal elements, illegal attributes, unclose container elements, malformed URLs and attribute values, etc.);
- Image-related problems (bandwidth consumption, images syntax, etc.);
- Document structure problems (both in tables and in forms);
- Portability problems (accessibility by various browsers and platforms, markup; inside comments, use of single quotation marks for attribute value, use of specific markup not supported by all browsers, liberal usage of file naming, etc.);
- Structural integrity problems (no index file for a directory, dead links, limbo pages, etc.);
- Security problems.

Table 11.1. Test Levels for Various Classes

Programs	Websites
Module testing	Syntactic testing
Integration testing	Security testing
System test	Service testing

The adoption of supporting tools [6, 7] allowed to set-up a test factory running almost automatically the following sequence of test classes:

- Check the document for spelling errors
- Perform an analysis of the images
- Test the document structure
- Look at image syntax
- Examine table structure
- Verify that all hyperlinks are valid
- Examine form structure
- Analyse command hierarchy

For more details on testing in the Internet domain, the interested reader is referred to [8]. An up-to-date state-of-the-art on such aspect has been provided in [10].

Process Improvement Actions: Object-Oriented (OO) Configuration Management and Document Control

Concerning CM, issues addressed included, among others: process management (life cycles for various objects, user roles, triggers, security control, etc.), release management (versioning, object control, dependency management, build management, bill-of-materials, variants and parallel releases, etc.), change management (status handling, report handling, etc.) [9]

The following detailed activities were fulfilled:

- Definition of rules for applying methods and tools within the pilot projects
- Application within pilot projects
- Definition of guidelines for companywide configuration management, for inclusion within a QMS standard operating procedure

Process improvement in CM resulted in a more severe distinction between the development environment and the production environment, the adoption of formal and tool-supported check-in/checkout procedures for items, and management of a repository of assets/utilities/programs for their re-use across services.

The Onion Configuration Management strategy was based on an OO approach. This relies on the consideration that every entity implemented during the development of Web projects must be treated as an object. Moreover, every action that can be performed on that object must be considered as a method applicable to the object.

This strategy very well fits with in the complex world of entities that the Web based projects have to be able to manage. Such a strategy also allows a high degree of flexibility because it is not mandatory to highlight in the very beginning the whole set of objects which will be used; rather it is possible to start with a small set of objects and methods and to take advantage of the possibility to define new objects and methods every time that this is needed.

Every entity belongs to a basic class called Asset. This class owns a set of properties that are inherited by every object descending from the class, namely: Owner, Description, Location, Class, Version Number, Construction Date, Verification Date, Approval Date, Responsible Person, Copyright, Access Control List, Configuration Control Method. On top of this basic class, others were defined, including: Order, Website, Program, Document, etc.

Concerning document control, an integrated environment was adopted, fully aligned with ISO 9000 requirement. This modular system was very useful in the light of setting up a QMS since it provides extensions for the management of additional ISO 9000 requirements (e.g., tool calibration, keeping of Quality Records, Supplier List management, etc.). In particular, the toolkit was very easy to introduce thanks to its strong integration with the Microsoft Office environment for the drafting of documents.

The most relevant features that proved to be suited for the specific environment were:

- Configuration identification (the definition of codes for the unambiguous identification of document and their related version allowed to constantly know the state of each document)
- Document management (handling several classes of documents, including: internal documents, external documents, fax, letters, contracts, Quality Records, etc.)
- A review and approval scheme based on a four-step mechanism
- A document matrix (identifying the responsibilities for preparation, review and approval of documents)
- The management of document distribution (for sake of confidentiality and security)
- The automatic management of document status, version, change history and authors; the management of company templates for all standard operating procedures and forms to be used in the company; meeting management (with tracking to closure of all action items)
- Tool calibration (keeping under control all the calibration activities)
- Time management (computing effort spent by project, work centres, and work category)
- Supplier management (keeping a supplier accredited list, with all relevant information)
- Nonconformity management (opening and tracking to closure of corrective actions)

Process Improvement Actions: Web-Based Quality Management System

The idea of setting-up a company Intranet designed for the management of the Quality Management System came across by observing that new technologies lead to more efficient and dynamic communication and thus to new infrastructures and work procedures for projects. Moreover, business process models are designed, information systems are established on Hypermedia platforms, and total quality management (TQM) gets a new vision when all effective processes of the organisation are made visible and accessible to the employees via Hypermedia and Internet systems.

Henceforth it was decided to manage the Quality Management System with a WWW support, as part of the companywide Intranet.

This involved the porting of documents in the WWW environment, the definition of access rules, the creation of hypertextual links across objects, the creation of modules through electronic forms, the linking with the mail systems etc.

The main advantages of WWW-based Quality Management Systems are:

- *Availability at large.* All people can have a direct, user-friendly access to all the items of the QMS.

- *Traceability.* The hyper-textual mechanisms embedded in the WWW are particularly suited for managing references within and across documents of the QMS, allowing to browse through the complex structure of a Quality Management System and to keep under control the overall architecture of the system.
- *Maintainability.* Only the most recent version of documents is always available on-line.
- *Distribution.* Thanks to the access control list, the distribution of controlled copies is greatly facilitated.
- *Deployment.* The availability of on-line forms (e.g., for tool procurement, anomaly management, training registration, supplier evaluation, etc.) is a powerful support to the adoption in the daily routine work of the defined practices.
- *Effectiveness.* The integration with the development environment (e.g., templates linked with the appropriate word processor, forms linked with the appropriate email for posting) provides a straightforward way to information circulation within the company.

The experience has proven to be very positive and thus now the company considers the WWW as the principal environment for the development, tuning, and maintenance of the QMS, and the WWW is where the company automatically derives the few paper copies that are still needed for the certification/surveillance audits.

CHECK: THE APPROACH TO MEASUREMENT

The following activities were foreseen for tracking the effectiveness of the Software Process Improvement Program:

- Process assessment
- Process metrics
- Analysis of Return On Investment

As far as quantitative measures are concerned, a small core set of basic metrics directly related to the business goals of the company was collected, including projects that did not benefit of the improvement actions, projects in which additional practices were piloted and projects in which the new practices had become daily routine work.

In so doing, it was possible to have a considerable data set upon which a management by metrics activity was performed. The set of indicators collected is summarised in Table 11.2, together with the quantitative goals defined (values have been set based on the experiences gained from earlier projects).

Table 11.2.   Quantitative Indicators[1]

Indicator	Definition	Target Goal
Timeliness for the customer	Planned service development time/actual time	> 80%
Reuse	% of common software modules re-used	> 50%
Fault density	Faults/KLOC	< 1
Testing effectiveness	Faults in testing/Total faults	> 80%
Software productivity	LOC/person-month	> 250
Asset productivity	Html pages/person-months	> 150

[1]More details can be found in [10].

ACT: BENEFITS ACHIEVED AND LESSONS LEARNED

Results and lessons learned are considered from the following perspectives:

- technical,
- business,
- organisational, and
- cultural.

At the end of this chapter an appraisal of the positive and negative aspects of the Improvement Program is given.

Technical Impacts and Lessons Learned

From a technical point of view, the following main achievements can be stated:

- Selection and procurement of tools
- Definition of a draft Quality Manual
- Definition of guidelines for testing and CM
- Deployment of enhanced practices from the pilot projects to the daily routine work
- Performance of training and internal dissemination activities

From a software engineering point of view, the following achievement can be stated:

- The introduction of more systematic testing methods and tools is of paramount importance for level 1 SMEs and can be done with success in a short time.
- The introduction of configuration management requires more care, both from a methodological and a cultural point of view.
- The development of WWW based multimedia applications cannot be ruled under a classic waterfall model but rather requires fast prototyping and Rapid Application Development approaches, that the company is setting as the next target for improvement.

Business Impacts and Lessons Learned

From a business point of view it was perceived that the adoption of more mature software development/maintenance practices results in increased confidence by the customers, which was reflected in positive returns from the market (the company is experiencing a 100 percent growth rate over 3 years)

Impacts at operational and business level were assessed in a quantitative way.

The following table reports the values of the various indicators for two projects.

Qualitative Indicators and Achievements

Indicator	Unit of Measure	Goal	Project 1	Project 2
Software productivity	LOC/person-month	> 250	1138	3346
Asset productivity	Html Pages/Person-Months	> 1500	300	2702
Testing effectiveness	% Faults in testing/Total faults	> 80%	78%	89%
Software fault density	Faults/KLOC	< 5	2.1	0.15
Asset fault density	Faults/Kilo-lines of HTML	< 3	not applic.	0.19
Timeliness	Planned service development time/actual time	> 80%	75%	80%
Software re-use	Re-used lines/ LOC	> 20%	10%	21%
Asset re-use	Object re-use Structure re-use + ½	> 50%	50%	50%

With respect to the main business goals of the software producing unit, the quantitative improvements summarised in the following table have been observed.

Qualitative Business Impact

Business Goal	Impact
Product quality	Better (increase) by 17%
Time-to-market	Better (reduction) by 10%
Cost	Better (reduction) by 9%

Onion's strategic goal is to consolidate as an excellence centre in all its business areas, offering advanced products and services to the local and international market. To this end, the company is planning to invest about 30 percent of its resources to research and development (R&D) in the next years, as well as achieving ISO 9001 registration in the medium term.

Organisational Impacts and Lessons Learned

The project was run in cooperation between the communications/technologies department and the consulting department, which has specific skills and experiences in software process improvement. Due to this organisational peculiarity, the project allowed us to transfer internally the process improvement culture previously owned only by a subset of people. This resulted in higher company integration, which is a key element for the strategic projects that the company runs with some major customers, requiring a strict combination of technical and consulting capabilities.

Moreover, due to the several interactions across people, the project facilitated a more clear definition of roles within the company.

At the same time, the company is more and more experiencing the adoption of a paradigm oriented toward a "flexible resource pool" with dynamic allocations and resource sharing across projects, rather than the permanent assignment of technical staff to a predetermined area/group. This goal albeit more complex from a resource management point of view—which is more and more done at company level, letting the detailed activity planning/tracking at Project Level—is felt to be very appropriate for SMEs confronted with a fast-changing market. In this respect, PI^3 has contributed to the strengthening of the positive mood and feel that is needed in a company willing to adopt a "resource pool" approach.

Cultural Aspects and Lessons Learned

Involvement of the people was positive, without major resistance in adopting new tooling and methods; a clear evidence of this is the fact that Project Leaders, besides their involvement in the pilot projects, autonomously planned to apply the new testing methods also to products already in field, for sake of sanity/regression checking.

Still, some barriers are present in the application of more rigorous configuration management methods and in test execution tracing/problem report management. This is due to the fact that such activities are sometimes foreseen as a project overhead which does not bring in tangible results in the short term; thus, such activities risk being assigned a lower priority when time schedule pressure is high.

In order to overcome this problem, we are looking at the definition of WWW-based support forms to facilitate the adoption of such practices by implementing a work style that is already familiar and accepted by the technical staff.

Another way to attack this issue is to stress internal dissemination of the enhanced practices by means of workshops held by the people who have already experienced the new solutions (this is felt much more convincing for the developers than a "theoretical" tutorial).

Moreover, an effort is under way to consider such activities in the light of continuous improvement, with a medium- to long-term plan consisting of ISO 9001 certification, which represents a challenging goal for the company.

Several additional skills have been acquired by the project staff as a result of the experiment (e.g., high-level knowledge of ISO 9000 and Software Process Improvement principles; knowledge of testing methods and techniques; knowledge of configuration management principles; in-depth knowledge of the procured tools); the nature of the experiment also implied considerable changes for the professionals involved, in terms of their way of working, their skills and disciplines, etc.

The impact of the experiment on human factors can be summarised as follows:

- People showed enthusiasm in using new tools.
- People accepted the idea of systematic testing (not just debugging) and independent verification and validation.
- People positively experienced the usefulness of project guidelines, provided these are pragmatic and built as much as possible bottom-up from the hands-on experience.
- People were a bit reluctant to adopt more rigorous activity tracing methods, when this is not felt as directly contributing to the project technical needs: bureaucracy is not welcome.

Strengths and Weaknesses of the Experience

This section provides a summary view of the usefulness of the Process Improvement program itself, identifying the strengths and weaknesses of the adopted approach and its overall benefit for the organisation.

The following aspects can be considered strong:

- Deployment in two pilot projects
- Involvement of people from different departments
- Combination of technical and methodological aspects

The following aspects show room for improvement:

- Parallel activation of two improvements (testing and CM) in a small organisation at the same time; this is good at rule definition level but is not easy at project level, where improvements have to be managed with care in order not to overwhelm the project staff that has to keep in any case the planned goals and schedules.
- Management of project guidelines within an overall framework; this was not foreseen at the beginning but soon came to be seen as a need by the company, which thus defined a first draft Quality Manual adhering to ISO 9001 before getting to the definition of detailed guidelines.

Overall, the PI³ project was felt to be successful. Nevertheless, if we were to repeat it, we would make specific changes to our approach in order to overcome the two identified weaknesses, namely: more accurate timing of deployment of improvements in the daily routine work and definition of company rules, adopting a top-down approach.

The issue of Process Improvement deployment is felt as critical, since for SMEs intensive software process actions might bring a disruption of the normal company activities. It is our opinion that this should not happen, provided the improvement actions are seen as a significant part of a global Process Improvement approach that the company should continuously apply.

Process Improvement in SMEs is a continuous, long-lasting process. Quoting from Ovid we could say, *Adde parvum parvo magnus acervus erit* "Add little to a little, and the amount will be large".

In any case, in order to avoid risks, the following provisions can be put forward:

- Care has to be taken in the detailed planning of the improvements in order to avoid the overlapping of the most effort-consuming activities.
- Improvements shall be extended to other projects adopting a bottom-up approach, that is to say, introducing additional practices in a controlled way and under the responsibility of the Project Leader, only after they have been discussed with and accepted by the involved designers.
- The measurement of quantitative results obtained by the pilot projects has to be the major criteria for deciding the deployment of additional practices into the normal company activities.
- Internal training and dissemination must have a big emphasis.

REFERENCES

1. M. Rohen, "ESSI: Objectives, Strategy and Implementation of Software Best Practice Actions," *Proceedings of ISCN 95 Conference*, Vienna, Sept. 1995.

2. R. Bache, G. Bazzana, *Software Metrics for Product Assessment*, International Software Quality Assurance Series, McGraw-Hill, London, 1995.

3. B. Beizer, *Software Testing Techniques*, Van Nostrand Reinhold, 1990.

4. Commission of the European Communities, *Information Technology Security Evaluation Criteria (ITSEC), Version 1.2*, CEC, June 1991.

5. Commission of the European Communities, *Information Technology Security Evaluation Manual (ITSEM), Version 1.0*, CEC, Sept. 1993.

6. ImagiWare, "Doctor HTML," http://imagiware.com/RxHTML.cgi.

7. N. Bowers, "WebLint: Quality Assurance for the World Wide Web," *Proceedings of 5th International WWW Conference*, Paris, May 1996, pp. 1283–1290.

8. G. Bazzana, et al., "Internet Testing Challenges," *EuroStar 96, 4th European Conference on Software Testing, Analysis and Review*, Amsterdam, Dec. 1996.

9. D.M. Marks, *Configuration Management*, McGraw-Hill, 1996.

10. G. Bazzana, et al., "Process Improvement in Internet Service Providing," *Proceeding of ISCN 96 Conference*, Brighton, UK, Dec. 1996.

Chapter 12

Alcatel's Experience with Process Improvement

Christophe Debou
Alcatel-Alsthom, Zaventem, Belgium

Daniel Courtel, Henri-Bernard Lambert
Alcatel Telecom France, Vélizy, France

Norbert Fuchs, Michael Haux
Alcatel Telecom Austria, Vienna, Austria

INTRODUCTION

Alcatel, as one of the biggest telecommunication equipment suppliers in the world, has been investing for years in quality initiatives for improving both process and products. This chapter presents experiences in process improvement that occurs in different entities of the company. First, the corporate software process improvement initiative started several years ago will be introduced with the first conclusions on CMM-based process improvement. Then two Alcatel entities will share their long-term history in improving product development processes with emphasis on software:

- Alcatel Telecom Austria is the first German-speaking company, which happened to be a finalist for the European Quality Award in 1995
- Alcatel E10 Switching Systems Division, which successfully implemented ISO 9001 processes and is now using the CMM principles to sustain improvements

The application domain is very similar to Chapter 10. Those two experiences demonstrate that results can be achieved with a different combination of improvement methodologies.

ALCATEL SOFTWARE PROCESS IMPROVEMENT INITIATIVE

Motivation

Telecommunication companies have gone through fundamental changes in the last decades. They have moved from an electronics-oriented (hardware design and production) organisation to almost being "software houses." The cost of software development of typical telecommunication systems like switching system accounts for 80 percent of the overall cost (20 years ago, that was the hardware part). Systems are becoming bigger (several million lines of code) and more complex to manage. One solution is to rationalise the product architecture to ease evolution with minimum software development effort. Another complementary one is to strengthen the way software is developed towards a more professional, disciplined, and controlled approach, that is, to introduce industrial process control in software development. The first step has been the implementation of an ISO 9001-based quality system. But it generally did not completely succeed in the software area where the certification was very often just an exercise for the sake of certification, not for real improvement.

Now, all major telecommunication companies have undertaken a corporate software process improvement programme (Siemens [7, 12] Nokia, AT&T, etc.). The top-level management of Alcatel Alsthom decided beginning in 1994 to initiate a continuous software process improvement programme using the SEI methodology to better address new challenges. The rising complexity of the systems is increasing the risk of delivering lower quality or with unacceptable delay that would imply high financial penalties. As a consequence of the globalization of telecommunication market, Telecom operators are becoming more schedule-driven than purely feature-driven. Furthermore, telecommunication operators or consortiums (British Telecom, Unisource, Bellcore, Eurescom, etc.) started visibility programmes for their suppliers covering the software development process.

Alcatel representatives visited several U.S. companies where SPI programme have been successfully implemented, to understand their main success drivers. The conclusion was a set of principles that would drive the initiative:

- The Capability Maturity Model [9, 10] will be the basis for assessing our software development capability and to guide but not dictate the improvements.
- All major development centres have to be assessed before they can produce local action plans (self-assessment supported by external coaches). Training of management and SPI staff has to be performed beforehand.
- Software Engineering Process Groups (SEPG) have to be established in each development centre together with a management steering committee.
- A dedicated budget should be allocated to SPI activities (about 3 percent of R&D effort).
- All SPI actions within a business division will be coordinated by a software process manager reporting to both local technical director and corporate SPI management.
- Improvement actions should be driven by business objectives and constraints on the one hand, by assessment findings on the other hand.
- Business and process performance indicators should be established to continuously evaluate the impact of changes on projects and on the organisation.

The corporate goal was to be equivalent to SEI level 3 by 1997. This is not to be considered a business objective or diploma per se, but more a means for action planning orientation rather than an end.

Those principles were fully supported by Alcatel Alsthom top-level management whose commitment has been made visible through Corporate support (financial, resources) for the business divisions to start up and sustain the initiative, and through continuous follow-up.

Approach Used

Figure 12.1 outlines a typical timescale of the SPI programme as usually done within one development centre. First, local management has to be exposed to the SPI concepts. The type

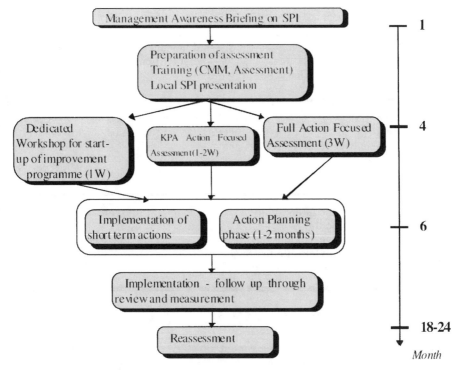

Figure 12.1. Time schedule of an SPI programme in one entity.

of approach will be then decided upon the estimated capability of the organisation, its size and "probable" level of commitment of local management. Then either a full 3-week assessment ("Action Focus Assessment [1, 8] refer to Figure 12.2) is performed or a more dedicated workshop less costly for the organisation but trying to address their specific concerns (particularly suitable for smaller organisations). Such workshops can include very small-scale assessment and/or some training on essential software engineering practices or the CMM. The 3-week assessment, in addition to conventional assessment schedule, includes 1 week for initiating the action planning phase ("Guidance for Action Planning").

The postassessment phase is crucial and starts with a detailed action planning phase. In parallel, short-term actions will be implemented to show management and practitioners that the momentum is being kept. During the implementation, performance indicators have to be collected on major projects in the organisation to evaluate changes. Those indicators should cover business aspects, process performance aspects, and conformance aspects (whether practices are applied at all and in the right way, which is work typically performed by a software quality assurance function).

LESSONS

After several years of experiences, some essential lessons can be drawn:

Tailoring

It is a dream to think that the same improvement approach can be applied everywhere. Each organisation inside a multinational company like Alcatel needs to be looked at carefully, to

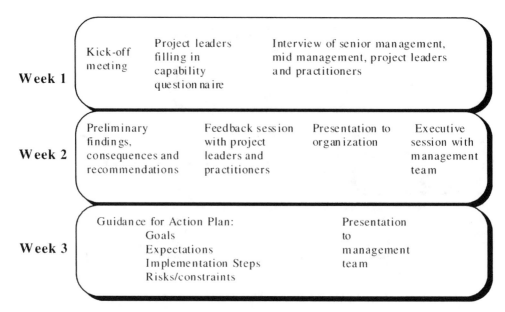

Figure 12.2.   Schedule of assessment.

understand what makes sense for it: assessment or software engineering practices training, heavy SPI organisation (SEPG, working group, steering committees, etc.) or light one (task force), use of corporate-funded external support for implementation or just a regular corporate follow-up. The first driver is certainly whether the site is part of a bigger organisation within the frame of master-slave relationships. It will inherit the main attributes from the overall programme. Then, the size of the development centre drives the decision. In big development centres, the expertise is usually there. What makes the difference is a push from local management to make things happen. Internal Small and Medium-size Enterprise (SMEs) needs a more pragmatic approach, straight to the issues with addition of external expertise.

Assessment First?

Before performing any CMM-based assessment, the readiness of the organisation to investing in SPI should be evaluated. An assessment is quite a heavy exercise for a development centre (3 weeks) and raises a lot of expectations within the organisation. If nothing happens after the assessment, then it can hurt the organisation more than it would have helped. Awareness training may be sufficient at first.

Strategy for Improvement

The assessment process is being overdocumented in conferences, books, and articles in comparison with what is written about improvement strategies. Assessment is only a starting point and is just a tiny part of the iceberg. Whether to use such assessment approach or such capability questionnaire does not account for a high probability in the success of the whole initiative. But the strategy to be used to bridge the gap between the assessment and the implementation of actions is much more critical and unfortunately not well mastered in the whole industry. The first experiences have shown that the delay between the assessment and the first impact on projects was much too big and led to the demotivation of practitioners and management. SPI was perceived as a long-term process, outside the daily business. To overcome this, an incremental approach was implemented to allow the delivery of a set of essential software engineering practices on critical areas (projects, key process area) every 4 to 5 months. Experienced consultants partly funded by corporate were brought in the organisation within the frame of formal contract between corporate and the local organisation, to accelerate the take-up of those new practices. The approach usually generates higher management attention as it is much nearer to the daily concerns and consequently get sooner the attention from all the organisation.

Link to Business

We experienced that the local programmes that had the most success were the ones where the business manager was convinced that it is worthwhile to invest in SPI. A key question is "How to convince him or her?" and how to speak to the business manager using the right set of business terms, that is, objectives, performance indicators, critical areas, and investigation of the risks of not doing it (competitive analysis, customer/market changes).

A continuous "proactive" follow-up by business management or responsible technical management was performed, also involving also the project leaders and mid-managers.

Strong emphasis was put on metrics. They were implemented from the start applying a goal-oriented measurement approach (e.g., Application of Metrics in Industry® [2]), including:

- Business performance, that is, indicators visible for customers, for example, fault reports after delivery
- Development performance, that is, how good is the software development, for example, what is the percentage of defects found in each testing phase
- Pilot performance, that is, how to evaluate quantitatively the results of implementation of a new process

On the other hand, SPI initiatives seemed to be less successful when

- management does not appear when expected (assessment presentation, etc.);
- the initiative is understood as being purely forced by corporate and not for self-improvement;
- ISO 9001 certification was just established with lots of documentation without a continuous improvement vision.

ISO 9001 versus CMM Assessment

Many criticisms were made of ISO 9001, and its real impact on quality and efficiency. To a certain extent, experiences show that most of the ISO 9001-certified organisations are still between a maturity level of 1 and level 3. However, an ISO 9001 quality system, if implemented correctly, basically uses the same concepts as SPI does (such as management commitment, budget, continuity).

A factor for success is a wise interpretation of ISO 9001 and CMM and a willingness for change on the part of management.

Cultural Issue

Trends in SPI basically come from the United States and everyone knows the difficulty of adapting technology and methods to other culture. Alcatel is a multinational organisation mainly present in Europe (France, Germany, Belgium, Spain, Italy) in terms of product development. And the attitude toward the methods and concepts vary from one culture to another and consequently the implementation. For example, one cannot approach assessments in Scandinavia (with their culture of openness) the same way as in Latin America! But wherever you are, as soon as you speak the local languages (not only the mother tongue but also "business language"), the probability of success is much bigger. And certainly it is rarely accepted in Europe to have a SPI guru who converses in an "ideal" and rather academic way (e.g., using phrases such as "the American miracle") and gives the impression that there is nothing else but the "bible" (CMM), emphasising primarily references and buzzwords more than the inherent concepts.

ALCATEL AUSTRIA'S EXPERIENCES WITH QUALITY APPROACHES

Motivation

Alcatel Austria's Quality initiative has a long history. It began in the 1970s with the introduction of the ITT Quality Program Quality Improvement through Defect Prevention which was conducted by the famous Group Quality Manager Philip Crosby. Recognition, certificates, and Quality awards of these previous days are still present in many departments of Alcatel Austria to remind staff of our longstanding experience in the field of Quality Management. In the early 1990s the board of directors stepped up the pace of Alcatel Austria's drive to Total Quality with the implementation of Time-Based Management and ISO 9001. In 1991 Alcatel Austria received external certification for the whole company and has since then passed a reaudit in 1994. End of 1995 the first internal audits according to the TickIT schema were performed (Software development specific interpretation of ISO 9000 based on ISO 9000-3).

Having received ISO 9001, a new challenge was sought to drive continuous improvement. A new process that could clearly discern strengths from opportunities for improvement was necessary. Therefore Alcatel Austria started a Total Quality process using the criteria of the European Quality Award (TEQA). Since 1992 self-assessments have played a major part in the yearly business review, since the company views the model of the European Foundation for Quality Management (EFQM) as a business model. It is a quality model that links all the aspects of the business, enabling employees to drive continuous business improvement through Total Quality Management. Alcatel Austria was the first and up to now the only Austrian company that applied for TEQA in 1993, 1994, and 1995. These systematic efforts made Alcatel Austria a finalist in 1995's award competition. It is the first time a German-speaking company got this recognition.

As software became a strategic element in Alcatel Austria, the board of directors decided in 1994 to start a specific activity aimed at the improvement of software development processes within the relevant divisions. The main quality attributes are cost, time to market, and reliability. To secure competitive advantage the Capability Maturity Model (CMM) has been selected which is already used within approximately 300 companies. In the meantime CMM was applied to all development divisions within Alcatel Austria.

In early 1994 the board of directors felt that the implementation of continuous improvements were not sufficient to react immediately to the fast changes in customer attitudes, market, technology, and competition. Therefore, the board commissioned an experienced consulting company to initiate a Business Process Reengineering project within one of the most critical business areas.

In the function of a central quality department the authors of this paper have been involved in all these activities. This experience will be used to discuss the different approaches and their nature of assessments.

Assessment/Improvement/Reengineering

In the last years a wave of quality awareness has swept over Europe. For various reasons approaches like ISO 9000, TickIT, CMM, or TEQA have been taken up by industry very rapidly. As a consequence, today industry is confronted with a lot of "new" quality approaches, slogans, and abbreviations. To put all these in context the following classification can be made (Figure 12.3).

The nature of process assessment is that the maturity of the processes stays unchanged. The assessment itself does not effect the processes; maybe the preparation does. Process improvement aims at continuous improvement and the ongoing optimisation. Process reengineering aims at radical change in the processes, hopefully an improvement but this is not guaranteed by the nature of process reengineering. Still about 70 percent of all process reengineering projects fail.

Both process improvement and process reengineering require an assessment first. You always have to know where you are before starting to change. Therefore the methods of process assessment are used and some approaches like CMM for improvement have even their own assessment method (SEI assessments).

Together with this development and the increasing process maturity, audit (assessment) methods have also improved. Every company should be able to see this improvement. Take, for example, a company that has stayed with ISO 9000 for 5 years.

After 5 years the nature of internal audits should have changed. Questions like "Do you have a quality policy?" seem to be childish after 5 years. With improving process maturity and understanding, the audits should develop in the following order:

Awareness Audits

Awareness audits are used to prove the applicability of a process description, the awareness of the employees, and to check the communication and information flow. The goal is to react as early as possible (changing process description, training employees), but also to improve the culture for quality.

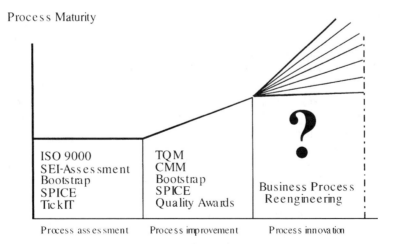

Figure 12.3.   Process assessment, improvement, and innovation.

Compliance Audits

Compliance audits aim at proving that standards are being followed, with the goal of obtaining a Certificate or an internal approval. ISO 9000 certification audits are a typical example here.

Improvement Audits

Improvement audits aim to show improvement potential with the goal of ongoing and preventive improvement. It is essential for improvement audits that auditor and auditee are working together as a team. Together they look for improvement potential based on their experiences and skills.

Assessment Audits

Assessment audits are used to assess a system of processes through a group of experts (assessors) with the goal to get a judgement relative to the environment (competition, state of the art, etc.). Thus this is akin to benchmarking. An example is the assessment procedure of the European Quality Award described below. The following sections will briefly present the approaches chosen by Alcatel Austria for process management and improvement.

ISO9001, TickIT, ISO 9000-3

The ISO 9000 series of international standards for quality management was first published in 1987. The content is not that new, of course, but has its roots several decades back in military standards. With the enormous international diffusion of ISO 9000 an introduction of the model seems unnecessary here. In September 1995, 80 ISO member countries adopted the series, and more are on the way [5]. According to the Mobil survey, over 95,000 certificates of conformance have been issued world-wide as of March 1995 [6].

Instead of just relying on ISO 9004 guidance for building a quality management system, the major role is still played by ISO 9001. ISO 9001 is the most comprehensive of the three "conformity" standards in the series and contains minimum requirements for a quality management system (QMS). The requirements focus heavily on documentation, that is, written process descriptions, procedures, etc. The 20 elements in ISO 9001 contain a mixture of life-cycle-dependent elements—like contract review, design control, and process control—and life-cycle-independent, supporting elements—like purchasing, document and data control, training—as well as management activities [4].

To ease the use of ISO 9001 in software developing organisations, ISO 9000-3 was first published in 1991 [3]. This guideline instead of the 20 elements uses a more logical structure with the chapters framework, life-cycle activities, and supporting activities. ISO 9000-3 should not add anything in the scope of ISO 9001, since it is a guideline, but should just clarify interpretation details specific for software business.

ISO 9000-3 is "just" a guideline. A software organisation may very well use it to get ideas for building its quality system in accordance with ISO 9001. An auditor may also use it as a guide. But auditing and certification is at the end nevertheless, according to ISO 9001. For software development there is also the TickIT IT sector certification scheme [11]. This scheme is based on the assumption that the existing accreditation system is too weak to enable effective auditing and certification in the IT sector. The main difference for audits are the special requirements on TickIT auditors' IT competence and qualification.

No matter if an organisation is using ISO 9001 for two-party agreement, or second- or third- party registration, internal QMS audits are required. These audits should be performed on a regular basis covering all of the organisation. Most readers should be familiar with the process of both external (certification and surveillance) and internal audits, so these are not discussed in more detail here.

Nevertheless one aspect should be stressed here in more detail: the process of how to select auditors. There are different possibilities for this process. You either can select few auditors having to spend a lot of time auditing, or you can select many auditors doing only few audits per year. Alcatel Austria decided from the very beginning to nominate a lot of internal auditors coming from all the different organisational units. About 20 auditors were selected, trained, and charged with doing two to three audits per year. These internal auditors are replaced every 3 years. This results in a lot of people who are, or who have been, auditors being spread over the whole company. The advantage is clear, which has been processed through a high education effort.

SEI CMM

Early 1994 Alcatel Austria's board of directors initiated a program for improving the software processes of the main Austrian development divisions. Based on experience gathered during several years of applied corporate research on software engineering topics the Austrian management decided to use the well-known SEI methodology for the improvement program. In parallel to these decisions, the Alcatel Alsthom corporate software process improvement program was started, based on the SEI CMM. Since local expertise was available in Austria, the Austrian managing director decided to set up a local Austrian specialist group (three persons) for supporting the program, while keeping all activities coordinated with the Alcatel Alsthom corporate functions. This Austrian group is part of the centralised quality department.

In which division should the improvement activities be started? Since the SEI assessment methodology (SPA) requires a certain organisation size to make sense, only three Austrian development departments were candidates. The smallest of these employed approximately 60 developers. In spring 1994, two of the divisions reported a high degree of interest in an assessment of their software development activities as soon as possible. The third division, while seeing the need for the quality improvement program, saw neither the possibility of freeing enough resources for doing the assessment, nor the possibility of investing in any resulting improvement actions. This division needed more time to plan for the program. In between this, the development department has been integrated in the corporate process improvement activities. For the other two departments, assessment dates were defined for mid-1994.

As mentioned above, local software engineering expertise was available, including knowledge of the SEI questionnaire and the CMM, and experience in building and auditing quality management systems. Anyway, it seemed necessary to take further training in doing assessments. This turned out to be a wise decision. Of the licensed SEI vendors, that is, companies officially providing assessment and training according to the SEI methodology (in 1994 all based in the United States), one could provide on-site training for the Alcatel Austria specialist group at short notice. The 1-week intensive training comprised detailed guidance for doing the SPA, including change management, SEI methodology, role playing, etc. What were the benefits from the training? Mainly this consisted in the following:

- Access to official, not public domain, SEI materials (such as forms, and checklists for the assessment process).

- Access to very good (partly SEI, partly vendor-specific) training material that was used for training Alcatel Austria's assessment teams. These internal trainings for Alcatel Austria's assessment teams were held by the above-mentioned specialist group.
- Complete case studies of SEI assessments and results.
- Advice from the trainer, who had participated in several assessments.

The following section briefly presents the SEI Software Process Assessment (SPA) methodology. The SPA preparation starts several weeks before the "real" assessment and includes selection of assessment team, selection of representative projects, training and briefing of participants, and collection of project leaders' answers to the SEI questionnaire. This questionnaire provides spot-checking of the situation in the organisation and is used by the assessment team to get a rough picture of the organisation's capability and to prepare interviews. During the following assessment week a systematic methodology including many group techniques is utilised to reach a consensus on the real problem areas and, last but not least, to reach a momentum in the change process. Due to the high involvement from the assessed organisation with assessment team members, project leaders and many (normally 20 to 30) practitioners from the projects, the credibility of the SPA method is high. Figure 12.4 indicates the whole process of an SPA.

The assessment team consisted of four experienced software professionals from the division assessed, and two division-external "consultants" from the centralised support group. During the first two assessments no Alcatel Alsthom corporate representative attended the assessments, though this might be the case in future assessments, and may bring some corporate synergies.

To summarise this discussion, the following are the main outputs of the assessments, with the most important first:

1. A change momentum
2. An action plan
3. The maturity level

The main results of the SPA are motivation to change things, belief in the possibility of improvement, and a visible commitment to software processes and quality. These effects underline the importance of a rigorous assessment approach with a focus on group dynamics. Compact assessment approaches (1-day assessment, or even 1-hour assessment using tool support) may be a solution for smaller organisations, where for instance the SEI SPA approach would be too heavy and where the motivation issues anyhow may be more under control.

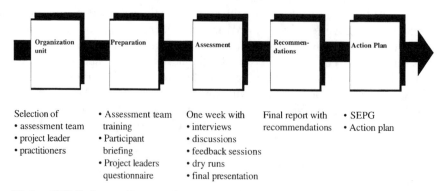

Figure 12.4. SEI Software Process Assessment (SPA) overview.

Another major result is of course the action plan. More on action planning follows later in this chapter.

The least important result of an assessment is the maturity level. Since an SPA is mainly done in order to initiate improvement, and not to prove a certain capability, the important result is to experience strengths and weaknesses. The CMM level merely assists in making the roadmap to better processes more visible.

The specialist group supported the division's own software people in planning improvement actions. This planning was finished within the month following the assessment. This time should be kept down in order not to lose the change momentum. One month is probably an upper limit. The action plan covers issues such as planned activities, input material, planned deliverables, and effort. The action planning is in fact essential for many reasons, not the least of which are the following:

- It provides an opportunity to do good planning and tracking, activities which are often weak in software projects. That is, an opportunity to "walk the talk."
- The plan will be accepted by top managers who thus show their commitment of resources.

In both divisions the first major action was to define the software engineering process group (SEPG). The SEPG was staffed with two half-time persons in one case, with one full-time and several part-time persons in the other case. At first the intent was to set up small working groups, coordinated by SEPG members, for each improvement area. However, this scheme did not really work, and the more viable solution was to let the SEPG do much of the work, while strongly interacting with developers.

During the design and implementation of changes it turned out that the planned efforts were not really needed. The estimates were too high! The lower amount of effort needed was due to several factors, notably synergies within Alcatel Alsthom and within Alcatel Austria. It turned out that diffusion of best practices from one project to another was a good way to save effort and have a "free" pilot. Within the international business divisions, processes were defined in common and some early starters with process improvement could provide useful input material.

The action plan must of course be tracked and updated. A good way is to define priorities for each action area and go for about three areas at a time. The detailed planning is then done in the SEPG for the actual three top priority areas. Progress tracking is accomplished in monthly SEPG meetings.

The coordination with the global Alcatel Alsthom SPI program varies between the business divisions. The minimum level of coordination includes:

- Sharing the main goal (to be equivalent to SEI level 3 by 1997) and means (the SEI CMM as a guide).
- SEPG reporting to the business division SEPG or process manager.
- Taking part in Alcatel Alsthom workshops and seminars related to the actual SPI activities.
- Furthermore, extensive use of the Alcatel Wide Web by some SEPGs improves the exchange of information like action plans, process definitions, etc.

TEQA

Each year since 1992, the European Foundation for Quality Management has presented The European Quality Award. The assessment of the participants in this competition is done against the EFQM model for total quality management. The award and the model are counterparts to the U.S. Malcolm Baldrige National Quality Award (MBNQA) and its criteria. The

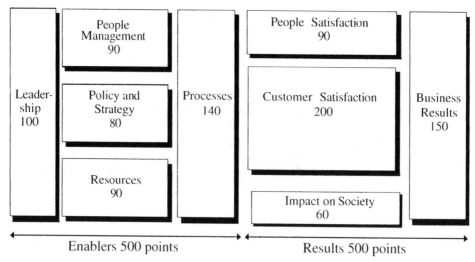

Figure 12.5.   The EFQM model for TQM.

models are similar, though the European model was from the beginning pushing a total management view, while MBNQA was more narrowly focused. For example, business results were part of TEQA from the beginning while MBNQA only lately has broadened the scope. The EFQM model is much wider than the process-oriented ISO 9001 or SEI CMM. We estimate that ISO 9001 covers less than 25 percent of the model, dealing only with enablers. The CMM in some way deals with all enablers but people management, while going rather into details of the key software development processes.

The process of participating in TEQA includes the following main steps:

1. Collect information and data on the nine EFQM model elements (Figure 12.5) from the organisation and write a report not exceeding 75 pages.
2. Perform a self-assessment in the company (see below).
3. Provide the company report to EFQM. EFQM assessors assess the company on the basis of this report.
4. If the company has more than approximately 550 points, an international assessment team is composed and will perform a site visit to validate the contents of the report, clarify issues, and check the real deployment.
5. EFQM summarises the results of the site visits, adjusts the scores from step 3, and presents the best companies with recognition (award, prizes).

Participating in TEQA is of course not the only goal with using the EFQM model. The model itself provides an excellent means for management to get a balanced company overview, and in combination with self-assessment, to initiate internal improvement projects. Self-assessment includes the following steps:

1. Select and train internal assessors from senior management, middle management, and other staff. At Alcatel Austria other staff includes centralised functions as well as young managers and trainees. In all about 30 people, split up in four assessor teams, took part.
2. Each self-assessor individually assesses the report using the TEQA scoring system, summarised in the following table:

Enablers	*Approach*—systematic? prevention-based? state-of-the-art?, integrated? PDCA cycle?	*Deployment*—is the approach used for all relevant areas and activities?
Results	*Results* as such—including benchmarking, trends, and causality	*Scope*—which areas and activities are covered?

3. In addition, each assessor notes strengths and improvement areas for each award criteria. The scoring should be objective; that is, relating to the written information in the report only, not taking into account his personal knowledge about the organisation.

4. The results of each assessor are collected and summarised.

5. Now each of the assessor teams works for one day together to reach a consensus. This is accomplished by letting the assessors with "extreme" results for a criteria present their argumentation and notes. Through further discussions a consensus is reached on each criteria; "consensus" here means less than 10 percent difference between the highest and the lowest score. During this process the moderator also notes the improvement areas discussed. These notes are summarised for the teams, and serve as an input for TQM improvement projects.

6. After the consensus process has been finished, the results are summarised and a company score is calculated.

LESSONS LEARNED

We have discussed a classification of various approaches, the development of assessments (or audits) through the stages awareness, compliance, improvement and assessment/benchmarking. The three process approaches used in Alcatel Austria, ISO, CMM, and TEQA, were discussed, their usage, and especially the related assessment techniques. In this chapter we will share our experience about the approaches' influence on the assessment style.

After some time using an ISO 9000 QMS the nature of audits has changed. This change was not caused by a conscious shift in the focus, like that used for the first steps of QMS introduction using awareness audits as described in Chapter 5. Several auditors started behaving more and more like change agents and improvement moderators. Why?—because they noticed the absurd situation of having to check ISO 9000 requirements and concentrating on the status quo after having had the QMS in place for some years. What happened was that they changed the way of asking questions. Instead of asking "Please show me . . ." they asked "Could you do it in another way?," "Who else could do it?," etc. During this transformation period it was also made explicit by the company's CEO that the ISO audits should not be narrowly focused. Thus, the audits had a much stronger improvement focus than before.

The assessments performed within the scope of a certain improvement approach have gone through an evolution, as indicated for ISO 9000 audits above. However, the main evolution has taken place at the organisational level—not limiting the four-stage evolution to one approach but going through the four stages with different approaches. The nature, or style, of the assessments had to reflect the approach. By using complimentary approaches and assessment/audit techniques to manage the evolution of the whole organisation through the four stages, the improvements can be supported in an orderly way. Table 12.1 shows how the approaches and evolution stages match each other:

Table 12.1.   Audit Nature Versus Selected Approach

Audit stage	ISO	SEI SPA (CMM)	TEQA
Awareness audits	Checked during implementation of QMS	Checked in SPA	Checked during site visit
Compliance audits	High	Low (no accreditation system, no registration system, etc.)	Low (as CMM but even less guidance on what to have to get certain points)
Improvement audits	Medium	High	Medium to high
Assessment audits	No-little (to some extent approach benchmarking)	No-little (to some extent approach benchmarking)	High, both approach and results benchmarking

To summarise the table above, the use of ISO 9001 can be recommended to define a basic QMS. Awareness audits are used to stimulate communication and to spread the quality management ideas and policies. Compliance audits are used to maintain the system, but don't forget to use these audits also to stimulate improvement. In order to continuously improve the software development process use CMM or SPICE (Software Process Improvement and Capability Determination) for best-practices hints and use assessments like SPAs to motivate people and build change momentum. Then EFQM/TEQA are used to validate the total management system and to benchmark yourself against others.

The evolutionary stages relate to the following strategic objectives with regard to process improvement and assessment:

- Create quality consciousness and support deployment of policies (awareness)
- Conform to a basic, internationally recognised, model for competitive or market reasons as well as for defining a first baseline for improvements (compliance)
- Drive improvements of software development in order to increase productivity, quality, decrease risks, etc. (improvement)
- Benchmark results and approaches with best in class, etc. (assessment)

The objectives of the approaches are reflected in the sources of inputs of the assessment, in the people involvement during assessments and in the outcome. Table 12.2 summarises these aspects.

During ISO audits, the main emphasis is on objective proof of living the QMS, mainly focusing on the "responsible" people in the organisation. In the SEI SPA not quite as much proof is requested, and the practitioners are heavily involved, bringing lots of input enabling the assessment team to validate the project leader interviews and to address issues lying outside the scope of the CMM, for instance communication problems. TEQA self-assessments require strategic and business knowledge as well as organisational overview, thus here the participation is focused on management. During the site visits performed by external assessors at the most successful TEQA applicants, deployment and understanding of the TQM principles and approaches are spot-checked at all levels of the company.

Table 12.2.   Inputs, Participants, and Results of Audits

Approach	Main Inputs	Highly Involved People	Results
ISO	QMS documentation Quality records	Line management Project leaders	Conformance y/n Corrective actions Remarks

SEI SPA (CMM)	The voice of the
	  developer
	Structured interviews
	  with project leaders
		Middle management
		Project leaders
		Practitioners
			CMM level
			Findings &
			  consequences
			Action plan
			Strengths

TEQA	Report describing organisation approaches and data/results (mapped to EFQM model)	Line and centralised management	Score Improvement areas Strengths Benchmarking

Finally, Table 12.3 illustrates the differences in the assessment nature for these three approaches by showing some example wordings used in problem findings.

Table 12.3.   Examples of Wordings in Findings

Approach	Typical Findings
ISO	. . . not documented . . . documented procedure not adhered to . . . missing requirement . . . responsibilities not clear . . . not provable
SEI SPA (CMM)	. . . not understood . . . lacking knowledge in. . . . . . not adequate . . . should be considered No perceived commitment to. . . Lack of mechanism to. . . Lack of widespread use of procedures. . . Lack of procedures, standards. . .
TEQA	PDCA cycle missing for. . . . . . no systematic improvement . . . show weak trends . . . lacks in continuity . . . effectiveness evaluation missing No competitor figures available . . . lacks in strategy-forming process deployment not . . .

CONTINUOUS QUALITY IMPROVEMENT IN TELECOMMUNICATION SYSTEMS DEVELOPMENT

Introduction

Alcatel 1000 Systems are developed by the Switching System Division of Alcatel Telecom. The two products, Alcatel 1000 S12 and Alcatel 1000 E10, both require considerable amounts of real-time software. A continuous Software Quality improvement process is used for both products.

This chapter describes the improvement process set up for the ALCATEL 1000 E10.

Alcatel 1000 E10 Improvement Policy

The aim of the Alcatel 1000 E10 improvement policy is to increase customer satisfaction, global competitiveness, and performance. To reach these objectives and to analyse problems and find solutions, a continuous improvement policy has been defined. To perfect the system engineering process, a continuous step by step evolution was used, taking into account the present practices. We have used emerging norms and standards in the areas as Quality Assurance and Process Improvements to strengthen and support this policy. Two major decisions were made:

> We use ISO 9001 norm as the reference of Quality Systems in each design centre, and show our customers, through ISO certificates, that we are deeply involved in mastering quality.

1. We use the SEI Capability Maturity Model (CMM) to reach ALCATEL 1000 E10 competitiveness objectives, through process optimisation and common quality culture improvement.
2. Each of these decisions was executed in successive steps, without any major breaks.

ISO 9000 Approach: A Step toward Mastering Quality

Commitment

Since 1991, each system and software design centre is individually involved in a ISO 9000 certification process. The objectives are to improve the customer supplier relationships, and to improve product and process quality.

The strong management commitment led to the implementation of Quality Systems in each design centre, and to ISO 9001 certificates between 1991 and 1994. These Quality Systems describe all the activities associated with Telecommunication Systems Developments, including system, hardware, and software aspects. The organisation and breakdown of these tasks were based on ISO 9000-3 norm, which describes ISO 9001 more specifically for software.

Since 1994, ISO 9000-3 has been used as the reference for our Quality Systems internal audits.

Quality Implementation

Two basic structures were defined to implement ISO 9001: the Quality System, and the Quality Organisation.

The Quality System, Figure 12.6 in each development centre, defines

- The quality policy, complemented by quantified and measurable objectives.
- The procedures, based on ISO 9000-3 types.

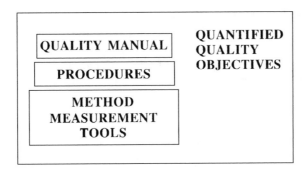

Figure 12.6.   Quality system.

- The methods, tools, and measurement plans.
- In some situations, more detailed information is gathered in a complementary Product Quality Plan. The detailed quality objectives are defined in these quality plans. Measurements are done throughout the development life cycle such as:
- Pre-delivery measurements.
- Post-delivery measurements in operations.
- End-of-phase and end-of-project reviews.
- Quality parameters at the development centre level.

Organisation and responsibilities are shared between Technical Department and Quality Department (Table 12.4).

- The Technical Department (TD) is responsible for product quality, development processes quality, and improvements.
- The Quality Department (QD) is an independent entity in charge of product and process quality assurance.

Table 12.4.   Quality Organisation.

	Technical Department (TD)	**Quality Department (QD)**
Quality System	Responsible for quality system definition	Conformity with ISO and, ISO 9000-3
Product Quality Assurance	Responsible for product quality	Give the green light
Process Quality Assurance	Applies the quality system procedures	Verify the use of quality system procedures

Improvement Implementation: Root Cause Analysis

Important improvements are implemented using two complementary approaches, one for products and one for processes.

Root cause analysis of product trouble reports

Exhaustive analysis of trouble reports is executed. Root cause analysis principles are used, in order to identify future preventive measures. This analysis can be done efficiently, since trouble report treatment is formalised, processes are defined, and measurement plans are executed during the product development life cycle. As an example, product performances were greatly improved after a root cause analysis of capacity problems: product performance controls were introduced in each step of product development.

Fault detection efficiency of processes

A root cause analysis is done on fault detection efficiency of processes, allowing us to identify:

- when the defect was incorporated,
- when it should have been found, if the process was perfect, and
- when it was finally detected, due to process problems.

As an example, this led us to identify gaps in our test coverage, and allowed us to define a global test strategy which increases test efficiency.

These two complementary approaches for root cause analysis, are used as the input for our Quality System improvements.

Achievements

After this first step was achieved, each ALCATEL 1000 E10 design centre enjoyed the following benefits:

- Use of a unique model for its quality structures: ISO 9001 complemented by ISO 9000-3.
- Definition of its own procedures and methods, based on local practices, allowing us to reach the quality, development cost, and planning objectives.
- Quality culture introduction, in all development teams.
- ISO certificates also increased our customer confidence in the mastery of quality.

The key success points for this first step were:

- the total management commitment to ISO 9000 certification;
- the decision to describe, as an initial reference, what is really done by asking the practitioners to write the procedures; and then to improve this reference;
- the use of the certification as a starting point for the improvement process.

From ISO 9000 to CMM

The mastery of quality and the fulfilment of our customers quality requirements cannot be considered the final step. Continuous product quality improvement is needed to survive in a competitive world: these improvements must be defined, refined, mastered and proved as beneficial for our clients.

The ISO 9000 benefits were used as a platform, to move from Quality Assurance to Process Improvement practices, by implementing the best practices in software development and process improvement.

CMM Approach: A Step toward Process Maturity and Improvement

Commitment

Natural evolution in quality improvement for both products and processes has driven Alcatel management to look for the best practices in these areas. The SEI CMM maturity model was chosen. This decision was made at the corporate level of Alcatel Alsthom, and implemented in all Alcatel units. For Alcatel 1000 E10, this model was considered as a complement to the ISO 9001 and 9000-3 norms, which were already implemented through the Quality Systems and Quality Organisations. The basic objective was to improve our competitiveness and quality level.

The following steps were defined:

- 1993/1994: Creation of Software Engineering Process Groups (SEPG) in each design centre, and training on the CMM model
- 1995: Self-assessment of each design centre using strengths and weaknesses of the assessments, definition of an improvement plan, common to all design centres
- 1996: Definition of standardised software process for Alcatel 1000 E10 Technical Department

Implementation of Improvement Structures

New improvement structures were defined, using the existing quality system, and quality organisation as a continuing evolution in order to implement this model.

Quality system and standardised process
The Quality System defined at the design centre level has evolved toward a standardised process used in all design centres, which is the basis of smaller and smaller local Quality Systems.

Quality organisation and SEPG
Quality Organisation was improved by the implementation of the Software Process Manager (SPM), the SEPG, and the improvement working groups (Their respective roles are explained in Table 12.5).

- The quality organisation is still responsible for implementing and ensuring products and process quality.
- The SPM is responsible for managing the improvement program process standardisation and improvement.
- The experts and participants in the working groups propose the improvements and supervise the pilot projects.

Improvement Implementation Institutionalised: Improvement Process

Working groups were implemented to complement the results obtained by root cause analysis of the ISO 9001 phase, and to institutionalise the improvement process.

Table 12.5.   Quality Organisation

	Technical Department (TD)	**Quality Department (QD)**
Process	**Standard process definition**	Conformity with ISO and **CMM**
Product Quality Assurance	Product quality	Green light and independence
Process Quality Assurance	**Applies Standard process**	**Verify standard process use**

The main improvement areas are:

- risk management,
- peer review,
- measurement,
- multiunit shared developments.

Each area is driven as a software project, including detailed planning, objectives, measurement, pilot project, and reviews.

Achievements

First results are the following:

- Reduction of improvement effort needed in each design centre.
- Self-assessments were well received by all employees, from managers to practitioners.
- Full set of improvement standards are being constituted.
- Visibility of standardised process coherence.

We also discovered that it is easy to find solutions for a specific problem, once it is seen as a real problem by the people concerned. It is much more difficult to obtain consensus when looking for the "best practice" for a given topic: this is a possible consequence of the problem solving approach, linked to ISO conformance model culture.

Some complementary needs were found when practising CMM. This can be CMM native, or linked to our assessment method:

- Only software aspects are covered, although we are providers of products with system, software, and hardware aspects.
- Customisation is needed in order to make CMM comprehensible to practitioners.
- The quantitative maturity level or KPA measurements were unreliable. Best-practice identification was thus more difficult to identify.

Experience

Looking backward, we can now identify the benefits of this incremental improvement approach.

ISO 9001, SEI maturity model, and self-assessments have together brought advantages for a number of domains.

CMM helped us to move from a product quality culture to a permanent process and product improvement culture:

- Increase in quality spirit and work force dynamics.
- "Improvement" is not only for experts, but also for all the practitioners.
- Improvement is managed as a project.
- Continuous process improvement becomes natural.
- Self-assessment experience is beneficial to all the employees.

The improvement approach combines the concerns of both customers and suppliers. Self-assessment allows all practitioners to bring their experience to the improvement approach, and is much less aggressive than the noncompliance verdicts of the audits: weaknesses as well as strengths can be more easily identified.

The CMM has been seen as a very useful complement to ISO 9001, for areas which are not at all covered in ISO conformance. Implementation of new best practices can be speeded up.

Measurement

CMM and associated improvement process implies the implementation of a reliable measurement program, with a historical data base, bringing:

- the adoption of the quality objective throughout the organisation,
- measurement framework adapted to maturity, and
- product and process improvement correlation.

Conclusion

ISO 9001 and CMM are complementary approaches to improve product and process quality for ALCATEL 1000 E10. ISO 9001 provides a low-cost framework.

Coupling ISO with CMM offers strong input to keep the Quality System alive, to reinforce common software quality culture, and highlight the best practices.

REFERENCES

1. C. Cox, Kasse T., Pinney D, "Guidance for Action Planning," *Proceedings of the SEPG 96*, Atlantic City, N. J., May 1996.

2. K. Pulford, A. Kuntzmann-Combelles, and S. Shirlaw, *A Quantitative Approach to Software Management*, Addison-Wesley, 1995.

3. *ISO 9000-3 Quality management and quality assurance standards—Part 3: Guidelines for the Application of ISO 9001 to the Development, Supply and Maintenance of Software*, ISO, 1991.

4. *ISO 9001, Quality systems—Model for Quality Assurance in Design/Development, Production, Installation and Servicing*, ISO, 1994.

5. ISO 9000, "Forum: Information letter," Sept. 1, 1995a.

6. ISO Press Release, Ref. 729, Oct. 5, 1995b.

7. E. Malmquist, "ESSI—Ericssons Systems Software Initiative," *Proceedings of the First E-SEPG Conference*, Amsterdam, June 1996.

8. T. Kasse, "Improving the Action Focus of Software Process Assessments," *Proceedings of the SPI '95 Conference*, Barcelona, Spain, Nov. 1995.

9. M.C. Paulk, B. Curtis, and M.B. Chrissis, *Capability Maturity Model for Software, Version 1.1*, CMU/SEI-93-TR-24, Feb. 1993.

10. M.C. Paulk, et al., *Key Practices of the Capability Maturity Model, Version 1.1*, CMU/SEI-93-TR-25, Feb. 1993.

11. *The TickIT Guide: A Guide to Software Quality Management System Construction and Certification to ISO 9001, Issue 3.0*, British Standards Institution, Oct. 1995.

12. A. Voelker and M. Gonauser, "Why Maturity Matters?," *Proceedings of the First E-SEPG Conference*, Amsterdam, June 1996.

Chapter 13

Software Process Identification:

A Case Study Using the ISO/IEC 12207 Software Life Cycle Processes Standard

Jean-Martin Simon
CISI, Lyon/FRANCE

INTRODUCTION

This chapter demonstrates how process standards can efficiently support the establishment of a quality improvement program within a company.

The ISO/IEC 12207—*Software Life Cycle processes* [1] standard is used as a framework for a certain phase of a process improvement programme. An improvement initiative, or internal project, usually runs through a set of phases. Such phase specific models usually are tailored to the company characteristics. One such characteristic could address the current "quality level" or "maturity" of the organisation, for software engineering activities and software processes management.

When starting an improvement programme the process improvement plan has to be fully adapted to the capacity of the organisation, and its people, to assure progress toward a higher level of quality. The case study described in this chapter deals with an organisation whose internal structures have been completely changed for becoming aligned with new business strategies of the company. These changes have brought new structures for the company's departments that perform software development activities, and especially changed practices like project management and project team building. People from different projects (with different software background, culture, and experience) shared their good and bad experiences and collaborated in defining best practices. To support this exchange of experience and establishment of good practices the company started a quality improvement program

- to harmonise the practices concerning software engineering and project management;
- to share experiences between all teams for defining the "best practices";
- to motivate each team member to follow a common vision and to align their goals with the business strategy of the company.

The improvement program, called IP in this chapter, has been established considering the variety of activities performed by the organisation (see Company Context below). The Project teams belong to departments dedicated to particular activities or services. Nevertheless, sometimes mixed teams were built when a project required different skills.

The IP described in this chapter was established for one branch of the Company. At highest level there is an annual quality improvement plan which is implemented by each branch of the Company. The improvement initiatives proposed in this plan might address various aspects of the organisation (people management, administrative procedures and practices, technological context, etc.). In this case study the focus will be put on the aspect of improving the software management and development processes of the company.

The IP comprises two phases:

- A preliminary and generic phase to organise and plan the tasks and develop the tools needed for the operational phase,
- The operational phase, performed for each department within the branch, and containing the following steps:
  1. The identification of the processes performed by the department; this case-study reports mainly on this step which uses the ISO/IEC 12207 standard as basic guideline.
  2. The estimation of the "quality level" or capability of the identified processes, by using an ISO/SPICE assessment-like approach.
  3. The determination of improvement actions.
  4. The performance of improvement cycles.

This chapter discusses the experience with steps 1 and 2, and gives examples of results, as well as some feedback about the method used and further necessary information about the experiment.

In the discussion below the department implementing the IP will be called the Unit, while the actions and tasks performed within the IP are part of the Project. The term *Standard* (beginning with a capital *S*) will refer to the *ISO/IEC 12207 Software Life Cycle* Processes standard.

Company Context

The Organisational Unit which performed the IP is a software house with different kinds of activities: software development, both in technical and business domains, software tools development, facilities management, and consulting and training activities. A major difficulty in the management of projects derives from the diversity of projects and/or activities. In this special case each practitioner put forth his or her particular preferences, in terms of technical practices, management approaches, or even for the current vocabulary. This is why the quality improvement program needed a federative approach, starting from a common structure as basis (the ISO 12207 standard [2]) and tailoring it according to the individual needs of the teams.

Starting Scenario

Even if the IP was mainly dedicated to software process improvement, it also contained complementary initiatives to train software practitioners, as well as to formalise the administrative and organisational context. These additional two aspects are not discussed in this case study.

By implementing a process improvement strategy, the plan was to introduce "best practices" to improve the quality of each activity or task. These best practices come from three major sources:

- Already existing skills and expertise
- State-of-the art (i.e., knowledge, external training, technical documents, etc.)
- Standards

The Project is managed and controlled by a Quality Manager who collaborates with Managers and Project Leaders from the Units. Within each Unit, people from middle management and project teams are also involved in meetings that are organised throughout the Project. The Quality engineers (i.e., those who work at project level for quality assurance and quality control) are bound to these meetings and work together with the above mentioned Quality manager who acts as a coordinator.

As it has been mentioned, each Unit is described by a set of characteristics. This also includes a specific quality maturity which ranges from the "rather informal" to some "well-defined" level, close to the ISO9001 requirements. This is why the Project had to be conducted Unit by Unit, but with cohesion, in order to rise the global level of the branch.

METHODOLOGY

The Project needed a detailed methodological framework to be performed successfully. This is why plans, operating guides (OG) and forms to be used along the steps of the Project have been developed. It is necessary, when performing a specific task, to collect data in a standard manner in order to facilitate their use during the next task.

These were developed during the preliminary phase and to be used during the operational phase. The development of such a methodological framework environment was regarded as important because the lack of methodological support during an improvement initiative is a common cause of failure. In [1], some key issues concerning the needs for supporting software quality improvement are described. Some of the issues described in [1] were observed in the organisation and formed the major motivation to the establishment of these plans, operating guides, and forms.

Below we describe the two-step model which was applied containing: the Preliminary Phase, and Operational Phase.

Preliminary Phase

During this phase, the development and successful acceptance of all the material needed for the operational phase must be managed. In this phase the standards to be used are selected, and by using them as a formal framework the OG, are built. As a result of the phase, each of the next phase's four steps are supported by an OG used by those who perform the Project in a particular Unit. To guarantee that all sessions and meetings are fruitful, each responsible is trained about the use of the OG and if possible, experiment it with the quality Manager for the first time of utilisation.

The four OG's are:

- operating guide 1 (OG1), for process and activity identification;
- operating guide 2 (OG2), to estimate the efficiency of the activities;

- operating guide 3 (OG3), to identify the improvement opportunities and to formalise improvement actions;
- operating guide 4 (OG4) describes the steps to plan, experiment, analyse, and implement improvements.

When writing an OG, a standard plan must be followed; it contains:

- introduction, reference documents, and responsibilities;
- expected goals;
- input data and documents;
- output results;
- tasks to be achieved;
- actions for quality control;
- forms to be used during the work sessions.

The success of the next phase is strongly dependent on the quality of the preliminary phase whose output products must be checked and validated carefully.

Operational Phase

The first step is to define the process model(s) that correspond(s) to the type of projects performed within the Units. One Unit might need more than one process model if its activities include different types of projects such as software development, servicing, consulting, etc. However, all process models are derived from the same starting point (the standard) following standard principles:

- For software project development, the process model will be close to the Standard, and if needed, will take inputs from other documents like [3].
- In case of services, some help can be obtained from [4].

In order to collect data about the internal knowledge and already existing practices of the organisation, a series of meetings (working sessions) are conducted with people from the Unit. These persons are from the middle management and/or involved in project teams as project managers. An informative session (about the IP) and training session (about the principles of the method used to establish the process models) are organised preliminary to these work sessions.

After having identified the Unit's process model and described the constituting activities, the second step of the phase deals with an estimation of the capability of the organisation to actually perform the proposed set of activities. This is done by investigating *how* activities are done, in terms of resources allocation, responsibilities, means available, tools, etc. and comparing the actual situation to a reference framework. This reference is an adapted subset of the *capability dimension* from ISO/SPICE [5].

This step is a kind of basic "process/activity assessment", but performed in an informal manner. The output of this estimation is then used as input for the next step which is dedicated to the identification of improvement opportunities. When identifying an opportunity, the business goals of the organisation as well as the customer's expectation are considered to have a realistic approach and not a theoretical one.

The improvement is driven according to Plan/Do/Check/Act cycles as suggested in [1] with the following steps (see also Chapters 5, 10, and 12):

- Selection and planning of a specific improvement action
- Implementation of the action after estimating the initial level

- Check of the results and the efficiency of the implementation
- Adjustment and decision to make the new experimented practice become the standard good practice of the Organisation

STANDARDS AND TOOLS USED

It was decided to base all work on standards that are well adapted for software engineering. The Project did not plan, for its first stage to define already a complete and companywide quality management system. In that case we would have based it on ISO 9001.

The standards that have been selected are a coherent set, with complementary aspects.

- ISO/IEC 12207 is a "process model," which organises processes in a logical manner, with tasks and activities.
- ISO/SPICE adds a capability dimension to a process model to obtain a "model for process management," compatible with the ISO/IEC 12207's process model.

Concepts and Principles of the ISO/IEC 12207 Standard

The origin of this standard comes from the need for a common framework to manage the software activities. Using a top-down approach, the processes performed for software acquisition, supply, development, and operation have been classified and described in terms of activities. Each of these processes is refined according to tasks. The standardisation of these concepts has been considered as a critical need for a common framework that can be used by software practitioners to "speak the same language to create and manage software in its environments". See [6] for a description of the standard by the project editor.

The ISO/IEC 12207 Standard provides a framework for the software life cycle, with the common sense of the term, as it does not involve any particular's one (V-shaped, spiral, etc.). Neither does it recommend any specific practices for implementing its requirements. The process model is supposed to be tailored either in the context of a customer-supplier relationship, or for internal use, considering the technological and managerial characteristics of the user of the standard. Even if the standard is primarily intended for use in a two-party contract this experiment demonstrates that it provides powerful assistance for managing software process improvement.

This section below gives a brief overview of the standard's content; nevertheless, the reader should refer to the original document for full details.

The software processes are classified into three categories. The Primary processes correspond to the main activities for software product elaboration and usage, from the initial need to the retirement. The primary processes are:

1. *Acquisition process.* Defines the activities of the acquirer, the organisation that acquires a system or software product.
2. *Supply process.* Defines the activities of the supplier, the organisation that provides the software product to the acquirer.
3. *Development process.* Defines the activities of the developer, the organisation that defines and develops the software product.
4. *Operation process.* Defines the activities of the operator, the organisation that provides the service of operating a computer system in its live environment for its users.
5. *Maintenance process.* Defines the activities of the maintainer, the organisation that provides the service of maintaining the software; that is, managing modifications to the software to

keep it current and in operational fitness. This process includes the migration and retirement of the software.

The Supporting Life cycle processes are the processes which support any other process as an integral part with a distinct purpose and contributes to its performance. When invoked, a supporting process helps the caller to achieve its goals. The supporting processes are:

1. *Documentation process.* Defines the activities for managing the documents produced as process work products.
2. *Configuration management process.* Defines the configuration management activities.
3. *Quality assurance process.* Defines the activities for objectively ensuring that software products are in conformance with their specified requirements and adhere to their established plans.
4. *Verification process.* Defines the activities (for the acquirer, the supplier, or an independent party) for verifying the software products in varying depth depending on the software project.
5. *Validation process.* Defines the activities (for the acquirer, the supplier, or an independent party) for validating the software products of the software project.
6. *Joint review process.* Defines the activities for evaluating the status and products of an activity. This process may be employed by any two parties, where one party (reviewing party) reviews another party (reviewed party) in a joint forum.
7. *Audit process.* Defines the activities for determining compliance with the requirements, plans, and contract. This process may be employed by any two parties, where one party (auditing party) audits the software products or activities of another party (audited party).
8. *Problem resolution process.* Defines a process for analysing and removing the problems (including nonconformance), whatever their nature or source, that are discovered during development, operation, maintenance, or other processes.

The last category, called Organisational Life Cycle category, is a set of four processes addressing the corporate level of an organisation to establish (define) and implement (provide resources and training) and improve the processes belonging to the two categories described above. These four organisational processes are:

1. *Management process.* Defines the basic activities of the management, including project management, during the life cycle processes.
2. *Infrastructure process.* Defines the basic activities for establishing the underlying structure of a process.
3. *Improvement process.* Defines the basic activities that an organisation performs for establishing, measuring, controlling, and improving its life cycle process.
4. *Training process.* Defines the activities for providing adequately trained personnel.

In order to better understand how the three categories interact together, Figure 13.1 illustrates the interaction between the Development process from the Primary Category, with the Supporting process called Quality Assurance.

Figure 13.1 describes the ISO/IEC 12207 [2] standard as a three-dimensional process model, encompassing the three previously described types of processes, such as primary, organisational, and supporting life cycle processes.

ISO/IEC SPICE Components Used

A full description of the SPICE project and products can be found in [3]. At the time of the experiment, SPICE had elaborated a set of documents to describe a model for software process

Figure 13.1. Process interactions.

management and interrelated guides to manage process improvement and the capability determination. Even if the SPICE software process model was actually a draft standard, its capability level concept has been considered here in order to estimate how the process and the activities were implemented and managed.

Operational Guidelines

When the work sessions are performed during the Operational phase, previously developed OGs and forms are used.

- OG1, for process and activities identification is supported by three forms:
   —one for identifying the activities of each process
   —one to describe the activities
   —one to estimate how the Support process, in the sense of the Standard, is used by the activities
- OG2 is supported by one form—the evaluation of the activities.
- OG3 and 4 have no specific forms to support them.

Samples of these forms are included below.

PERFORMING THE PROJECT

Process and Activities Identification

The project is conducted by at least two people, one with some strong software Quality background, and the other from the Unit, with the support of the above-mentioned OG1 document.
   The description of the processes uses the following definition of a software process:

A set of activities done to achieve (a) goal(s), using inputs elements (or information) to produce output elements (or information), in order to provide a product or a service.

These activities must:

- be linked together so that one activity's inputs correspond to the outputs of the previous activity.
- allow the identification of some parameters reflecting the progress of performance.

- be composed of elementary practices, reflecting the ability of the Unit's members.
- include the definition of indicators to provide quantitative data on the performance and the quality of the process.

For each kind of major business activity of the Unit, the expected results are:

- a list of activities included in each process, with their constitutive tasks;
- a process diagram inspired by the process representation given in the Standard;
- the description of each activity.

It is also necessary to identify the people acting in the Unit in terms of functions, as well as the kind of relations between them. They might be in a customer-supplier relationship, or might only collaborate together or by themselves.

The data is collected during working sessions using a standard form. Form 1 below illustrates a primary process called Supply, for the facilities management projects, with its activities.

Detailed Description of Each Activity

Each activity for an identified process is then described by the characterisation of its

- starting and ending conditions;
- input and output work products;
- methods, techniques and tools that might be used;

ACTIVITY CONTEXT :	FACILITIES MANAGEMENT
PRIMARY PROCESS	*SUPPLY*

N°	ACTIVITY NAME	TASK DESCRIPTION (*sample*)
2	Answer to the call for proposal	• Create standard documents and files • Study the call for proposal • Establish responsibilities and roles • Customer site audit (unformal) • Plans the proposal • Define preliminary contract with the customer
3	Build the contract	• Formal audit of the site's customer • Establish Committees and roles • Establish and validate the contract • Contract acceptance
4	Establish the Plans	• Establish the Management plan, Quality plan, etc.
5	Project planning	• Identify tasks and tasks requirements • Tasks planning and tracking
6	Project performance	• Process performance • Process tracking • Review and committees
7	Prepare the reversibility	• On site audit and hard point identification • Site description • Reversibility planning
8	Reversibility	• Transfer hard and soft back to the customer • Help customer for operation during reversibility
9	Buying	• Define needs • Select suppliers • Perform buying

High level tasks description

Form 1.

- verification and validation practices;
- responsibilities and authorities.

The collected data is put together in Form 2.

After having described all the activities, for every identified process, the process model can be established. As an example, again in the case of Facilities Management, the process model corresponds to Figure 13.2 which is close to the standard model for software process management described by the Standard. Even if some processes were not fully implemented, it has been decided to keep them in the model to have a global process reference which can be used during the next phases for process improvement.

Compared with the Standard process model, the Supporting Process Perform Problem Resolution was distributed to the other processes, as it was considered to be too generic.

Estimating the Performance of the Support Processes

By using the description of the Support Processes, as they are defined in the Standard, the applicability of each of these processes was estimated for all the previously identified activities. This was done by compiling a rating with the following scale:

- A Support process might correspond to the unknown practices.
- A Support process might be implemented in an elementary way.
- A Support process might be implemented informally.
- A Support process might be implemented formally.

The results, obtained for the Supply process, again for Facilities Management projects, are described below in Form 3. The formula in Form 3 is applied to calculate total measures in the range between 0 and 1, with 1 as complete and 0 as missing a standard application.

Quality Requirements

All the tasks performed during the operational phase should satisfy the quality requirements. The following quality parameters were selected to be checked during quality control:

- Exhaustiveness of the process/activity description.
- Reusability: descriptions must be usable, each time they may concern a standard activity reusable by another Unit.
- Comprehensiveness of the descriptions.

ACTIVITY CONTEXT :	FACILITIES MANAGEMENT
PRIMARY PROCESS	SUPPLY

N°	Activity	Starting condition	Ending condition	Input work products	Output work products	Method, technics and tools	Verif. & Validation	Resp.
1	Initialisation							
2	Answer to the call							
9	Buying							

Form 2.

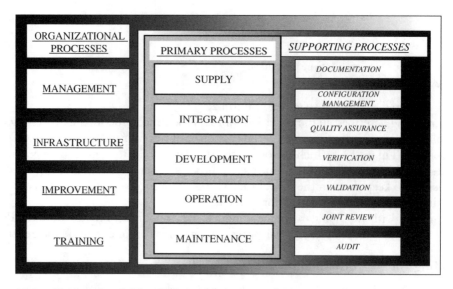

Figure 13.2. Process model for facilities management.

ACTIVITY CONTEXT :	FACILITIES MANAGEMENT
PRIMARY PROCESS	*SUPPLY*

N°	ACT.	Doc.	Conf. Man.	Qual. Assur.	Verif. Valid	Joint Rev.	Audit	Prob. Res.	Total
1	Initialisation	2	/	/	2	0	0	0	**0.27**
2	Answer to the call	1	/	2	2	0	0	/	**0.33**
3	Build the contract	2	2						
4	Establish the Plans	2	2						
5	Project planning	2	2						
6	Project performance	2	1						
7	Prepare the reversibility	0	0						
8	Reversibility	0	0						
9	Buying	2	2						
		0.48	**0.43**						

These ratings indicate :
1. the global implementation of a specific Support process, i.e; How a Support process is invoked by the activities
2. the use of the Support processes by an activity,

These values allow comparisons and are imputs for the identification of improvement actions.
Ratings are calculated according to the rule :

rating = SUM (significant values) / (3x nb. of significant values)

Form 3.

Note: The quotation is made using the following convention:
   / = The Support process is not in the scope of the activity
   0 = The Support process is in the scope of the activity but is not implemented
   1 = The Support process is partially and irregularly implemented
   2 = The Support process is frequently implemented
   3 = The Support process is always implemented, using standards and/or guide

Estimating the Efficiency of the Activities

In order to estimate how the activities of a process are performed, an assessment is done according to the document OG2. This is mainly done by rather informal interviews, with some documents analysis (concerning procedures, standard, project documents), if needed.

The assessment is conducted according to the basic concept described by the capability dimension described in the SPICE (V1) model for process management. This results in a profile that indicates which are the activities with a low or with a high level of good practices.

The implementation of OG2 is performed by a software quality expert who knows the concepts of process assessment well, in collaboration with practitioners from the Unit.

Some specific quality controls are done to ensure that the results of these estimations are:

- reproducible: if possible, profiles must be appraised independently by at least two distinct people.
- exploitable: for the selection of actions for improvement.

The form used for OG2 looks like Form 4 below.

The form used for OG2 looks like Form 4 below.

ACTIVITY CONTEXT :	FACILITIES MANAGEMENT
PRIMARY PROCESS	*SUPPLY*

N1 = Performed N2 = Planned and tracked N3 = Well defined ÚÄÄÄ **Level / n°** ⇓ Requirement ÄÄÄ¿ ⇓	N° : *Activity* *ÀÄÄ⇒*	1 Init.	2 Answer to call		9 Buying
N2 / 2	Measures are used for corrective actions				
N2 / 1	Measures are available				
N2 / 2	Quality control is performed				
N2 / 1	The Organization has described a standard way to performed the activity (or has current practices)				
N2 / 2	Configuration management is accomplished				
N2 / 1	Activity is performed according to the predictive documents				
N2 / 6	Performance of the activity is planned				
N2 / 5	Individuals are skilled and trained				
N2 / 4	Tools are used				
N2 / 3	The performance of the activity is described in predictive documents				
N2 2	Responsibility is established				
N2 / 1	Resources are available for the performance of the activity				
N1 / 1	Activity is performed and produces/uses work products				

Adequacy scale :
1. No implementation : *White*.
2. Medium/light adequation : *Horizontal*
3. Full or strong adequation with the requirement : *Vertical*

Form 4.   Estimating the efficiency for the Supply process activities

Next Steps

On the basis of the defined process models, with the use of the quality level estimations, the improvement cycles are initiated using the OG3 and OG4 guidelines.

LESSONS LEARNED

The Method

The successful achievement of any quality improvement plan depends on many factors. They involve a number of prerequisites before starting the improvement.

For the project described in this chapter, the following set of actions have been identified as critical success factors:

- A plan has to be established with identified tasks, schedules, and resource availability. This plan is used as a road map by the quality manager in charge of the project and helps him or her to manage the tasks and schedule. The improvement plan must be established in detail, as in a normal software development project.
- If possible, a quality plan should be also defined, or at least some quality requirements must be identified and checked during the project in regard to the document to be delivered and results expected.
- The Operational Guidelines are very useful, first, to give a common framework when many people are doing the same tasks in different contexts; and second, because they oblige you, when writing these documents, to have a coherent and global approach. They are also intensively used during the briefing and training sessions.

The impact of this managed approach for quality improvement will be visible on a longer timescale and requires a higher initial cost to organise and prepare the methodological tools to be used during the operational phase. Nevertheless, it is a requirement for success in a company with many different business segments and types of projects, that wishes to achieve and a plan to establish an improvement strategy across all these different types of segments.

Using Standards

The two standard ISO12207 and SPICE components used during the Project guide an Organisation toward an improved quality management for software, offering:

- a formal and common framework applicable and adaptable;
- concepts and efficient tools for quality management such as those concerning *software process models, model for process management*, etc.;
- a proposed set of good practices that can be integrated into the standard process definition of the Organisation.

REFERENCES

1. J.A. Lowell, *Improving Software Quality*, Wiley, 1993.
2. ISO/IEC 12207, *Information Technology—Software Life Cycle Processes*, 1st ed., Aug. 1995.
3. ISO/IEC 9000-3, *Quality Management and Quality Assurance Standards—Part 3: Guidelines for the Application of ISO 9001 to the Development, Supply and Maintenance of Software*, 1st ed., June 1991.

4. ISO/IEC 9004-2, *Quality Management and Quality System Elements— Part 2: Guidelines for Services,* 1st ed. Aug. 1991.

5. SPICE project, *Baseline Practices Guide, SPICE Project Document, Version 1.00,* 1994.

6. R. Singh, *International Standard ISO/IEC 12207 Software Life Cycle Processes, Software Process—Improvement and Practices,* Vol. 2, Issue 1, Wiley, 1996.

Chapter 14

Experience with a Lean Team Model and Open Architecture Culture

Gerhard Rutschek
FESTO GmbH, Vienna

Richard Messnarz
ISCN, Dublin, Ireland

INTRODUCTION

This chapter describes a process improvement experiment which was supported under the European Systems and Software Initiative (ESSI). ESSI experiments follow a standard approach (as described under Types of Improvement Projects in Chapter 1 "Road Map for Readers") with a state-of-the-art analysis as a starting point, a baseline project in which the improvement is actually tried out over a period of 18 months, an experiment which introduces improved processes and technologies into the baseline project, and a dissemination phase at the end to spread the lessons learned across the organisation and the wider EU community.

The baseline project for this experiment was the software project ODB Online Database. The starting situation for the improvement were the large maintenance problems which arose during the former project Visualisation of Industrial Processes (VIP). ODB is a toolbox for process control systems with an open architecture. The idea of toolbox means that the system will never be finished and is open for further enhancements based on standardised interfaces. Engineering becomes easier, because due to standardised interfaces it becomes easy for outsourcing parts of the development. Also, if there is a need any program on the market can easily be connected to the existing ODB architecture based on the standardised interfaces. This leads to an open system architecture which can easily be enhanced, adapted, and tailored.

A number of improvement actions have been performed during the ODB baseline project resulting in a role-based team model as a defined way for software development, and an open architecture philosophy for both the software and the team members (especially in outsourcing situations).

Here it is important to mention that FESTO SWE is a small software competence centre with a number of partners in Eastern Europe, where East European partners are used as outsourcing development units as needed.

Thus the experience described in this chapter specifically addresses small software competence centres which utilise a number of contracted partners to either outsource work or to distribute the development tasks of a larger project between distributed small teams.

Introduction to FESTO Vienna and the SWE Profit Centre

The company FESTO has 50 locations worldwide with about 3,250 employees. Its business areas can be characterised as pneumatic, cybernetic, didactic, and "tooltechnic." The product range covers everything from individual components such as valves, cylinders and accessories, through to pre-assembled and ready-to-connect modules including customer-specific designs. One percent of the 800,000,000 DM turnover is used for vocational and further training programs, and 5 percent for research and development. FESTO has achieved a worldwide ISO 9001 certification. For example, the FESTO quality assurance system meets the requirements of this standard in all areas from design, development, production, and assembly right up to aftersales service.

FESTO Vienna has 130 employees. The firm has partners nearly in all Eastern countries and coordinates the Eastern European market. The software engineering department named SWE includes approximately 10 software engineers working on hardware and software projects, among them special solutions, for example, for banks.

FESTO Austria has a reputation for good partnerships with neighbouring countries of the former Eastern block. The first joint ventures were started in 1982. Today, in addition to numerous agencies, representatives, and automation centres, FESTO Austria has wholly owned subsidiaries in Hungary, Bulgaria, the Czech Republic, Slovakia, Poland, Russia, Romania, the Ukraine, Slovenia, and Croatia. An agency office has been established in Tashkent to provide service for Usbekistan. In all these countries, FESTO Vienna offers full range of products and services on behalf of the FESTO international firm.

FESTO's main emphasis is in the field of process automation and one of the major tasks of the software division Vienna is concerned with the development of software to control and overview industrial processes. The two processware tools VIP and ODB have been developed in FESTO SWE. Vienna is the know-how centre for the Eastern European market, for example, know-how about databases, ODBC, object orientation, and distributed systems. It is evolving to become a know-how centre for the entire company.

Figure 14.1 illustrates the general organisational structure of the customer (baseline) project and the ESSI project. In Figure 14.1 IICM is the acronym for one of the Austrian research institutes in Graz, and HPM is the acronym of a development training organisation.

GLOSSARY

ESSI	European Software and System Initiative
ESA PSS 05	European Space Agency Software Engineering Standards
LOC	Line of Codes
ODB	Online Database
ODBC	Online Database Connection
SA	Structured Analysis
SWE	Software Engineering
URD	User Requirements Document
VIP	Visualisation of Industrial Processes

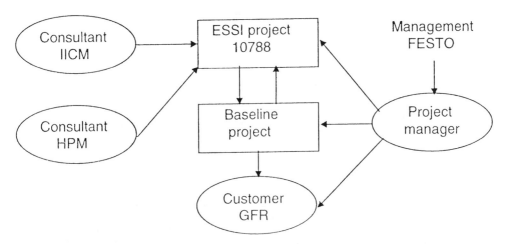

Figure 14.1. Organisation.

Starting Scenario

The predecessor project of the ODB was VIP, a Visualisation of Industrial Processes. In particular, it dealt with industrial processes (manufacturing, power plants, systems integrated in buildings, etc.) and implemented a system, that provides a graphical interface to overview data and processes. The first version was delivered at the end of 1988. Further versions were distributed in 1991 and end of 1993.

VIP represents a PC-based control and visualisation system. It works in a DOS, NOVELL and desk-view environment. Till today around 1300 licences were sold abroad. ViP required 18 man-years and consists of 1 MB runtime-code, with all tools it needs approximately 6 MB. VIP exists also in a mini and a didactic version.

During the project VIP the following critical problems came up:

- *No structured documentation.* After the introduction of Structured Analysis (SA) no consequent updating of design charts and documents followed. Working with a missing structured design resulted in vague definitions and descriptions of the interfaces. The actuality of the documents stayed behind and they have been rarely updated. No visibility of the work process existed, a life cycle model was missed.
- *Faint project planning and controlling.* There was no consequent project tracking, so bug fixing problems occurred during the outsourcing, because of unclear contracts and functional descriptions.
- *No problem tracking.* No error documentation and problem analysis were taken through and the monolithic construction of the program caused troubles during the maintenance.

A big problem was that VIP was realised to be a monolithic program. The description of the internal interfaces was missing or was rarely described so that it was hard to find the responsible module in case of a bug. In a monolithically built system an adaptation or change for newer requirements is very expensive, you have to step through the whole system. Changing parts or installing new modules is very complicated. Any change has an impact on nearly all system components and usually leads to an uncontrolled number of additional changes. Thus, maintenance of a monolithic system leads to even-increasing maintenance efforts.

In the later versions an overlay system was realised, but again no distribution of tasks was done. The system consisted of one big part. It was not split into smaller ones, which would communicate together by well-defined interfaces. In case of a change the whole system had to

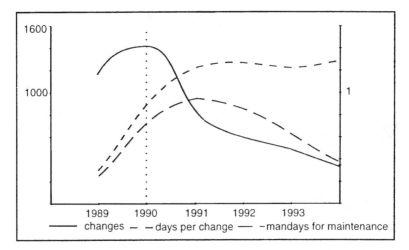

Figure 14.2.   Maintenance situation of VIP.

be recompiled and delivered. This is also a reason for the fact that nearly 40 percent of corrections were done after delivery. Due to these big troubles a new version including major corrections, was delivered 2 years after the delivery of the first version.

Figure 14.2 contains two scales. The left scale shows the number of changes performed and recorded within a year. The right-hand scale illustrates the average number of days duration per change (around 0.25 to 1.1 days).

The numbers presented were analysed by a review of all old code and the changes noted and formed the basis for comparison with the achievements in the ODB project (after installation of the improvements).

The analysis in Figure 14.2 led to a conclusion that over 40 percent of the changes were actually made after delivery which was far too much.

From the point of view of reuse it was not possible to separate functions from the system. So reuse was absolutely impossible.

Also from the aspect of project management it was impossible to create clear responsibilities, because due to the monolithic system architecture all personnel were responsible for all modules.

The goal of the improvements implemented in the project ODB (Online Data Base) was to avoid these problems and find a new way of working and system architecture favouring component software and reusability.

At the time the BOOTSTRAP Assessment was ordered already up to 70 percent of the staff was doing maintenance and it was visible that VIP would run out of the market within the next 2 years.

PROCESS ANALYSIS

BOOTSTRAP Assessment

In 1992 a BOOTSTRAP assessment was performed resulting in a detailed representation of weaknesses and strengths of the software division at FESTO Vienna. Based on this process quality profile an Action Plan to improve the software development environment was set up. Figure 14.3 shows the major weaknesses identified in form of a fishbone diagram.

Figure 14.3. A summary of the identified process weaknesses.

Comments on Technology:	Comments on Organisation:	Comments on Methodology:
(-)A project management tool was purchased, but never used. (-)They used no tools for analysis and design.	(-)no quality manual (-) no formal method to produce quality plans (-)high dependency on the qualifications of the individual engineers (-)no concept or model for software development	(-)no formal procedures to produce development plans (-)no test plans and no concepts and methods for testing (except for acceptance testing, which was performed) (-)no quality plans (-)no methods for analysis and design
(+)They are aware of the state of the art, but had problems to motivate the project-co-workers to learn new methods. (+)They had in-house developed testdata generators.	(+)training programmes for managers (+)quality is a strategy of the company (+)resource management	(+)purchased software was evaluated (+)prototyping (+)acceptance testing (+)maintenance

The whole department was on the way to becoming a profit centre which has to prove its profitability and its independence from funds. For this it was necessary to improve the development process, in order to decrease the blocked capacity for maintenance so that people get free for new profitable development in ODB avoiding the problems learned in the past with VIP.

In addition, the BOOTSTRAP assessment resulted in a quality profile showing the maturity levels of about 30 processes, which highlighted the above-described problems.

THE IMPROVEMENT PROJECT

ESSI Proposal and Schedule

The ESSI Project started in May 1993, at a time when Austria was not yet a member of the EU.

The results of the BOOTSTRAP Assessment showed the current status of the SWE practice, the conclusions out of it were the required status of the SWE practice upon completion of the experiment. Expected achievements were the evolution of a phased plan, good commercial impacts, and the transferability of the experience to other projects.

Team Model Requirements

The goals of the model and the developed philosophy are:

- Strict use of standard interfaces (e.g., ODBC).
- Division of the whole work in objects with clear assignment of responsibilities in the team.
- Clear object-interface definitions. Each object has to be a task, which is able to run as a standalone program. Only the interfaces are defined. The code inside must only follow the rules of quality.
- Reduction of maintenance costs.
- Increasing the reuse of already developed modules.

The goal of the project was to design a guideline and software life cycle model focussing on reuse and the development of open architecture concepts. This concept should first be tried out in the new ODB product which should finally provide standard interfaces and a stable database architecture in the middle.

This interfacing is also a good way for outsourcing. You can plan with small, easy-to-outsource tasks, because the outface of the modules is fixed like the conditions of a contract. This idea follows the strategy of cohesion and coupling and information hiding. The interface of a task is a technical part of the contract with the outsourcing group—we call this "Programming by contract." This interface is written down for both partners and, if it is necessary, both are able to simulate the foreign part. It is much easier to maintain small functions than to debug the entire system.

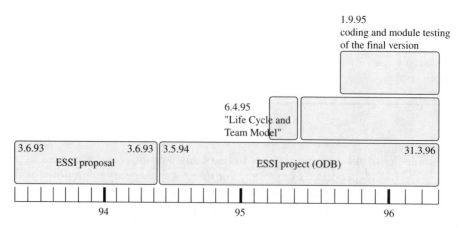

Figure 14.4. Time schedule of the ESSI project.

The software development team model and the architectural design guidelines should favour the design of systems which are completely distributed. Each functionality is an independent task with well-defined interfaces. This concept makes finding out the module responsible for a bug easier. By debugging the interfaces between different modules and simulating the interfaces a powerful way for catching real-time bugs is given.

The costs of single independent modules should be measured in the future to detect critical modules early and to derive information about the quality of the (outsourcing) team that develops the module.

Improvements Achieved After the Experiment

The estimated productivity of the VIP project was nearly 20 Lines Of Code (LOC) per person-day. With the prototype under UNIX of the ODB a productivity of 25 LOC/person-day was reached. The real number of 38 LOCs was reduced to 25 (to only 65 percent) due to increased documentation and design, which formed additional effort due to new architectural design and requirements definition guidelines (not just looking at code development but at the overall effort).

Due to the implementation of the new team model, the clear roles and interfaces (between modules and the people responsible for the modules) the team spirit increased and a better basis for constructive discussions in the team was obtained.

The clear interfaces and the module architectures (according to the new guidelines) led to a situation in which each member of the team was accepting ownership of his role which led to an effective parallel development of modules.

The maintenance of VIP was reduced to nearly one-third of the previous effort.

A version of the control system with a connected bug tracking system has been installed. Thus, according to the maintenance guidelines each change request and bug report is recorded and automatically statistics of the quality of each module (i.e., subcontractor) are generated. Also members of the team will be like self-responsible subcontractors (module owners) in the future.

Functions for creating interfaces to ODB have been packed into toolboxes which provide support in linking additional software to ODB in a defined and testable way.

IMPROVEMENT ACTIVITIES PERFORMED

Organisation

Based on the fact, that in a small team (1) the resources (e.g., time) are limited and (2) each team member has to fulfill several roles at the same time, the design of an adapted teamwork and development model was needed.

Small teams need lean documentation. Lean does not mean "not complete." Only the information really necessary should be included and overly long documentation avoided.

Based on experiences made during the ESSI project the following guidelines have been developed.

THE LIFE CYCLE AND TEAM MODEL

Most existing life cycle models focus on process steps and document flows. However, in small teams the team members are playing several roles at the same time so that the focus was put on which roles are played in a small software team, the roles' responsibilities, and the interaction of the roles. Only after the role playing framework has been agreed, have the documents supporting the required teamwork style been defined.

The roles have been identified in a set of interviews conducted with the team (based on practical work experience), taking into account the roles proposed in the German defence standard (V-Standard), adapting the ESA PSS 05 guidelines, and using structured analysis and structured design methods. It has been designed for teams with less then 10 persons.

PROGRAMMING BY CONTRACT

Concerning the role of the module owner the team model is based on the new approach of "Programming by Contract." A module corresponds with a data process following the (SA) notation and has clearly defined data and control inputs, which are the incoming arrows in SA, and produces a couple of data and control outputs, which are the outgoing arrows in SA. Each module is delegated to a responsible person and a kind of contract is made: Each module has one clear input and output situation and the supplier has only a guaranty for this prearranged input and output situations.

These module ownership arrangements are documented in a management file which is the basic instrument for monitoring the project. The project manager can easily supervise who has taken which module to which contracting conditions, which contracts are already finished, which module parts of the system were already generated, tested, taken over, and integrated.

Each module owner refines his or her module with SA and hands over the newly created modules to subcontractors. The project manager has to control, that the interfaces and feedback loops of the modules cause no deadlock situations.

Each module owner tests his or her module and documents the used test data. During the module acceptance the test data in full is given to the higher subcontractor. Two kinds of modules can be distinguished: elemental baseline modules, which are the building blocks of the integration, and integrated modules, which consist of baseline modules. During the acceptance of elemental modules a complete test is demanded, during the integration the complete testing gets more difficult, so that during the integration well-defined test data, but not completeness, is wanted. All collected test data are given to the maintenance making the retesting easier.

OTHER ROLES

Beside the above-described module owner role a complete set of 12 roles has been identified, analysed, and defined. After the definition of these roles the next step was the creation of interaction diagrams describing teamwork scenarios.

Project Manager

The project manager

- plans of the project (time, effort, resources);
- ascertains the requirements together with the client contact person, whereby the requirements made during the project acquisition are refined and completed;
- designs the context diagrams and the system modules and constructs the first module description;
- analyses errors;

- gives contracts to module owners;
- watches over the project using the module contracts;
- writes the project diary; and
- prepares the project conclusion report.

Customer Contact Person

The customer contact person

- is a representative from the client's side, responsible for technical requirements, who is the technical interface to the customer;
- keeps contact with the project manager during the whole project; and
- reviews the requirements.

Additional roles were reviewer, finance and control, support, etc.

THE CONCEPT OF REUSE

The concept of reuse based on three principles:

1. Development of competencies and independent and configurable tasks instead of products (Fig. 14.4).
2. Cutting each aspect of the work into small tasks under the aspects of objects (Fig. 14.5).
3. Using standard programmes and interfaces.

Figure 14.4 illustrates the "configurable independent tasks" philosophy. Basic system components form a core element (ODB, Maintenance System) and can be configured for different environments simply by data adjustments.

All other components can be linked through standard interfaces, and further components can easily be connected through these interfaces. This way the system becomes highly flexible, changeable, and configurable.

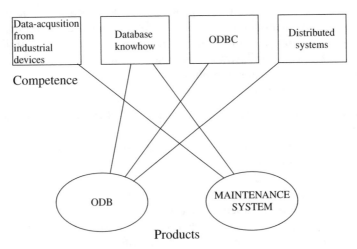

Figure 14.4.   Configurable and independent competencies.

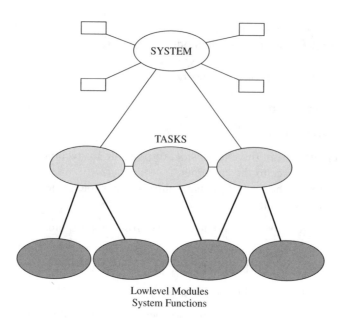

Figure 14.5. Object driven decomposition in team tasks and modules.

Figure 14.5 generalises the example from Figure 14.4 and defines a system as a number of configurable tasks that can be easily integrated by simple adjustments and through standard interfaces.

It is not just a functional decomposition, rather it is like a set of independent objects with each object having a standard set of connectors to build larger compositions.

A Sample Part of a Role Interaction Model

Three metaphases have been established: project acquisition (usually not part of software development models but essential for small profit centres), realisation, and maintenance.

Each metaphase contains a number of role plays (work scenarios) described in form of interaction models. Figure 14.6 illustrates a sample part of a role interaction model which is performed within the project acquisition phase.

In the project acquisition phase

- A customer (in German, *Kunde*) defines a request and forwards it to the sales department (in German, *Vertrieb*)
- The sales department determines the responsible division head (in German, *Abteilungsleiter*) and forwards the request.
- The division head installs a technical engineer (in German, *Techniker*) who contacts the customer contact person (in German, *Kunden Kontakt Person*) and starts writing a first draft of a requirements document (in German, *Pflichtenheft*).
- The technical engineer provides the division head with a first requirements document who then makes a first cost estimation and draft offer (in German, *Anbot*).
- The draft offer is reviewed by the finance and control (in German, *Geschaeftsfuehrung*).
- After review, the offer is sent to the customer who either defines a new request (all previous steps are run through again) or sends an order (in German, *Bestellung*).

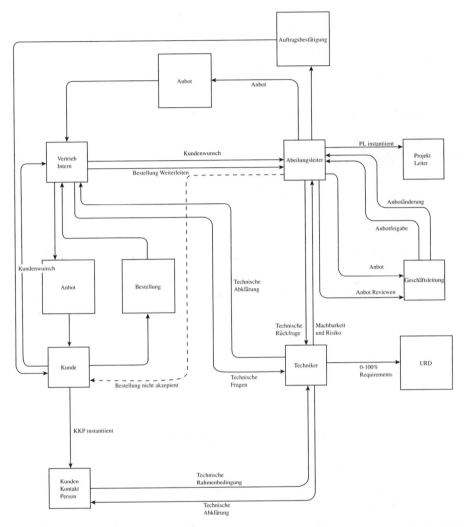

Figure 14.6.   Sample part of a role-playing in the model project acquisition phase (titles in German).

- After the receipt of the offer the responsible division head installs a project manager (in German, *Projektleiter*) who is responsible for the realisation phase.

Data-Collection Plan

The collection of data is focused around the following questions:

- What maintenance efforts do single models cause?
- In which modules do the most errors appear?
- How big are the modules?
- How critical was the error?
- In which size module were the delivery dates passed over?
- Which part of a module consists in reuse components?
- What is the relationship between effort and the size of a module?

The project manager writes the project diary, which documents the dates, activities, and efforts, based on the finished module contracts. Each module contract contains a starting date, a delivery date, and an approximation of the related efforts. After the acceptance the real efforts and the real delivery day are written down in the project diary.

Each module owner tests his or her module and protocols all test data. In this protocol the efforts of testing are also listed.

The project leader draws up an acceptance test protocol, in which the kind and number of errors are documented.

Internal Dissemination

The Lean Life Cycle and Team Model has been ISO 9001 certified in 1995 and is used as guideline for further projects. With this model the department SWE has no problem realising the audits.

THE EFFECTS ON THE ODB BASELINE PROJECT

Figure 14.7 shows a graphical representation of the baseline project ODB and how the open architecture and team guidelines have been implemented to actually achieve an open architecture.

From the business point of view an open architecture offers flexibility on the market, because the same system can easily be adapted to different market segments, such as

1. manufacturing plants,
2. buildings,
3. power plants,
4. etc.

KEY LESSONS LEARNED

Technological Point of View

- *Lean teams need lean documentation.* Lean does not mean less, but only that necessary things should be written down.
- *Open system.* The open system allows one to buy modules with expert know-how and include them in the system.
- *Parallel working.* Parallel working on the project is only possible with a concept like the Programming by Contract, because each group can simulate the interface from a task, which will be developed by an other group.
- It is better to invest in a cheaper tool and in good (mostly expensive) training than to invest a lot in the tool and forget the importance of skills, training, and methodology. A fool with just a tool remains a fool.
- Develop only what is not available on the market. The question of price occurs only if a good price for the number of licences you need is not possible.
- What is important is the interface and not the code inside.

The Results from a Business Point of View

The complete system is realised in a distributed manner which makes bug tracking easier. By debugging the interfaces between different modules and simulating the interfaces, a powerful way for catching real-time bugs is achieved.

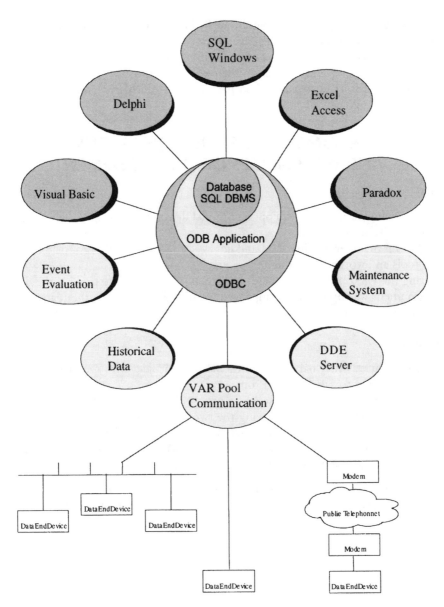

Figure 14.7.   The baseline project ODB.

The lessons learned from a business perspective were the following

- A prototype before full development is much cheaper than a system that is wrongly developed.
- The baseline component shall be kept independent from application software as a basis for future configurability.
- *Reusability.* Because of the exact input and output definitions of the several modules it is easy to reuse them in other projects. A second smaller project followed, in which 70 percent of the code was reusable.

- *Easy handling of extension.* In a monolithically built system an adaptation or change based on new requirements is very expensive, since you have to step through the whole system. Changing parts or installing new modules is very complicated. In a toolbox the changes of some modules have no impact on the remaining system.
- *Maintenance.* Effort decreased by 66 percent due to a better understandable structure and architecture.

A SUMMARY OF THE STRENGHTHS AND WEAKNESSES OF THE EXPERIMENT

Strengths

- The implementation of a development model driven by team spirit, which was accepted by the entire team.
- Each team member was involved and engaged in the installation of new methodologies and tools and worked with them.
- During the ESSI project and the development of the baseline project, the development environment was dramatically improved from both viewpoints, the managerial and the technical.

Weaknesses

- Sometimes it was very hard to align the baseline project with the process improvement experiment, and to satisfy the customer.
- In the first phase there was a separate process improvement manager and a customer project manager. This idea of having the two managers failed. The first ESSI manager had the opinion that a model had to be made by himself and experts, and this model had to be accepted by the team. This idea failed too. Models must grow from experience and should not be idealistically established by external experts.

The case study and measures concerning tailoring and reengineering at the end of Chapter 3 stem from a project aligned to the experiment outlined in the the present chapter.

Chapter 15

AIMing for Increases
in Software Process Maturity

Some Irish Case Studies

Éamonn McGuinness,
aimware Ltd., Ireland

INTRODUCTION

This first part of the chapter introduces five companies in Ireland who committed to and executed process improvement projects. This part of the chapter also relates many of the experiences of the five companies under the headings of these following fundamental aspects of process improvement:

- Sponsor's Role
- Assessment Variations
- Improvement Life Cycle
- Resourcing and Managing the Project
- Role of Training and Coaching
- Process Automation
- Results Obtained
- Sustaining Improvement
- Experience with Clusters and Networking
- Summary and Benchmark Questions

The chapter goes on to draw together the main lessons of the above five companies into a process improvement life cycle. This life cycle is constructed to give companies a step-by-step approach to software process improvement, that will hopefully help them avoid the traps and pitfalls that dogged the above five companies. The process improvement life cycle description is annotated with a case study of its proposed implementation in a sixth company.

CASE STUDY COMPANIES INTRODUCED

This first part of the chapter relates some of the experiences of five companies in Ireland who have invested in software process improvement and got a return on those investments. Their experiences are organised into what might be regarded as key aspects of process improvement, as listed above. Not all of their experiences can be related in a short chapter of this nature but it is hoped that enough samples are included to get across the main lessons of software process improvement. It is not the intention to profile each company equally under each heading, but rather to use the experiences of whatever company best illustrate the point. At the end of this first part of the chapter, it will be possible for the reader to ask himself or herself 10 questions in order to benchmark the efforts of their own organisations against the experiences of these five companies! How will you score out of 10?

"Factory" is the computer integrated manufacturing department of a large factory with 50 software engineering staff and are responsible for software ranging from personnel and finance on one side to factory support and product test on the other end of the spectrum. "Financial" is a commercial software organisation and develops, markets, and sells software for the international financial markets from their base in Ireland and employs over 100 software engineering staff. "Insurance" is the in-house information technology department of a large insurance company in Ireland and they have over 20 people in the software development group of the Information Technology department. "Telecom 1" is one of the R&D arms of a multinational Telecom provider that also has a large manufacturing base in Ireland and this firm employs over 30 software engineering staff. "Telecom 2" is the in-house Information Technology Directorate of a very large Irish organisation and this directorate employs, close to 250 computer staff. (*Note:* The companies are deliberately not listed until the end of the chapter, so that the reader can concentrate on the main lessons, without the distraction of whatever perception he or she has about the company in question. . . if any!)

Sponsor's Role

The "Factory" pursued (and still pursues) an aggressive policy with respect to software process improvement. Indeed some of the engineering staff wondered at times if the stretch goals were too ambitious but when the going got tough the sponsor got going! He set the goal with the group, continuously monitored the projects and cleared all roadblocks for the process improvement efforts. Sometimes this involved difficult negotiations with business managers on deliverables and time-scales. When these negotiations were getting difficult, he had his own senior manager publicly support the improvement efforts of the software group. He participated actively in the process improvement steering team but was careful not to lead it. He even participated in one SEI assessment of his own group. (The Software Engineering Institute is a U.S. government and industry-sponsored body which focuses on products and technologies for software process improvement. It is located at Carnegie Mellon University.) The group was in no doubt where the sponsor's beliefs and priorities lay!

"Financial" and "Insurance" also had strong sponsors who were largely responsible for starting their organisations on the road to process improvement. The initial results were impressive but both sponsors were changed in the middle of the project. These changes were signalled in advance and actions were taken to reduce the risk of any negative impact. These actions were not effective enough. Both projects flagged for a period in the middle and indeed in "Financial" the arrival of a new senior manager with an interest in process improvement probably saved the project from mediocre results. "Telecom 1" and "Telecom 2" both have their process improvement efforts sponsored by senior managers responsible for the respective departments (i.e., the R&D Director and the Information Technology Director). These sponsors have been visible and vocal in their support for process improvement. Indeed, in "Telecom 1" the sponsor reviews the progress of the process improvement project at a monthly meeting and has been known to spend a full day reviewing the progress and giving leadership to the project! "Telecom 2" makes use of a "Customer First Program" to drive cultural change and the process improvement has been driven from the very top of the organisation as a major element of the way "Telecom 2" will do their business in future.

Lesson 1: Process improvement gives mediocre results, flags, or fails without a serious level of senior management sponsorship with an accompanying vision.

Assessment Variations

> "If you don't know where you are, a map won't help!!"

This is a quote from the first page of the first chapter of Watts Humphrey's now famous book [1]. If I had a dollar for every time I saw the above "saying" quoted! I must admit to using it in my own MSc. But the irony of it is that:

> "If you don't know where you are, a map is the *only* thing that will help!!"

I spent 10 years in the Irish Army and one of the first exercises we did in basic training (boot camp) involved being driven in a covered truck to an unknown destination and basically dropped off in the middle of nowhere. We were given a map and a compass, so we could find out where we were and get back to base. Humphrey's book and subsequent versions of the CMM[sm] (CMM is a Service Mark of Carnegie Mellon University)—the SEI's Capability Maturity Model [2] have been the map to help those software souls who are lost. I'm not saying that any of the five organisations were lost, but they all used various form of assessments to find out exactly where they were and to understand the choices of destination open to them.

"Factory" uses Software Engineering Institute (SEI) assessments. They have twice used the 5-day version and at other times they have tailored it down to 2 days to get an interim profile of how their process is progressing. They have also used directed workshops (also known as search conferences) with project teams that serve the dual purpose of giving each project a profile and of educating engineers as to the motivations of process improvement. "Financial" runs an internal audit program that highlights areas that need improvement. "Insurance" was involved with a testing improvement program and it chose to assess its testing practices by looking at process, product, and resource metrics. "Insurance" found, for example, that on average 44 percent of project effort was devoted to testing. The firm benchmarks taken at the end of the improvement project to assess the progress made with the new testing practices. "Telecom 1" decided to use directed workshops on the SEI CMM to educate the teams on the model but also to identify the practices that were missing or were in need of improvement. A year later the company invested in an official SEI assessment of the latest type—the SEI CBA IPI, which is the CMM-Based Assessment/Appraisal for Internal Process Improvement [3]. "Telecom 2" started their process improvement efforts with an SEI assessment. Indeed, the senior management sponsor opened the assessment by appealing to all involved to be open, honest, and participate actively. On the last morning of the assessment when the final findings (strengths and opportunities for improvement) were being presented to a packed room of software staff, the senior manager asked if everyone was in agreement with the findings of the assessment. As the assessment team sat nervously, no dissenters emerged! That is the hallmark of a good assessment. He then charted the way forward for the group. A good assessment will deliver at least three results:

1. A benchmark against a recognised model
2. A set of improvement priorities
3. A group who have actively participated in the "assessment," reached consensus, and who are motivated for the upcoming improvement.

Lesson 2: Any of the variations of assessment (or combinations thereof) used by the five companies should work and deliver the positive results needed to initiate a process improvement program.

Improvement Life Cycle

Of course there is no point in working everyone up into a frenzy about improvement if there is no willingness to do something about the results! All five companies have used some modified form of the Shewhart or Deming [4] cycle for improvement, for example:

Status—Where are we (e.g., with respect to some recognised software quality model)
Vision—Where do we want to be on this model
Plan—Plan the project necessary to deliver on the vision
Design—Design the new approach and pilot it
Implement—Ensure that the changes are adopted organisationwide
Manage—Settle the changes in and measure the costs and benefits

The SEI, which has contributed so much of their process improvement models, methods and results to the public domain have recently released a process improvement model depicted here, called IDEAL^sm [5] (IDEAL is a Service Mark of Carnegie Mellon University). See Figure 15.1.

"Financial," having traversed the wheel of improvement a few times, did find that the shorter the life cycle the better. They found that shorter spins are better! Long life cycles (as in software development) tend to be unfocused and can fizzle out.

Lesson 3: The message from the experiences of the five companies is: Define an improvement approach or life cycle and follow it.

Providing Resources and Managing the Project

Improvement does not happen by accident. It has to be planned. As with all major undertakings, a project is usually the best mechanism to achieve the desired results.

"Factory" uses, the classic improvement structure of Steering Team, Project Manager and Improvement Teams. "Factory" has a full-time Software Quality Assurance (SQA) person who looks after Quality Assurance and Quality Improvement. This person is the process improvement project manager. There was a personnel change after the first spin of the process improvement wheel. The first SQA person was promoted and a new person was appointed. While the first SQA person was very successful (hence the promotion), the new blood was seen as a good idea for the second spin. This revitalising of the improvement effort is not unusual. In "Factory" the project manager has the backing of a steering team composed of the project managers. These are the people who can and do commit to action, and so have been a very successful team, and indeed have been formally recognised in the company as such. There are also many improvement teams of engineers that work on the different processes that they have decided to improve. The teams then present and hand over their work to the wider group, who use the results as part of their day to day efforts. As soon as the work of the team is done, the team disbands. Everyone in the group has been on a process improvement team at one stage or other. Everyone in the group spends up to 10 percent of their time on process improvement.

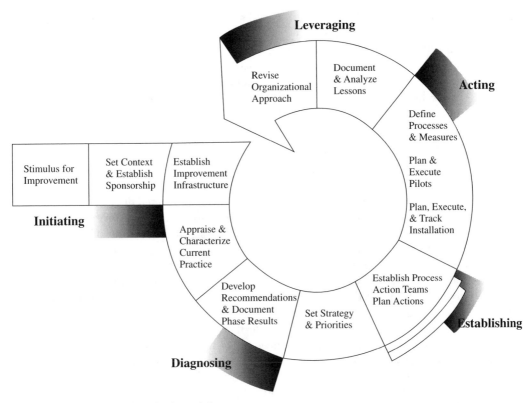

Figure 15.1.   The SEI ideal model.

"Factory" is now starting the third major spin of the process improvement wheel. The steering team, project manager, and the new process improvement teams are in place and they are about to finalise on the exact goals and an associated plan. They have found through experience that it does not happen by accident!

Lesson 4: They know that for them, improvement has to be a project with a stretch goal and an associated plan that is rigorously tracked. The other four companies used similar structures or variations on the theme.

Role of Training and Coaching

"Factory" made good use of customised workshops where engineers were facilitated in exploring the SEI CMM model, best practices in a particular software engineering area (e.g., software testing, software project management, etc.) and their own processes. These were really structured group coaching sessions rather than formal training courses. "Telecom 1" also choose to use this approach a lot. It had the added benefit of "buying in" engineers to the improvement efforts. These sessions helped them influence the improvement efforts in the direction that would most benefit them. "Financial" found a combination of these workshops and individual coaching sessions the most beneficial. They labelled this approach, "Just in Time Training." "Insurance" made good use of these workshop sessions and used the experiences to make short easy-to-use guidebooks for the department, for example, Guide to Reviews and Guide to Metrics Collection. "Factory," "Telecom 1," and "Telecom 2" all invested in SEI CMM assessment skills transfer and coaching. This is where they had a combination of training courses (with extensive exercises and role-playing) and coaching sessions by having an experienced assessment leader facilitate them in the initial assessments.

Lesson 5: The experiences of these five companies underline that you should think more laterally when you think of "training" and try and determine the objectives and the best method. The methods that worked very well for these companies include goal-oriented workshops, coaching sessions, short guides, and on-the-job training.

Process Automation

We software people spend our lives automating other people's jobs but seem to forget about ourselves. Why should we be the cobbler with holes in our shoes?

As with the areas described above, the companies profiled selected different approaches to the challenge of process automation. "Telecom 2" targets automation sooner rather than later, as the group is so large and the projects are complex with significant technical integration and project coordination, that they say they need automation to really institutionalise the key process areas effectively. They would, for example, define and pilot their Project Management approach and support it very early on with groupware tools. "Factory," while it makes extensive use of tools, preferred to define and implement a lot of key process areas before considering process automation. While the approaches are different, they are both of course defining the processes before they automate them! "Financial" makes heavy use of automation for their process. The firm makes the point that the investment in setting up automated product support (e.g., Testing) is usually underestimated while the benefits are normally overestimated but do have great potential if introduced correctly. Most of the companies use point solutions for Project Management (e.g., AutoPlan, Microsoft Project, etc.) and Configuration Management (Intersolv's PVCS, ClearCASE, etc.).

Lesson 6: Four of the five companies have deployed or are about to deploy Groupware tools (e.g., Lotus Notes) in support of their process implementation. In the words of the Quality Manager at "Financial," this makes the process an inescapable part of everyday life—to follow the process is easier than not to follow it. "Telecom 2" call their automation, "the working and living environment for the duration of the project."

Results Obtained

"Factory" was assessed at SEI Level 2 in October 1994 and SEI Level 3 in November 1995. The firm has internal product, process, resource, and productivity metrics that report on items such as customer satisfaction, cycle time, productivity, in-process faults, released defects, etc. These are monitored to gauge the success or otherwise of the process improvement efforts. For example, one of the Q4 1995 charts showed a marked increase in the number of in-process faults, which was offset by a decrease in the number of post-release defects. These results were the fruits of introducing an updated Review process. "Financial" have achieved ISO 9001/TickIT certification. The firm has also reduced their postrelease defects by 50 percent. (See Figure 15.2.)

"Insurance" has reduced postrelease defects by 30 perent departmentwide. "Telecom 1" has put in place the processes needed for SEI CMM Level 2 and most of the processes needed for SEI CMM Level 3. The firm has been ISO 9001 certified for many years. "Telecom 2," acting on the recommendations of the SEI CMM assessment (i.e., the voice of the engineers—people feel ownership of the improvements and take actively part in it) has implemented two key process areas and are close to completing the definition of the third.

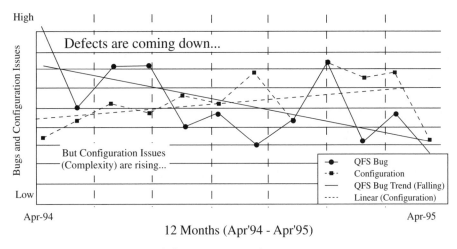

Figure 15.2. Benefit analysis—defects are going down.

Lesson 7: Large organisations have to survey extensively all of the methods and approaches on the market, before piloting and implementing a "best of breed" solution across their group. Once implemented, metrics help to verify success or further improvement potentials.

Sustaining Improvement

Process improvement and maturity is a lot like physical fitness. One has to endure some pain to achieve the level of fitness required and it requires some level of effort to retain the level, though not as much as in initially achieving it. If some effort is not continuously injected into maintaining the level of fitness (or process maturity) then the level of maturity (or fitness!) achieved will be gradually eroded. Sad but true!

"Factory" use the SEI assessments, the team-based approach, and the part-time SQA project representatives (who provide SQA support to projects other than their own) as the main mechanism, to sustain and improve the levels of process maturity. The firm eases off the pressure a little after achieving a particular goal to allow all the processes to settle in before they reapply the pressure with a fresh goal and a new project plan. The SEI CMM is the model they look to for suggestions on what to improve next. They are currently looking at companywide metrics implementation and process automation. "Financial" have defined and implemented a lot of the processes and are now focusing on improving some of them in the light of changing business requirements (e.g., Configuration Management) and in automating more fully other areas (e.g., Testing). The firm is looking at SEI CMM and SPICE [6] as models that help with process improvement prioritisation and requirements. They are also using internal company Special Interest Groups (SIGs) to focus on certain key areas and to keep the momentum going. "Insurance" is implementing departmentwide the new practices that were successful on the pilots (i.e., Testing and Reviews). "Telecom 1" is using the SEI CMM as a model to help drive their process improvement efforts and is using an SEI CBA-IPI assessment as a pit stop to gauge strengths, and opportunities for improvement but also to get people signed up for the next phase of the improvement. "Telecom 2" is also using the SEI CMM as a road map for improvement but is progressing deliberately with the key processes because they are investing in automation and full institutionalisation as they proceed.

Questions Critical for SPI Success	Your Score Yes or No!
1. Strong, visible and active senior management sponsorship is needed	
2. A clear picture of the starting point is necessary (preferably against a recognised international model, e.g., SEI CMM, ISO 9001/TickIT)	
3. A focus on the results required is essential. Stretch goals do work and may be needed to rock some people from their comfort zones. Focusing on the results needed should also keep the long term in mind (e.g., not just get ISO 9001 or SEI Level 2 by 1998—i.e., invest for the long haul, for the capability to be gained).	
4. Make the improvement a project that is well managed. Since it is difficult enough to deliver on the day job (i.e., delivering software) it proves to be even more difficult to deliver on process improvement. The latter requires more careful project management or it will fail or deliver mediocre results.	
5. Ensure strong participation of as many of the people as possible. It is best if it is done by the people for the people! Imposed solutions tend to be resisted fiercely and may have a longer implementation schedule.	
6. Software Development needs an approach and so does Process Improvement. Select a life cycle of phases and activities that will deliver the desired result.	
7. Commit real resources to the effort and if necessary reprioritise some of the other work to get the improvement started. Engineers will really appreciate the seriousness of these actions!	
8. Take one bite of the elephant at a time. Don't allow too much to be tackled especially until some benefits are delivered. All of the models are broken into key areas, so there is no need to tackle them all at once.	
9. Provide automated support as early as possible. It is one way to help the institutionalisation.	
10. Have a vision of where you want to go after the initial improvements (whether onward and upward or stand still) and devise an appropriate strategy to meet this goal.	
Your Total Score out of 10 is	→

Lesson 8: Improvement is not easy the first time but keeping it going without erosion of the once achieved level of fitness requires continuous investment, improvement, and a strategy. Companies need to have a strategy after the first spin of the process improvement wheel that determines how they will go up the maturity ladder or alternatively how they will stay where they are, because companies have fallen down!

Experience with Clusters and Networking

Three of the above five companies were involved in two different clusters of companies to help improve process improvement (i.e., companies coming together to work jointly on process improvement). These have obvious advantages such as reducing costs, providing synergy, moral support etc. They also have limitations. It is best if companies are at the same process maturity level and are facing the same challenges. In joint sessions it is annoying for a company to listen to some simple process explained that they have in place and similarly it is frustrating for the other company to listen to advanced process concepts discussed, when they do not have the basics in place. One of the advantages is reduced costs through joint training sessions but it has proved difficult to keep everyone on the same project plan, as invariably business pressures affects the progress of some companies more than others. Therefore a higher degree of coordination is needed to keep the project on track. Who pays for this? Networking, on the other hand, does not provide the potential benefits of clustering but is a lot cheaper! The difficulty according to companies has been finding the right people to network with! Ireland is served in this regard with the EU and Government-funded Centre for Software Engineering. The Irish Computer Society also has a Software Engineering SIG.

Lesson 9: Clusters are a good idea if the companies are at similar maturity levels and have the same goals and are really committed to doing something about them. Process Improvement can sometimes be a lonely and thankless job, so it does help to have a network of peers who are in the same boat!

Summary of Case Studies and Benchmark Questions

The above five companies would not claim to be perfect when it comes to Software Process Improvement, but they have seen many aspects of their approaches succeed and fail. Some of the main aspects critical for success are listed here. You can use these to benchmark your improvement ideas or projects.

Ask yourself 10 questions based on the above points and the thought process will either confirm that you are on the right track or give you ideas on how to improve your process improvement efforts.

I would go so far as to say that unless you score well on these 10 points, you should reconsider your improvement efforts. I hope you score well with process improvement and that this part of the chapter is of some help.

AN "IDEAL" PROCESS IMPROVEMENT LIFE CYCLE

This second part of the chapter draws together the main lessons of the above five companies into a suggested process improvement life cycle. This life cycle is constructed to give companies a step-by-step approach to software process improvement, that will hopefully help them avoid the traps and pitfalls that dogged the above five companies. The process improvement life cycle description is annotated with a case study of a proposed implementation in a sixth company (aimware). The main life cycle stages come from the SEI CMM IDEAL process improvement life cycle model.

The quality quest at aimware is interesting in that the company attempted to inject quality into the company at the start of the company's life cycle . . . which meant it was in place for the start of the product life cycles. aimware is used here as a case study to explain the various stages of the proposed improvement life cycle.

Case Study Background—aimware Ltd.

aimware is in the business of developing software for the software process. The company has developed a software product to help companies achieve higher levels of software process maturity based on the SEI CMM model. The product is being further developed in partnership with European-based U.S. companies and indigenous companies. The aimware product suite consists of software which computerises the documentation templates and work-flows of the software process. It also contains the option of a fully documented set of processes which adheres to the SEI CMM and/or ISO 9001/TickIT models.

Initiating Phase

In this sample "IDEAL" Plan, the "Initiating" phase has three main steps:
   Initiating

1. Recognise or get improvement impetus.
2. Set improvement business context and goals.
3. Ensure Senior Sponsorship is in place.

Recognise or Get Improvement Impetus

Companies typically need a jolt to get them into software process improvement. This can come from increased customer pressure in the face of visible and mounting product quality problems. It can come from purchasers that mandate certain levels of quality against some international software quality model (e.g., ISO 9001 or SEI CMM Level 2 to bid for contracts). It sometimes comes from within, when companies recognise that they cannot keep going the way that they are going! These companies have to get projects back in control . . . if indeed they ever were in control! In some companies it is a corporate dictate/objective that all subsidiaries gradually improve their processes.

The inference in all of the above is that the status quo is not good enough. The impetus is then the reason that companies enter into the improvement cycle. It is the pressure that starts companies on the road to improvement. It is very important to recognise this impetus and call it out loudly and clearly. It may not be the best reason in the world for starting process improvement but it is typically a real pressure that can keep the flame alive when other pressures mount and rise up against the process improvement project.

Set Improvement Business Context and Goals

Many improvements start, but few finish! Many of these failed initiatives start in the technical department as the technical staff know that they have to improve. However, they sometimes forget to tie these efforts to the overall business goals. This means effort expended on the process improvement is the first project to be sacrificed in the face of other business pressures. Preventing defects from reaching the customer is a good business goal to have! There are, however, many other goals that can tie software process improvement to the business in question. Most companies can examine their goals in respect of the Time, Quality, and Cost variables. Indeed, most companies, while ambitious in all three directions, are usually more focused on one of the three. For some companies (e.g., commercial software houses) time to market is critical and therefore reducing cycle time is key. For other companies, reliability (e.g., aircraft control software) is crucial and therefore minimum defect levels are the goal. Some companies are driven primarily by cost (e.g., in-house IT departments) so keeping projects to budget is critical. In most companies, the driver is a combination of all three but it is important to understand where the real emphasis lies. In other companies the emphasis varies in the different software producing units (e.g., the Maintenance group focus on minimising defects whereas the New Products group might focus on time to market). It is essential to see what is driving the company and then ensure that the process improvement is goaled on delivering or helping to ensure the achievement of these overall objectives. If the process improvement can be seen to contribute to these overall goals it has a much better chance of prospering. Clearly, numerical, objective, and measurable goals are best. Examples are provided in the next section.

Ensure Senior Sponsorship Is in Place

If the idea for process improvement did not come from the top of the organisation then it is essential to have a very senior manager sponsor the effort. If I might be so bold as to suggest that one should seriously consider stopping the process improvement effort at this early stage if there is no sponsorship in place, or at least delay the project until the sponsorship is evident and visible.

What does a sponsor do?

- Resources the project (money, people, etc.)
- Gives the project direction and focus as well as visible and vocal support
- Reviews the project to ensure it is on target and delivering the results
- Changes the focus of the project as appropriate
- Ensures that the project has the support of the organisation
- Helps the project through difficult times (resource conflicts, etc.)

Case Study: aimware Impetus, Business Context, and Business Sponsorship

aimware impetus

aimware is in the business of process improvement—with focus on services but in particular, on associated automation software. Having this expertise and knowledge meant the company had incentives, both internal and external, to implement its own Quality System and then have it certified. Internally because the firm knew the potential benefits of process improvement, and externally it was felt that customers would recognise the value of working with a company that practice what it sells. In essence, how could aimwave justifiably sell the ideas, concepts, services, and products of software process improvement if they did not "buy" them! They had to eat their own dogfood!

aimware business context and goals

Recent statistics from Watts Humphrey, the "Edison" of the Software Process world, suggest a high defect rate on average for code written. Most of the code does eventually get taken out during the software's life cycle, some of it in compilation, some in testing, some during inspections, etc. But some code only makes its way out, when this is least expected or wanted! The first key thing to notice about this defect rate is that it appears to be consistent across senior and junior engineers alike. The second is that there are differing costs associated with fixing bugs at the different life cycle stages. Thus, a bug fixed at the design stage is much less costly than a defect encountered at the coding stage.

In addition to this, it is commonly recognised that testing is the least efficient means of getting rid of defects. Although testing is absolutely necessary in a properly constructed process, ideally it should serve only to catch the bugs not caught at earlier stages. Using it as a general method for catching and correcting bugs is costly and inefficient.

As a business manager, it pays to have an effective means to deal with the problem of defects. Prevention is cheaper than detection and a good process allows the early capture of most defects. Thus, having a Quality System is more than just an added extra—it is crucial to the profitability of software development companies. That is why aimware ultimately is committed to having an improving software process. The current aimware objectives for software quality are included here by way of example.

The objectives are in six dimensions and their achievement or otherwise will be measured as described in the italics that appear in the parentheses below:

1. *Process:* Aim for and achieve SEI CMM Level 4 or higher by December 1999 (as benchmarked on an official SEI assessment).
2. *Product:* Reduce postrelease defects by at least 50 percent from the baseline (Jan. 1997) within 1 year, by at least 70 percent within 2 years and by 90 percent within 3 years(to be verified by checking the software engineering database).
3. *Cycle Time:* Be capable of shipping two minor releases and two major releases every year within 2 years of the baseline (Jan. 1997) (to be verified by examining the software engineering database).
4. *Productivity:* Ship at least 30 percent more functionality in each major release than is shipped at the baseline date (to be verified by examining the software engineering database).
5. *Cost and Benefit:* No major increases in headcount or technology spending over the current business plan to achieve the profit levels specified (i.e., the above gains to be realised by increasing effort and focus on quality!) (to be verified by examining the business plans).
6. *People:* Be capable of attracting and retaining the best people to aimware as the company will operate in a high-quality working environment compared to the relative chaos of some software development environments (To be measured in terms of hiring costs and personnel turnover rates and associated costs by comparison to other local software companies).

aimware business sponsorship

Process improvement is not cheap! Investments are heavily needed at the formation of quality initiatives, and plans and budget must be sufficient to continue the investment. The key here is budget and plans, as having quality built-in as part of the business plan is essential. Process improvement has to be budgeted for and scheduled in the same way as any other successful element of the business. There is extra investment required upfront but it is believed that this is certain to lead to longer-term gain. Short-term pain for long-term gain is the paradigm.

Summary–Initiating Stage

It may be possible to start a process improvement pilot without this level of sponsorship but serious company wide improvement is very unlikely to succeed without senior management sponsorship. Thus it is essential to ask the following three questions before exiting this stage . . . successfully:

1. Do we recognise or know where the improvement impetus is coming from?
2. Have we set measurable improvement goals in line with the business direction?
3. Is the requisite level of Senior Sponsorship in place?

Diagnosing Phase

In this sample "IDEAL" Plan, the "Diagnosing" phase has two main steps.
Diagnosing Phase

1. Decide which `measures' to take, for example,
   a. Process, e.g., CMM Assessment
   b. Product, e.g., Defects pre- and postship
   c. Resource/Cost, for example, Size and cost of projects

  e. Revenue, e.g., Cost and benefit
  f. Productivity, e.g., Size and/or cost over time
2. Take the "measures"

Decide Which Measures to Take

It frequently happens that process improvement does indeed take place successfully in some companies. This usually happens when there is a push for ISO 9001 certification. Unfortunately, the only measure taken is the binary measure of whether certification has been achieved or not! When this measure turns from "No" to "Yes," the impetus for process improvement sometimes fades. Similarly, although there may be a warm and fuzzy feeling about the certification, many companies cannot quantifiably say what the improvement achieved in real terms. Some within the organisation say that it had been a waste of time and bureaucratic, while others say that it was a great benefit. And so the debates rage, fuelled by emotion, charge, and counter-charge . . . but no concrete evidence! With the latter in mind, it is best to measure the effect (or lack of effect) of the process improvement program, so that companies know whether or not there is a benefit to be gained from process improvement costs within their environs. Similarly it is difficult to chart an exact course for the process improvement project without knowing where the company is, with respect to process improvement. Unfortunately, no one measure alone is sufficient and six types of measure are discussed here for companies to consider. With measures like these companies can find themselves on the process improvement roadmap and select a route to drive on.

Process Measures—For Example, CMM Assessment

A good process gives a company a very good chance (but no guarantee!) of a resulting high-quality product. There are now many international software quality models against which companies can benchmark themselves, for example, SEI CMM, ISO 9001/TickIT, ISO 9000-3, BootStrap, or SPICE. The choice of model is maybe less important than the use of the model. Unfortunately many companies merely assess to get certified or to achieve a certain CMM level. While there are obvious business pressures to achieve certification, when this is taken too far, the long term results are less than impressive. Staff tend to get disinterested as they see management more interested in the perception of a CMM level, than the reality of process improvement. Also one of the main purposes of the assessment (i.e., highlight areas that need improvement) is thwarted. A good assessment will deliver at least three results:

1. A benchmark against a recognised model (e.g. SEI CMM, ISO 9001, etc.)
2. A list of key software areas that need immediate improvement (within 12 months)
3. A group who have actively participated in the "assessment," reached consensus, and who are motivated for the upcoming improvement

I must confess a preference for assessing with the maturity-based models, like the SEI CMM, where software groups are given interim targets to shoot for on the road to software engineering excellence.

Product—For Example, Defects Pre- and Postship

As was explained above, a good process implies a good chance of a good quality product, but no guarantee! To ensure that the software product is indeed of high enough quality, a software group should measure the number of defects found pre- and postship. These figures should start to improve as the process improvement program kicks in. A group will not know how much the product quality is improving unless it is measured from the start. These measures are also an indicator that the process improvement is working as planned and delivering the correct benefit.

Resource/Cost—For Example, Size and Cost of Projects

Of course, it is possible to spend a lot of time and resource on process improvement and to have defect levels coming down . . . but at what cost? We could all probably get near zero defects if we had unlimited resources and time. More often than not we need to achieve improvements in process and product quality with the same resources. It is important therefore to measure the size, effort, and cost of software projects. The size measure can be either the traditional "lines of code" or the newer "function points." Alternatively, if you are convinced of neither and sick of the endless debates about the relative merits and demerits of each, then make up your own size measures. If you look long enough and hard enough you will find something. (See sample below.) So what, if you are not using an industry standard measure and cannot benchmark yourself against the "Top Ten" lines of code performers or the "Fortune 500" function point performers. All you really need is some way to compare your own performances (past, present, and future).

Revenue—For Example, Cost and Benefit

All this investment, time, and effort had better make you more money, give you happier customers, and keep your staff from getting frustrated with chaotic software practices. There is only one way to find out—measure!

Productivity—For Example, Size and/or Cost Over Time

Productivity is the measure that helps you combine some of the above measures in an appropriate fashion. Some companies are interested in how much functionality (measured in terms of size) they delivered in this period of time compared to the previous period of time. Many companies investing in process improvement would like to see more software being delivered, with less defects, in a shorter space of time, with the same or less resources!

Take Measures

There are no right or wrong measures to take . . . but it's vital to get a balanced set that

- accurately reflects past performance
- checks to see if the goals set in the "Initiating" stage were too severe or too easy;
- gives a baseline with which to compare future performances against;
- sets the direction and pace for the required improvement.

Getting a balanced set of measures implies measuring the different dimensions, for example, process, product, cost, resource/effort, size, time, etc. This stage of the improvement (the Diagnosing) is the time to take these measures. Many companies start the improvement with no measures and of those that do measure, it appears that the majority measure in the process dimension only. Clearly, the information may not be there for all dimensions but either a study can be made to extrapolate this information from the various sources within the company or a set of actions can be started to get this information measured over a period of months. Remember, we are not talking about measuring everything that moves in the software process but rather about taking a few key indicators. And finally as you will doubtlessly have heard and read elsewhere, you must not use these measures to judge individual performance within your organisations, as you will soon be receiving measures that you cannot rely on—and you would deserve no better!

Case Study: aimware Measures

aimware started the Quality definition and improvement project as soon as the business plan was written for the company. Provision was included for time and money in the business plan to invest in Quality, in addition to equipment and people. These initial endeavours were successful. As a result of these efforts, aimware is now registered to ISO 9001/TickIT. The certificate is valid from May 7, 1996, which is not bad since the company was only incorporated on December 7, 1995. All the typical components of a software quality management system are in place that one would expect from an ISO 9001/TickIT certificate, including but not limited to continuous improvement through audits and corrective actions. aimware sponsored an SEI CMM search conference in-house at the end of July 1996. This is a style of SEI assessment without a lot of the overhead of an official assessment. This brought further ideas and consensus on what to improve and these improvements required months to put in place. These are essentially the elements necessary to go from ISO 9001/TickIT to a strong SEI CMM Level 3.

Aimware plans to examine the records in the software engineering database, talk to the people on the ground, and take the various measures that accurately measure the past performance. This will enable aimware to recalibrate the process, product, cycle time, productivity, cost/benefit, and people objectives set at the Initiating stage of the improvement life cycle.

Summary—Diagnosing Stage

It is essential to have indicators like these before exiting this stage . . . successfully:

1. Process Quality and Maturity
2. Product Quality
3. Cycle Time (Time to Market)
4. Productivity
5. Cost and Business/Profit Benefits
6. People Factors

Establishing Phase

In this sample "IDEAL" Plan, the Establishing stage has the following four steps:
    Establishing Phase

1. Set Strategy and Priorities (refer to CMM and business priorities)
2. Finalise Improvement Infrastructure
3. Establish Process Improvement Teams (PITs)
4. Plan PIT team actions

Set Strategy and Priorities (Refer to CMM and Business Priorities)

An organisation that set objectives as part of the Initiating stage of the process improvement lifecycle should now know if they were realistic or not. The process objective might have included the achievement of CMM Level 4 within 12 months, as they thought they were a strong CMM level 3. But when the process measure was taken in the Diagnosing stage, they might have turned out to be a rock solid CMM Level 1. This then is the time to recalibrate the improvement objectives set at the Initiating stage against the real feedback of the Diagnosing stage. At the end of this step, the objectives or priorities have been finalised. Also, at this step the improvement strategy will need to be set. How many key areas will be tackled? What key areas will be tackled first? What tool support will be used? What will the project structure of the improvement be? How will training be delivered?

Finalise Improvement Infrastructure

The technology infrastructure needs to be put in place. It has been the author's experience that long-term institutionalisation of processes needs good tool support. People will adhere to best practices for the early part of the improvement but long term compliance requires automated support. This should not be so shocking to us software folk, who after all spend most of our waking working hours automating the business processes of others! The technology infrastructure should include a software engineering database that can house process defining artifacts such as policies, processes, standards, procedures, and templates, as well as process implementation artifacts such as plans, reports, defects, risks, issues, metrics, etc.

Establish Process Improvement Teams (PITs)

The improvements will not be delivered by accident. Resources need to be committed to the improvement. The improvement needs to be a real project with real people! It is best to staff these teams with people who want to improve and know something about the area in question. These teams need to be given some time and space to deliver on the required actions (e.g., on average a half a day each week).

Plan Process Improvement Team Actions

If the improvements are planned there is a good chance (no guarantees) that they will be delivered! These people are likely to be very busy and committed to the 'real' work of developing software. Thus this improvement work will be playing second fiddle most of the time. This means that as soon as the pressure comes on for the "real" work (maybe due to poor processes!) the secondary task of improvement will be shelved. It tends to be very hard for these people to switch back into the improvement team work after the latest crisis. Recognising this as fact, it becomes imperative to rigorously manage (i.e., plan and track) the improvement work as a mini project.

Case Study: aimware Priorities, Technology Infrastructure and Resources

Priority
aimware recalibrated the objectives from the Initiation stage against the results of the Diagnosis stage. From a process point of view, other subobjectives to aim were added at this stage as follows:

1. Control project performance quantitatively
2. Measure software product quality and set new targets for each project
3. Manage the achievement of these measurable targets on each project
4. Know the organisation is process capability in quantitative terms
5. Plan process management activities in quantitative terms

6. Identify common causes of defects and prioritise them
7. Plan and execute defect prevention activities systematically
8. Achieve organisationwide involvement in continuous process improvement
9. Systematically evaluate new technologies for quality and productivity improvements
10. Incorporate the relevant new technologies into the organisation

Technology Infrastructure

aimware has a software engineering database capable of managing the software process assets (e.g., policies, life cycles and procedures, etc.) as well as the artifacts created as a result of having these policies (e.g., defect reports, metrics, plans, etc.). This workflow-enabled database not only helps engineers do a better quality job, but it is also the way the job is done, so process deployment and fidelity is ensured.

PIT Teams

Based on the aimware experience of making the large effort to get to ISO 9001/TickIT, we needed one senior resource on the project 1 day a week and three other people 1 day every 2 weeks (or 10 percent of their time.) This serious commitment of resource is what gave aimware the early results. To achieve the next massive jump (e.g., SEI Level 4 or higher) aimware needed an even more serious resource commitment for the project. It is estimated as follows:

one Senior Quality Project Manager:	2 days/week for 3 years = 135 days
10 Engineers, Marketing reps, etc.:	0.5 day/week for 3 years = 675 days
One Senior Manager:	1 day/month for 3 years = 36 days

Allowing for just over 10 percent contingency, this is at least a 1000-person-day project which is roughly equivalent to 5 person years over 3 elapsed years. This amounts to a serious effort!

Summary—Establishing Stage

To successfully exit this stage you should have:

1. set the Improvement Strategy and recalibrated the Priorities;
2. finalised the Improvement Technical Infrastructure;
3. established Process Improvement Teams (PITs);
4. planned PIT team actions and committed real project resources.

Acting Phase

In this sample "IDEAL" Plan, the Acting stage encompasses the following six steps for each key area to be improved:
    Acting Phase

1. Define process, tool support, and measures
2. Plan pilots
3. Execute pilots
4. Plan company/group wide implementation
5. Installation
6. Support and Track installation

These six steps are likely to form the basis of the action plans or mini project plans for each of the Process Improvement Teams.

Define Process, Tool Support, and Measures

Using their collective wisdom and some basic research (e.g., on the Internet and through books and courses, perhaps) the team decides how best to perform the process in question. The process might be improved testing or improved project management or some such key area of the software process. The team is to be governed by the overall improvement objectives set earlier in the project. They draft a new process or amend an existing one in order to describe how the process should be performed in the future. The process also illustrates how tools should support the implementation of the process and also explains how it is measured, to verify success or otherwise.

Plan Pilots

The team knows that there are some rough edges in their new process and piloting the process on a real project will smooth these out. They also know that most projects are busy enough with the "real" work, so that they need to plan in advance to get the processes piloted. This does not always pose a large problem if the team leaders are also on the PITs. They generally find the time to try out their newfound ideas!

Execute Pilots

The processes are tried on the designated projects and they usually run into some difficulty, so it is important to have a process coach ready to help out, so that the good is not thrown out with the bad when the teams get frustrated.

Plan Company/Group Wide Implementation

What works in one area needs to be transferred to other areas—it does not seep out by accident! This step should go well if the different teams are feeding back to the larger group what worked and what did not work. At this stage it is a good idea to give the larger group the opportunity to review and improve the processes in question. They see which processes were useful and at the same time see that they had an opportunity to influence them. This helps them feel more ownership of the new processes.

Installation

The new processes are now ready to be rolled out to the other projects. Again it may not be possible to do this all at once, so a staged plan may be required.

Support and Track Installation

One cannot assume that the process will be in place overnight! Indeed, it might not be used at all. It will be vital to support, coach, and facilitate the new projects, when they are installing the new processes. It will also be necessary to check (through audits, reviews, etc.) how the new processes are being deployed. As a result of these checks you will find some combination of the following:

- People need coaching as they do not fully understand how to perform the process.
- People need "pushing" as they are not bothering to perform the new process.
- The process needs changing to better suit the environment.

Case Study: aimware "Acting" Out Process Deployment

Any practices found to be useful or better than those aimware currently has, make it into the process database and all staff are trained and coached on their use, so that the practices become everyday processes. It should also be noted that aimware personnel are all working on the one very large project with the subprojects being frequent deliveries. This has the advantage that whatever is determined by experiment to be successful, is implemented and piloted by everyone straight away. It does not, however, mean that the practices are institutionalised immediately. It will be aimware's challenge to ensure that all practices are identified and evaluated, and the good ones are committed to the organisation's process database and are implemented for each of the subsequent projects and deliveries.

aimware staff have weekly meetings where Quality Improvement is a standing agenda item. This "slot" promotes the best practices of late and follows up on outstanding improvements. Thus, aimware engineers on one subproject are engaged in auditing other subprojects and better practices are replicated through these events. aimware has external audits with the ISO 9001/TickIT registration and these audits also promote and disseminate best practices. aimware has a software engineering database where company processes can be stored, reviewed, and referred to. Changes and improvements are managed and disseminated through this system. There is a constant focus on process improvement as was described above and this continues to disseminate the quality message and the best practices. After this project aimware will doubtlessly have even better internal dissemination practices, as communication is a large focus of the higher levels of process maturity.

Summary—Acting Stage

At this stage companies need to tackle each required improvement in a systematic manner and the following steps seem as good as any the author has come across:

1. Define process, tool support, and measures
2. Plan pilots
3. Execute pilots
4. Plan companywide or groupwide implementation
5. Installation
6. Support and Track installation

Leveraging Phase

In this sample "IDEAL" Plan, the Leveraging stage has the following three steps:
Leveraging Phase

1. Analyse and document lessons learned
2. Consider taking a break
3. Start the next "IDEAL" Loop

Analyse and Document Lessons Learned

This phase can be as simple as it suggests, that is, some form of postmortem to analyse the results achieved. The results should be pretty evident if the measures were in place as described in the previous sections. What will be less evident is how people feel about the exercise, what they saw as the advantages and disadvantages, the costs and the benefits, etc. It is very important to see what lessons can be learned or what should be avoided on the next turn of the process improvement wheel. It is also a good idea to publish any successes, so that credit can be given where it is due.

Consider Taking a Break

It sometimes happens that organisations race up the software maturity ladder and get burned out very early on. It is often a better idea to let the improvements that were introduced really sink into the organisation before driving for the next level. This is not the same as saying that an organisation can defocus on software quality until the next great push. Quite the opposite, there will be a certain amount of effort and focus required from everyone to maintain the benefits realised during the recent push. It is a little like levels of physical fitness in that regard.

Start the Next "IDEAL" Loop

Small improvements should keep happening at this stage, through whatever processes were put in place. But in order to get a real push for another level of process maturity and thus performance, it will be necessary to lead the organisation through another spin of the "IDEAL" wheel.

Case Study: aimware Will Leverage the Results

What lessons do aimware hope to have learned by this stage?

aimware wants to show that it is possible to build Quality into the beginning of a company (and not just the beginning of a product/project life cycle). The firm wants to show that dramatic results can be achieved if young (and maybe not so young!) companies adopt a Quality approach from the outset. aimware wants to show that it is cheaper, easier, and faster for companies to do this, than to wait until they are forced to do so by customers and poor product quality levels.

What are dramatic results? aimware was registered to ISO 9001/TickIT 5 months to the day after the company was incorporated. The firm embraced Quality on Day 1. It has been profitable for the company to do so. aimware now wants to aim for higher levels of Quality and specifically for SEI CMM Level 4! Why?

- SEI CMM Levels 4 and higher are about measuring process and product and improving based on this quantitative feedback. aimware, like many companies, has good numerical controls on the business side—the firm now wants the same controls on the Quality side of the business . . . to make more *profit*!
- It is important and relevant for aimwares business.
- aimware staff are tired of people saying that Quality is impossible. As a group of professionals they have been helping companies improve their software quality for years and now they want to do it themselves . . . to show that it is not so impossible!
- To show that it can be done (and by a small company).
- Because it's out there!
- *It's profitable:* it's a professional way of executing and improving the performance and business
- *It's marketable:* it's a way of setting aimware apart from the competition
- *It's people conscious:* it's a mechanism to regulate the work rate, so that software staff have the time to produce first-class work and enjoy it (and not be always delivering to impossible schedules).

At the end of the project, aimware will have the capability to:

1. Announce to customers that they have achieved SEI CMM Level 4, thus giving them greater confidence in the company's capability and hopefully winning *more business* for aimware.
2. Deliver a far higher-quality product to customers, thus *reducing rework*.
3. Be capable of shipping two minor releases every year and 1 major release every 6 months and thus be faster to market, thereby being *more responsive* to the rate of change of customers' business.
4. Be far *more productive* by shipping at least 30 percent more functionality in each major release than is done today, thus delivering value for money to customers
5. Incur no major increases in headcount or technology spending over the current business plan to achieve the profit levels specified (i.e., the gains will be realised by increasing effort and focus on quality!) which will mean *remaining competitive.*
6. Attract and retain the best *people* to the company, as this is the key to achieving all of the other commercial objectives.

What next? Assuming aimware does reach SEI Level 4, the firm will be in a natural optimising or improving loop. The actual improvement decisions that will be taken will be decided based on the data that is being returned from the process and product quality. aimware will have defined a process for continuous process improvement companywide. Most improvements should at that stage come from the engineers through this process. Assuming that this all works according to plan, aimware will take a break and let the improvements really sink in. They may well look at ISO-SPICE after a few months or a year, if the business justification is there. Another model for continuous improvement that particularly interests them is the People Capability Maturity Model. This is all in the future!

Summary—Leveraging Stage

The following simple steps form the core of the Leveraging stage.

1. Analyse and Document lessons learned
2. Consider taking a 'break'
3. Start the next "IDEAL" Loop

Results Achieved—The Proof Is in the Eating!

aimware used the lessons above as the basis for the initial process improvement spin of the IDEAL wheel (December 1995 to December 1996). By using these lessons, aimware was recommended for ISO 9001/TickIT certification on the firm's fifth birthday (fifth month of operation, not fifth year—and not 5 months from the start of the ISO project—5 months from the incorporation of the company!).

We will have to wait a few years to see exactly how aimware fares when using this approach the second time out, as described above.

SUMMARY AND CONCLUSIONS

Many process improvements have failed—many more than have succeeded. Looking at the success indicators of the first five companies, it is possible to identify the ingredients of a profitable process improvement approach. The sample IDEAL model combines these and other required attributes into a life cycle of stages and steps to follow to achieve successful and profitable process improvement.

REFERENCES

1. W.S. Humphrey, *Managing the Software Process*, Addison-Wesley.

2. C.M. Paulk et al., *Capability Maturity Model for Software, Version 1.1, Report CMU/SEI-93-TR-24*, Software Engineering Institute, Pittsburgh, Pa.

3. CBA: *CMM Based Appraisal, SEI Lead Assessor Training*, Course Materials, Software Engineering Institute, Pittsburgh, Pa.

4. W.E. Deming, *Out of Crisis*, MIT Center for Advanced Engineering Studies, Cambridge, Mass., 1986.

5. B. Peterson, "News, Software Engineering Institute," *Software Process Improvement & Practice*, August 1995, pp. 68–70.

6. T. P. Rout, "SPICE: A Framework for Software Process Assessment," *Software Process Improvement & Practice*," Aug. 1995, pp. 56–66.

RECOMMENDED READING

W. S. Humphrey, *Managing the Software Process*, Addison–Wesley.

"If you don't know where you are, a map won't help"
Humphrey's book and subsequent versions of the CMM—the SEI's Capability Maturity Model have been the map to help those software souls who are lost! Read the book to understand the choices of destination open to your software group. A must for your bookshelf.

P. R. Scholtes, *The Team Handbook*, Joiner Associates.

Do you want to visit the first principles of quality management? Much of the software process work today is based on the labours of W. Edwards Deming. This book will lead you on an easy stroll through the first principles of quality and change management. The book is a practical book to working on or with teams. Many software folk grew up as "techies" and have no formal training as "teamsters." This book is full of instructions, illustrations, and worksheets, each one in turn showing how to implement quality improvement principles. Essential reading for the people dimension of the software process.

T. Gilb and D. Graham, *Software Inspection*, Addison–Wesley.

Anyone who knows Tom will tell you that he gives away all his slides, books, processes, etc. on disk at every course. He is generous with his material, to say the least. This book is no different. It contains everything from the Self-Assessment test, to the One Page Inspection Handbook, to sample procedures to blank forms to be used in the process. The book is a nice mix of the Inspection process and case studies of the process being applied in real companies. The foreword is written by Watts S. Humphrey and he is generous in his praise of the book. Enough said!

ACKNOWLEDGMENTS

The author would like to thank the five organisations for inviting him to be a part of their process improvement projects and for allowing him to publish some of their experiences, so that others might benefit from their efforts. The five companies profiled are:

1. "Factory": Motorola Manufacturing in Dublin
2. "Financial": Quay Financial Software, Dublin (a CSK company)
3. "Insurance": Voluntary Health Insurance, Dublin
4. "Telecom 1": Tellabs, Shannon, Co. Clare, Ireland
5. "Telecom 2": Telecom Eireann, Dublin

Chapter 16

Success Factors and Barriers for Software Process Improvement

Khaled El Emam, Pierfrancesco Fusaro
Fraunhofer, Germany

Bob Smith
ESI, Spain

INTRODUCTION ·

Software process assessments are a powerful tool for initiating Software Process Improvement (SPI). However, it is well known that not all assessment-based SPI efforts are successful. There have been a number of suggestions as to why this might be the case. Through systematic investigation of this phenomenon across many organizations, we can potentially identify the most critical factors that make or break an SPI effort. Results like these can be of wide practical utility to SPI professionals to plan and manage SPI efforts in their organizations, and consequently raise the success rate of SPI efforts. In 1995 the SEI reported a study that examined the factors contributing to successful SPI after a CMM-based assessment. Within the SPICE Trials, a similar study has been conducted with organizations that have performed assessments using the emerging International Standard on Software Process Assessment. In total, 18 organizations in Europe, Canada, and Australia participated, covering 19 assessments. They provided responses to a questionnaire 1 year after they conducted their assessments. The questionnaire characterizes the degree to which the organizations have been successful in their SPI efforts, and factors that are believed to be either detrimental or important for successful SPI. Using robust data analysis techniques, we identify which of these factors are most strongly related to the success of SPI efforts, and which factors have no impact. In the chapter we present the method of the study, the results, and a discussion of how to interpret the results and their limitations. We also compare our findings with those of the SEI study to identify the consistencies between them. We close with practical recommendations on ensuring successful SPI based on the results of both studies.

PARADIGMS

Two general paradigms for software process improvement have emerged in the software engineering community: the analytic and the benchmarking paradigms (see Chapter 7). With the analytic paradigm one relies on "quantitative evidence to determine where improvements are needed and whether an improvement initiative has been successful." The benchmarking paradigm, on the other hand, "depends on identifying an 'excellent' organization in a field and documenting its practices and tools." The benchmarking paradigm for process improvement is also referred to as assessment-based Software Process Improvement (SPI).

As well as identifying the strengths and weaknesses of an organization, one of the main goals of conducting a software process assessment is to "support, enable, and encourage an organization's commitment to software process improvement" [2]. If an assessment does not create a climate for successful SPI then it can be argued that it has not been an effective assessment.

It is clear, however, that many organizations need support with assessment-based SPI, and specifically, many require guidance on how to do it. For example, one survey conducted by the SEI identified that respondents had a high requirement for information on how to sustain organizational commitment to SPI, and on implementing organizational change [6]. Another survey of users of the emerging ISO/IEC 15504 Software Process Assessment international standard[1] found that they required further guidance on sustaining organizational commitment for SPI.[2]

A recent study conducted by the SEI empirically evaluated various organizational factors that were believed to promote or hinder successful SPI [7]. Such studies are very valuable because they identify the factors that are the most important to pay attention to during an SPI effort.

In this chapter we conduct a study similar to that of the SEI with another sample of organizations going through assessment-based SPI. In particular, our sample of organizations had used the emerging ISO/IEC 15504 international standard as the basis of their assessments. We conducted a follow up survey approximately 11 months after the assessment. Our results identified the factors that tend to have a big impact on the success of assessment-based SPI. We provide recommendations based on the results from our study and those from [7].

The following section provides some background information on the SEI study and on the specific hypotheses that we pose. A further section describes the data collection and analysis methods. In a subsequent section we present the results of our study and discuss their implications and limitations. We conclude with a summary of the chapter and directions for future work.

BACKGROUND

Review of the SEI Study

In the SEI survey [7], a sample of representatives from 61 assessments (in different organizations) were contacted. These assessments were conduced at least one year prior to the survey. Three respondents per organization were sought: (1) the project level software manager most knowledgeable about the assessment, (2) the most knowledgeable and well-respected senior developer or similar technical person available, and (3) an organizational level SEPG manager,

---

[1]More specifically, these were respondents who were involved in the SPICE Project, which developed the first version of the ISO/IEC 15504 document set.

[2]K. El Emam, J. N. Drouin, and V. Hailey, "A Survey of the Needs of the SPICE User Community," Presentation at the *International Syposium on Software Engineering Standards*, Walnut Creek, 1997.

or someone with equivalent responsibilities, if such a person existed. In total, responses from 138 individuals representing 56 of the 61 organizations were returned. This gives an average of about 2.5 responses per organization. The pooled observations from all three roles were used for the analysis, giving a total of 138 observations.

In that study, respondents were asked about the extent of success their organizations have had in addressing the findings and recommendations that were raised as a result of the assessment (we will refer to this variable as *SPI Success*). A series of questions were also asked about factors that may have an impact on SPI Success. These questions can be categorized as Organizational Factors or Barriers. Subsequently, bivariate associations between each of these factors and SPI Success were investigated.[3] Only the results of statistical testing of this association are presented. A chi-square test was used for these purposes.[4]

The unit of analysis about which conclusions ought to be drawn for this kind of study is the organization. However, since pooled observations are being used, the unit of analysis was actually the respondent. For inferential statistics this pooling effectively increases the number of observations. The power of statistical tests [11] is affected by the number of observations [1]. Therefore, the pooling artificially inflates the power of the statistical test, and increases the chances of finding a result that is statistically significant.

The implications of this are as follows. Relationships that were found to be statistically nonsignificant, even after the pooling, have quite strong evidence against them. However, relationships that were found to be statistically significant ought to be investigated further.

Based on this, the current study only considers the relationships that were significant in [7] to see if we find them to be statistically significant or not. The "Organizational Factors" and "Barriers" that were found to be statistically significant in [7] are summarized in Figure 16.1.

Hypothesized Relationships

In addition to the "Organizational Factors" and "Barriers" summarized in Figure 16.1, we also considered another set of factors in our study: "Process Factors". These are factors related to initiating an SPI effort and that have been claimed to be necessary for successful SPI. These are: creating an action plan for SPI, creating Process Action Teams, and piloting process changes.

Also, in the current study we consider two dependent variables instead of one:

- SPI Success: "how successfully the findings and recommendations of the assessment were addressed," and
- SPI Influence: "the extent to which the SPI effort was determined by the findings and the recommendations of the assessment." These two variables consider different aspects of success.

The former considers the extent to which the organization was able to act on the findings of the assessment. This is the same dependent variable that was presented in the SEI analysis [7].

The latter considers the extent to which the assessment results had an influence on the overall SPI effort of the organization. It has been suggested that assessment models in general do not cover all areas that sponsors of assessments and assessors believe they should cover.

---

[3] A bivariate association looks at the relationship between only two variables.

[4] A *chi-square* test, as applied in the SEI study, is a statistical test that is used to find out whether there is an association between two variables when both variables are on a categorical scale. In the bivariate analysis that was performed, one variable was either an *Organizational Factor* or a *Barrier*, and the second was *SPI Success*. They are categorical in the sense that they were responses to a question with a fixed number of response options (categories).

Organizational Factors
Senior Management Monitoring of SPI
Compensated SPI Responsibilities
SPI Goals Well Understood
Technical Staff Involved in SPI
SPI People Well Respected
Staff Time/Resources Dedicated to Process Improvement
Barriers
Discouragement About SPI Prospects
SPI Gets in the Way of "Real" Work
"Turf Guarding" Inhibits SPI
Existence of Organizational Politics
Assessment Recommendations Too Ambitious
Need Guidance About How to Improve
Need More Mentoring and Assistance

Figure 16.1. Organizational factors and barriers that were found to be related to SPI success in [7].

Therefore, it can be argued that SPI efforts should not be driven primarily by the findings of an assessment. However, in practice, assessments do identify weaknesses that are not in the assessment model. Therefore, one can also argue that it would be expected that SPI efforts should be driven by the findings of an assessment since the assessment findings would cover the relevant areas of the assessment model, as well as other identified weaknesses not covered in the assessment model.

If an organization is performing SPI based on multiple sources of information (that is, not only assessments), then the relationship between the three types of independent variables (Organizational Factors, Process Factors, and Barriers) and SPI Influence may be weak or nonexistent. If during our empirical study we *do not* find a relationship between these independent variables and SPI Influence, then the existence of multiple sources of information would be one of the possible interpretations.

We would expect that there would be a positive relationship between the organizational and process factors, and both dependent variables. Also, we would expect a negative relationship between the barriers and both dependent variables.

It is also reasonable to hypothesize that if the SPI effort is determined by the findings of the assessment, then there is a greater possibility of the assessment findings to be addressed. Therefore, we hypothesize a relationship between the two dependent variables. The overall model that we are testing is depicted in Figure 16.2. Note that we have put the organizational and process factors together as "Success factors."

While the relationship between the two dependent variables may seem intuitively obvious at first, there are two reasons why it ought to be modeled explicitly:

- A barrier or success factor may have an impact on SPI success only through SPI Influence. One of the advantages of testing such multistage models is to identify important independent variables that may be having an indirect effect on the final outcome.

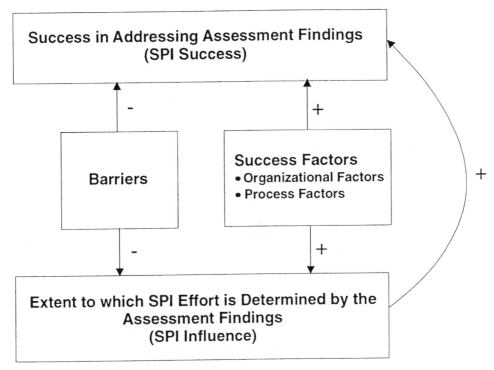

Figure 16.2.   Model being tested in our study.

- Consider the situation whereby an organization has multiple sources of information about the strengths and weaknesses of their practices in addition to assessments. Furthermore, consider that all the sources of information identify the same strengths and weaknesses. In such a case SPI Influence may be low but SPI Success may be high. Therefore, a positive relationship between SPI Influence and SPI Success is not as obvious as would initially seem. If we *do not* find a positive relationship, then the explanation above may be one of the possible interpretations.

The objective of our study was then to test all of the above hypotheses as depicted in the model of Figure 16.2.

RESEARCH METHOD

Data Collection

During Phase 1 of the SPICE Trials 35 assessments were conducted (see [5] for an overview of the SPICE Trials). A questionnaire, fashioned after the one reported in [7], was developed and sent to the Sponsors of assessments conducted during Phase 1 of the SPICE Trials. This was done approximately 11 months after the completion of data collection for the Phase 1 Trials.[5] A copy of the questionnaire is available from the authors. We used a persistent follow-up procedure to increase the response rate.

---

[5]The Phase 1 Trials lasted approximately 1 year. Therefore, assessments conducted at the beginning of the trials may have been performed up to 23 months before our survey.

We obtained responses from 18 sponsors (each questionnaire was answered by only one sponsor). One of the Sponsors was responsible for two assessments. Therefore, this gives a 54 percent response rate. This is a respectable response rate from which we can draw some tentative conclusions (see [10]). Of the 19 assessments that were covered by our responses, 5 were conducted in Australia, 1 in Canada, and 13 in Europe.

Data Analysis

Two types of analyses were performed: summarize the sample's achievements with assessment-based SPI, and investigate the bivariate relationships according to the model in Figure 16.2.

Sample Summary

The objective of this analysis was to get a better understanding of the sample's achievements with assessment-based SPI. We performed two general analyses. The first was to describe the sponsors' perceptions about their progress with SPI, and the second to evaluate the extent to which the assessment has promoted buy-in for SPI within the organization.

For the description of sponsors' perceptions, we used percentages of respondents who are supportive (as opposed to critical) of their experiences with assessment-based SPI. For example, assume that a question asked the respondents to express their extent of agreement to the statement, "The assessment was well worth the money and effort we spent; it had a major positive effect on the organization," and that it had the following four response categories: "Strongly Agree," "Agree," "Disagree," and "Strongly Disagree." As shown in Figure 16.3, the "Strongly Agree" and "Agree" responses would be considered supportive of assessment-based SPI, and the "Disagree" and "Strongly Disagree" responses would be considered to be critical of assessment-based SPI.

In addition, to determine the extent of buy-in, the respondents were requested to give their perceptions about the extent of buy-in for SPI for before the assessment and since the assessment. This was done for four different roles in the organization: participants in the assessment, the organization's technical staff, the organization's management, and the assessment sponsor. A Wilcoxon matched-pairs test was used to compare the "before" and "since the assessment" responses [14]. Hypothesis testing was all one-tailed since we expect the effect to be directional: an assessment increases buy-in.

Bivariate Relationships

We follow the general approach in the previous study of [7], whereby only bivariate relationships are considered. This is particularly important for the current study as the number of observations is not very large, therefore a multivariate analysis is not feasible.

In [7], a chi-square[6] test was conducted to determine if there was any association between the two variables. In this sense, the two variables were treated as being on a nominal scale with

Supportive Responses	Critical Responses
Strongly Agree	*Disagree*
Agree	*Strongly Disagree*

Figure 16.3.   Scheme for defining supportive and critical responses.

---

[6]We assume that the test used was Pearson's chi-square test in this discussion.

no ordering implied amongst the response categories. However, when there is an ordering amongst the response categories, a chi-square test does not take advantage of this information. A more powerful approach would treat the data as being at least on an ordinal scale.

We choose to use the Pearson correlation coefficient to evaluate the magnitude of bivariate relationships, and an approximate randomization procedure for inferential tests [4]. This has a number of advantages. First, it provides us with an easily interpretable measure of the effect size (i.e., how big a relationship is; the chi-square value is a measure of effect size but in general it is not easily interpretable). Second, it can be applied for situations when both variables are dichotomous (i.e., the phi coefficient), when only one variable is dichotomous (i.e., the point biseral correlation), and when both variables are continuous. This gives us one measure of effect size that is applicable for all of our variables. Third, by using an approximate randomization procedure for statistical inference [4], it is not necessary to make distributional assumptions.[7] Since this is not a commonly used procedure in software engineering empirical research, an overview of this procedure is provided in the Appendix.

Given that all our hypotheses are directional, we employ one-tailed tests. The empirical distributions generated using approximate randomization procedures are not necessarily symmetrical. Therefore, to calculate p values the appropriate tail is used (i.e., upper tail for a hypothesized positive correlation, and lower tail for a hypothesized negative correlation).

Interpreting the Results

Because of the small sample size that is used in our study, the results have to be interpreted carefully. The small sample size would potentially result in low power for the statistical tests. Therefore, if we find a result that is statistically significant then this is quite strong evidence that there is a relationship. If we find that a relationship is not statistically significant, then this may be due to low power, and further empirical investigation is necessary with larger samples.

Another important consideration is the magnitude of the relationship. Cohen [1] has provided some general guidelines for interpreting the magnitude of the correlation coefficient. He considers a value of 0.1 to be a small magnitude, a value of 0.3 to be a medium magnitude, and a value of 0.5 to be a large magnitude. Following these guidelines, we therefore consider values equal to or greater than 0.3 to be of practical significance. This also means that if a relationship is of practical significance but is not statistically significant, then this may be due to the low power, and therefore deserves further empirical investigation on a larger scale.

In our results we provide the values of the correlation coefficient (denoted as r). This should be useful for future researchers investigating these phenomena during the planning stage of their studies, especially in performing a power analysis to determine the appropriate sample size to use [1].

---

[7]Some Monte Carlo studies have found that the traditional parametric t test for determining the probability of obtaining a value as large as r under the null distribution (with r = 0) is quite robust to violations of the normality assumption [3]. However, many of these studies generate data from specific nonnormal distributions, and it is not clear to what extent these nonnormal distributions are representative of software engineering data. Another Monte Carlo study compares the Type I error rates of the parametric approach with the approximate randomization approach [12]. This found that the Type I error rates are similar for both approaches and both are liberal. Again, since we do not know the nature of the distributions of software engineering data, it is not clear to what extent these can be generalized to software engineering. To err on the conservative side, we still use the approximate randomization approach since it does not make distributional assumptions. So if the nonnormal distributions used in [12] are representative of software engineering data, then we do not lose or gain anything by using an approximate randomization test (in terms of Type I errors). If they are not representative of software engineering data, then the approximate randomization test is the safer option to take.

RESULTS

Description of Sample

We received a total of 18 responses to our questionnaire. However, some of the assessments were done too recently for any accurate information about the progress of SPI to be collected. Therefore, we excluded all observations that were conducted less than 30 weeks before the response time. This left us with data from 14 valid assessments and subsequent SPI efforts. We consider the response that covers two assessments as one observation since it was within the same organization. The variation of elapsed time since the assessment is given in Figure 16.4. This indicates that the organizations from which we have data have conducted their assessments from 44 to 90 weeks before responding to the questionnaire. This provides sufficient time for SPI efforts to have started and for some progress to have been made.

Our results on the perceptions about assessment based SPI are summarized in Table 16.1. Counter to what has sometimes been heard, all of the sponsors do not believe that software processes have become more bureaucratic due to their SPI efforts (see question 1). Neither do they believe that other important issues facing the organization have been neglected (see question 2). Almost all of the sponsors (93 percent) do not agree with the statement that things have deteriorated (see question 3). Almost three quarters of the respondents (77 percent) disagree with the statement that there has been disillusionment due to a lack of improvement (see question 4).

However, a sizable group of respondents (54 percent) believe that SPI is costing more than they have anticipated (see question 5). Approximately three-fifths do not believe that the assessment has had a major impact on the organization (see question 6). This may be due to there not being sufficient time since the assessment for SPI to have taken root, or may be due to the fact that the organizations have not been able to act on the recommendations and

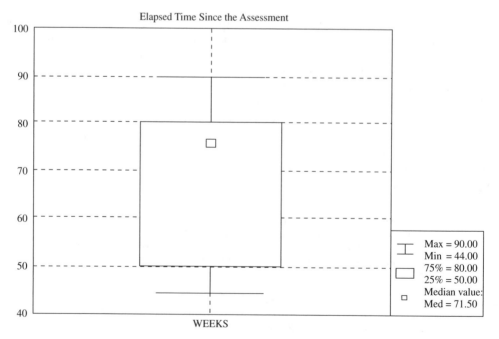

Figure 16.4.   Distribution of elapsed time since the assessment.

Table 16.1.   Percentages of Supportive and Critical Responses on the Assessment Based SPI

No.	Question	Supportive Response Categories	Critical Response Categories	Percentage Supportive
(1)	Software processes have become more rigid and bureaucratic; it is harder to find creative solutions to technical problems	• Strongly Disagree • Disagree	• Strongly Agree • Agree	(14/14) = 100%
(2)	Because of the assessment, we have neglected other important issues facing the organization	• Strongly Disagree • Disagree	• Strongly Agree • Agree	(14/14) = 100%
(3)	The assessment was counter-productive; things have gotten worse	• Strongly Disagree • Disagree	• Strongly Agree • Agree	(13/14) = 93%
(4)	There has been a lot of disillusionment over the lack of improvement	• Strongly Disagree • Disagree	• Strongly Agree • Agree	(10/13) = 77%
(5)	Process improvement is costing more than we expected	• Strongly Disagree • Disagree	• Strongly Agree • Agree	(6/13) = 46%
(6)	The assessment was well worth the money and effort we spent; it had a major positive effect on the organization	• Strongly Agree • Agree	• Strongly Disagree • Disagree	(5/14) = 36%
(7)	Nothing much has changed since the assessment	• Strongly Disagree • Disagree	• Strongly Agree • Agree	(4/14) = 28%
(8)	Process improvement was overcome by events and crises; other things took priority	• Strongly Disagree • Disagree	• Strongly Agree • Agree	(3/14) = 21%
(9)	Process improvement is taking longer than expected	• Strongly Disagree • Disagree	• Strongly Agree • Agree	(2/13) = 15%
(10)	Process improvement has often suffered due to time and resource limitations	• Strongly Disagree • Disagree	• Strongly Agree • Agree	(1/14) = 7%
(11)	Process change has been easier than we expected	• Strongly Agree • Agree	• Strongly Disagree • Disagree	(0/14) = 0%

findings from the assessment. To deal with this issue, we can consider the recommendation that it can be very important to make some "quick wins" to ensure that the assessment is seen to have had an impact and to maintain momentum.

This is further reinforced by the finding that only 28 percent disagree with the statement that nothing much has changed since the assessment (see question 7). It is interesting to note that 79 percent believe that SPI was overcome by events and crises (see question 8), indicating potentially that the organizations were not in a state that is ready for long-term SPI initiatives (i.e., there were other more important things to attend to). Some further reasons are forth-coming from the following responses: 85 percent believe that SPI is taking longer than expected (see question 9), and not surprisingly 93 percent believe that SPI suffered due to time and resource limitations (see question 10). None of the respondents believe that SPI has been easier than expected (see question 11).

Two general problems emerge from the above descriptive statistics. First, that expectations of organizational sponsors may not have been managed optimally, given that many believe that SPI costs more than expected, and is taking longer than expected. Second, in many cases insuf-ficient resources were made available for SPI, and insufficient priority was given to SPI. This can lead us to the conclusion that an SPI effort must be treated as a project in its own right with a plan, resources- and commitment. However, these problems do not seem to have damp-ened the enthusiasm within the organizations for assessments and assessment-based SPI.

One of the major objectives of an assessment is to create "buy-in" for SPI within the orga-nization. We investigated four different roles. The results of this are summarized in Table 16.2. It can be seen that participants in the assessment and the organization's technical staff increased their buy-in since the assessment. However, the organization's management and sponsor were not perceived to have increased their buy-in. This is evidenced by the results in the previous analysis, whereby the insufficient resources and priority were given to the SPI initiatives.

In summary then, the distribution of the success of assessment-based SPI efforts that are considered in this study are skewed, with more toward the low success end, and less observa-tions toward the high success end. The assessments did not manage to significantly increase the buy-in of the organization's management nor sponsor, and this explains the low priority and low resources given to the SPI effort in many of the assessments. However, this does not seem to have created disillusionment about SPI within these organizations. In addition, there is sufficient variation for conducting a bivariate analysis.

Bivariate Relationship Analysis

Our bivariate results are presented in a series of tables. In each table we provide a description of the factor that is hypothesized to have an impact on the dependent variable. This is the same

Table 16.2.   The Ability of the assessment to Create "Buy-in" for Various Roles in the Organization[1]

Role	p
Participants in the assessment	**0.00**
Organization's technical staff	**0.00**
Organization's management	0.18
Assessment sponsor	0.12

[1]Significant results are in the expected direction.

wording that is used in the questionnaire. This is then followed by the coefficient of correlation (r), and the one-tailed p value obtained from the approximate randomization procedure. When unexpected results were obtained, they are enclosed in the parentheses and explained in the text. For all tests we use an alpha level of 0.1 to determine statistical significance. When an r value is significantly different from zero, the p value is bolded for highlighting.

Of the organizational factors, we found that only "SPI goals being well understood" and "Technical Staff involvement in SPI" to be critical for success in addressing the findings from an assessment (see Table 16.3). All organizational factors were found to be critical for increasing the possibility that the findings from the assessment have a big influence on the overall SPI effort (Table 16.4).

None of the barriers were found to be related to success in addressing the findings from the assessment (see Table 16.5). In fact, for four of the barriers the correlation coefficient was

Table 16.3. Organizational Factors Affecting how Successfully the Findings and Recommendations of the Assessment were Addressed (SPI Success)

	r	p
Senior management monitoring of SPI	0.42	0.12
Compensated SPI responsibilities	0.29	0.22
SPI goals well understood	0.61	**0.03**
Technical staff involved in SPI	0.46	**0.07**
Staff Time/Resources dedicated to SPI	0.18	0.40
SPI people well respected	0.38	0.13

Table 16.4. Organizational Factors Affecting the Extent to which the SPI Effort was Determined by the Findings and the Recommendations of the Assessment (SPI Influence)

	r	p
Senior management monitoring of SPI	0.56	**0.04**
Compensated SPI responsibilities	0.57	**0.03**
SPI goals well understood	0.52	**0.05**
Technical staff involved in SPI	0.78	**0.00**
Staff Time/Resources dedicated to SPI	0.51	**0.06**
SPI people well respected	0.79	**0.00**

Table 16.5. Barriers Affecting How Successfully the Findings and Recommendations of the Assessment were Addressed (SPI Success)

	r	p
Discouragement about SPI prospects	-0.32	0.21
SPI gets in the way of real work	-0.09	(1.00)
"Turf guarding" inhibits SPI	-0.07	(1.00)
Organizational politics	-0.02	(1.00)
Recommendations too ambitious	-0.23	(0.62)
Need guidance about how to improve	-0.27	0.26
Need mentoring/assistance	0.23	0.30

in the opposite direction. However, it should be noted that if the value of r in the population is zero, some samples drawn from this population would have negative correlations. A two-tailed test indicated that the probability of finding an r value this large or larger approaches 1 (shown in parentheses in the table).

In Table 16.6 we see the results for the second dependent variable. There are two relationships that are statistically significant, however, they are in the wrong direction.[8] This particular situation has been discussed by Goldfried [8]. In such a situation, we ought to revert to a two-tailed test (at an alpha level of 0.1), however, the probability of rejecting the null hypothesis when it is in fact true needs to be adjusted. According to Goldfried's recommendation, we use an effective alpha value of 0.066. In this case, we find that both barriers have an impact on the extent of the SPI effort being influenced by the results of the assessment: "Organizational politics" and "Recommendations being to ambitious." (see Table 16.5).

Although unexpected, these findings do have a reasonable interpretation. The term "organizational politics" has a wide interpretation. However, one possibility is that such politics can prevent the organization from straying beyond the findings of the assessment (i.e., following the findings of the assessment is "safe" since SPI efforts based largely on these can be defended rationally). For the second barrier, it is plausible that ambitious recommendations drive organizations to try harder to address them, hence they become a major influence on the SPI effort.

The process factors' influence on success in addressing the assessment findings are shown in Table 16.7. As can be seen, "Creating process action teams" is a necessary ingredient for addressing the findings from the assessment. Piloting process changes does not have an influence, and neither does creating an action plan. The former may be because the organizations did not yet have an opportunity to progress far in their SPI efforts to have started many pilot programs. However, the lack of influence of action planning is a surprise result, which may be

Table 16.6. Barriers Affecting the Extent to Which the SPI Effort was Determined by the Findings and the Recommendations of the Assessment (SPI Influence)

	r	p
Discouragement about SPI prospects	-0.30	0.20
SPI gets in the way of real work	0.18	(0.60)
"Turf guarding" inhibits SPI	-0.26	0.17
Organizational politics	0.54	**(0.05)**
Recommendations too ambitious	0.51	**(0.08)**
Need guidance about how to improve	-0.23	0.30
Need mentoring/assistance	-0.34	0.17

Table 16.7. Process Factors Affecting How Successfully the Findings and Recommendations of the Assessment Were Addressed (SPI Success)

	r	p
Creating an action plan	0.43	0.15
Creating process action teams	0.55	**0.06**
Piloting process changes	0.06	0.61

[8]This means that the direction of the relationship is opposite to the one that was originally hypothesized.

due to the low power of the statistical test (note that the magnitude of this relationship is not small at 0.43).

None of the three process factors seem to be important for increasing the extent that the assessment findings influence the overall SPI effort[9] as shown in Table 16.8. This could suggest that these activities are being performed without a full understanding of what SPI is aiming to achieve. Perhaps these recommended activities are being performed to follow the "accepted wisdom," but also perhaps without training and without understanding what the assessment results really mean to the organization. This could be important in explaining why a large proportion of assessment-based SPI efforts do not achieve their potential. Certainly further investigation is required to identify what factors will help an organization implement SPI successfully.

The relationship between the two dependent variables had an r magnitude of +0.48, and a p value of 0.08. This is statistically significant at an alpha level of 0.1. This indicates that the more the SPI effort is determined by the assessment findings, the greater the possibility of the findings being addressed.

Table 16.8.   Process Factors Affecting the Extent to Which the SPI Effort was Determined by the Findings and the Recommendations of the Assessment (SPI Influence)

	r	p
Creating an action plan	0.40	0.12
Creating process action teams	0.39	0.19
Piloting process changes	0.40	0.12

Recommendations

The recommendations presented here are focused on maximizing the effectiveness of software process assessments for the purpose of SPI. Assessments are considered effective if their findings determine an organization's SPI effort, and if the organization is successful in addressing the findings of the assessment.

We found that the more an organization's SPI effort is determined by the findings of an assessment, the greater the extent to which the assessment findings are successfully addressed. Therefore, it is important to ensure that the SPI effort is determined by the assessment findings.

To increase the possibility that the assessment's findings determine the SPI effort of the organization, the following factors were found to be important:

- Senior management monitoring of SPI
- Compensated SPI responsibilities
- Ensuring that SPI goals are well understood
- Technical staff involvement in SPI
- Staff and time resources should be made available for SPI
- SPI people are well respected

---

[9]However, note that this is a tentative conclusion since the magnitude of all three relationships is greater than 0.3. Not finding the relationships statistically significant may be due to the small sample sizes.

Surprisingly, it was found that increased so-called "organizational politics" and "ambitious recommendations" from the assessment tend to increase the extent to which the SPI effort is determined by the assessment findings and recommendations. Therefore, these two factors are not necessarily a bad thing!

Ensuring that the SPI effort is determined by the assessment findings is not the only factor that affects the success in addressing the assessment findings. Other factors that should be taken into account are:

- Ensuring that SPI goals are well understood
- Technical staff involvement in SPI
- Creating process action teams

In fact, the first two factors are critical for both our dependent variables, and can therefore be considered as important ingredients of a successful assessment-based SPI initiative.

These recommendations present an initial empirically based road map for ensuring successful SPI. However, there is also the possibility that some of the factors found nonsignificant in our study are important. Our small sample sizes may have contributed toward their nonsignificance in the statistical sense. Therefore, future empirical investigations ought to consider closely these factors. Specifically, the following factors had relationships with the success in addressing the assessment findings and recommendations whose magnitude was sufficiently large, but were not statistically significant, possibly due to the small sample sizes:

- Senior management monitoring of SPI
- SPI people well respected
- Discouragement about SPI prospects
- Creating an action plan

The following factors had relationships with the extent to which the assessment findings influenced the SPI effort whose magnitude was sufficiently large, but were not statistically significant possibly due to the small sample sizes:

- Discouragement about SPI prospects
- Need for mentoring and assistance
- Creating an action plan
- Creating process action teams
- Piloting process changes

Limitations

The particular approach we have used for data analysis does not make large sample approximations, and hence addressing some of the potential difficulties in analyzing a small data set such as the one that we had in this particular study. However, one limitation in this kind of study, where many bivariate relationships are investigated, is the heightened probability of obtaining a statistically significant result by chance, by virtue of conducting so many inferential tests. This can be addressed by using, for example, a Bonferroni procedure (see [13]). But if we do so then the adjusted alpha level would be quite low, and with small sample sizes the power of statistical tests would be substantially diminished. Therefore, just as this is a follow-up study of [7], it is important that the current study be replicated to increase our confidence in the findings and to address limitations. A further motivation for replication is to increase our confidence in the generalizability of our findings.

CONCLUSIONS

The objective of this study was to investigate some of the important success factors and barriers to successful assessment-based SPI. Our study is a follow-up study to one reported by the SEI in 1995. We used data from the SPICE Trials collected through a survey. In total we used data from 14 organizations that have conducted an assessment. An initial multistage causal model explaining SPI success was developed and tested. This model may be a useful starting point for further research on this topic.

Our results indicate that many organizations struggle with achieving successful SPI based on process assessments. The two most critical success factors were found to be that the SPI goals are well understood and the involvement of technical staff in the SPI effort. These two factors were also found to be important in the SEI study.

Of interest as well are the questions raised by this study. Combined with the results of the SEI study, we have only identified a small number of success factors and no important barriers to SPI success. Given the investmant by organizations in assessment based SPI, it is of critical importance to further improve our understanding of assessment based SPI: we could not find support for many of the commonly cited recommendations about how to go about a software process improvement effort.

REFERENCES

1. J. Cohen, *Statistical Power Analysis for the Behavioral Sciences*, Lawrence Erlbaum Associates, 1988.

2. D. Dunaway and S. Masters, *CMM-Based Appraisal for Internal Process Improvement (CBA IPI): Method Description*, Software Engineering Institute, CMU/SEI-96-TR-007, 1996.

3. S. Edgell and S. Noon, "Effect of Violation of Normality on the t Test of the Correlation Coefficient," *Psychological Bulletin*, Vol. 95, No. 3, 1984, pp. 576–583.

4. E. Edgington: *Randomization Tests*, Marcel Dekker, 1980.

5. K. El Emam, J.N. Drouin, and W. Melo, eds., *SPICE: The Theory and Practice of Software Process Improvement and Capability Determination*, IEEE Computer Soc. Press, 1998.

6. D. Goldenson, *Software Process Needs Analysis: Customer Perspectives*, Software Engineering Institute, June 1994.

7. D. Goldenson and J. Herbsleb, *After the Appraisal: A Systematic Survey of Process Improvement, its Benefits, and Factors that Influence Success*, Software Engineering Institute, CMU/SEI-95-TR-009, 1995.

8. M. Goldfried, "One-Tailed Tests and Unexpected Results," *Psychological Review*, Vol. 66, No. 1, 1959, pp. 79–80.

9. P. Good, *Permutation Tests: A Practical Guide to Resampling Methods for Testing Hypotheses*, Springer–Verlag, 1994.

10. M. Igbaria, J. Greenhaus, and S. Parasuraman, "Career Orientations of MIS Employees: An Empirical Analysis," *MIS Quarterly*, Vol. 15, No. 2, 1991, pp. 151–169.

11. E. Noreen, *Computer-Intensive Methods for Testing Hypotheses: An Introduction.* John Wiley & Sons, 1989.

12. J. Rasmussen, "Computer-Intensive Correlational Analysis: Bootstrap and Approximate Randomization Techniques," *British Journal of Mathematical and Statistical Psychology*, Vol. 42, 1989, pp. 103–111.

13. J. Rice, *Mathematical Statistics and Data Analysis*, Duxbury Press, 1995.

    S. Siegel and N. J. Castellan, *Nonparametric Statistics for the Behavioral Sciences*, McGraw-Hill, 1988.

15. Visual Numerics, *C Functions for Statistical Analysis*, Visual Numerics, Inc., 1996.

APPENDIX

In this appendix, we give an overview of the approximate randomization procedure for testing hypotheses. This procedure does not make distributional assumptions, as do parametric tests of hypotheses. Here we only consider the case of the correlation coefficient as a test statistic.

One must first define a null hypothesis. Then, one must generate the null distribution for this hypothesis. As with parametric tests, one then calculates the p value by considering the lower, upper, or two tails of this null distribution. The p value is the probability that a value as large (small) or larger (smaller) could have occurred under the null hypothesis.

The null hypothesis being tested is that the two variables (independent and dependent) are not associated with each other. If this is the case, then any of the possible permutations of the variables against each other is equally likely. An exact randomization procedure would list all of these permutations. Except for small samples, this exact procedure is not feasible. Therefore, approximate randomization tests are employed. These randomly shuffle one of the variables against the other, and the statistic (in this case r) is computed for each shuffle. The shuffles are repeated a large number of times and r is computed for each. The computed values of r are then null distribution from which the p value is calculated. The random shuffling essentially samples from all possible permutations.

A flowchart illustrating the procedure is depicted in Figure 16.5. This is for an upper-tail test using the correlation coefficient. After each shuffle, it is determined whether the pseudo r value is equal to or greater than the obtained r value (i.e., the value without shuffling). If this is the case, a counter, *nge* in the flowchart, is incremented. After NS iterations the proportion of times that the pseudo r was equal to or larger than the obtained r is the p value. This calculation of the p value has to be adjusted slightly since the obtained value of r is also one of the possible permutations. This adjustment, however, has little effect when NS is large.

For the current study a program for conducting approximate randomization tests was developed using a commercial statistics library [15]. The random shuffle was implemented following a procedure described by Good [9]. For all tests, an NS value of 999 was used.

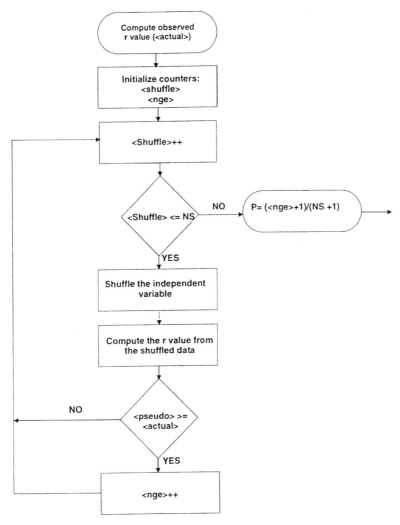

Figure 16.5. Flowchart showing the approximate randomization procedure for an upper-tail test using the correlation coefficient.

Chapter 17

Applying Quantitative ISO Auditing Techniques— The BICO Approach

Susanne Lanzerstorfer
QUEST, Unterstinkenbrunn 78, A–2154, Austria

Hans Scherzer
APAC, Mariahilfer Straße 89A, A–1060, Vienna, Austria

INTRODUCTION

So far assessment and certification are kept as different approaches. Typical arguments are: "While SEI/CMM, SPICE, etc. offer an improvement path, ISO 9001 just offers a certificate without guidance to create an improvement cycle by stepwise achieving higher grades maturity—from the initial level up to the optimising level." The major question behind the BICO project was "Why not combine the ISO 9001 certification approach with the maturity level architecture?"

In this case an ISO 9001 audit does not only result in a set of nonconformances but in detailed process maturity profile (similar to the one in BOOTSTRAP [5, 11]) for the 20 ISO 9001 attributes providing information about both, the nonconformances and the improvement potentials in the different attributes.

This chapter provides an overview of the Benchmarking and ISO Combined (BICO) method, the development of which was supported by the Austrian government. Most assessments and/or certification audits are very expensive, whereas the BICO approach was to develop the assessment and certification methodology especially for small and middle-sized firms, with lean assessments, and ISO 9001 certification support, at moderate prices (compared to SEI [9], BOOTSTRAP [5], and others [6] [12]) affordable also for small firms. This approach was driven by the fact that more than 70 percent of the Austrian software market consists of very small software firms, and a large computer firm in Austria is usually smaller than a middle-sized firm in countries like Germany. This specific need led to the development of BICO.

THE BICO METHOD

General

BICO is a tool-supported, quantitative method for assessments [1] and process improvement, which is in conformance with ISO 9000 and takes into account SPICE and SEI/CMM. Until now, the BICO methods and tools are applicable in environments, in which development plays an important role. The BICO method is based on an acknowledged quantitative assessment model and results in an ISO 9001-conformant questionnaire. A toolset that allows fast compilation and easy-to-understand visualisation of the data collected during the audit, supports the process improvement. The quantitative assessment results reveal the actual status and identify the improvement potential. The BICO model guides the target organisation on the way toward higher quality and productivity by process improvement based on the assessment results and its business goals.

BICO was developed by APAC in cooperation with QUEST, partly funded by the Austrian authority, and mainly addresses the needs of very small organisations. QUEST was responsible for the verification and validation and the field tests. BICO shall either be applied by process improvement experts within the target organisation or by a consultant. With regard to the figures concerning the number of deployments, it has to be taken into account that APAC is a very small company of about 10 employees. As this chapter concentrates on the deployment of BICO, only a short overview of BICO will be presented.

BICO Life Cycle

BICO is not only a method and a toolset for quantitative process assessments but also supports continuous process improvement. It is based on the Plan-Do-Check-Act [10] approach. The major goal of the BICO process is to improve quality and productivity. The BICO material is structured into the following modules (Figure 17.1):

Phase Independent:

BLCM-PM	Project Management Module
BLCM-PC	Project Controlling Module
BLCM-QA	Quality Assurance Module (includes overall V&V, BLCM metrics, and BLCM V&V)
BLCM-DB	Database Module (data stored without reference to the source)
BLCM-PRO	Product Management Module
BLCM-TE	Training and Education Module
BLCM-IF	Interface Module (providing interfaces to map the results on other quality assurance system models)

Phase Dependent:

BLCM-PIP	Process Improvement Preparation; Planning and Design of the Improvement Process
BLCM-PI	Process Improvement Module
BLCM-A	Audit Module (includes the tool ASAP-F and ISO 9001-conformant questionnaire)
BLCM-AN	Analysis Module (includes the evaluation tool ASAP-B)

Selection of the
improvement measures

Taking into account the rule that for any process
- the organisation is more important than the method
- the method is more important than the technology

The prioritising of the improvement measures is based on:
- the audit results
- the business goals
- the risk involved, if the measure is not implemented
- the return of investment gained by the implementation of the improvement measure

---

Figure 17.1.   Selection of measures and prioritisation.

The module BLCM-A supports the following types of audits: quality system audit (entire organisational unit), project quality system audit (project), project status audit (plan vs. actual schedule, costs, and resources), evaluation of the process capability of proposers (at large international companies, competitive invitations to tender), and any combination of the types mentioned above.

This list and the short description of the contents of the modules give an overview of the scope of the BICO method.

The BICO improvement process is based on the rule $O > M > T$ which means that organisational aspects are more important than methodology, and methodology is more important than technology.

Much attention is paid to the process of the selection of the improvement measures and process improvement planning.

The BICO Audit Process

Usually the BICO process starts with a BICO audit. The BICO audit process, which is well-defined and documented in the module BLCM-A, is supported by a tool that runs on a small palmtop PC for onsite data collection. The tool accepts questionnaires in several formats without any restrictions on the contents or structure as long as the questionnaire is compliant with the required format and syntax. APAC uses a proprietary questionnaire that takes into account ISO 9001 [2], ISO 9000-3 [3], and CMM/SEI V1.1 [9] and ESA PSS05 [4]. Two different questionnaires are used for project assessments and system assessments. Both questionnaires consist of about 200 questions. The compilation and visualisation of the results is performed with another tool that runs under Windows 95 and offers state-of-the-art simulation and visualisation. The compilation is based on a proprietary algorithm that allows scoring in higher levels, even if the requirements of lower levels are not fully satisfied. The output may be structured in several ways, the most commonly used structure being in according with ISO 9001 [2,3,7,8] attributes. The resulting profiles will be discussed in the case study. The scoring ranges from 1 to 5 with a granularity of 0.25.

The process was designed to meet the requirements of very small or small organisations that cannot afford a full-scale SEI-assessment [9] or similar expensive approaches. The main purposes of most of the BICO audits are to identify weaknesses and improvement potentials, to visualise the results in a way that everybody understands, and to establish buy-in for the process improvement process. Most of the assessed organisations design and produce software as well as hardware. The disadvantage of this approach is that the results are not comparable with the results of other assessment methods without additional data selection and compilation. The benefit of this approach is that the customer's needs are met. The BICO method, being based on the experience of the authors, shows that process improvement in small organisations can be achieved more efficiently and effectively if the entire organisation is involved. The BICO audit process also resembles the experience of the authors, in that strict accuracy doesn't pay in terms of the necessary effort required to achieve it. It is much more important to trigger improvement, to buy-in, and to identify large improvement potentials. If one visualises the progress with a profile 1 year later, this is more help in increasing the motivation to support the improvement process than strict accuracy.

Under normal conditions the BICO audit method allows assessment of an organisation of about 20 employees within the following time constraints: planning of the audit, and evaluation of the quality management documentation, 8 hours; on-site assessment, 8 hours; data compilation and report generation, including a proposal for process improvement, actions, 8 hours; presentation and discussion of the results, 4 hours.

Benefits of BICO

If applied successfully, the BICO method offers the following benefits:

- The audit process results are strength/weakness profiles of the system and of the evaluated projects.
- The profiles visualise clearly, where the ISO 9001 requirements are satisfied, and give the customer enough information to start with process improvement.
- As BICO maps the results onto the SEI Capability Maturity Model, BICO doesn't stop at the ISO 9001 level but supports the customers on their way to TQM.
- A well-defined method helps to identify the most effective improvement measures.
- BICO helps to increase quality and productivity.
- The benchmarking tells the assessed organisation absolutely how they rate independently and also rate in comparison with their competitors.

DEPLOYMENT OF BICO

General

During the early stages of the BICO project the typical target organisation was identified. The major characteristics are:

- Less than 150 employees
- Awareness for quality assurance (some of them were already ISO 9001 certified)
- Software development is an important part of their activities, but typically they deliver systems that also include hardware and engineering services
- High-tech products (e.g., image processing, air traffic control, large and high-performance lottery systems, aerospace business)

As the BICO project was only scheduled for one year, only part of the BICO procedures could be validated during the project. The audit procedure was excessively validated during the project, and the feedback was taken into account for the final product. The validation of all other procedures and material needs more time and depends on a target organisation. To improve the quality of the product, APAC installed lessons learned database, where not only the feedback of the application of BICO is stored, but also identified lessons learned from similar approaches as far as available through publications and discussions. APAC has installed a change board that meets twice a year to review the lessons learned and to agree upon updates of BICO.

BICO Audits

Originally, the BICO audit module was designed to perform quality system audits. During the first deployment of BICO, it was identified that there was also a need for project status audits (plan vs. actual of schedule, costs, and resources), evaluation of the process capability of proposers (from large international competitive invitations to tender) and any combination of the types mentioned above. The BICO audit module was updated to meet the requirements of the additionally identified types.

The more organisations, issuing invitations to tender, realised that low process capability of the contractor substantially increases the project risk, the more they looked for a quantitative method to evaluate the proposers process capability. APAC and QUEST developed a handbook for the quantitative evaluation of the process capability of proposers, which is based on the BICO audit module. Of course, a necessary precondition for the successful application of this handbook is that the call for proposals defines process requirements, which will be applicable during the project. The proposers are required to show in the proposal how they intend to meet these requirements. The evaluation of the process capability of the proposers is mainly based on the information provided in the proposal.

The following BICO audits have been performed from 1995 to 1996 in the organisations mentioned in Table 17.1:

QMSA	Quality System Audit	11
PQMSA	Project Quality Management System Audit	15
PSTA	Project Status Audit	18
PRPA	Evaluation of the Process Capability of Proposers	5
MIXA	Any combination of QMSA, PMSA, PSTA	1
	TOTAL	39

The audits were split among nine organisations. Table 17.1 provides some information about the target organisations:

Table 17.1

Code	Employees	ISO 9001	Area	Audits	Trigger
A	20	No	Image processing	QMSA	Customers, ISO 9001
B	7	Yes	Quality engineering	QMSA, PMSA	Process improvement
C	12	No	Banking devices	QMSA, PMSA	Customers
D	100	Yes	Lottery systems	QMSA, PMSA	Process improvement
E	6	No	Embedded systems	QMSA	Process improvement, ISO 9001
F	150	Yes	Air traffic control	QMSA, PMSA, PSTA	Process improvement
G	500	No	Air traffic control	PRPA	Risk minimisation
H	100	No	Air traffic control	PRPA	Risk minimisation
I	20	No	Air traffic control	PSTA, MIX	Customer

Additional data was collected at each environment but no correlation between the collected data and the results could be identified.

Accuracy of the results. As already explained above, accuracy was sacrificed for efficiency. An accuracy of about +20 percent accuracy is expected. The accuracy was tested by interviewing different people of the same environment. Most of the audits were performed by two auditors, who scored independently. Comparing the results, this goal was met with three exceptions.

Correctness of the results. Our interpretation of correctness in this case is based on the premise that the profile will visualise the status of the audited environment in a way that doesn't give rise to severe contradiction at the presentation. This goal was met with one exception.

The influence of incorrect answers on the result is not particularly important, as the auditor asks different people the same questions and respectively discusses the same topic with them. Furthermore, the answers they give are verified by objective means as much as possible (e.g., documents, quality records). To draw the correct conclusions and to derive the next steps, the collected data and the results were accurate enough. Normally, the target organisation will start process improvement in the areas with the highest improvement potential and the highest potential for return of investment, and this is again an argument for not concentrating on strict accuracy.

No correlation of strengths and weaknesses with the characteristics of the environment of the target organisations were detected, but the following weaknesses were found in every organisation at the first system audit, before the improvement process began:

- Verification and validation
- Design
- Statistical methods (metrics)

Correlation of system maturity with project maturity. A correlation of the product quality with the process maturity could only be identified in the case study described below. This does not mean that the product quality does not correlate with process maturity, but that there was not enough data to verify this.

Comparison of the results of project audits with the quality system audit of the same organisation. In each project areas could be clearly identified, where the process maturity of the project was much higher than the system level. In some cases, project practices in some areas were really state-of-the-art. This very well supports the approach, to base organisationwide process improvement on a project's best practice.

The most significant benefits of the BICO audits were:

- Accurate high-level management information
- Buy-in
- Visualisation of the maturity level supports easy understanding of the current status
- Easy identification of improvement potential
- Quantitative basis for the next steps
- Comparison of the actual profile with former profiles clearly showed success and failure of process improvement programs

We derived the following conclusion from our audit experience:

Common sense is the most valuable tool of a process improvement expert. If you are an expert, you don't need a quantitive assessment to identify major improvement potentials, but you need the visualisation of the results to buy-in. And anyway, it is a reliable metric to measure your own qualification!

Process Improvement Based on BICO Audits (BICO Life Cycle)

APAC and QUEST have performed 10 quality system audits until now. Five audits were followed by process improvement actions. Three audits were a follow on action after process improvement actions. With one exception, the audits didn't really trigger the process improvement activities as all organisations had already decided to do some process improvement when they ordered the audits. The BICO audits helped with buy-in, to communicate the actual status, and made it possible to measure the improvement some time later. One organisation, a branch of a very large company, ordered the BICO audit as a customer requested it. As the customer realised the low maturity level of the contractor he insisted on process improvement actions. Under the customer's pressure the organisation started some process improvement actions but never began them seriously. The intention was to make the customer believe that the situation had improved. It is no surprise that the initiative failed and the project crashed.

At four organisations APAC or QUEST supported the improvement process. All improvement processes that were supported by APAC or QUEST were successful, which means that quality and productivity were improved. One organisation decided to hire a student who should implement an ISO 9001 conform process. It resulted in a very long process that is as yet not finished but success can be expected.

As an improvement process is mainly a management process and the organisation had not the necessary human resources de facto, APAC or QUEST managed the process. Only one organisation explicitly ordered the management of the process improvement. It can be said that without a professional management none of the organisations would have reached the goal so soon.

Within all organisations that improved their process the consultancy effort was above 300 hours. The benefit of the strong involvement of a consultant is the know-how and power behind the measures but the disadvantage is that the system is mostly designed by the consultant and he knows most about the system. A good consultant will try to involve the customer as much as possible.

The goals of the customers to start with process improvement were to improve quality and productivity. Only one customer identified the ISO 9001 certificate as the major goal.

CASE STUDY

Background

This is a success story and shows what can be achieved by applying an adequate method for process improvement. In all honesty, if we could tell a failure story, we would rather tell a success story. But, we have only experienced success.

The first BICO audit was performed at the target organisation in March 1995. Based on the results of the audit, the auditors defined, together with the quality assurance manager, a 2-year process improvement (PI) program. The major PI activities were scheduled for the first year. The second year was dedicated to consolidation and fine-tuning. During the third year follow-up project status audits (PSTA) were organised to ensure that the process improvement on system level is put into practice at the projects. After 1 year of process improvement activities, a second BICO audit clearly showed what was achieved. The results of the follow-up project audits showed that most project managers have put into practice the improved practices but it also showed that changes are not possible if they are not supported by the majority of the affected.

Before the first BICO audit, the auditors had already supported the company in project-related quality assurance matters, but knowledge of the entire organisation was very limited.

Target Organisation

Short description of the target organisation:

Frequentis Nachrichtentechnik Gesellschaft M.B.H

Vienna/Austria

- 450 employees
- 12,200 million ATS turnover
- Air Traffic Control Systems, Command and Control Centres, Terrestrial European Trunked Radio (TETRA)
- Program oriented
- Very strong management commitment
- Holds ISO 9001 certificate for 5 years

Starting Point

FREQUENTIS was one of the ISO 9001 pioneers in Austria and achieved ISO 9001 certification in 1993. It is part of the company philosophy to outsource tasks which can be performed by a subcontractor at least as well as internally. It is a very good idea to subcontract internal audits for the sake of independence. At FREQUENTIS, a system audit is performed twice a year, and every large project has to be audited at least once during the project life cycle. For 1998 the General Management of FREQUENTIS requires for large projects with more than 5 percent of software development a project status audit twice a year. Every year, one system audit is performed as a normal ISO 9001 internal audit by another consultant and the second system audit is performed by the authors with the BICO method.

In March 1995 the first BICO audit took place.

Some surrounding information:

- The audit was planned for 3 1/2 days.
- The audit was preceded by the evaluation of the quality management documentation.
- The audit partners were informed about 2 weeks in advance.
- The audit team consisted of two BICO auditors and the quality manager of FREQUENTIS.
- The audit was fully in accordance with ISO 9000.

Scope of the audit:

- Quality system audit including quality system documentation
- Project quality system audit of four projects

The audit results were delivered to the quality manager for review within 3 days and consisted of profiles for the quality management documentation, the quality management system implementation, one profile for each audited project and the 30-page audit report.

The result of the first BICO audit of the quality management system at FREQUENTIS in March 1995 clearly showed the improvement potential (Figures 17.2 and 17.3).

Figure 17.2 shows the results of the nonsegment assessment, and Figure 17.3 the average values from the essessed projects.

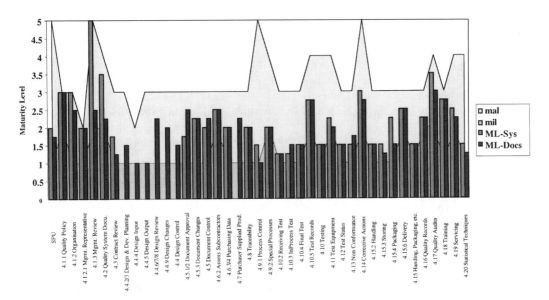

Figure 17.2.   Organisational ISO 9001 maturity profile of Frequentis in 1995.

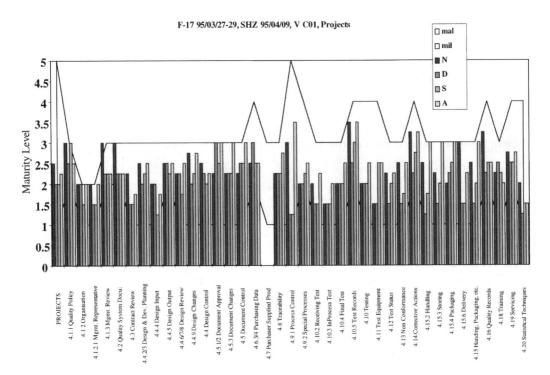

Figure 17.3.   Project average ISO 9001 maturity profile of Frequentis in 1995.

Explanation of the major elements of Figure 17.2, visualising the scores of the quality management system documentation and the quality management system implementation:

- The light grey area shows the possible scores depending on the attribute.
- The middle grey bars show the values scored by the quality management system documentation.
- The dark grey bars show the scores of the implementation of the quality management system.
- At the bottom of the chart is the ISO 9001 quality attribute, to which the bars belong, is shown.

Explanation of the major elements in Figure 17.3, visualising the scores of four projects:

- The light grey area shows the possible scores depending on the attribute.
- The bars show the values scored by the different projects.

Summary of the interpretation of the profiles outlined in Figures. 17.2 and 17.3.

- Poor quality management documentation.
- Project independent implementations mostly do not exceed the scoring of the quality management documentation.
- Projects' processes are much more mature (with one exception).
- The following weak areas could be identified in all projects: contract review, design input, document control (includes control of hardware and source code as well), special processes (safety, reuse, embedded systems), testing, delivery, and metrics (statistical techniques).

From the audit, the auditors knew that the deficiencies in the projects are mostly related to software development. Additionally, and not visible in the profiles, the auditors identified weaknesses in project management and controlling.

The areas of deficiencies and the associated improvement potential were explicitly addressed in a 30-page audit report, which became the basis for the next step.

Process Improvement Activities Started After the First BICO Audit

The audit report, including the profiles, was distributed among the key personnel of the projects, the department heads and the general management. In a presentation, the results were explained by the auditors.

Taking into account the risk involved and the potential for return of investment, the improvement actions were selected and prioritised as described above (matrix). A very important factor was the very strong management commitment, and it was possible to start process improvement in all weak areas.

The following process improvement activities were started:

- Update of the quality management documentation to reach at least the average level of the project implementation
- Development of state-of-the-art procedures in work instructions for software development, document control (includes control of hardware and source code as well), safety, reuse, verification and validation—the other identified weak areas were covered by the update of the quality management documentation.

A project was initialised. The goal was, to base the definition of the procedures on the best practices already identified in projects, and to include as many experts of FREQUENTIS in the process, as could be justified by the potential of return of investment. The moderation of the process and the technical guidance was outsourced to APAC. The quality manager of FRE-QUENTIS was responsible for the overall project management. The project planning resulted in the following schedule (Figure 17.4).

The development of the procedures and documentation was accompanied by organisational measures. The position of the quality management was enforced, central configuration management was installed, and a safety manager was installed.

Progress meetings were held every 2 months and corrective actions were initiated where necessary.

Additionally, a project management handbook was developed and a trainee program was established. Concerning the special processes the initiative to install an independent safety management and Availability, Reliability, and Maintainability (ARM) unit has been started. The formal safety and ARM program process was started.

Results of the PI Activities

The process improvement project was finished about three months late but with a very high quality of the produced material. The following charts show the results of the BICO audit in March 1996. Figure 17.5 shows the updated profile compared to Figure 17.2. The improvement in maturity of the quality management documentation and of the implemented process can be easily identified. On the chart, which compares 1996 with 1997 (Figure 17.7), it can be seen that there where no major improvements except in the area of Contract Reviews and Statistical Techniques as the second year of the process improvement initiative was dedicated to fine-tuning. In general, significant improvements can be demonstrated comparing the 1995 profiles with those from 1998 (Figure 17.8).

Figure 17.6 shows the updated profile compared to Figure 17.3.

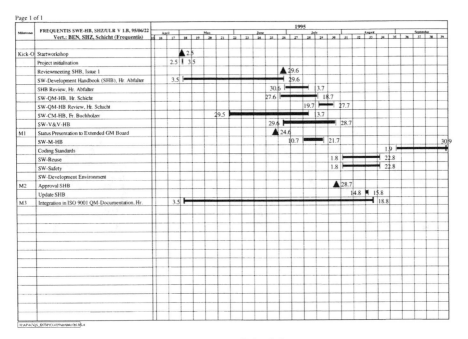

Figure 17.4. A Sample Improvement Project Schedule.

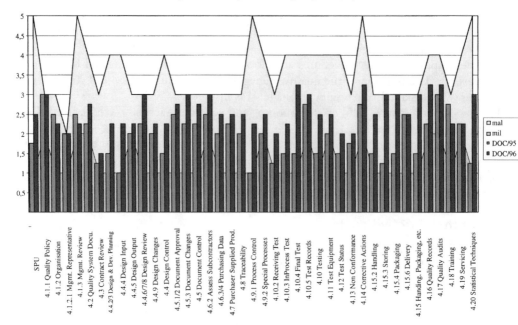

Figure 17.5. Comparison of the quality management documentation 1995–1996.

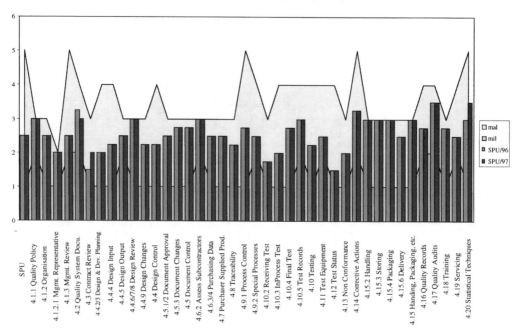

Figure 17.6. Comparison of the quality management implementation 1995–1996.

FRQ-SPU 1996 und 1997, SHZ, 97-09-09,97-09-10,97-09-15, V 1.0

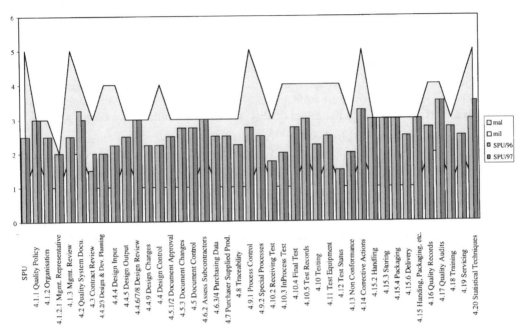

Figure 17.7.   Comparison of the quality management implementation 1996–1997.

Comparison of FRQ Projects (95 and 98)

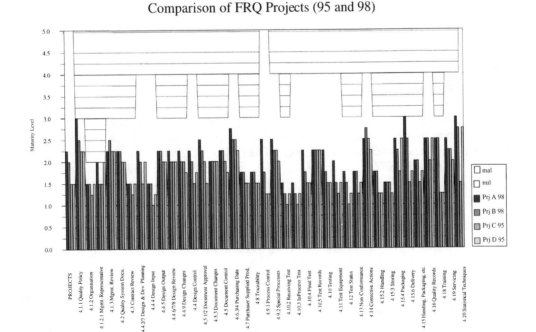

Figure 17.8.   Comparison of the project process maturity 1995 and 1998.

Output. Updated quality management documentation and the work instructions listed in the schedule.

Costs and benefits. The costs for consultancy were 15,000 ECU per audit plus the establishment of an action plan the internal effort was about 1500 hours. It is too early to calculate quantifiable benefits, but the improvement of product quality, which is associated with substantial savings, is evident. Redesign of hardware components was reduced by 30 percent, thus, a better process helps to identify errors very early, which reduces costs, and the higher product quality will reduce maintenance costs. [13]

Project process maturity. [13] In 1996, 1997, and 1998, APAC also performed some project audits, the results of which prove most of the projects have at least the process maturity of the system. This is proof that the implementation of the defined procedures works. At the first BICO audit in 1995, high variance was detected. The process maturity is not mainly triggered by the customer any more, as it was before, which reduces the risk to a great extent.

Lessons learned. Management commitment and a strong project management are key success factors; distribution of information about what is going on, helps buy-in very much.

During the first quarter of 1998 the most important projects with software development were assessed. The results proved that:

- There was an overall improvement especially in the area of project management.
- There is still substantial improvement potential in the testing process and the design process.
- Due to the fast growth of the organisation the processes have to be redesigned.

Acceptance and Human Aspects at the Target Organisation

What people think about an audit and how they interpret the results depends very much on the hierarchical level, the know-how about processes, and quality assurance.

The audit results were presented to an extended management panel that consists of the general management and the important project managers. They asked for many details but didn't question the overall results. The visualisation of the results was considered very useful at management level but engineers relied much more on the detailed audit report. The reason for this was that the charts do not tell very much if you don't know the model on which the calculation of the profile is based and if the charts are not properly explained.

When the initiative started many persons at the lower hierarchical level felt that the audit was a tool of the general management to supervise and criticise them and they did not see the potential that the identification of weaknesses offers. Whether people see the difference between an error and failure depends on the culture of an area. Three years later the benefit of audits was accepted even at the lower hierarchical levels.

Sometimes the employees use the audit to communicate information to the management that they wouldn't otherwise tell them. This is also a very important aspect of an audit as the management learns what they should know anyway and the employee can communicate what bothers them.

The auditors also identified some cases where the audit was used to fight other groups within their organisation, either by telling lies or by disclosing the right information to bias the situation. This situation is very dangerous and the auditor should prevent it. In one case at a project audit that was not part of this case study, the auditor had not identified the motivation of the audited person correctly. The audit report led to very strong contradictory conclusions and caused a lot of harm though the data was mostly correct.

What an involved person expects from and what he or she gets from an audit depends very much on his or her motivation.

Future Outlook

The major improvement goals were achieved within the first year. The second year was dedicated to fine-tuning and consolidation. The third year was dedicated to more fine-tuning and monitoring as well as to the verification and validation of the results of the implemented improvement measures. The goal of FREQUENTIS is to optimise quality and productivity. Process improvement is supported by the management as long as there is a proven potential that it will result in less risk and higher productivity. Higher process quality has to pay off. As there is no proven evidence that achieving very high maturity levels will pay off from the commercial point of view, no large-scale process improvement programs are planned for the near future. Of course, continuous fine-tuning will be carried out but this does not necessarily result in a higher maturity level.

The authors expect that FREQUENTIS will also order a BICO system audit every year. It cannot be expected that the new profiles will show dramatic improvement compared to the last profile. Sometimes relatively small enhancements cannot be identified in the profile but may be identified in the audit report. If an organisation does not have the explicit goal of reaching higher process maturity the importance of the profile diminishes and the importance of the detailed audit report rises. In this case the profile may be used to identify areas that have become weaker and to compare the project's maturity level with the overall quality system level.

REFERENCES

1. R. Messnarz, Design of a Quantitative Quality Evaluation System (QUES), dissertation, Dec. 1994.

2. *EN ISO 9001*, 1994.

3. *ISO 9000-3, Part 3, Guidelines for the Application of 9001 to the Development, Supply and Maintenance of Software.*

4. *ESA PSS-05-0, Issue 2, Software Engineering Standards.*

5. V. Haas, et al., "Bootstrap: Fine-tuning Process Assessment," *IEEE Software*, July 1994.

6. *Trillium Questionnaire, Telecom Software Product Development Capability Assessment Model, Version 3.0*, 1994.

7. *DIN ISO 10011, Guidelines for Auditing Quality Systems, Part 1-3* 1992.

8. *EN ISO 9004-1, Quality Management and Quality System Elements—Part 1: Guidelines*, 1994.

9. *Key Practices of the Capability Maturity Model V 1.1, CMU/SEI-93-TR-25*, Feb. 1993.

10. *The ami Handbook*, 1995.

11. P. Kuvaja, *Software Process Assessment and Improvement/The Bootstrap Approach*, 1994.

12. *TickIT, Guide to Software Quality Management System Construction and Certification using EN 29001*, 1992.

13. S. Lanzerstorfer, *Positive Correlation between Process Maturity and Product Quality as well as Project Performance*, 1996.

Chapter 18

Summary and Outlook

Richard Messnarz
ISCN, Ireland

THE BOOK'S MESSAGE IN GENERAL

What Makes Europe Different from the United States

What makes Europe distinctive from the United States is that Europe is still divided into many different nationalities and borders with many cultures and different approaches to work and life. Even if the European Union (EU) establishes a joint currency and common policy on the market it is to be expected that all different nationalities will preserve their cultural differences as much as they can. This has a direct influence on work politics, social rights, and how software process improvement and market competition are approached. An integration of workforces across borders, nationalities, and boundaries takes time and the ESPRIT programme (a European Research Programme) has been supporting the formation of transnational consortia and cooperations across Europe for about a decade now.

This shows first effects and the next framework program (starting at 1999) will focus even more on new networking and cooperation environments which will effectively support a further European transnational and transcultural integration and the formation of workforces working together on joint research, development, and market strategies.

In the United States the integration process started long ago (in 1776) and it took much time to create a common language, a common market, a common foreign policy, and a strong worldwide influencing defense system. Due to the cold war in the twentieth century the Department of Defense (DoD) came to occupy a very central role in many research activities by simply having been forced (under Russian competition) to be the major funding organisation for new technical directions.

Europe, on the other hand, has always relied on the United States for its defense policies (indirectly through the North American Treaty Organisation [NATO]) and thus has not so much focused on military- and defense-funded research. The ESPRIT program focused much on businesses such as banks, insurance companies, software houses in general, and so forth while the defense-focused sector remained rather small.

The book reflects this European multienvironment issue and illustrates that certain results and approaches have been used differently in different regions of Europe compared to the United States.

It might seem contradictory for a U.S. citizen but in fact one needs to know this basic multicultural European understanding to be able to effectively transfer know-how between the United States and Europe.

The Effects of a Multicultural European Interpretation

The same basic situation is solved completely differently in different countries (e.g., compare Chapter 12, dealing with Alcatel France, with Chapter 8, dealing with Siemens Germany) and still leads to successful results. An old European saying from the Roman Empire (approx. 40 B.C. to 450 A.C.) said "All roads (and not only one) lead to Rome," and this is still true in an interpreted sense for technology transfer in different European cultures and regions.

In software process improvement the U.S. approach with the CMM (Capability Maturity Model) is a pragmatic approach which certainly (with a large "push" through the DoD) is used across the United States in the same way. And I could imagine that all companies are happy that only a one-way road is provided (with not too many exits to allow them to leave the road too early).

In Europe, however, it is nearly a must that before a company from country A uses a methodology from country B they create their own adapted version B_A which they claim to be working perfectly for their own region.

This might sound complicated but in many cases this brings surprisingly good results and a set of complementary approaches which can be combined with pragmatic solutions (e.g., CMM) which are documented in this book, such as:

- Chapter 2: Creating a business understanding in addition to assessments.
- Chapter 3: Creating a teamwork-based definition of software processes to conceptualize not only processes but also the effective work of people behind the processes.
- Chapter 3: Instead of one assessment method hundreds are developed and (see above) nearly every region does so.
- Chapter 4: Creating a goal analysis strategy aligned with assessments.
- Chapter 5: Developing guidelines and proposed metrics sets for detailed measurement of product quality and process performance.
- Chapter 6: The situation is the same in the United States and Europe. Business managers want to be able to estimate the return on investment before they provide a budget to an SPI team.

This is also the reason why you did not find a structure like

- Part I: a one-way methodology (step-by-step, with not too many junctions)
- Part II: a set of companies that used this one way and show the goals they have achieved

Instead, you found an architecture like

- Part I : A mixture of methodologies and approaches;
- Part II: A set of companies that used different selections from the methodologies, combined them, and achieved results.

A SET OF EUROPEAN SUCCESS CRITERIA

The sections below discuss SPI drivers from a European perspective and compare them in part with the United States.

SPI Driven by Business

In the United States the use of assessment methods became inevitable in the mid-1980s. A large part of the software systems funded by the DoD were actually never used because their quality was not sufficiently checked and error behaviour could not be predicted, making it a hazard to use such systems in critical situations.

As stated above, in Europe (with the exception of the UK) defense was not the most important business. Rather, it was banking, insurance, manufacturing (cars), and so forth.

So it was much easier in the United States to motivate companies to use approaches like CMM because the larger funding was channelled through DoD and organisations were eager to search for this funding. So they tried to satisfy CMM requirements as soon as they could.

In Europe this was much more difficult. Defence is not the strongest driving force. Rather, it is market demands (to show ISO 9001 compliance for achieving customer confidence), supplier relationships (to satisfy the customer and get further contracts), and the ambition to achieve a competitive structure for the future organisation.

Even the European Systems and Software Initiative (ESSI) did not see the assessments as a certification tool (who is allowed to receive funding?), but rather as a tool which supports the identification of companies' weaknesses and permits them to get funded to improve their infrastructure and work processes to develop faster, at higher quality, within better organised environments. This is a consulting rather than certification (e.g., SCE) approach.

This strategy goes back to one of the early findings of the European ESPRIT project BOOTSTRAP in 1992 which compared the maturity levels of organisations in the United States and Europe. At this time the United States showed a majority of organisations on level 1 and only few on higher levels, but these few were the worldwide leaders. However, Europe did not show as many worldwide leading software companies than the United States. Rather, over 75 percent of the software companies in Europe are very small (as reported in the EU ESSI Initiative), but (and that was interesting to note) a majority of these smaller firms were at a maturity of around 2. The idea was born that with a big shift of all these smaller and middle-sized companies from 2 to a higher level a better competitive structure of Europe could be achieved in general.

The major question in Europe is (and was), if there is no "must" through a defense force, what can motivate business managers to provide necessary funds and support for SPI initiatives?

Chapter 2 discusses these different motivations of business managers and Chapter 7 analyses the cost and return on investment from SPI.

These business-driven viewpoints can also be found in the statements from leading European companies published in this book:

- Mr. Daniel Courtel (process improvement manager) from Alcatel Telecom, in Chapter 12 : "It is a decisive aspect to strengthen the way of developing towards a more professional, disciplined and controlled approach, through Software Process Improvement."
- Mr. Aldo Lora (business manager at Italtel), in Chapter 9: "In the market of global solutions for mobile communications a greatly deal of effort is currently invested into software process improvement which is seen as a major level to increase a company's capabilities."

- Dr. Axel Voelker (head of Process Improvement Group) from Siemens ZL, in Chapter 8: "For all divisions in Siemens worldwide, where software is a relevant factor, a software process assessment and improvement programme shall increase the organisation's maturity level and put software development on a realiable basis for industrial development within Siemens."

People as an Asset of the Company

While Europe was surrounded by two ideologies, an extreme communist view in Eastern Europe and a strong capitalist view in the United States, most European nations went through a political process that created a kind of social capitalism in the last century.

In Italy, for instance, the Communist Party is very strong and all other parties had to create an alliance to keep the Communist Party out of power as long as there was the cold war. France, for instance, has a history over hundreds of years of revolutions in which the principles of *liberté, fraternité*, and *egalité* were kept alive, which led to well-defined social rights and labour laws which protect employees and their rights.

Also in Germany, the big electronics firms have founders who were socially conscious people and who created a synergy between their company and the social rights and social support of people.

Thus, employees have many more rights and protection than in the United States. This created a much more people-oriented approach in Europe, and motivation became a key asset.

It is not enough in Europe to merely define processes and assess them and if they are not properly executed to set staffing consequences or exchange people. This is the reason why many European organisations try to establish processes with a teamwork culture that allows people to identify themselves with the process and to actively work with others in a highly motivating environment.

Chapter 3 discusses this people and teamwork-based software process definition, and Chapter 14 illustrates such a role-based example.

Goals as a Translation of Different Viewpoints

Let us assume that all previously described SPI drivers are satisfied and that

- An assessment produced a strengths and weaknesses profile.
- A business manager is motivated to provide funds because he sees the weaknesses and estimates a business benefit by investment in SPI.
- The people are motivated to improve their work processes.

Even if the above points are clear it is still (in a people-centred environment as described above) a huge task to reach a critical mass of people that follow the vision and are motivated to achieve the business manager's goals in SPI.

A major problem relies in the fact (stated in Chapter 3) that business managers, middle managers, and practitioners speak different languages. It seems hard to find a consistent architecture of goals that links the objectives of these three groups in such a way that success and the achievement of goals becomes traceable.

A goal tree then becomes a translator of SPI understanding across different groups in an organisation.

Chapter 5 describes such goal analysis strategies, experiences, and results. Chapter 6 illustrates a set of measures and guidelines to evaluate the achievement of goals in quantitative terms.

Experience with this goal-based approach is illustrated in Chapter 12 dealing with Alcatel, and a goal-measurement driven approach is discussed in Chapters 9 and 10, dealing with Italtel.

An SPI Shop with a Large Selection

The above-described multimethod-driven European perspective also leads to a number of adaptations, changes, and transformations to assessment models before they are used in different regions or industry sectors. This explains the incredibly large set of assessment models and methods explained in Chapter 4, and the different contributions from experience detailed in Chapters 13, 15, 16, and 17.

A EUROPEAN-LIKE INTERPRETATION OF SPI

From a European perspective, therefore, SPI is much more complex, acceptance is much harder to achieve, and the general strategy is much more multidimensional-driven than one-way.

On the one hand, this leads to more options to make things wrong; on the other hand, it yields a variety of methods which, if they are used in a proper combination, can be very powerful.

SPI then becomes a philosophy which, like a puzzle, combines methods and builds bridges between different sets of

- assessment methods
- goal analysis strategies
- measurement tools
- paradigms and strategies to establish people motivation and teamwork processes
- improvement planning techniques

to achieve certain goals originating with business managers and directed at making the organisation more competitive. Business orientation is a must to justify the budget for SPI. People management and motivation is a must to get a critical mass of people to follow the SPI vision. Goal trees are a must to translate the business managers' viewpoints into practical objectives for the SPI teams. And pragmatic assessment methods (CMM, BOOTSTRAP, TickIT, Trillium, etc.) are just one tool to evaluate the strengths and weaknesses before applying a combination of all the other approaches (from business orientation to goal analysis).

IEEE Computer Society Publications

The world-renowned IEEE Computer Society publishes, promotes, and distributes a wide variety of authoritative computer science and engineering texts. These books are available from most retail outlets. Visit the Online Catalog, *http://computer.org*, for a list of products.

IEEE Computer Society Proceedings

The IEEE Computer Society also produces and actively promotes the proceedings of more than 141 acclaimed international conferences each year in multimedia formats that include hard and softcover books, CD-ROMs, videos, and on-line publications.

For information on the IEEE Computer Society proceedings, send e-mail to cs.books@computer.org or write to Proceedings, IEEE Computer Society, P.O. Box 3014, 10662 Los Vaqueros Circle, Los Alamitos, CA 90720-1314. Telephone +1 714-821-8380. FAX +1 714-761-1784.

Additional information regarding the Computer Society, conferences and proceedings, CD-ROMs, videos, and books can also be accessed from our web site at *http://computer.org/cspress*